Empire Islands

Empire Islands

Castaways, Cannibals, and
Fantasies of Conquest

Rebecca Weaver-Hightower

University of Minnesota Press | Minneapolis | London

Chapter 3 was originally published as "Voracious Cannibals, Rapacious Pirates, and the Empire Island," *Journal of Commonwealth and Postcolonial Studies* 8.1–2 (2002): 81–107.

An earlier version of chapter 6 appeared as "*Cast Away* and *Survivor:* The Surviving Castaway and the Rebirth of Empire," *Journal of Popular Culture* 39, no. 2 (2006). Copyright 2006 Blackwell Publishing; reprinted with permission from Blackwell Publishing.

Published by the University of Minnesota Press
111 Third Avenue South, Suite 290
Minneapolis, MN 55401-2520
http://www.upress.umn.edu

LIBRARY OF CONGRESS CATALOGING-IN-PUBLICATION DATA
Weaver-Hightower, Rebecca.
    Empire islands : castaways, cannibals, and fantasies of conquest / Rebecca
    Weaver-Hightower.
        p.   cm.
    Includes bibliographical references and index.
    ISBN: 978-0-8166-4862-7   ISBN-10: 0-8166-4862-X   (hc : alk. paper)
    ISBN: 978-0-8166-4863-4   ISBN-10: 0-8166-4863-8   (pb : alk. paper)
    1. Islands in literature. 2. English fiction—History and criticism. 3. English fiction—
English-speaking countries—History and criticism. 4. Castaways in literature.
5. Imperialism in literature. 6. Cannibalism in literature. 7. Pirates in literature.
8. Monsters in literature. 9. Psychology in literature. 10. Psychoanalysis and literature.
I. Title.
    PR830.I75W43   2007
    823.009'32—dc22
                                    2006100756

Printed in the United States of America on acid-free paper

The University of Minnesota is an equal-opportunity educator and employer.

12 11 10 09 08 07   10 9 8 7 6 5 4 3 2 1

For
Jack Weaver and Betty Nester Weaver
Dana
and Marcus

and in memory of
Matilda Weaver-Hightower

Contents

Introduction
Islands and the Narrating of Possession

Gilligan's Island. Robinson Crusoe. Fantasy Island. We are fascinated with islands, both real and imaginary, mysterious and elemental. Combining the allure of sexy sunset beaches with the titillation of risk, islands evoke romance and danger. This lure of islands permeates literature. Particularly popular are stories, written during fifteenth- through early twentieth-century Europe's colonization of much of the world, which typically tell of a person—most often a single man—stranded on an island, a castaway. He is forced to survive, usually on wits and coconuts alone, the perilous situations that island life often brings: hunger, loneliness, madness, fierce weather, cannibals, pirates, and monsters, real or imagined. Also prevalent are twentieth-century postcolonial stories of castaways that revise many of the trope's key elements. What is it about this story that gives it such endurance and appeal? Why the island?

Empire Islands will engage with those questions by providing a detailed unpacking of the psychological draw of the castaway genre and analysis of how it worked as a tool of European imperial culture. One of the central tenets of this book is that by helping generations of readers to make sense of (perhaps feel better about) imperial aggression, the castaway story, in effect, enabled the expansion and maintenance of European empire. *Empire Islands,* then, reads hundreds of years of castaway narratives. Though these are often called "Robinsonades," after their progenitor novel, Daniel Defoe's *Robinson Crusoe* (1719), I prefer "island narrative" or "castaway narrative," since this project includes narratives set on islands that aren't strictly speaking *Robinsonades,* including those (such as *The Tempest*) written before *Robinson Crusoe,* and others (such as H. G. Wells's *The Island of Dr. Moreau* and Edgar Allan Poe's *The Narrative of Arthur Gordon Pym*) that, while set on islands, don't explicitly respond to Defoe's story. Understanding of this psychological power of castaway tales requires analysis of how they made imperial expansion and control seem unproblematic and natural, like the innate processes of the human body. These tales, this book demonstrates, accomplished this

FIGURE 1. Cover by David Holzman from George Lamming, *Water with Berries* (New York: Holt, Rinehart, and Winston, 1971).

feat by presenting stories in which castaways could control the naturally bounded space of the island as they control the naturally bounded space of their bodies. The island-like book that colonial readers hold in their hands, then, contains a story of a body-like island. Moreover, the body that the island represents is a manly body, meaning that *Empire Islands* engages and challenges previous critical work examining discourse of the colonizable land as a female body.

Demonstrating this trope of the book as island-cum-body is the striking image from the cover of George Lamming's 1971 *Water with Berries* (see Figure 1), his revision of Shakespeare's *The Tempest*. This is the image with which I conceptually began this book. It shows a black man whose body is an island. His grave face sits atop his island mountain/body gazing into the distance, his arms palm trees, with fronds or fists upraised as if in defiance or frustration. Over each arm sits a hazy mountain, suggesting powerful muscles flexed in readiness for battle. The artist, David Holzman (as he explained in a personal communication on September 9, 2003), trying "to get the feeling of the book . . . rather than repeating a narrative from the writing," places the man/island atop an image akin to the London Houses of Parliament and Tower Bridge, with the phallic or syringe-like steeple of Big Ben pointed straight up into the throat of the man/island as if threatening penetration. Despite the steeple, this illustration makes clear that this island is not Prospero's; it is Caliban's. This island is neither a woman to be dominated nor is it a man in denial of his feminine side. The man/island may have Parliament at its foundation, but underneath even Parliament is the blue sea, calm for the moment but also powerful, perhaps maternal, enclosing every island, even England. That the skin of the man/island is also tinted blue suggests that the sea has permeated his skin, while the angry green sky behind his head heralds a storm. Surrounding the entire image, as the sea surrounds an island, is a purplish border flowing down into the name "George Lamming," reminding that both this body and island are enclosed within the formerly colonized Lamming's book. This image and the novel it covers capture the aim of *Empire Islands*, which is to reveal how the castaway story presents such a psychoculturally powerful fantasy of *natural* command of landscape through the manly body that generations of postcolonial writers (such as Lamming) were compelled to dismantle it as part of anticolonial struggle.

Lamming's story does in narrative what Holzman's cover does in image, which is to recast the castaway story and transform the island/body/

book trope from a colonial tool into a postcolonial one. Lamming wrote the novel, as he explained in a 1973 interview, as a revision of Shakespeare's *The Tempest* in order to demonstrate violent anticolonial resistance, which fulfills he says "a therapeutic need for a certain kind of violence in the breaking" of colonial ties (Kent 91). Taking its title from the famous speech in which Caliban protests Prospero's psychological cruelty to him, *Water with Berries* focuses on a group of Caribbean expatriates living in London who are planning a revolution on their home island against neocolonial despots. Just as Holzman's image redraws the body/book/island connection of historical castaway narratives, Lamming's story retells Shakespeare's, making Prospero into a plantation owner and Caliban into a black intellectual.

Scores of other postcolonial writers have "written back" to the castaway story; Derek Walcott, for example, chose to revise Defoe's *Robinson Crusoe* in his 1978 play *Pantomime*.[1] In Walcott's version, Harry, a white English hotel owner, modifies *Robinson Crusoe* for the stage, with himself as Friday and his Afro-Caribbean servant, Jackson, playing Crusoe. But Harry's play never moves out of rehearsal, for once they begin, the racial role reversal so distresses Harry that he abandons the play. He fears that a performance of *Robinson Crusoe* with a black Crusoe and a white Friday "could get offensive . . . I mean, there'd be a lot of things there that people . . . well, it would make them think too much, and well, we don't want that . . . we just want a little . . . entertainment" (125). Angered and annoyed, the black Crusoe-to-be, Jackson, speculates that their argument symbolizes a larger struggle over changing imperial roles: "This moment that we are now acting here is the history of imperialism," he says. "It's nothing less than that" (125). And that is just Walcott's point: In *Robinson Crusoe* and its adaptations and revisions exist histories of and struggles against imperialism. That is *Empire Islands'* point as well: By looking more closely at the psychological work of castaway narratives, we can better understand how they aided the management of cultural anxieties and desires of empire and why so many postcolonial writers had no choice but to write back to them.

Historical Scope

That both Lamming and Walcott hail from Caribbean islands, as does their compatriot, Aimé Cesairé, who also decided to target *The Tempest* in his own *A Tempest* (1969), might explain the coincidence of these island-set revisions. Yet, what should we make of that fact that dozens of other writers from nonisland nations spanning the globe have also chosen to "write back" to colonial island tales, in fact, choosing to rewrite the castaway island tale more often by far than any other genre or story?[2] To address that query, *Empire Islands* jumps back in time from those postcolonial revisions to analyze in depth a range of colonial castaway tales in terms of imperial myth and psychological fantasy, exploring the subconscious appeal of the island form to generations of colonial writers and readers and investigating how those stories of island colonization affected the way people (both of the colonizing and colonized cultures) thought and felt about real-world empire.

Because literature informs and so often is informed by historical events, where possible I note relationships between historical events of empire and the literature accompanying them over the five-hundred-year scope this study covers. In order to investigate the power of such a long-lived literary subgenre as the colonial castaway tale, one must look at a large number of them, starting at the beginning (if one can even determine such a date). *Empire Islands,* then, spans five hundred years of literature, starting with the first acts of modern European colonization in the "New World" (traditionally said to begin with Columbus's late fifteenth-century voyages) and Shakespeare's *The Tempest* in 1611 and continuing through scores of castaway tales. This book will analyze some familiar titles, such as *Robinson Crusoe, The Swiss Family Robinson, The Mysterious Island,* and *The Coral Island,* alongside some less familiar ones, such as *The Life and Astonishing Adventures of John Daniel* and the pantomime *Robinson Crusoe, the Lad Rather Loose O' and the Black Man Called Friday, Who Kept His House Tidy,* ending with twenty-first-century postcolonial and neocolonial film and literary revisions, such as *Cast Away* and the television series *Survivor.*

Though the texts discussed in this work follow a long tradition of island narratives, including Thomas More's *Utopia,* Homer's *The Odyssey,* texts in the *isolario* genre, and the Sinbad tale of Sir Richard Burton's *The Book of the Thousand Nights and a Night,* the fifteenth through twentieth centuries saw an explosion in the number of island narratives, with literally hundreds of variations produced in response to European empire. *Empire Islands* stresses the historical significance of these colonial castaway narratives by tracking how they document evolving attitudes to empire, with the shift from single castaway to group of castaways mirroring shifts in imperial ideologies, from being oriented in individual corporate financial ventures to national ideologies of (as Kipling calls it) "The White Man's Burden." As historians have noted, colonization endured longer than simple profitability justified. Island narratives evolved as imperial policy and colonial practice itself evolved—from early (fifteenth and sixteenth centuries) fantasy-based narratives like Renaissance traveler's tales, to the eighteenth century's more realistic island tales, to the nineteenth century's jingoistic island tales—yet the remarkable narrative consistency of the stories suggest psychosocial significance in addition to historical import.

Though *Empire Islands* is historically grounded, the tracing of these narrative consistencies and speculation on their psychosocial significance is its primary labor. Previous critical examinations have remarked that castaway stories often depict colonization as benign—both *unavoidable,* since the castaway moored on a deserted island was forced by God, fate, or nature to take control of the space, and *legitimate,* since in most island narratives the island is *terra nullius,* meaning no indigenous island people precede the castaway or contest his claim though they often join him, as Friday does Crusoe. This book adds to those previous discussions by showing how island stories in particular link those fictional and real world acts of empire to psychological experiences of the body, making colonization seem natural, as well. By showing how many of these island texts connect the right to authority over the colonial landscape (in this case the colony, not the imperial center) to one's right and ability to command one's own flesh, *Empire Islands* will demonstrate how the literary island setting provides a space where European imperial cultures could play out fantasies and process anxieties of empire through fantasies and anxieties of the body.

The Island as Body

This analysis of literary links between land and body expands upon previous investigations of somatic metaphors for landscape, both island and continental. As Leonard Barkan remarks, the human body has long provided humanity with its most fundamental narrative metaphors for perceiving the world[3]: "In the life of the primitive man, the self, and hence the body, is the only wholeness which can be grasped. Anthropomorphism is *faute de mieux,* [literally "for want of a better"] this man's only cosmology" (8). Anthropologist Mary Douglas in *Purity and Danger: An Analysis of the Concepts of Pollution and Taboo,* makes general claims about the body as symbol in Western and non-Western cultures, explaining that "just as it is true that everything symbolizes the body, so it is equally true (and all the more so for that reason) that the body symbolizes everything else" (122). "The body is a complex structure," she says. "The functions of its different parts and their relation afford a source of symbols for other complex structures" (115). Islands and empires, this book will argue, are clearly such "complex structures."

A range of theorists explains the historical scope in the West of this notion of the representative body. Barkan notes that pre-Renaissance culture envisioned a unity between the human body and the cosmos, with the human body as a microcosm of the natural world. So, for example, a walnut was considered to duplicate the human head, with the meat of the nut being shaped like the human brain and the shell the skull. Though still a crucial epistemological construct, early modern culture saw this analogy between the human body and the world become less literal, moving from the realm of science into art and myth. In *Body Criticism,* Barbara Stafford explains how the body as symbol endured during the eighteenth century, during which "the human body represented the ultimate visual compendium, the comprehensive method of methods, the organizing structure of structures. As a visible natural whole made up of invisible dissimilar parts, it was the organic paradigm or architectural standard for all complex unions" (12). The body as epistemological system endured throughout the nineteenth and twentieth centuries, as well.

An excellent example of a somatic allegory exists in an early piece of colonial literature, Fineas Fletcher's 1633 poem *The Purple Island or The Isle of Man,* which uses a body metaphor to explain the workings of the island-state that symbolizes the fledgling British Empire at large. Early in the poem, Fletcher describes the island as geographically partitioned into three political regions, which he equates to the body's heart, head, and digestive system, a metaphor he proceeds to explicate at great length in the rest of his 171-page poem. Fletcher employs a rubric familiar to his readers, using their own flesh to make clear England's political entrails. As well as providing an easily digestible metaphor for his readers, Fletcher's equation of the island-state with the human body paints England's political system as a naturally occurring organism straight from the hands of the creator, which would provide powerful incentive to obey the state. Such metaphorical connections between the land and the monarch's body were not unusual in early modern culture, says

Ernst Kantorowicz in *The King's Two Bodies*. Like such texts, which use the body to explain complex political systems and to encourage obedience, it is my argument that island narratives, which grew out of Modern perceptions of the individually owned and commanded body, provided a psychological mechanism to help readers accept and consent to their government appropriating land in the name of empire.

Moreover, as other critics have noted, psychological links between *female* bodies and land were used throughout early colonial literature to legitimize acts of colonization by white men. My project adds to these arguments by exploring how the employment of the island as a literary-geographical space to be controlled builds a slightly different imperial fantasy, not one of controlling the land as one would *another's* *female* body but of controlling the land as one would one's *own male* body. This distinction is important to make if we are to better understand desires to colonize a place and what makes such actions psychologically bearable. *Empire Islands* addresses those issues through its reading of island stories for clues about the subconscious of cultures and writers, about why readers would respond to certain narrative choices over others, and about why a writer would make the discursive choices he or she did. Island narratives exist among many types of texts of empire, including other types of novels, diaries, letters, newspapers, poetry, travel tales, reports, plays, cartoons, films, paintings, and other artistic expressions—all metaphorically gathered around the fireside of empire, and many working, as do island narratives, to legitimize imperial behaviors, perhaps (or not) drawing upon the same psychosocial mechanisms. It is my hope that turning an attentive eye to these island tales will aid in discriminating the other faces around the hearth (the other genres) and help us begin to understand how a variety of texts can create the psychological space for working through anxieties and desires.

Why the Island?

In order to examine this question of the power and appeal of the island narrative, we need to return to the question with which I began this introduction, "Why the island?" As with their postcolonial successors, what drew so many colonial writers who wished to compose tales of exploration and adventure to choose the *island* as their setting, over and over again?[4] One explanation could be that these writers desired to test their subjects against the tensions of solitude and the demands of ingenuity. Since, however, significant sections of continents in the sixteenth through nineteenth centuries were barely charted, self-reliance and resourcefulness could have been tested as well in a variety of nonisland venues. Second, we could understand perhaps why English writers, who were historically entangled in struggle to command their own island (including Scotland and Wales) and their nearest neighbor, Ireland, would subconsciously link the island geographical form to fantasies of colonial domination.[5] As Lawrence James notes in *The Rise and Fall of the British Empire*, "the first colonization of North America was contemporaneous with the far larger settlement of Ireland, mainly by Presbyterian Scottish immigrants. Between 1620 and 1642, 120,000 colonists arrived to help undertake what Sir Francis Bacon revealingly called 'the reduction to civility' of the Gaelic-speaking, Catholic Irish" (14). Thirdly, we might explain the popularity of the island setting by remembering that many famous *nonfictional* accounts of imperial exploration (Columbus's, Dampier's, Cook's) primarily concerned islands.[6] Yet, based in analysis of scores of those island tales, *Empire Islands* will show that these explanations are insufficient. The appeal of the island as fictional setting (and perhaps the appeal of the island for real-world colonization) is more deeply rooted, stemming, in fact, from the island's ability to enable a fantasy that colonization writ large is "natural," or oriented in organic systems of the body and natural world.

To explain this fantasy of colonization as natural, let me start with a moment that I will return to often throughout this book, one that is virtually universal in colonial castaway narratives. Mary Louise Pratt in *Imperial Eyes* calls these moments the "monarch-of-all-I-survey," though her reference is to nonfictional, nonisland travel narratives (201). Often in travel narratives, as travelers "discover" a place by visually surveying a landscape already familiar to the native guides who brought them there, they declare sovereignty over the space in the name of the monarch they represent. As with Mungo Parks naming "Victoria Falls," Pratt explains, the simple act of viewing, often from a position of elevation, provides a feeling of and a legal justification for ownership.

We can see similar moments in almost all fictional castaway tales. The castaway (a man, or later, a small group of people) first suffers through a night or two of dark despair at being cast away, and perhaps a day of rescuing provisions from the wrecked craft. But in an action that typically leads to acceptance of his fate, as I will show in chapter 1, soon after landing on the island, the castaway ascends to a place of geographical elevation to survey the space. This is the monarch-of-all-I-survey moment. Though his immediate motive may be to ascertain if he is indeed stranded on an island rather than a continent, that moment also provides him a sense of ownership as he scans his new home and visually appropriates it. That scene proves crucial to the protagonist's gaining a sense of island possession. In that moment he becomes a "castaway colonist," a term I often use instead of "castaway" to foreground the story's imperial undercurrents, reminding that the character, in terms of the story, has not so much been cast away *from* something as brought *to* the island by colonial ambition and that the story concerns his relationship with the island more than the home he left. I also refer to the castaway as "colonist" to disrupt the story's typical promotion of the protagonist's fate as act of God or nature and not the result of his own actions, since, despite being brought to the island by a storm, many fictional castaways were former colonists, as was Crusoe, or were intending to be colonists, like Wyss's aptly named Robinson family. In that oft-repeated monarch-of-all-I-survey scene, before climbing the mountain or hill or promontory, the castaway is a *survivor,* but afterwards, he is an *owner.* What happens in that moment to lead to such a dramatic change in identity? A compelling explanation (and an explanation for the appeal of the island) exists within psychoanalytic theory and its concepts of the body.

The I-Land and Psychoanalysis

Psychoanalytic theories of the body image, the gaze, the skin ego, and especially of incorporation describe how, on a subconscious level (as is most mental activity), human beings experience the world through their bodies. According to psychoanalysts such as Sigmund Freud and Melanie Klein, humanity's most basic process of imagining a relationship between the self and the world occurs through the body, a fact we can see most clearly in young children, who experience much of the universe through their mouths. Babies, Klein says, understand the world as what enters and exits their mouths and bodies, through the acts of sucking, consuming, repletion, and expulsion. In early childhood, Freud says, toddlers continue to experience their environment orally, often putting objects they desire or want to understand into their mouths. Didier Anziu expands that notion to argue that babies understand the world and their place in it through their skin, which develops into an adult "skin ego," a way of perceiving our bodies, possessions, others, and immediate surroundings in relation to our skin. As adults we continue to subconsciously process our universe in terms of what is inside and outside our bodies. As we mature, our culture trains us not to directly express and act on those incorporative impulses, but they continue to undergird how we psychically manage our bodies and our world. It's no coincidence that Western capitalists often refer to ourselves as "consumers."

Such notions of the body provide a pervasive and powerful psychical mechanism in island narratives. Much of what happens, in fact, in that moment of mountaintop surveying, the "monarch-of-all-I-survey" moment, can be understood through the concepts of incorporation and the gaze. The castaway's behavior in and after that scene suggests that in that moment, as he marks the boundaries of the island with his gaze, he begins to symbolically incorporate the island. As I will explain in detail in chapter 1, the castaway's words and behavior in that scene and after demonstrate that in that moment he initiates a subconscious connection between the island and his body that will develop in the rest of the narrative, a connection that leads him to imagine command over the space he "civilizes" at the same time he disciplines his body.

Castaway colonists spend much of their time on the island trying to turn it into a more "civilized," Western space like that they left, building huts, treehouses, pens, bowers, bridges, gardens and/or fortifications that resemble their lost home, both making the space familiar and marking their rights over their territory for would-be transgressors. The island form is crucial here. Like the castaway's body, the island is naturally bounded (often being observed in its entirety from that mountaintop vista). The island form exerts a psychological appeal important to stories of adventure and exploration. By its very nature and because of its firm boundaries and natural borders, the island could mirror perceptions of a human body bounded by skin and could thus enable writers and readers to fantasize about naturally ruling and owning land as one would one's own body.

Let us take a minute to explore this concept of the human body as "naturally bounded" and individually owned and controlled, which cultural historians such as Norbert Elias argue is a modern rather than medieval or pre-modern notion. This conception in the late twentieth and early twenty-first centuries has grown into a cultural obsession, making billions of dollars for the diet, health, bodybuilding, cosmetics, and plastic surgery industries, as well as being concretized in legal decisions such as *Roe v. Wade* (the U.S. Supreme Court decision that legalized abortion under the argument that we have private bodies that we have the right to control). Elias argues in *The Civilizing Process* that, as Europe passed from its feudal into its Modern era, a fantasy of the body as atomistic began to replace an earlier notion of the body as owned by God or king within a feudal system. Elias argues that in Erasmus's 1530 *De civilitate morum puerilium* (translation, *On Civility in Children*), which outlined the proper handling of bodily functions, we can see reflected such transitions from medieval to early-modern cultural perceptions of the body. Medieval folk, "people who ate together in the way customary in the Middle Ages, taking meat with their fingers from the same dish, wine from the same goblet, soup from the same pot or the same plate," he explains, "stood in a different relationship to one another than we [Modern people] do" (69). As well, as Gail Kern Paster remarks, with this Renaissance privatization comes the "shame threshold," which is the increase in shame that bodily functions began to carry as people distanced themselves psychically and linguistically from bodily functions. This distancing of the body from food and from each other's bodies, as the new rules about proper bodily behavior make evident, indicates a shift from a feudal, group identity to identities based in economic individualism, coinciding geographically and chronologically with increases in commerce and international trade and the formation of notions of consumption inherent in modern capitalism.[7] As Anthony Synnott likewise observes in *The Body Social:* "Indeed only 100 years after Erasmus's book, the new realities of the individual as *alone* (divided from others), secular (divided from God), and dual (internally divided) are succinctly expressed in the Cartesian '*Cogito, ergo sum*' ["I think, therefore I am"]" (19).

Not coincidentally, simultaneous with these changes in body perception and identity came increased production of castaway narratives. Again borrowing Synnott's words: "increasingly after the Renaissance everyone is an island—which is what Descartes implied and Donne protested against" (19). With these new fantasies of the human body as a distinct and bounded space, I contend, the island, with its natural geographic borders, becomes the perfect imaginary space for an individual person to inhabit and solely command—to, in short, colonize. Because both body and island were understood as discrete entities with observable and fixed boundaries, the island form would enhance fantasies of one person being able to control all of the space between those boundaries, just as one supposedly controls the contents of what lies within the boundaries of one's skin. By looking further into this imagined connection between the island and the human body, *Empire Islands* aims to further our understanding of how these texts function as narratives of possession, and how the castaway (and reading public) could begin to imagine colonization as legitimate.

The island narratives themselves suggest that, as well as repeatedly depicting the *desires* of their imperial reading public, they chronicle *anxieties* inherent in colonization, which they also significantly dramatize through stories of the castaway's body. After conquest, the imperial machine devoted much of its energy to maintaining order in the colonies—setting up court systems, building roads and infrastructures, mediating indigenous disagreements, and subduing hints of resistance. The fear of rebellion and the question of the morality of imperial conquest created constant anxieties in the colonizing culture, anxieties rearticulated through island narratives. Just as the desires of empire were played out on the island colonist's literary body, so were anxieties, for as Douglas explains in *Purity and Danger,* the body's "boundaries can represent any boundaries which are threatened or precarious" (115). Island narratives symbolize these anxieties in stories of fictional colonists struggling to harden and masculinize their bodily borders in a delusion of exerting greater mastery over what enters and leaves the boundaries of their skin (which I will explore at greater length in chapter 2). The ideology of self-protection here is masculine, for gender—masculinity, really—is all-important in these island narratives. It divides the powerful from the disempowered, the disciplined from the nondisciplined, the animal from the human, and the white from the nonwhite. As I will explore in chapter 3, stories of being captured by pirates or cannibalized, of going native or being tattooed demonstrate anxieties over loss of bodily control, which symbolize loss of colonial order, while plots of maintained manly self-discipline perhaps helped to assuage such anxieties for the colonial reading public.

Readers and Recodification

In order to understand how reading island narratives might affect how readers respond to colonization, *Empire Islands* situates its investigation of the psychology of *literary* colonization within the historical realities of colonization (colonial events and developments, the actual writing of the island narrative, and the apparent need to frequently reproduce the fantasy). *Empire Islands* will argue that these island stories provided a potential means through which "ordinary" citizens could process certain anxieties and desires about their empire—in short, to process fantasies. Psychoanalysts examine their patients' fantasies to unearth the causes of repetitive behavior. Similarly, yet conversely, this analysis looks at the repetitive behavior (the production and consumption of the castaway narrative) for insight into the "patient's" (the culture's) fantasies. Jacqueline Rose's *States of Fantasy* (1996), quotes Freud's articulation of fantasies as "protective fictions," and then further explains fantasy as "a way of re-elaborating and therefore of partly recognizing the memory which is struggling, against the psychic odds, to be heard" (5). I want to keep in mind throughout this study this notion of fantasy as articulation of desire, defense against fear, and evidence of repressed reality, as I examine how island narratives functioned as cultural fantasies.

We can understand how island narratives could help the cultural management of anxiety and desire and why such work would be performed by literature by looking back at how Gilles Deleuze and Félix Guattari explain psychic recodification in *Anti-Oedipus: Capitalism and Schizophrenia*. Freud, they argue, in describing the *natural* psychological development he labels the "Oedipal conflict" recognized a pattern of desire and blockage not just inherent to human psychology but inherent in Western capitalism.[8] That is, Freud unintentionally mapped a sociocultural pattern onto the individual psyche—onto a narrative of a rite of passage—where he could discuss a cultural and economic system in terms of natural masculine development. He transferred (in Deleuze and Guattari's words, "psychically recodified") the societal system of European capitalism and its social conflicts onto a model of the individual psyche, displacing a macrocosm of real-world anxieties and desires onto a microcosmic model of the "normal" mind and body. Of course, as we know, the European capitalism that Freud described in terms of the individual was predicated on a system of colonization.[9] So, as Deleuze and Guattari define it, Freud's theory of the oedipal conflict describes an economic, political, and social system of colonial conflict. It is fitting that just as much of the modern world economically, politically, and socially descends from the legacy of empire, Freud's primary theory of how human beings confront identity springs out of the anxieties and desires of empire.

I use Deleuze and Guattari's theories because they help explain how castaway narratives could serve as a microcosm of larger imperial desires and anxieties, since many of these island narratives map desires and anxieties of a sociocultural phenomenon (colonization) into a representative narrative contained in a specific space (often the physical and psychological space of the novel) and onto the individual mind and body of a man. A complicated and ambivalent social system, then, becomes contained in a subgenre, in the pages of a book, and in one man's head. Just as Freud made the oedipal model seem natural as he internalized it and inserted it into "normal" psychosocial development, the authors of island narratives make imperial ideology seem natural by internalizing it and describing it in terms of the natural and logical behaviors of a castaway colonist surviving and "naturally" managing his own body. Producers of island narratives (both writers and the publishers who requested or responded to such tales) could thus subconsciously internalize the problems and paradigms of empire into a tale of a single, male colonial body—incorporating and thereby controlling—a single, uninhabited, bounded space. And in their pervasive consumption of island narratives, generations of colonial readers could recognize and more easily manage their recodified, psychosocial, real-world desires.

I use the term "psychosocial" throughout *Empire Islands* because this study looks at the complex nexus of the psychological and the sociological in island narratives. That is, I examine how the narratives participate in *psychological* processes by aiding individual psyches in managing the anxieties of colonization. At the same time, this study's analysis of how the narratives recodify the larger colonial cultural system in their island castaway stories presents *sociological* explanations. In many ways, *Empire Islands* demonstrates the theories Kelly Oliver outlines in *The Colonization of Psychic Space,* in which she develops "a theory that operates between the psyche and the social, through which the very terms of psychoanalysis are transformed into social concepts" (xiv). Like Oliver, I hope to show that, when it comes to empire, the psychological and sociological are intertwined and interdependent.

Methodology

I would like to take a minute to say more about my methodology as a researcher. Though *Empire Islands* draws upon arguments of psychoanalysis throughout, I use a "situated psychoanalysis," what Anne McClintock explains as "a culturally contextualized psychoanalysis that is simultaneously a psychoanalytically informed history" (*Imperial Leather,* 72). In short, though focused on reading literature to understand colonial impulses, like Ranjana Khanna's *Dark Continents,* one must remember that psychoanalytic theory was founded simultaneously with, in response to, and complicit with those same colonial impulses. Concepts of a circumscribed self as articulated in psychoanalysis need an Other with which to contrast, and where better to find that Other than through the process of colonization? In a study such as this one, which attempts to use psychoanalysis as a window into the colonial soul, it is even more important that terminology and theories be thoroughly contextualized since, as Khanna explains, psychoanalysis, along with psychology and psychiatry, was "employed by European colonizers . . . to assist in the analysis, pathologization, and repression of colonized peoples, sometimes reworking the basic assumptions of those fields to achieve this" (26). Historians of psychoanalysis, like Rubin Fine, have analyzed how the field grew out of and alongside historical situations rooted in early colonialism, as scientists of the seventeenth and eighteenth centuries began to look at mental illnesses as psychological diseases produced by sociocultural factors instead of as resulting from imbalance in the humors or demonic possession. With Freud's probing of the subconscious and recognition of neuroses as defense mechanisms, the family and European bourgeoisie society (which, as Edward Said argues, was built on scaffolds of colonialism) also came under scrutiny as causative agents. The self that psychoanalysis delimits is essentially a Modern and, because European, *imperial* self, even if directly disenfranchised from the spoils of empire because of class, gender, race, or religion. (Freud himself felt that his Jewish heritage, for example, factored negatively into his career.) Though Freud is not himself explicit in such connections between psychoanalysis and empire, he does imply a historical and ideological linkage in the subtitle of *Totem and Taboo,* "Resemblances Between the Psychic Lives of Savages and Neurotics," with the neurosis he describes being a Modern condition. As Freud explains, the psychic life of the colonized, "the savage and semi-savage races . . . assumes a peculiar interest for us, for we can recognize in their psychic life a well-preserved, early stage of our own development" (3). Remembering that Freud was working in an era where recapitulation theory (the notion that development of the species mirrors the development of the individual) was king, "us" and "we" were no doubt assumed to be Modern people living in the colonial so-called center, for whom colonized people are necessary for contrast.

Also concerning methodology, *Empire Islands* plumbs the subconscious thoughts and drives of generations of writers (as much as can be deduced from their stories) and readers (as much as can be deduced from their choice of reading material). While psychologists and psychoanalysts read the narrative and language of free association, hypnosis, or dreams to search for insight into the subconscious, I use literary texts. Like a psychologist or psychoanalyst, I read texts' narratives and language, as well as their illustrations, sales records, and any information I have about their use, all for insight into individual and societal subconscious and to speculate on the sociopsychological effects of literature. Experience tells us as readers and teachers that narrative does affect thought, though the tangible results, moments when someone's opinions were changed or anxieties assuaged through the reading of a book, are often elusive and illusory. Such evidence was especially slippery for this project since so many of these works and people are distant historically and since readers would not necessarily be aware of reactions (because often subconscious) or able to record them. Of course, we also need to recognize that not all readers would react to the same story in the same way, though publishing industries must have assumed a critical mass of similar readings, or they wouldn't have kept republishing the same essential story in different guises. Despite this risk of overgeneralizing, *Empire Islands* studies the psychosocial consequences of generations of readers consuming so much island literature.

The nature of *Empire Islands* also demands that, as well as reading texts for their stories, I analyze the texts' physical properties for evidence of their use, intention, and reception, thus occasionally invoking a certain edition's illustration of a scene for evidence of the text's message to its readers, for its possible effect on readers' and illustrators' perception of the story.[10] I have found through examination of scores of these volumes that my own reaction to the text is indeed affected by its packaging, that a striking illustration shapes my response to a certain scene or character. Generations of readers may have been similarly affected by the packaging of island narratives, which justifies reading illustrations and other material elements, where appropriate, for further clues into (at least what publishers perceived to be) readers' and cultures' elusive psyches. As well, examination of the production history of these texts can provide fascinating insight into a collective production of ideology. My analysis reads these texts as cooperative projects in which many people (authors, editors, illustrators, publishers, translators) participated in the production of colonial ideology. Moreover, these publishing conventions often created a critical practice of their own. One can see, for instance, how illustrations of *Robinson Crusoe* build upon and modify earlier illustrations, creating an interesting dynamic of intertextuality; and how a tradition evolved in the nineteenth century of publishing new editions of *Robinson Crusoe* prefaced by a heroic biography of Defoe. Both practices create a hidden relationship between editions of the text and the many hands over the years that touch them, a tradition as strong as that between author and reader.

In my struggle to understand the specters of reader psychology, I have needed to borrow tools and language from distinct yet compatible disciplines and theoretical camps. Like the four blind men in the fable, each one feeling and describing a different part of an elephant's body (one its trunk, one its side, one its leg, and one its tail), different approaches to cultural analysis (such as those found in literature, postcolonial studies, anthropology, geography, and psychoanalytic theory) can describe the same animal (in my case the psychology of modern, imperial, culture) using varying language and protocols. Only by piecing together their narratives, as does this book, can one gain a three-dimensional description of the beast we call empire.

Island Overview

It would be helpful to forecast how *Empire Islands* as a whole develops the ideas just outlined. What I have outlined so far, how island narratives play out desires for natural and secure colonial authority, is fleshed out, so to speak, in the first chapter. Drawing on psychoanalytic theories of perception of bodies and space, the chapter analyzes certain repeated colonial actions, which function to give castaway colonists imagined control over their space. These colonial deeds, which Patricia Seed calls "rituals of possession," include mapping, building structures, domesticating animals and plants, even changing the topography to better suit the castaway's needs. All of these further the castaway's process of psychically linking his changing body to the changing island space, thereby giving him a sense of natural command over the island as his command over his body (his "discipline") increases.

Chapter 2 builds on this discussion of discipline and desire, focusing on how the narratives construct the island fantasy so that "natural" control becomes equated with white imperial manhood, masculine fortitude, and natural law. Though island narratives occasionally contain

more than one male protagonist (sometimes a female, as well), the stories consistently show that the most masculine white man (with defini-
tions of "masculine" shifting over time) *earns* island ownership through
his discipline and fortitude. Women and the other island-stranded men
need to be protected and commanded by this disciplined man, because
lacking his perfect restraint, they cannot plan or think as well, resist their
physical needs, or maintain cheerful and focused minds. *The Swiss Family Robinson,* for instance, details how the castaway father dominates his
wife and rears his four sons to be good colonists, transferring his fatherly,
masculine rule over their bodies into an internalized island law.

   The book's third and fourth chapters analyze the island narrative
as manager of trauma, specifically the colonist's fear of the breakdown
of this imagined natural, imperial control. In answer to a need to feel
secure as well as justified in imperial aspirations, the narratives enact
dramas of the successful *repulsion* of threats to the body, which symbolize threats to the island and empire. Chapter 3 focuses on anxieties of
counterincorporation, in which the castaway colonist feels threatened by
cannibals and pirates with the loss of both island and body, in stories
that reverse the incorporative acts that gave him that authority. So, for
instance, island narratives often pair cannibal and pirate invasions (as
in *Robinson Crusoe* and *Masterman Ready*), with the cannibals standing
for threats to the colonist's island and body by indigenous forces and
the pirates standing for threats to the colonist's body and island from
competing "bad" colonizers. Chapter 3 also examines the *allure* of the
cannibal and the pirate and how many island narratives include stories
of the castaway being *forced* to be a cannibal (such as Poe's *The Narrative
of Arthur Gordon Pym*) or pirate (such as Ballantyne's *The Coral Island*) in
ways that leave the character free of moral responsibility and allow the
reader to safely play out these abject fantasies.

   Chapter 4 extends this discussion of feared loss of control, moving
from chapter 3's analysis of counterincorporation into an interrogation
of *counter-transformation.* In a reverse of the story of domestication outlined in chapter 1, the colonist fears being transformed *by* the island, being infected (as Prendick fears in *The Island of Dr. Moreau*) by a "bestial
taint" (95), that is "degenerating" or "going native." Many texts, such as
Jules Verne's *The Mysterious Island,* include a wild man character with
which to contrast the disciplined castaway, or they include an island "indigene" (human, animal, or monster) that has already been infected by
the island's savagery, an event the texts often mark on the character's

body with tattoos, darkened skin, or animalistic or monstrous features. The chapter also investigates colonists' relationships with island animals and castaways' attempts to use science and law as antidotes to the island's savagery, thereby sealing the boundaries of their own bodies, making them impregnable to "infection."

The book's fifth chapter examines texts of resistance to the repeated psychological drama of self-justification. It examines how primarily eighteenth- and nineteenth-century burlesque performances and pantomimes interact with imperial ideology in a complex manner, how they both dissipate and concretize popular ambivalence toward empire for different audiences at different times. These popular dramas, such as Gilbert and Sullivan's *Utopia Limited,* Thomas Duffett's *Mock-Tempest,* and Geoffrey Thorne's *Grand Christmas Pantomime Entitled Robinson Crusoe, or Harlequin Man Friday, Who Kept the House Tidy, and Polly of Liverpool Town* (1895), use humor both to recognize and encourage their audiences' latent dissatisfaction with violent and self-threatening imperial practices. Because they also provide a controlled space for the venting of these resistant energies, as Mikhail Bakhtin explains in his discussion of carnival in *Rabelais and His World,* these theatrical experiences could also undermine the mobilization of this dissatisfaction, perhaps ultimately serving as a tool of empire, not of resistance.

The book's final chapter explores why contemporary, supposedly postcolonial audiences continue to find the island fantasy pervasive and attractive, as suggested by U.S. versions of the island fantasy in television (such as *Survivor* and *Temptation Island*) and film (such as *Cast Away* and *The Beach*). The chapter argues that by looking at these late twentieth- and early twenty-first-century cinematic versions of the castaway story, we can see an American-based neo-imperial fantasy at work. I am particularly interested in looking at how the United States, which many see as the world's neo-imperial power, draws upon traditional colonial discourse. We have certainly seen U.S. history echo dual representations of islands as sites of desire and anxiety. A nonisland nation (though it often thinks of itself as a political island), the United States has historically incorporated islands it desires, as states (Hawaii) or protectorates (Puerto Rico and the Philippines). Yet simultaneously, islands form sites of anxiety in the United States, because the only attacks on U.S. soil since its own civil war targeted islands—Hawaii on December 7, 1941, and more recently, Manhattan on September 11, 2001. The assertions *Empire Islands* makes of a subconscious link between islands, masculine bodies, and the national imagination could also help to decipher claims that the attacks on Pearl Harbor and on Manhattan challenged the national masculinity of the United States—especially if one thinks of the twin towers in the World Trade Center as national phalluses.[11] In this neo-imperial age of expanding global corporatism, international terrorism panics, Western hoarding of medicine and technology from the third world, and tyrannies of information (everything from medical records to satellite images), now more than ever we need a nuanced understanding of imperialism's internal logic, which demands that we continue to investigate the psychology of empire. *Empire Islands* aims to contribute to that exploration of the psychology behind colonialism to better understand the complexities of colonizers, the mental processes that enabled them to legitimize their colonial aggression, the compulsions that led writers to construct and continually replay the same island fantasy, and the cravings that led to these stories' continuing popularity with readers.

1. Monarchs of All They Survey

THE story is familiar: a castaway, brave and lucky, survives a shipwreck and initial despair to make the perfect home of an alien island, meanwhile evolving, himself, from survivor to colonist. The latter, that crucial *psychological* transition from survivor to colonist, occurs in tale after tale through a well-known series of events, including one oft-repeated scene in which the castaway views the island from an elevated site, often from a mountaintop. But what happens, we might ask, in the castaway's mind during those familiar events? What leads to his sense of possession? And what can tracing this psychological transition from survivor to colonist in the literary realm bring to our understanding of real-world colonization? Answering these questions and understanding the ideological function of island narratives within imperialism demands that we pause to examine in greater detail this transition from survivor to colonist, focusing in particular on that repeated scene of mountain-top surveying.

Published during high empire (just a couple of years before the world witnessed England's Queen Victoria declare herself Empress of India), Jules Verne's *The Mysterious Island* (1875) provides the perfect terrain for seeking answers to these questions.[1] The novel begins, as is typical of island narratives, with its five protagonists' narrow escape from a tempest-caused shipwreck, though in their case, the "ship" was a hot air balloon in which they escaped captivity of the U.S. Civil War's Confederate Army. After five horrific days of toughing out a storm while suspended over the sea in a slowly deflating balloon, four of Verne's five protagonists (and their dog) crash on a piece of land they later learn is an island, and they soon discover that they are separated from the fifth castaway, Cyrus Harding, whose knowledge and leadership they know assures their survival. Thus they spend their first few days on the island desperately searching for Harding, instead of (as in other island narratives) scrambling to salvage what they can from the wrecked craft, symbol of their old world, before it vanishes. Crusoe, for instance, after surviving his shipwreck and his first day of complete shock and stupor, in a panic unloads every movable object from the wrecked ship onto the island. Verne intentionally adapted that element of the castaway story, choosing to strand his characters without a ship or any provisions from their balloon excepting two pocket watches, a pad of paper, the clothes on their backs, and their wits. As he says in his authorial commentary, they must "from nothing . . . supply themselves with everything," which they do, beginning with the customary desperate quest for shelter and food and with an uncustomary search for their leader (36). In Verne's version it is the culmination of that search (like the unloading of the ship in other tales) that marks a transition into a new segment of the adventure and the beginning of the castaway's mental shift from survivor to colonist. When they do joyously find the injured Harding and he murmurs, "Island or continent?" (53), the book's and the castaways' attention shifts to the quest to learn the answer to that question, the typical second concern of the castaway. When assured of the basic necessities, Verne's castaways, like others, transition from panic to stay alive to consideration of long-term future, climbing the levels of desire and concern that Abraham Maslow would later map into a "hierarchy."

As briefly explained in my introduction, castaways typically attempt to answer that crucial question of "island or continent" by ascending to an elevated position where they can survey the entire land mass. Pratt explains in her analysis of similar moments in so-called nonfictional travel narratives that the dramatic narration of the monarch-of-all-I-survey scene was necessary to "render momentously significant what is, especially from a narrative point of view, practically a non-event" (202). Yet, if the actual "discovery" was a nonevent, she says, the text narrating the occasion was enormously important in documenting the "discovery" for other imperialists and crucial for granting the adventurer legal claims over the gazed-upon space. As L. J. Davis also notes in "Known Unknown Locations: The Ideology of Novelistic Landscape in *Robinson Crusoe*" the ability to produce descriptions of the land granted legal rights: "Since natives could not describe their own space they could not be said to own it in the same way as the European—and here the ability to describe land has its legal consequences as well since deeds and land claims require a specialized kind of linguistic notation" (100). As Pratt explains with Mungo Parks's claim to Victoria Falls, the simple act of seeing the landscape and describing that moment in text, even though the falls were, of course, previously known to the African guide who brought

Parks there, gave him the psychological and legal sense of ownership necessary to name the falls and claim it for England. The monarch-of-all-I-survey scene found in island narratives is equally key to providing the fictional colonist with a fantasy of power over the land he views, and as in real-world travel narratives, such fictional texts also enable their readers to establish and maintain a fantasy of legitimate ownership over colonized lands symbolized by the fictional island.

The often-dramatic presentation of that monarch-of-all-I-survey moment attests to its import to the castaway's developing imperial identity (as does the fact that so many postcolonial writers needed to dismantle it in their texts of "writing back"). As Verne's castaways climb an extinct volcano to behold island shores on every side, for instance, they wonder, "Did the sea surround this unknown land?" a thought to which they respond with delight mixed with fear. Two of the castaways, reach the summit just at twilight, when the fog that has shrouded the island since their arrival briefly and dramatically lifts. Seeing by moonlight the "horizontal line" of the island meeting the sea, they exclaim "An island!" in a "grave" voice. At that moment, darkness suddenly falls, "the lunar crescent disappear[ing] beneath the waves," swathing their panorama in shadows (72). These first two castaways to reach the summit have their excitement tempered by apprehension, but the other castaways ascending the peak the next morning display more frank delight and anticipation. They cry, "'The sea, the sea everywhere!' . . . as if their lips could not restrain the words which made islanders of them" (74), their enthusiasm momentarily supplanting their anxieties.

This moment was more vividly and dramatically described in nineteenth-century island narratives such as Verne's than in earlier versions, such as the seventeenth-century *Tempest* or the early eighteenth-century *Robinson Crusoe,* perhaps indicating that as the European imperial enterprise continued, increasing effort was put into masking capitalistic motives behind aesthetic or moral ones. Yet that virtually every castaway narrative includes this monarch-of-all-I-survey moment attests to the scene's centrality to the ideological work the texts perform across historical boundaries. On the one hand, this dramatic moment encapsulates the combined trepidation and desire—the ambivalence—castaway colonists typically feel at learning they are island-bound, an ambivalence likely shared by real-world explorers such as Columbus, whose anticipation of gain and glory was tempered by fear and, perhaps on some level, guilt. Though concerned by the many hazards of island isolation (including going mad, attack from natives and wild animals), these literary castaways are in equal measure intoxicated by the spectacle of the island and by their new possession's potential. While standing "mute and motionless" on that summit, Verne's awe-struck characters, for instance, "surveyed for some minutes every point of the ocean, examining it to its most extreme limits . . . From the ocean their gaze returned to the island which they commanded entirely" (74, 75). The scene is often fraught with tension, as it is in Verne's book, mirroring (in Homi Bhabha's words in "Of Mimicry and Man") the "colonial ambivalence" of the larger culture. Perhaps, by showing ambivalence as a normal element of imperial exploration instead of as a specter of subconscious angst, such scenes add the individual and cultural acceptance of that ambivalence.

The surveying moment's significance, as well, comes from its initiation of the psychological processes crucial to the castaway's transformation from survivor to colonist: to his gaining a sense of possession of the space. In island tale after island tale, during and after the monarch-of-all-I-survey scene, the castaway moves beyond his initial despondency to embrace his new role of colonist. Verne's characters, for instance, resolve just before departing their mountaintop "not [to] consider ourselves castaways, but colonists who have come here to settle" (78). The psychological shift from castaway to colonist so marvelously expressed in that statement, its importance, and its psychological power for both character and reader will be the focus of this chapter. Throughout this chapter I revisit this moment from *The Mysterious Island* and others like it because they are crucial to understanding the psychology behind island narratives, specifically how certain repeated plot elements of island narratives dramatize and enable desires of empire while helping to assuage anxieties. More than later chapters, this one is grounded in psychoanalytic theory, particularly in theories of incorporation, which provide a powerful mechanism to explain how the "monarch-of-all-I-survey" moment in island narratives initiates the transition from survivor to colonist. To that end, the chapter first lays out the psychoanalytic theories most useful for unpacking how the colonist and reader imagine gaining ownership of the island, in particular Melanie Klein's theories of *projective identification*. Then, I explore more fully how the narratives dramatize first projection and then identification, ending by examining the text itself as a sort of island and our reading of it as incorporation.

Psychoanalyzing Possession

Better understanding of how literature and island narratives in particular participate in sociohistorical processes such as empire requires speculation on how such texts could psychologically and emotionally involve readers in their adventures, without, of course, slighting the important geographical, historical, and sociocultural differences between readers. We can find clues to potential effects on readers of that typical moment of island surveying in artistic depictions of that scene, such as one by the noted American artist N. C. Wyeth, who illustrated a number of island narratives, including a 1920 edition of *The Mysterious Island* (see Figure 2). Wyeth's artful illustration works to place the reader within that moment of mountaintop observation. He paints the five protagonists at the volcanic summit underneath an enormous white-clouded blue sky, emphasizing the immense horizon, their isolation and mastery over the space, each character captured in emotion as he looks to where the land meets the sea. The characters' bodies seem to overlap, forming one combined entity at the island's center. Though each character gazes over only a portion of the island, together they can survey all of the island's boundaries from that one elevated spot.[2] In the background behind the men, one side of the island joins the sea. On the right, Neb, the former slave, and Top, the dog, view the island's eastern boundaries, while two other survivors, Jack Pencroft and Gideon Spilett, scan the western shores off to the left. It is interesting to consider that Wyeth's 1920 illustration of that paradigmatic moment of imperial possession (an illustration that, published in New York, would have been at least partially aimed at U.S. readers) was released to the world at the end of what was, at that time, the world's bloodiest and costliest world war (a war partially caused by a race for colonies) and at the beginning of the rise in global importance of the United States. The castaways Wyeth paints are Americans engaged in an allegory of imperial possession, an occurrence reminding us of the role of the United States in the drama of empire, even while disavowing colonial ambitions.

The genius of Wyeth's composition lies in its *non*-depiction of the island's final side and in his employment of multiple tools of perspective to include the reader. The group's leader, Cyrus Harding, and the boy, Herbert, look towards the island's unseen shores over the reader/viewer's right shoulder. Wyeth's configuration craftily locates the island's undrawn boundary behind the reader/viewer's back, placing the reader

FIGURE 2. *Marooned* by N. C. Wyeth, from Jules Verne, *The Mysterious Island* (New York: Scribner, 1920), 79.

on the mountaintop with the other castaway colonists. This effect, of making the reader/viewer part of the scene, is enhanced by Wyeth's drawing of mysterious shadows crossing Herbert and Harding's bodies, shadows which could be cast by another body, perhaps the reader/viewer's, which further places the reader/viewer imaginatively just in front of the castaways, facing them. Situating the reader/viewer *with* the protagonists on that mountaintop, surveying the boundaries of the island with them, encourages the reader/viewer to participate in that moment's fantasy of island ownership and colonization.

Such attempts to invite readers into the action are not limited to illustrations, for the narratives often strive to insert readers into the story through their plot as well. Readers are encouraged by the familiar story of island survival to participate in the drama of colonization and speculate on their own ingenuity. If in the same situation, readers are guided to wonder, could they match the castaway's cleverness? Would they survive and prosper or descend into savagery and perish? Much of the appeal of the island narrative genre, in fact, stems from its ability to pull readers into the colonial adventure with the protagonists. As Walter de la Mare remarks in his classic study of island narratives, "we [the readers] are autocrats there [on the imaginary island]—monarchs of all we survey, from its vines and goats to its stars and its ocean" (44). Through imaginatively sharing the castaway's adventures, beginning with the monarch-of-all-I-survey scene, readers can share the castaway's sense of possession of the island. Although seemingly innocent within the narrative, this moment of mental surveying symbolizes an aggressive act of real-world imperialism; the monarch-of-all-I-survey scene initiates a fantasy that seeks to buffer readers' encounter with any guilt resulting from their participation or complicity in such actions, however limited.

Psychoanalytic theory provides a valuable interpretive frame for understanding just how the monarch-of-all-I-survey scene catalyzes the castaway's fantasized command of the island. We should not be surprised at the applicability of psychoanalysis, considering the field's roots in and co-evolution with European imperial culture. As explained in my introduction, a variety of psychoanalytic theories (grown out of empire and Western capitalism) postulate a psychological relationship between fantasies of controlling one's body and fantasies of controlling objects and space. Theories of incorporation, in particular, prove constructive for explaining how the fictional castaway psychologically grants himself ownership of the island and how these perceptions of ownership involve the male body as a locus for control. (As I will explain later in the chapter, theories of the body image and the skin ego are equally useful for exploring the importance of bodily boundaries.) Freud explains that human beings, as sexually embodied creatures, obtain a necessary sense of management of the sometimes-overwhelming world outside the body by imaginatively taking it into their bodies. Just as children put objects they desire to know or control into their mouths, Freud says, adult subjects also psychically incorporate and thus imagine they control objects they desire or fear. As noted in the introduction, because the behavioral patterns Freud posited as innate can also be understood as recodifications of entrenched economic, social, and psychological systems of capitalism and exchange, it could be that children simply express in a more overt manner than adults their ongoing training into those cultural systems. Understanding incorporative impulses as socially constructed instead of as innate, however, makes them no less powerful.

Generations of theorists have refined Freud's ideas of incorporation, including Melanie Klein, who, from her work with children and babies explains *destructive* impulses of incorporation as responses to fears of a threatening figure. Children undergoing an oral-sadistic phase and coping with fears of being re-imprisoned in their mothers' bodies, she says, would fantasize about projecting themselves into the mother's body in order to control her from within or would fantasize about devouring her insides by sucking at her breast, resulting in her destruction. Though I remain a bit wary of Klein's methodology (she reads children's preverbal fantasies through their play), I do find her articulation of the violence inherent in incorporative fantasies to be compelling. Some castaways' behaviors towards the island, their compulsive efforts to remake the island, are quite violent, as with the castaways in *The Mysterious Island,* who blow up parts of the island to make it better suit their needs (which I will discuss at greater length). In adulthood, as well, Klein and Freud say, incorporative fantasies might involve both mastery and destruction, responding to both latent fear and desire.

Klein's second important development of Freud's work involves her theorizing incorporation as a two-part process of "projective identification." In incorporation, she argues, subjects first *project* themselves onto an object by psychically filling the object with characteristics of themselves, in essence seeing the object in terms of how they imagine themselves. Subjects then *identify* with the objects onto which they have psychically projected themselves, recognizing themselves in the fantasy projected onto the object and consuming that fantasy. Through this combination of projection and identification, Klein explains, a person can imagine incorporating an object that is like him/herself, even if that object is feared.[3] Both Freud and Klein postulate that, because sub-jects desire to incorporate objects with which they can identify rather than those they see as Other, incorporation requires both projection onto and identification with the object. Again, we could understand this need for projection as an aspect of incorporation as part of a capitalistic cultural construct, since consumers—even of the colonial era—seek to incorporate objects that reflect a desirable image of themselves, even if that image is of one who consumes "exotic" (desirably Other) or "risqué" (threatening) objects.

Projection and the Eye-land Gaze

Klein's theory of projection is particularly helpful for understanding the castaway colonist's initial thoughts and actions upon ascending the is-land summit and how these thoughts and actions relate to his gaining a sense of control over the island space. By analyzing a castaway's behav-ior, we can gain insight into his thoughts, particularly his use of sight to survey the island and to project identity and needs onto it in preparation for incorporation. Typically, during his first few days on the island, and particularly while standing on the island's summit, the castaway surveys the island, visually cataloging its flora and fauna, being especially inter-ested in other human inhabitants or dangerous animals. These initial acts of viewing the island enable castaways to classify the island as *terra nullius*, that is, as empty and thus available for colonizing. In *The Mysteri-ous Island*, however, the castaways during their initial few days can't see the island because of its heavy fog. Until their monarch-of-all-I-survey scene, the fog frustrates their attempts, keeping in question the island's availability (perhaps forecasting their eventual discovery that the island was previously colonized by Captain Nemo). Yet at the appropriate mo-ment, the island sheds its fog, enabling their panoptic gaze and their initial feelings of command of the space.[4] As persuasively illustrated by Pratt, a slippery slope of normalizing authority begins with visual surveys of landscape, which can lead to literal mapping, and then to cognitive appropriation, culminating in legal and physical appropriation.

Belief in the eye or its gaze as agent of control was not new to the island narrative. As cultural historians explain, vision has long been understood in terms of the power (or the fantasy of power) it grants the viewer over the objects or subjects being viewed.[5] Both David Lindberg and Thomas Laqueur analyze the first-century Greek anatomist Galen, who postulated that the "male" eye reached out from the viewer through hollow optic nerves stemming from the mind to seize and transform the object being viewed. Galen thought this act of vision *physically* joined the viewer with the viewed, granting the viewer power over the viewed. Centuries later (not coincidentally during a period of increasing European colonization and heightened popularity of island narratives) early-modern scientists continued to perceive the gaze as agent of control, despite competing Aristotelian theories that contrastingly perceived vision as the act of a passive eye accepting the forms that light brings to its optic nerve. Early-modern anatomists, Sergei Lobanov-Rostovsky explains, resolved this difference between Galen's active theory of vision and the Aristotelian passive theory by coalescing the competing theories of vision into the concept of the *gaze*. In this combined principle, the wielder of the gaze projects his power out of his body through his eyes to command the object being viewed. In the eighteenth century, the Austrian physician and hypnotist Franz Mesmer's theories of the effects of "animal magnetism," later called "mesmerism," built upon such fantasies of a controlling gaze. In Mesmer's popular (but highly scientifically contested) theory, one person could hold a "magnetic" influence over another person initiated through a powerful gaze or magnetic wand.[6] Freud also talked about the desire to see, which, as Peter Brooks explains in *Body Work,* he labeled a drive and termed "scopophilia," in contrast with the drive to know, "epistemophelia," both drives producing an erotic pleasure when satisfied. In island narratives' plots of the gaze as agent of control, we find historical and ideological parallels of such "scientific" theories of the gaze, just as psychoanalytic theories of incorporation describe fantasies of commanding or incorporating objects with a gaze.

This gloss of the history of the gaze contextualizes some of the castaway's typical actions of viewing, surveying, and charting—which I see as behaviors of psychical projection. One of these typical actions involves the castaway colonist as he views the island, describing it as he needs it to be for his ownership of it, which may or may not correspond to any "reality" of what the island actually shows him. The act of narrating this mental map of the island, of course, means that the castaway colonist inscribes the island as filtered through the screen of his wants and fears, thus projecting his needs onto the island's space and onto the space of the book's page. In *Robinson Crusoe,* for example, after unloading his ship, Crusoe, as is typical, ascends the highest hill on his island. At first, as did Verne's protagonists, he reacts with ambivalence, seeing "to [his] great Affliction" that he is "in an Island environ'd every Way with the Sea" (40). As well as describing his "affliction," Crusoe's initial description of the island reveals his beginning subconscious incorporation of it, as he projects his needs, desires, and fears into the island. With little evidence, he labels the island "barren" (though later descriptions contradict this first statement), thereby establishing that the island needs a good colonial steward like himself. He also declares it "un-inhabited, except by wild Beasts, of whom however [he] saw none," thereby erasing any competing claims for it (40). Further, the presence of wild beasts, Crusoe reasons, establishes that the island needs his civilizing influence. Crusoe's reasoning here is, of course, in keeping with real-world imperial discourse. Through texts such as Kipling's "White Man's Burden," colonial powers worked to convince the public at home and the people they would colonize that colonizable people were in need of imperial guidance and that such guidance was the "white man's" (in Kipling's case, the Euro-American's) duty.

Interestingly, despite its work as a tool of colonial ideology, *Robinson Crusoe* presents "official" European colonization in a negative light (contrary to Defoe's own pro-colonization views, as reported by Michael Seidel). In order to better portray Crusoe's island colonization as innocent and good, the novel contrasts his benevolent behavior on the island with his earlier life as a slave owner and colonial sugar planter in the Brazilian colonies (for a brief time, in fact, he is a slave himself). Indeed, the voyage he undertakes that strands him on the island involves the colonial slave trade. However, after being stranded on the island, he experiences a religious conversion and criticizes his previous colonial ventures, calling his past life "my wicked and hardned Life past" (96). Yet, he doesn't criticize his colonization of the island, nor does he even label his habitation as "colonization," though he uses the colonial term "plantation" to refer to his settlements (110). Crusoe recognizes his sovereignty over the island, calling himself "Lord of the whole Manor; or if I pleas'd . . . King, or Emperor over the whole Country which I had Possession of" (94), yet the novel presents his island colonization as benevolent, accidental, innocent, and humanitarian, and de-emphasizes his colonial motives by repeatedly comparing the castaway Crusoe with his earlier selfishly colonial self.

Crusoe's initial reactions to the island's animals (real and imagined) as voiced in his monarch-of-all-I-survey moment also hint at a complicated set of anxieties about empire. First, Crusoe's assumption of wild beasts suggests fears of being killed and eaten. Soon afterwards, he survives an earthquake and begins to fear "being swallow'd up alive" by the island (61). Again Klein's theories of the destructive part of incorporation provide a useful approach for understanding these fears. Crusoe's phobia of the island eating him mirrors unconscious childhood fears that the mother wants to reabsorb the child into the womb (which chapter 3 further examines in arguments that the desire to incorporate always carries the simultaneous fear of/desire to be incorporated). Second, Crusoe's assumption of wild beasts, if resulting from his reading of fantastic travelers' tales that typically contained fabulous animals, could also index anxieties of prior travelers and a priori occupation of his island; he fears *not* being the first European on his island as much as he fears being the first European on the island. Finally, Crusoe's reaction to the animals he actually sees is just as telling as his reaction to the animals he only imagines. He sees a bird, shoots at it, and declares that his shot "was the first Gun that had been fir'd there since the Creation of the World" (40)—a phallic fantasy that provides a brief glimpse into Crusoe's desperation to assert himself the first and sole monarch of all he surveys, even as he fears what he sees.

In other castaway narratives, such as Ralph Morris's *A Narrative of the Life and Astonishing Adventures of John Daniel* (1751), this process of projection leads castaways to anthropomorphize the island, to not only project onto the island their needs for it but to project onto it their own agency, feelings, and motivations. After the two castaway colonists in that tale (John Daniel and "Thomas," who is later revealed to be a woman disguised as a man) "conquer" their island mountain, as John Daniel explains, "we plainly then perceived that the land we inhabited was an island, which to our apprehensions might be about ten miles over, the way we came, and might be the transverse way, near as long again" (54). As with other castaways, they admit their "apprehension" at the recognition of the island, but soon transfer that anxiety into fantasies of incorporation. Their visual mapping of the island according to their position on it, according to "the way [they] came" suggests projection and identification, as well.

A second clue to their evolving mental incorporation comes through Thomas and John Daniel's striking paucity of detail (compared with Verne's description) of the island as they see it; instead they tell about their projection of themselves and their experience onto the island. Excepting the size of the island ("about ten miles over, the way we came, and might be the transverse way, near as long again"), the castaways only describe one feature of what they see before them: "wherever there was any large savannah, or plain, we were sure to see a river, or brook running along it" (54). Otherwise, in language suggesting projection, the entirety of the two-page narration concerns why they spent the night on the mountaintop, focusing on their relationship with the island and demonstrating their anthropomorphism of it. As John Daniel explains, "the prospect we enjoyed upon this mountain, *inviting* our eyes longer than we had purposed to stay there, we could not possibly reach our lodging by day light" (55, emphasis mine). By saying that the mountain "invites" their eyes, John Daniel and Thomas ascribe to it their own voyeurism, imagining that its view coerces their stay despite their original "purposes." John Daniel personifies the landscape, in effect naturalizing his own projection of colonial desire through a nature that seems to want his presence on that mountain and that embraces him and "Thomas" in what he later calls a "snug hollow" (55). John Daniel's fantasy that the island encourages their stay is further revealed in his description of it providing for them an evening meal. While climbing the mountain, Thomas and John sight birds eating acorns, which, as John Daniel explains, "*induced* us freely to make the experiment ourselves" (54), meaning that later John and Thomas were "*supplied* with so large a quantity of the nuts, we were not so solicitous for returning [from the mountain to their shore camp], as we otherwise must have been" (55, emphasis mine). The island, in John Daniel's language, "invites" them to consume it, showing them what and how to eat ("inducing" their experimentation) and then "supplying" them with so much food that they were discouraged from leaving, prolonging their incorporation of the island and its products. This fantasy of a fecund land inviting colonization must have been seductive during the mid-eighteenth century, when John Daniel's narrative was published. As the British continued to fight the French for hold over North America—a contest in which key to claiming land were assertions of the vibrancy of one's settlements— fantasies of "inviting" land could make successful settlements seem like evidence of the land itself choosing its conquerors.

Such language insinuating John Daniel and Thomas's projection of their behaviors and wishes onto the island mountain continues throughout the next segment of the scene. As John and Thomas "began to form a design of establishing there a place for a signal, in case we should happen to see any vessel passing by," John Daniel admits that they were "now *persuaded* there were no inhabitants in the island" (55, 56, emphasis mine). The mountain, while enabling their incorporation, also solicits their ownership by "persuading" them of its emptiness, its status as *terra nullius,* perhaps offering itself to them. In the following sentence, John Daniel remarks that they "could form no prospect of relief, but from what we might providentially observe, from the height of the mountain" (56). Significantly, this "relief" from despair or perhaps solitude, which "providence" has enabled them to observe from the mountain, does not contain hope of rescue but instead comprises elements of their future as colonists: the island's natural resources, its lack of natives, and its wish to be consumed. The highly suggestive language in this description reflects as much of Thomas and John Daniel's need to project their desire to be colonists onto the space, as it does the scene that their eyes actually encountered. In that moment Thomas and John Daniel begin to accept their fate, transitioning from castaway survivors to castaway colonists.

Naming and Mapping

After such mental charting often come two other behaviors equally important to the castaway's transition to colonist, which are also typically initiated in the monarch-of-all-I-survey scene: naming the island and mapping it. After the colonists mentally chart the island, they often give it a name, labeling its geographical features after their experiences there or after themselves. This trope of naming could be read as further evidence of their projection, for, as Pratt explains when discussing the naming involved in natural history, "naming brings the reality of order into being" (33). The family of castaway colonists in *The Swiss Family Robinson,* for instance, names the island and its attributes according to their adventures. After the Robinson father and his two oldest sons climb the island's promontory to survey it, they return to their camp, where the family as a whole chooses to name the island "New Switzerland" after the European homeland they left and to which they feel akin. The rest of the island they designate after their experiences, calling the bay where they first landed, "Safety Bay," as the mother says, "in token of gratitude for our escape" (94); the shore where they first camped "Tentholm"; their tree house "Falconhurst"; the prominence from which they surveyed the island "Prospect Hill"; and the place where they looked in vain for other shipwreck survivors, "Cape Disappointment." Such actions of self-naming provide further insight into the projection taking place in the castaway's subconscious, for after the act of naming the place, the castaway behaves increasingly as if the island is his space, his colony.

We find clearly expressed the psychological shift in perception that follows island naming in the Robinson father's articulation of their motives for mapping and naming the island: "It will become more and more troublesome to explain what we mean unless we do so [name parts of the island]," he explains. "Besides which we shall feel much more at home if we can talk as people do in inhabited countries" (94). This mapping and naming, which mark a further stage in their projection of themselves on the island, will make the Robinsons "feel much more at home," in that they will be able to better see themselves reflected in the space. Yet at the same time, the wording here suggests an as-yet incomplete authority, an ongoing struggle to establish ownership, for Mr. Robinson forecasts that with naming they will "talk *as* people do in inhabited countries," suggesting that they are at that moment different from those people, that they do not yet inhabit their own country (94, emphasis mine). Such exertions to quickly map and name the island remind that anxieties of insecure possession often accompany desires of ownership.

In some island narratives, the characters take a further step in establishing possession by transcribing their mental charts of the island onto physical space, either onto a piece of paper or wood. In eighteenth- and nineteenth-century Europe, the act of writing itself carried legal, social, and psychological power. As Daniel Lord Smail notes in *Imaginary Cartographies,* documentation often equaled reification: "All maps, linguistic or graphic, are sites for the expression of power, state or otherwise, even if changing technologies of map production allow for changes in the expression of that power" (8). And in his analysis of early-modern European mapmaking, *The Self-Made Map,* Tom Conley also links a rise in mapmaking to early-modern shifts in perception of individuality, as he says, in "the new importance afforded to the emerging *self* and to the self's relation to the idea of national space. In this domain . . . there seems to be a correlation between mapping and the growth of a new medium— literature—in early modern print culture" (2). In other words, maps, names, and I add island narratives all reify one capitalistic relationship to space (ownership of land) through another capitalistic relationship to space (possession of the printed document), all of which, I argue, can be traced back to fantasies of controlling the space of the body.

Verne's characters in *The Mysterious Island,* for instance, by inscribing their mental map of their island onto paper and making a physical record of their incorporative moment, enhance their sense of and claim to mastery over the landscape. As in the other narratives, Verne's castaway colonists begin by visually surveying the island and then designate their ownership through naming it. Verne indicates in the monarch-of-all-I-survey scene that the island was "spread out under their eyes like a map and they had only to give names to all its angles and points. Gideon Spilett would write them down, and the geographical nomenclature of the island would definitely be adopted" (79). As this passage attests, colonial authority here slips between visual acumen and cartographic dominance, for to assume control over the island, they had "only" to view it, name it, map it, and inscribe that mental mapping and mastery onto physical space. Interestingly (like Jacques Derrida's argument that the U.S. Declaration of Independence gained authority from its signatures, while simultaneously and paradoxically granting the signers the power to make the declaration in the first place), it is this act of naming and mapping that simultaneously gives the castaways the authority and recognizes their authority to map and name it. Conley theorizes the importance of real-world mapmakers' signatures (which are both image and text) using some of the same logic: "The writer or cartographer labors at creating the aura of the language and the lands of his patron, but he also gains currency, ascendancy, and even a sense of adequacy through the gesture and reminder of his own presence located in the inscription" (21). In castaway novels, moments of naming the parts of the island and inscribing those names into a text demonstrate how colonists such as those in *The Mysterious Island* project themselves onto the landscape to receive a sense of control over the island, attempting to document and fix their shaky sense of "ownership" of the territory, and inscribe their mental projection of the island onto another physical space, the surface of a map.

Often those scenes of projective mapping contain other clues to the castaway's psychological state and to the anxieties and desires inherent in the move from survivor to colonist. Occasionally that moment of mapping reveals the fictional colonists' initial sense of the island's alterity, an alterity that they labor to transform into familiarity. Again, Freud and

Klein's theories prove useful for explicating significant events in the island narrative, for subjects sometimes fantasize incorporating objects they find threatening, hence the necessity for projection to psychically transform the object into something more familiar and suitable for incorporation. Some passages in island narratives hint at such needs to transform alterity into familiarity to prepare for incorporation. Just as Crusoe first sees what he later describes as his "little kingdom" (100) as a "barren" isle (40), occasionally other castaway colonists describe the island as threatening, foreign, or Other. Several texts depict castaway colonists' original sense of the island's alterity by having them initially imagine it in terms of an Other body—perhaps a nonmale (female) or nonhuman (monster or animal) body. Verne's castaway colonists, for instance, first see in their island's shape the body of a giant sea monster or whale, which seems "strange," dangerous, and unnatural: "Its strange form caught the eye," Verne narrates, "and when Gideon Spilett . . . had drawn the outline, they found that it resembled some fantastic animal, a monstrous leviathan, which lay sleeping on the surface of the Pacific" (75). They further note that various parts of the island resemble different parts of the monster's body, a perception they reflect by choosing to name some of the island's features after those monstrous parts, for the monster names, they say, "will impress themselves better on our memory, and the same time will be more practical" (79). One island cape, then, is named "Serpentine Peninsula," another becomes "Mandible Cape" after the jaws it resembles, and a third, which looks like a claw becomes "Claw Cape" (80). This moment illustrates both the initial alterity of the Other before made familiar and the profound ambivalence involved in the transition from survivor to colonist—the fear of being consumed *by* the island instead of consuming it—a fear, again, that Klein recognizes in her analyses of destructive incorporative impulses.

A third explanation for some castaways originally seeing the island as Other can be found in analyses of critics like Annette Kolodny, Rebecca Stott, and Anne McClintock. Seeing the land as Other (particularly as female), they argue, provides another way of imagining colonial control as legitimately stemming from the "natural" male authority over the female or the animal.[7] Just as Freud transposed cultural systems onto a model of natural order of the mind, island narratives transposed cultural systems of European colonialism onto the "natural" system of the island-cum-female being controlled by the male colonizer. In characters initially imagining the island as Other exists a different, though complementary, ideology of naturalized male authority. As I will further explore in chapter 2, the colonist might initially conceive of the land-scape as a female or Other body, but according to the logic of projective identification, he must remap it to be like him, that is, as a male human body, thus imagining his masculine control of the island as innate, like his perceived control of his own body. Michel Tournier, in fact, reworks this trope in his castaway tale *Vendredi* (1967). When Robinson, Tournier's castaway, first lands on the island, in his despair he thinks of it as "the Island of Desolation" (20). When he sees the island in its entirety in the monarch-of-all-I-survey scene, however, he begins thinking of and calling the island "Speranza, the Island of Hope," a name he took from a "hot-blooded Italian girl he had known when he was a student" (47), noting that "viewed from a certain angle the island resembled a female body, headless but nevertheless a woman, seated with her legs drawn up beneath her in an attitude wherein submission, fear, and simple aban-donment were inextricably mingled" (47, 48). Tournier takes this imag-ining of masculine control over the female-embodied-island to an ex-treme, as he has Robinson have intercourse with the island (inserting his penis into its ground), produce "children" (striped mandrake flow-ers), and get jealous of Friday, who also has intercourse with the island. Though Tournier's story first clearly designates the island as a female body, as Robinson gains control over the island by civilizing and taming it, he comes to think of it as an extension of his own body, and then fi-nally comes to think of himself as a part of it. Many island narratives like-wise depict the island's state of original femininity as *unnatural,* in that in nature's order, the white, male, disciplined, colonizing body commands the landscape. The island narrative thus restores what in this logic is the *natural* order (land controlled by/mapped as the white male body) to the landscape.

Some island narratives register that transition from Other to self through naming, as do Verne's castaway colonists, who mark their initial sense of the island's alterity and their increasing sense of ownership by naming some parts of the island after a whale/monster's body and other features after men like themselves. Just after deciding on the monster designations, they discuss naming the island's other geographical fea-tures after themselves (as one of them suggests) but decide that they "prefer borrowing names from our country . . . which would remind us of America" (79). So they name the island "Lincoln Island" (after, as they say "a great citizen . . . who now struggles to defend the unity of the

American Republic" [81]), one of the island's bays "Washington Bay,"
a lake "Lake Grant," and the island's primary mountain "Mount Frank-
lin" (79). All of these names come from prominent U.S. statesmen, men
the castaways admire and aspire to resemble, symptomatic of the characters' placing their fantasy of themselves (their ideal ego) onto the island. Laura Mulvey's "Visual Pleasure and Narrative Cinema" in relation
to film-viewing explains the process of projection of the ideal ego that
precedes identification. As Mulvey explains, the male film viewer experiences castration anxiety from viewing the female form on the screen but
finds that he can *identify* with the male protagonist, his "more perfect,
more complete, more powerful ideal ego" (842). This identification parallels the projective identification evident in these "monarch-of-all-I-survey" moments. Like Mulvey's male viewer who identifies with his ideal
ego on screen, the images of themselves Verne's protagonists choose to
project and later identify with are representations of their ideal ego.

Like the Robinsons, Verne's castaways also project their collective
identities onto the island by naming parts of the island for their experiences there: a river providing good drinking water becomes "Mercy
River," an islet where they first washed ashore before moving to the larger
island "Safety Island," and the "precipice . . . from whence the gaze could
embrace the whole of the vast bay" they name "Prospect Heights" (80).
Verne's wording in this passage, as he describes how Prospect Heights
provides a spot for the castaways' "gaze" to "embrace the whole of the
vast bay," uncannily resembles the larger incorporative process of which
the naming is a part: the fantasized reaching out of the body's boundaries to encompass/embrace the desired landscape. As well, naming the
precipice in that way recognizes the need for continued incorporative
maintenance, as castaway colonists from that site can regularly police
the island's borders, an action seemingly necessary for them to feel their
ownership secure.

Because these narratives are transmitted through text, any act of
mapping or naming obviously becomes transcribed into the text of the
narrative, upon the protagonists' uttering the words. But occasionally,
island narratives include printed maps of the island in their pages, even
if the rest of the story lacks illustration. These maps, like Wyeth's illustration of the monarch-of-all-I-survey moment from the *Mysterious Island*
discussed earlier, are constructed so that they could affect the reading
of the text by bringing the reader into the acts of mapping and projection. The maps typically fall into two groups: either showing the reader

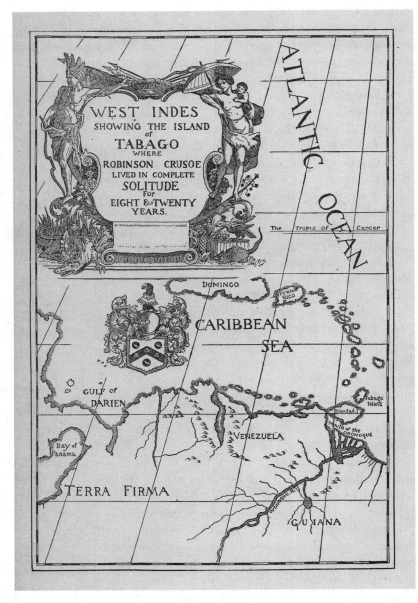

FIGURE 3. Frontispiece map by Louis Rhead and Frederick Rhead, from Daniel Defoe, *The Life and Adventures of Robinson Crusoe* (New York: Harper and Bros., 1900). By permission of the Hubbard Imaginary Voyages Collection, Special Collections Library, University of Michigan.

the region of the castaway colonist's island, thereby orienting the story within the reader's previous knowledge of world geography, or representing the island according to the castaway colonist's experiences there, likely also orienting the story within the reader's prior knowledge of the genre. A 1900 Harper and Brother's edition of *Robinson Crusoe*, for instance, locates the story within the reader's previous knowledge of world geography (see Figure 3) by giving a map of the Caribbean region where Crusoe's fictional island supposedly exists, and where the island that the real castaway, Alexander Selkirk, does exist. Note, however, that though it marks other island colonies, the map does not mark the site of the particular fictional island, an occurrence which, while frustrating the reader's desire to see the island, reminds that the fictional island is uncharted.[8] As well, by making the island a no place, literally a "utopia," this map allows the reader to project this island fantasy onto the real islands pictured. The second type of map, represented by an example from a 1910 Routledge and Sons edition (illustrated by J. D. Watson), maps the island as a palimpsest of Crusoe's adventures (see Figure 4). The map includes such designations as "first landing of savages," "second landing of savages," and "Spaniards washed ashore," as well as marking the different fields of Crusoe's crops at the island's center. Significantly, the map also charts what Crusoe *did not* know, showing the parts of the island Crusoe did not explore (marked on the maps as "unexplored"), and designating the island's exact distance from other islands, which would of course be beyond Crusoe's knowledge while on the island.

Ricardo Padrón's *The Spacious Word*, which focuses on the history of cartography and the psychological significance of maps, brings an interesting historic dimension to the differences between the two maps. Padrón traces a cartographic revolution from itinerary maps made by travelers charting distance and space from one spot to another "as a series of stopping places and obstacles on the body's trip through it" to a different type of gridded map, one that imagines space as a surface with multiple routes, one that presents space as a consumable entity and positions the viewer not as a fellow traveler experiencing the journey but as an abstract being above the landscape in space (61). This cognitive shift in cartography and space coincided with the early modern period, with shifting perceptions of the body and with the exponential growth of European colonization and the castaway narrative. While arguing that this shift signals a cognitive leap, Padrón also demonstrates that the two types of perceptions of charting space continue to coexist in maps and in literature

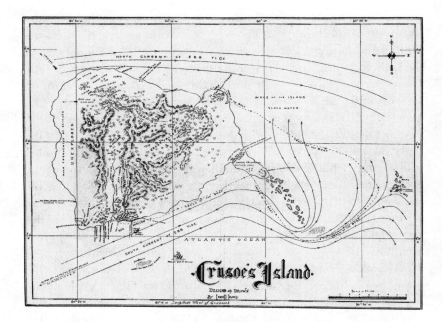

FIGURE 4. Frontispiece map of Crusoe's island by Ernest H. Tugwell, from Daniel Defoe, *The Life and Adventures of Robinson Crusoe* (New York: Routledge and Sons, 1910). By permission of the British Library, 12980.a.14.

that describes landscape as a "give-and-take between two tendencies, a give-and-take that can manifest itself within the writings of a single author and even within the confines of a single chart or a single text" (84). In the two maps of Crusoe's island, and in many of the acts of mapping within island narratives, coexist these two conceptualizations of space: the tension between the itinerary map and the gridded map, between imagining space in terms of a series of routes from where one has been and will go again and space as a chronological totality consumable from a position of elevation. Mirroring these dual conceptualizations are the castaway, in some scenes experiencing the adventure as an itinerary and in other scenes in command on the mountaintop. Through such maps the reader likewise can experience the adventure (itinerary) while positioned above the page (gridded), looking down. Mapping the literary island in this way contributes to the mapping of larger imperial space in terms of itinerary (how the colonizers have and could exist in and civilize the space) and ownership.

Both of the Crusoe maps come in twentieth-century reprints aimed at readers likely at least familiar with the basics of the castaway tale, yet the purpose of both maps still seems to place readers in a privileged position of knowledge by equipping them before the story begins (the maps are typically frontispieces) with information Crusoe does not possess, including the events of the story to come, thus pulling readers into the story's action. Such a map could invite projective identification by soliciting readers' projection of former knowledge of the tale or colonial desires onto its space and then allowing them to identify throughout the reading of the novel with the information there, as they compare text and map to order their reading experience. Moreover, by placing readers in the panoptic position of being able to view all of Crusoe's adventures at once, the map allows them to participate in the narrative's fantasy of omniscient control of time and space. Certainly the map invites readers familiar or unfamiliar with the story to incorporate both novel and island, for it places readers in an omniscient position. Like the castaway colonist, who in his monarch-of-all-I-survey scene can at once visually mark the entire boundaries of his island, readers could survey the entire island and text by looking at its map from an even more ascendant position over the space and time.

Like Wyeth's illustration of the monarch-of-all-I-survey scene, these illustrations, published in 1900 and 1910 were released in a world on the cusp of social and economic changes that would culminate in the end of European empire as the world then knew it. One must wonder, then, how the inclusion of such maps would have affected readers' sense of involvement with the castaway story, and perhaps with their nations' imperial aspirations. The passive participation in the story begun with these maps and with the monarch-of-all-I-survey scene continues with readers' witnessing of the next typical phase of the castaway story, in which the castaway transforms the island.

Rituals of Possession

As explained in my introduction, castaway colonists spend much of their time on the island trying to turn it into a more "civilized," Western space like that they left. They build huts, treehouses, pens, bowers, bridges, gardens and/or fortifications that resemble their lost U.S./European home, both making the space familiar and marking their rights over their territory for would-be transgressors. Crusoe, for instance, builds two homes on the island (both surrounded by layered walls and fortifications), makes furnishings for them, constructs a bower, plants fields, and manufactures pens for the animals he traps and domesticates. Maximillian E. Novak offers in "The Economic Meaning of Robinson Crusoe" that Crusoe works obsessively because he enjoys the work and "prefers this type of work to idleness, and it seems to be part of his character rather than part of his religion" (98). Likewise, Ian Watt explains Crusoe's drive to work as resulting from Calvinist doctrine, which saw work as proof of salvation (*The Rise of the Novel*, 1957). I would argue that neither explanation, though both are fascinating, explains the corresponding psychological impulses undergirding Crusoe's work ethic and societal links between work and religious salvation.

As well as marking his territory and transforming the island into a "civilized" home, these actions further suggest the castaway colonist's subconscious projection of himself onto the island. Like Crusoe, Wyss's Robinson family builds all over their island. By the novel's end, they have built three elaborate homes surrounded by fountains and trellises, several farms, gardens and orchards, barns and pens for their animals at each home, a bridge, a ship, and a port. Verne's protagonists, too, build all over their island, hardly taking a day's rest from their labors, eventually constructing an elevator for their home and even a telegraph! All of the colonists supplement these large building efforts with the painstaking manufacture of smaller "civilizing" implements (pots, ovens, clothes,

shoes, candles, and various tools) that also serve to mark their maintenance of what Pierre Bourdieu calls their *habitus* and their resistance to
the temptations of "going native" (a fear I will discuss further in chapter
4). The habitus, as Bourdieu explains it—a mental and physical embodying of the totality of the classed, raced, nationalized, chronologically placed environment in which a person develops—becomes a nearly
inescapable sense of how the world should work, a part of one's body
and its functioning in society. The habitus is expressed through the language, habits, bodily movement and expressions, and even the tastes for
music, food, sport, and so on that an individual evinces. Thus, individual
"choices" are to some extent predictable by class, race, gender, historical
placement, even age; choices are not really so "individual" as popularly
believed.

With Bourdieu's habitus in mind, we can see why castaways must
re-create, as accurately as possible, their home on the island, projecting their history, culture, desires, and anxieties onto the space. This impulse is *embodied;* all of the habits and choices they reproduce that are
part of their habitus involve their body's existence and functioning in
the world—what it consumes, who it touches, where and how it lives.
Habitus determines whether one consumes American cheese or brie,
white bread or wheat. The mechanism of incorporation, whether literally ingesting food or psychically consuming spaces, always-already has a
filter of habitus on it. Thus, the castaway's changing of the island to fit his
already-existing habitus so that it can be incorporated, in fact, provides
evidence that incorporation is taking place. Were bringing the island
both literally and psychically into the body *not* taking place, there would
be no need to alter the island to fit the habitus. To live on the island as
it is upon their arrival (a possibility not forestalled by descriptions of the
island in any of the narratives) would open castaways to the possibility of
being consumed by the island instead of consuming it.

It is striking how closely fictional acts of transforming the island mirror the maneuvers of real-world colonizers who appropriated land, both
of which stand for psychological processes of seizing possession under
the guise of "normal" or "natural" behaviors. These actions, which in
Marvelous Possessions, Stephen Greenblatt calls "rituals of possession,"
have been analyzed by the historians Keller, Lissitzyn, and Mann in *Creation of Rights of Sovereignty through Symbolic Acts* and by Patricia Seed in
Ceremonies of Possession in Europe's Conquest of the New World, 1492–1640.
As these critics explain, real-world colonizers performed certain rituals

to demonstrate to themselves, their countrymen, and competing European colonizers their colonial authority over the space they claim. The natives witnessing the acts, if, as Greenblatt remarks, any did, weren't the intended audiences for the colonists' efforts, for they wouldn't have understood the colonists' language or the symbolic importance of the actions. As Seed remarks, "Colonial rule over the New World was initiated through largely ceremonial practices—planting crosses, standards, banners, and coats of arms—marching in processions, picking up dirt, measuring the stars, drawing maps, speaking certain words, or remaining silent" (3).[9] Such real-world "deeds" to establish possession included changing the landscape (for example, cutting trees), constructing enclosures (such as building fortifications or homes), and putting actions into writing (for example, making a map or a legal pronouncement before a notary public)—activities also ritually and sometimes metaphorically performed in fictional narratives.

Instead of depicting such actions as ritual performances to establish ownership to competing powers, of course, island texts present mapping, naming, building, and changing the landscape as natural and innocuous, as the *logical* behavior of anyone stranded on an island. The novels, though, typically lack evidence that the castaway colonists couldn't live off of the island as it was—learning to live in a simpler way instead of expending so much energy to transform the island. As if to point out that the typical behaviors of the colonial castaway colonist are not natural or logical, *post*-colonial revisions of island narratives often relate a different, obverse set of plot elements. Jean Giraudoux's island protagonist, Suzanne, in *Suzanne and the Pacific* (1923), for instance, does not expend the tremendous energy to build a house, but instead sleeps in a bower of trees. Instead of planting crops, she eats the fruit from the trees and vegetables growing naturally. In fact, when Suzanne finds and reads an old copy of *Robinson Crusoe,* she scoffs at what she sees as Crusoe's wasted energy. "Don't work three months to make yourself a table," she longs to advise him. "Squat" (226). Through his unconventional girl-Crusoe, Giraudoux deconstructs the subgenre's arguments about what are natural and logical castaway behaviors.

Yet in the colonial-era island narratives, by choosing one way of life over another, the castaway colonist seemingly separates the logical from the necessary, demonstrating that he purposefully maintains his civilized demeanor, though his efforts to transform the island are, in fact, ideological elements of a cultural system he labors intensively to project onto the landscape. Occasionally, the texts depict actions meant to serve as rituals of possession that are clearly not necessary for survival. The Swiss Robinson family, for example, as well as transforming their island, performs rites to mark their possession of it. Each year the family marks the anniversary of their landing with a self-produced and self-witnessed ritual spectacle of races, feasts, cannon fire, and ceremony. This yearly "thanksgiving day" ritual augments the hundreds of seemingly logical daily rituals the family performs that transform the island and similarly mark their island ownership, such as marking the calendar to keep track of the Christian Sabbath, performing other Christian rituals, washing daily, and dressing in European clothing. These rituals of transformation and possession like the more "necessary" acts function as part of the projective-incorporative process, for they aid in the psychic assumption and maintenance of island ownership and naturalize that control. These activities, like real-world rituals of possession, enable the fictional colonist and the texts' readers to imagine a sense of secure ownership of the space, and like real-world rituals of possession (colonial authority had to be continually reasserted beyond initial contact), fictional rituals of possession must be repeated to maintain their viability.

We can see rituals of possession, as well, in how the castaway colonist chooses to literally ingest the island through the food he eats. Choosing not to simply eat the island's native flora and fauna, castaways feel compelled to assume control of their food supply instead of hunting/gathering. When they have seeds from Europe, like Crusoe, John Daniel, and the Robinson family, they plant crops on the island. When they don't have seeds, like Verne's protagonists, they domesticate the island's plants (transplanting them into bowers and fields, choosing the best specimens to nurture), though the texts give no indication of a need for such work, no evidence that they could not simply live off of the island's resources without imposing their control over its ecosystem. In *Robinson Crusoe,* for instance, out of the fear of his domesticated food (the corn and rice) running out, Crusoe plants corn for three years before he allows himself to eat "the least Grain . . . and even then but sparingly" (59). He also captures and domesticates the island's wild goats so that, instead of simply hunting them, he commands that food source from breeding to table.[10] Likewise, Frederick Marryat's *Masterman Ready* describes nearly every meal that its castaways consume and tells how they domesticate and manage their food supply—even to the extent of creating pools for the controlled breeding of fish and turtles to eliminate dependence on the natural bounty of the sea.

Remembering that these island worlds were often imagined, there is no reason why the writer couldn't have created an environment replete with fruit and plants for the castaway to harvest without extensive labor. The writer's and character's compulsion to control the food supply certainly suggests the need for the colonist to project himself onto the island before he can, in a literal sense, incorporate it. In keeping with the ideology of the uncolonized space as lacking and in need of their help, the castaway must either take command of (domesticate) the island's indigenous products, or, instead, plant and harvest the European plants/animals he brought with him. This compulsion to control what he ingests discloses the colonist's desperate fantasy to control what he incorporates.

Food often symbolizes the male protagonist's power over other's bodies (and his control of the island), as well as over his own body. In *The Tempest*, for instance, Prospero conjures and dangles a feast in front of the hungry eyes of the Milanese only to snatch it away, demonstrating his power over the island and the newly shipwrecked characters. Food symbolizes island control for Caliban, as well, for when he bemoans handing over control of the island to Prospero, he reminds him that he [Caliban] originally shared the secrets of the island's food: Prospero gave him "water with berries in't" and Caliban "showed [him] all the qualities o'th'isle, / The fresh springs, brine pits, barren place and fertile" (1.2.334, 337–38). When Caliban swears loyalty to the comicals later in the play, he illustrates his devotion again through offers of food. He suggests, "I'll show thee the best springs; I'll pluck thee berries; / I'll fish for thee" (2.2.154–55). Control over food represents command of the island for all of the island's inhabitants, for the reader, and for the author. In an earlier discussion, Antonio and Sebastian jokingly represent the island itself as a piece of fruit that could be carried in Gonzolo's "pocket," exchanged for an apple and reproduced in other islands from its "kernals" being sown in the sea (2.1.88–90). These lighthearted comments recognize a connection between control of the island and its food.

Though island narratives typically sanitize out of their pages the acts of colonial violence that preceded or accompanied these "civilizing" behaviors in real-world colonization, in several of the texts, characters do explicitly mention their work as part of creating a colony for later incorporation into their home country. The castaway colonists of *The Mysterious Island,* for instance, vow to "make a little America of this island," to "build towns," "establish railways, start telegraphs, and one fine day, when it is quite changed, quite put in order and quite civilized . . . offer it to the government of the Union" (78), a plan that is ironically fitting, considering the debates to come in the late nineteenth century over U.S. imperial aims in the Philippines, Hawaii, and Cuba. It seems that Verne sees that the United States' post–Civil War reconstruction and reassertion of its unity involves imagining itself as a colonizer, not colony. The Swiss Robinson family likewise claims their island for Switzerland and envisions it as a future colony. Perhaps such promises of future joining to their home nation helped to legitimize these personal acts of colonization, though it is interesting to note that in neither case does that promise become fulfilled: In *The Mysterious Island,* the island blows up, and in *The Swiss Family Robinson,* the family never quite relinquishes possession. Thus the castaway gets to join the club of legitimate colonists without having to pay the dues.

Identification: The Island Skin Ego

The second half of Klein's theory, identification, is equally useful for unraveling the processes whereby the castaway becomes colonist. As with "projection," the term "identify" is used to describe a range of cognitive experiences whereby subjects encountering other subjects or objects discover in those others qualities of themselves or traits that they wish to assume for themselves. According to Klein, identification accompanies and combines with projection to result in incorporation, so it is not surprising that some of the castaway's behaviors in the monarch-of-all-I-survey scene suggest identification, as well. The colonist both projects his perception (or fantasy) of his identity and culture onto the island and identifies with the projected fantasy he sees reflected back at him from the island. But, as Jacques Lacan remarks in his discussion of the mirror stage of child development, that recognition of the self in the island/mirror is always fundamentally misrecognition, since what the child sees is *not* the self but only an image of the self. In this case, what the colonist sees in the island, as a reflection of what he wants to see and be, is also misrecognition, a projection of desire more than reality, an optical illusion necessary to the formation of colonial identity.

We can see this cognitive process in island narratives most clearly when castaway colonists, in the act of viewing the island, actually articulate a change in their perception of identity. In *The Swiss Family Robinson,* for instance, the Robinson father and eldest son, Fritz, conduct a "most careful survey of the beautiful landscape," from a mountaintop, one which "failed to show [them] the slightest sign or trace of human beings" (32). This monarch-of-all-I-survey moment affirms the island's suitability for their needs, a fantasy that their description of the island in such terms shows that they have projected onto the space. They express feeling "a shade of loneliness stealing over [them] as [they] gazed on [the island's] utter solitude" (32). As well as marking the ambivalence typical of the discovery of being island bound, this reaction is significant in that they react to the island's "utter solitude" by recognizing their own sympathetic "loneliness"; Mr. Robinson and Fritz's perceptions of themselves in that moment are altered through identification with the island.

They work through this loneliness, however, by finding in the island's seclusion a second, more acceptable identity for themselves as colonists instead of castaways. Mr. Robinson decides in that moment to cast their situation in terms of a choice and not an accident, saying, "Cheer up, Fritz, lad. . . . Remember that we chose a settler's life long ago, before we left our own dear country" (32). This shift from feeling lonely to considering themselves as "settlers" signals an ongoing psychological process of identification. In this moment of self-willed shift in identity, Mr. Robinson, desperate to assert control over the situation, reaffirms his *choice* and identity as a colonist, not castaway. Mr. Robinson's next sentences suggest that, as well, he will model a contentment with providentially bountiful isolation, a contentment he sees in the island. He continues, "We certainly did not expect to be so entirely alone—but what matters a few people, more or less? With God's help, let us endeavor to live here contentedly, thankful that we were not cast upon some bare and inhospitable island" (32). Like the naturally solitary, but not-bare and not-inhospitable island with which in that moment they identify, they resolve to find peace in their lack of company and to be at home in their sea-bound secluded colony.

A similar self-willed cognitive shift as a result of island identification exists in *The Mysterious Island* in a similar need for the castaways to pretend that they made a choice to be colonists. In their monarch-of-all-I-survey moment, Verne's castaways likewise find in the island they view an acceptable fantasy of themselves, deciding to "not consider ourselves castaways, but colonists, who have come here to settle" (78). The act of viewing in the monarch-of-all-I-survey moment, as well as allowing them to project their needs onto the island, allows them to reabsorb those needs—that "improved" self-image and identity as solitary owner that the empty, available, bountiful island reflects back to them. And as "colonists," the characters enjoy an economic relationship to the island and a sense of capitalist ownership which, as "castaways," they would lack.

This budding identification with the island affects how the castaway colonist perceives his body, as well as how he perceives his status on the island. The obsessive repetition of certain behaviors suggests that, because of subconscious psychical operations centering on his body's control of space, the castaway begins to psychically correlate his body with the island. In effect, the castaway colonist transfers his need to feel secure on his island onto his flesh; he treats the island as an extension of his body and his body like a smaller island needing fortification of its boundaries.[11] Crusoe, for instance, soon after his monarch-of-all-I-survey moment, becomes obsessed with protecting his body, despite little evidence of any real threat except those he concocts from reading earlier travelers' tales. After he has had ample time to see that the island is safe, and before he sees the renowned footprint, Crusoe admits to his obsession with his bodily safety. Again, he fears being consumed by animals ("My Thoughts were now wholly employ'd about securing my self against either Savages, if any should appear, or wild Beasts, if any were in the island" [43–44]); and he fears being consumed by the island itself ("The fear of being swallow'd up alive, made me that I never slept in quiet, and yet the Apprehensions of lying abroad without any Fence was almost equal to it" [61]). Crusoe's fears of threats from within and without, which at this point in the narrative are both groundless and all-consuming, lead him to create extra bodily protections.

To protect his fragile body against a fantasy threat, he fortifies his island, building excessive layers of enclosures on the island to thicken his symbolic skin. When first on the island, Crusoe describes protecting his body by "barricad[ing]" it "round with the Chests and Boards . . . brought on Shore" (40) and erecting his home as a fortress, surrounded by rows of sharpened stakes to impale any man or beast threatening his body. When building yet another layer of fortification, he describes, "I began my Fence or Wall; which being still jealous of my being attack'd by some Body, I resolve'd to make very thick and strong" (56). Interestingly, a year after Crusoe planted the stakes in the ground, he finds that, as if by magic, they have grown root and have formed a living barrier—a hedge—which, as he explains, "at first [made] a fine Cover to my Habitation, and afterward serv'd for a Defence" (77). This change from deadwood weapon (the stake) to living wood hedge suggests that the island itself participates in defending his body. The fortifications extend Crusoe's body boundaries, providing additional psychical layers of toughened skin to protect his vulnerable boundaries, giving him the tenuous sensation of being secure on his island and in his body. The near-paranoid Crusoe, who projected onto the island his need for it to be uninhabited-yet-hostile, barren-yet-potentially-bountiful, also identifies with his projection so that his perception of his own body alters into being vulnerable-yet-secure.

The work of the neurologist Paul Schilder, specifically his concept of the "body image," can help to explain Crusoe's behavior, in particular why he begins to treat the island as if it is an extension of his body. Schilder explains the "body image" as the perception human beings have of the size, shape, and placement of their bodies. When working with stroke victims and amputees, Schilder noted that his patients' mental perceptions of their bodies were often distorted because of their injury. While stroke victims frequently experienced their bodies as missing limbs or parts they could not feel, amputees often included missing limbs in their mental perceptions of their bodies, even feeling sensations as if the amputated limb were still there (called Phantom Limb Syndrome). As Schilder explains, the body image can also be altered under more "ordinary" circumstances to contain objects near to or involved with the body (such as a frequently used cane). "Anything which participates in the conscious movement of our bodies is added to the model of ourselves and becomes part of these schemata: a woman's power of localization may extend to the feather in her hat" (13). The body image can be extended, as well, to include the world around the subject, for, as Schilder says, "we do not perceive our own body differently from objects in the outside world" (122). The feminist cultural theorist Elizabeth Grosz has built on Schilder's work with biological body images to explain psychological perceptions of the body. As Grosz explains, because the body image is "formed out of the various modes of contact the subject has with its environment through its actions in the world" it also provides "an anticipatory plane of (future) action in which a knowledge of the body's current position and capacities for action must be registered" (67). We can see this articulation of the body image reflected in the island map, which, in turn reflects the castaway's fears/desires about the island and his body. In the map, he creates a physical portrayal of what is, in a way, his body image, his anticipated and hoped for future actions as colonizer, as well as his growing perceptions of himself as linked to the island. As well, Schilder's theories help to explain how one's perception of one's body can be distinct from reality and how the body image can be psychically linked to one's environment. In these island narratives, the most important characteristic of the castaway's life is his isolation on that bounded isle. The island and his immediate fortified environment become for the castaway part of what Schilder calls the "model of ourselves." Crusoe's labors to shore up his body with concentric circles of boundaries, with the largest being the island shores, reflect his altered body image; his body and his island have become subconsciously sutured together.

Crusoe is not the only castaway colonist to exhibit such a shift in bodily perception. We see similar fortifications constructed in other island narratives, as well. The castaway colonists of *The Mysterious Island* go to extreme lengths to construct a home in a cave within the island, illustrating the deterritorialization and reterritorialization that Deleuze and Guattari discuss in *Anti-Oedipus*. Despite having seen no "savages" on or off the island or even any threatening animals, excepting a solitary cougar viewed from a great distance, they fear a threat, and the need to, as Pencroft remarks, "fortify ourselves against savages with two legs as well as against savages with four" (115). As Verne's language here suggests, building a stronghold would supplement fantasies of security and ownership earlier initiated through their gaze, for with a fortified home such as the one they envision, they shall "not be obliged to watch every night, or to keep up a fire," making them feel safe enough, they imagine, to suspend their visual policing of the island space (114). The castaways are well prepared to build a structure, having already constructed a kiln for brick, pottery, and iron tool making. As Pencroft remarks, "neither bricks nor tools are wanting now. After having been brickmakers, plotters, smelters, and smiths, we shall surely know how to be masons!" (115). They possess all of the materials necessary for building a secure brick dwelling but instead seek a cave because, as Harding remarks, "A natural dwelling would spare us much work, and would be a surer retreat, for it would be as well defended against enemies from the interior as those from outside" (115).

Let us pause for a moment over this significant statement, examining first the assumption that moving into a cave would save effort. (The striking claim of the cave's security from enemies from within and with-out I will examine in chapters 3 and 4.) While at first seemingly contra-dicting the tendency to avoid utilizing the island "as is" in favor of impos-ing Western habits and structures, creating a cave dwelling does not save the colonists much, if any, effort. In fact, the extreme effort they expend makes their cave-reconstruction function as yet another ritual of pos-session. According to Harding's careful plan, to make their cave-home, they must first lower the level of Lake Grant by three feet to expose the underwater entrance to a cavern they suspect is there, a feat they accom-plish by exploding a passage in the lake's basin with nitroglycerin, the creation of which also requires a long and complicated process of inven-tion. Once they lower the lake's level and discover the passage to a cav-ern in the granite under Prospect Heights, they reconstruct the cave to make it a suitable dwelling by using more nitroglycerin to cut windows and a door in the cave walls and by hauling bricks and other materials into the cavern to construct walls and partitions. Finally, they gather ma-terials for and weave a 100-foot rope ladder to allow them to enter their cave, since their newly made door is 80 feet above the ground and since they plan to dam the lake to again cover the natural entrance to the cav-ern. These efforts, which cause great violence to the island (reminding of Klein's notion of the oral-sadistic violence of incorporation), hardly seem less than those required to build a brick or wood dwelling.

The second part of Harding's sentence provides a perhaps more candid explanation of their psychological need to live in a cave. Their cave dwelling, which they call "solid, healthy, and secure" (142), they be-lieve would be safer than a house, even a sturdily built brick one. First, its walls, literally encased within the thickness of the island's body, they feel would be more solid than those of a house, perhaps better pro-tecting them from tempests like the one that stranded them (though they seem unconcerned about cave-ins). Secondly, they imagine that they can exert greater command over the entrance to their cave than they could to a house, though they worry excessively about making even the entrance to a cave more secure. As they explain, "if it is easy for us to reach our dwelling by this passage [the natural passage], it will be equally easy for others besides us," so they require "a rope ladder, which, once drawn up, will render access to our dwelling impossible" (136). In this fantasy, if they reconfigure the cave's entrance, they will be able to control what enters and leaves their cave orifice just as they fantasize they control what enters and exits the orifices of their bodies.

Because the cave, which functions as an additional level of fortification of their bodies, also acts as a metaphorical skin for their vulnerable bodies, a "naturally" thickened and protective and thus psychologically comforting skin, they fantasize that it will protect them better than a house. Yet, at the same time, they must reconstruct the cave so that they imagine they are encasing themselves within the island's body on their terms (just as they decided to consider themselves colonists and not castaways). This fantasy is similar to that found in Thomas More's early island-set colonial fantasy *Utopia* (1516). More's island also resembles a large body, circular in shape with an interior body of water that can only be reached through a naturally protected rocky harbor, which only Utopians themselves know how to navigate. More's harbor functions like a permeable orifice, one that is strictly controlled so that only desirable objects (those that have already undergone projective identification) will be incorporated, while undesirable objects (enemies) can be kept from penetrating the body's skin.

This compulsion to assert command over the to-be-colonized space suggests a profound insecurity with the enterprise, one shared by real-world colonizers as they likewise sought to refashion colonial space on their own terms. As L. J. Davis notes in "Known Unknown Locations: The Ideology of Novelistic Landscape in *Robinson Crusoe*," we can draw a comparison between Crusoe's efforts to "civilize" the island and other transformations of space by European monarchs to demonstrate and solidify power, such as the British rebuilding of New Delhi as their orderly, planned colonial center in the early twentieth century. After deciding that Calcutta had become too violent for their work, the British planned and built their own colonial space in New Delhi, instead of simply constructing new buildings in the old city of Delhi. "England's industry in building over the preexistent Delhi" Davis says, "is not unlike Crusoe's remarkable reshaping of his environment" (97). Like the castaway, the British must have imagined that a new city would be more "solid, healthy, and secure" for their vulnerable bodies in the dangerous climate and culture, a "naturally" thickened and protective and thus psychologically comforting skin.

As a "natural" structure, the cave also links castaways in *The Mysterious Island* to the land, providing a bodily connection or interface (literally an "inter-face") between them and the island. Again, psychoanalytic theory can help to explain such behaviors of citadel building, which while protecting the castaway colonists' bodies, also provides a further juncture between the body and the island. The work of the psychoanalyst, Didier Anzieu in his study *The Skin Ego* (1989), proves especially helpful here, for his explanation of the role of skin in fantasies of incorporation illustrates how psychological boundaries can provide fantasies of both protection and connection. Like Lacan, Klein, and Freud, Anzieu bases his theory on speculation regarding how babies come to experience themselves as individuals, a realization that Anzieu argues involves children's experience of their skin. As Freud's and Klein recognize, a newborn experiences itself and its relationship to the world through its body, first through the mouth and then through the stomach and intestinal fullness it feels after feeding. As Anzieu explains: "If the mouth provides the first experience, brief and vivid, of a differentiating contact, of a place of passage and an incorporation, repletion brings the infant the more diffuse and more durable experience of a central mass, a fullness, a centre of gravity" (36). According to Anzieu, we all, then, first experience ourselves as beings who consume the world.

Anzieu adds a third sensation to that foundational moment of self-identification, which involves the baby being held, caressed, and pressed in its mother's warm arms, a skin experience followed by the different (possibly cold or painful) sensations of its washing, rubbing, and dressing.[12] "These activities," Anzieu explains, "lead the child progressively to differentiate a surface which has both an inner and an outer face, in other words an interface, permitting a distinction between inside and outside" (36–37). As well as knowing the world through the feeling of our consuming bodies, then, we also know the world as that which brings sensation to the boundaries of our bodies, which leads us to first know ourselves as bounded entities. Because this experience of the world as primarily divided into inside or outside the skin remains constant, if latent, throughout life, incorporation and what Anzieu terms "the skin ego" as a means of imagining one's relationship with the world always exists on the subconscious level. The skin, according to Anzieu, becomes the site for playing out fantasies of control and desire, which explains how it and the additional boundaries the castaway colonist constructs provide an interface between the colonist and the island environment he desires to command. The colonist's skin and its corresponding island borders form important spaces for recognizing boundaries between self and other, between what one controls/owns and the outside world. The skin's importance to self-identity and to perceptions of control and ownership makes the island an ideal setting for fantasies of colonization, for the colonist's desire to visually police his island's borders during the monarch-of-all-I-survey scene, to fortify them, or to physically patrol them on foot or by boat builds on this fantasy of being able to control the boundaries of the body and what enters and leaves the boundaries of the body (which I will discuss in detail in coming chapters).

Fantasies of the skin and of the body's boundaries as linked to the desirable/threatening island are threaded throughout the narrative, as the castaway colonist adapts to island life, defends against threats, and eventually prepares for return to the home he left. Of course, we should also remember that, as with Freud's and Klein's theories, it is easy to see how Anzieu's theories of natural development also describe realities of colonization. Skin was (and continues to be) one of the most overdetermined bodily sites for classifying identity—second perhaps only to the genitalia. In colonial cultures of the seventeenth through twentieth centuries, people were often classified by the state of their skin—its color (race), cleanliness (class), softness and hairiness (gender and class), smoothness (age), and by the products adorning it (clothing, jewelry, and cosmetics, or lack of same, all denoting class). Such skin-based classifications were of course crucial at every level of colonial culture, providing both an interface between the person and the culture, a way for individuals to declare and maintain identity within a particular social group, and providing a site for creating protective psychological barriers between self and others, a way for individuals to distinguish themselves from other social groups. Anzieu's theories of the importance of skin to identity, then, could be said to psychoanalyze the cultural group, as well as the individual.

Reading as Incorporation: Adventure Tales, Bedtime Stories, and Cultural Training

At the close of this first chapter, we must return to the issue of the role of these island narratives in real-world empire. Of course, we can't return to the fifteenth and sixteen centuries to ask those living during the ages of first imperial exploration about their responses to travelers' tales and early island narratives. Unfortunately, we also lack many firsthand accounts of reactions of island narrative readers living during the time of high imperial expansion in the eighteenth and nineteenth centuries. We do, however, have evidence of the popularity of the subgenre and of some of its uses as a model to pass on tenets of good imperial behavior, especially for children, both of which provide clues into the island fantasy's ideological function. Kevin Carpenter's bibliography *Desert Isles and Pirate Islands,* listing more than five hundred island narratives published in England between 1788 and 1910, attests to the island tale's popularity. Cultural historians, such as those quoted in Humphrey Carpenter and Mari Prichard's *The Oxford Companion to Children's Literature,* provide insight into the subgenre's consumption by children, designating the Robinsonade as "the dominant form in fiction for children and young people" during the late imperial period (458), and noting that an 1888 poll found *Robinson Crusoe* (in abridged form for children) and *The Swiss Family Robinson* to be the two favorite books of the children polled.[13] Indeed, as Diane Loxley has argued, castaway tales were crucial to the training of British boys in hegemonic imperial masculinity. One of *Robinson Crusoe*'s most famous fans, Samuel Taylor Coleridge, claims to have read it before the age of six and remained a lifelong fan of the novel.[14] Another fan, Rousseau, famously remarks in *Emile* (1762) that *Robinson Crusoe* would be the first book to be read by his fictional pupil and would form the basis of his education. One revision of *Robinson Crusoe* for children, Joachim Campe's *Robinson the Younger* (1789) even includes the framing device of a father relating an even more sanitized version of the Crusoe tale to his children as a bedtime story. Another, Racey Helps's *Little Mouse Crusoe* (1948) casts the Crusoe story with animals, Crusoe being an adorable mouse and Friday a hapless turtle. With vivid illustrations, and covers depicting important moments in colonial psychology, such island narratives packaged empire for children and provided an important vehicle for their enculturation into imperial society.

As well, the packaging of the island narrative suggests that it was used (if not intended) as a tool of imperial ideology for people in colonized countries. Derek Walcott attests to the importance of *Robinson Crusoe* in the colonial education and enculturation of children in the West Indies. "Crusoe is a figure from our schoolboy reading," Walcott explains. "He is a part of the mythology of every West Indian child" ("The Figure of Crusoe" 37). The island narrative genre's popularity, as Walcott recognizes, led to it becoming (or resulted from its) position as a staple of Western imperial mythology. Versions retelling the island story in pictures or in words of one syllable (such as Charles Lamb's *Lamb's Stories from Shakespeare Put into Basic English* [1932], *Robinson Crusoe in Words of One Syllable* [1868], or *The Robinson Crusoe Picture Book* [1879]), suggest that the fantasy was, as well, passed on to children and adults with limited literacy in English, like the poor or the newly colonized. All three groups (children, the poor, the colonized) would have been targets for such imperial propaganda and asked to model their behavior after the industrious, forthright, and pious, castaway colonist—the model citizen and capitalist. And as Martin Crotty remarks, as imperial adventure stories, island narratives were often marketed for and consumed by British boys, the next generation of imperial administrators.

Critics, including Karl Marx, have recognized *Robinson Crusoe*'s importance as a model of modern capitalistic industry and as a vehicle for spreading literacy (which Benedict Anderson aptly calls "print capitalism"). John Robert Moore argues that as the first English novel "widely accepted among all classes of English and Scottish readers," *Robinson Crusoe* "created a new reading public" (222). Industrial capitalism, other critics note, relied upon the expansion of empire and imperial ideology. As L. J. Davis remarks, "At roughly the period that Europe was creating the representation of its colonies, its novelists—at least Defoe—were colonizing another kind of space—a space perhaps more complete and total because it was inside the mind of some captives of the novel—the middle class reader" (96). Popular and frequently reproduced, castaway island narratives shaped a positive image of the colonial enterprise and spread fantasies of imperial legitimacy, for "the enterprise of empire" so says Said, "depends upon the *idea* of *having an empire*" (italics in original, *Culture and Imperialism* 11).

The cultural uses of island narratives significantly mirror the stories they presented, since island narratives both recodify the larger dynamics of colonization and consumption and psychologically enable those processes by presenting them as natural. While the fictional colonist imagines natural colonial control through incorporation of the island (recodifying the larger process), readers could participate in that fantasy through their consumption of the island-like book, psychologically enabling imperial expansion, individual by individual, and, as earlier noted, through their consumption of book illustrations, such as Wyeth's illustration of *The Mysterious Island*'s monarch-of-all-I-survey scene. We should remember that while the island narrative subgenre was being developed, so were (as Ian Watt argues) the novel, (as Benedict Anderson argues) the nation-state, the modern subject and literacy (the spread of the practice of consuming words), and (as Firdous Azim argues) Western imperialism. In island narratives we see mirrored those notions of consumption and individuality that undergird modern, Western imperialism. Like the fictional colonist, readers of island narratives incorporate the island by consuming the book.

This idea of reading as consuming goes beyond metaphor; Mary Jacobus's *Psychoanalysis and the Scene of Reading* equates all acts of reading with psychic incorporation. Building on typical cultural incorporative metaphors for reading (eating, savoring, devouring books), Jacobus explains the reading act in terms of oral incorporation, as "the way we imagine putting the world inside us, disposing of its dangers by making its meanings ours, cannibalistically consuming it, recycling it, savoring its borrowed sweetness as our own" (31). Readers' consumption of words, Jacobus suggests, allows them to incorporate their desires while digesting inoculated fears. Characterized by their bounded space, books, like islands, make juicy morsels for fantasies of incorporation. Martin Gliserman also sees the reading act as essentially embodied. As Gliserman says, "the body in-forms the text; the text embodies its writer; the reading reader embodies the body of the text" (11).

Returning to Klein's theory of projective identification helps to explain a possible real-world reading of island narratives, just as it does the consumptive fantasies enacted in the text. The fictional island and the book's pages are, in a very real sense, *projections* of real-world imperial desires for safe and natural colonization of the colonial culture that produced the narratives. By reading the text, the culture then *identifies* with its created (in Foucault's words in "Of Other Spaces") heterotopia, that is a fantasized utopist, well-ordered space. The reader consumes/reads the book qua island, recognizes "self" in the book/island mirror (like the Lacanian child during its mirror stage), and, ironically, models this self after that often unattainable and sanitized fantasy. The act of incorporation becomes complete as the culture uses that discursive microcosm as justification for its real-world colonial actions. By transferring fantasies into the island narrative for easy consumption, the colonial culture projects its imperial ego ideal onto the island narrative, just as Verne's colonists project their ego ideal onto the island by naming it Lincoln Island.

Homi Bhabha takes up a similar discussion of the ego ideal in his analysis of the emblem of the English book. In "Signs Taken for Wonders: Questions of Ambivalence and Authority Under a Tree Outside Delhi, May 1817," Bhabha notes that the colonial (for him English) book "as a signifier of authority . . . acquires its meaning *after* the traumatic scenario of colonial difference, cultural or racial, returns the eye of power to some prior, archaic image or identity" (168–69). In short, the book gains its power from colonizers' attempts to re-create or project their fantasy of a stable identity, which may or may not exist but is rather a glorified, imagined past, onto the book's pages. "Consequently," Bhabha remarks, "the colonial presence is always ambivalent, split between its appearance as original and authoritative and its articulation as repetition and difference" (168–69). The same can be said for the particular example of the English book under discussion, the colonial island narrative; its attempts to create a mirror of an ideal colonial reality reveal its ambivalence about the reality it neither can (nor seeks to, since that reality is flawed) accurately depict.

As Bhabha notes, an important characteristic of the "colonial presence" is its "articulation as repetition and difference," an articulation we can see at work in the castaway narrative subgenre. Through five hundred years of republication and revision of the island fantasy, Western imperial cultures repeated the cycle of projection, identification, and consumption. The perpetual reproduction of the story—the repetition of the projection—can be read as rituals of possession on the literary level. The basic story of the colonial island narrative (the castaway colonist domesticating the island into his own little colonial world) was immensely popular and frequently repeated. As one anonymous reviewer claimed of *Robinson Crusoe,* by 1871 the novel had been "translated into all languages that can boast a literature" (reprinted in Rogers *Defoe: The Critical Heritage* 199). The island fantasy had to be constantly re-inscribed and disseminated in series of colonial texts because the real-world incorporation that the texts enabled, the always unstable colonial contest, demanded self-justification through institutions of the church, state (military and scientific establishments), and media (entertainment, song, literature, news, drama, and later, film). Western imperialists needed to be able to constantly identify with the ego-ideal projected into the page and to consume it to fuel further expansion.

Replaying the fantasy of natural and successful colonization, these texts enable real-world incorporation of land—which is, of course, colonization. As Said reminds when discussing the participation of fiction (novels in particular) in the imperial enterprise, "we must continue to remember that novels participate in, are part of, contribute to an extremely slow, infinitesimal politics that clarifies, reinforces, perhaps even occasionally advances perceptions and attitudes about England and the world" (75). The prototype of the novel genre, *Robinson Crusoe,* Said reminds, "is certainly not accidentally . . . about a European who creates a fiefdom for himself on a distant, non-European island" (xii). Like an island and a body, a novel creates a self-contained space with boundaries one can consume and police with the eye. Like an island, a novel presents an inviting space for the construction of a self-controlled and easily-incorporated world, a world that, as my next chapter will investigate, was governed by the rules of masculine discipline and patriarchal law.

2. Disciplined Islands

White Fatherhood, Homosocial Masculinity, and Law

MOST fictional castaways are men. And in their behavior, most are essentially interchangeable: they remain strong in the face of adversity, stoic when confronted with despair, equipped for every threat and challenge, disciplined in mind and body. They are manly men, and when more than one male is stranded together, the white man most strongly displaying behaviors of strength, stoicism, and self-discipline becomes leader and commander of the island.

In the examination in chapter 1 of how bodies can provide subconscious means for imagining control of island space, I left aside for that moment that those bodies, of course, are classed, raced, and gendered. I temporarily sidestepped that the bodies linked to and controlling the island in these tales are consistently masculine, white, and male, and that these bodies often become more and more disciplined as the narratives progress. The time has now come to both investigate connections between the body fantasy traced in chapter 1, the castaway's gender, and the discipline that the men who imagine themselves island owners work so hard to maintain, and to study the effects of the castaway story's gendering on its readers and on its value as colonial myth. This chapter, then, continues the analysis begun in chapter 1 of the castaway's psychological transition into island ownership, but here I specifically focus on links between fantasies of controlling the land and fantasies of self-controlling the white, masculinized body.[1] This chapter will argue that island tales often depict castaways who become colonists as earning that island ownership by performing certain manly deeds, deeds that strengthen the subconscious correlation between island and body initiated in the monarch-of-all-I-survey scene, a correlation that becomes recodified through the notion of discipline. In short, as noted in chapter 1, incorporating the island leads the castaway colonist to think of the island as an extension of his body. Yet, as this chapter will show, it is only the castaway who can maintain a fantasy of bodily discipline (often a white, Western, fatherly man) who can successfully perform and sustain that incorporation to become island owner. The island tests the castaway's discipline and fortitude, but if he can pass those tests, beginning with his reaction to the disaster that strands him, he will be able to psychically incorporate and command the island.

Frederick Marryat's castaway narrative *Masterman Ready* (1814), which shows men both passing and failing the shipwreck test of discipline and manhood, provides a good starting point for this discussion.[2] Published just the year before the British Empire celebrated Queen Victoria's Diamond Jubilee, Marryat's tale, as is typical, starts with a stormy shipwreck. The ship's crew mutinies when a falling beam strikes senseless the captain, exemplifying failure of discipline. Though they had worked "well and cheerfully" under the captain's leadership, upon his mortal injury, they "no longer felt themselves under control" (31). Sinking into despair, they get drunk, and abandon ship in the last remaining lifeboat, leaving behind their charges, the (ironically named) Seagrave family of colonists bound for New South Wales, Australia. In contrast, that same storm sequence illustrates retained discipline through the older seaman, Masterman Ready, who becomes the Seagraves' savior. Ready rationalizes the crew's actions to Mr. Seagrave as "the law of nature," for "when it is a question of life, it is every one for himself" (34). Yet Ready, unlike the other sailors, has the fortitude to master his self-preserving "nature" and risk his life to save the Seagraves, thus passing that test of his self-control. Instead of leaving as the sailors urge him to, Ready bravely rides out the storm with the Seagraves, sharing his experience and courage, even fortifying the despondent (and thus comparatively more feminine) Mr. Seagrave during the crisis. As well as providing contrast with the crew's undisciplined behavior, Ready also provides a differing example of fate. After abandoning ship, the crewmen completely lose control of their lifeboat and drown, whereas had they kept their heads and stayed under Ready's sound command, they would have survived. The characters that maintain their self-control, Ready and the less physically hardy but stout-hearted Seagraves, survive the wreck, while those who lose their self-control (the ship's crew) are consumed by the raging waters.

Such tests of the castaway's self-discipline suffuse island narratives, typically bringing rewards for those who pass them, including command of the island and (unofficially) any other castaways. After bravely riding out the storm, for instance, Masterman Ready navigates the sinking ship to a deserted island, where he, in time, transforms the island into a home for himself and the Seagraves, who surely would not have survived without him. The "master man" of just about everything, who is "ready" for any situation, and who "masters" each "man" around him, instills his discipline and knowledge in the Seagraves, in effect "readying" them for survival on the island. The old seaman's ability to harness his own instincts and channel those energies into bridling nature gives Ready authority over his fellow castaways and over the island on which they become stranded. In fact, as island leader, Ready acts as a wise father and teacher to the Seagrave family, even to the true family patriarch, Mr. Seagrave, a man whose socioeconomic status would, in the metropole, make him Ready's social superior. Marryat explains in his introduction that he purposefully divided what he labels the unrealistically knowledgeable father in *The Swiss Family Robinson* into two characters, each with his own domain of knowledge, as he says "to show the practical man in Ready and the theoretical in the father of the family" (xii), but Marryat does not own up to giving Ready greater significance (except in naming the novel after him). Nevertheless, the novel restores social order (as does J. M. Barrie's 1918 castaway parody *The Admirable Crichton*) and eliminates Ready as a source of law and masculine competition for Mr. Seagrave by ending with Ready's death just as the Seagrave family is about to be rescued and returned to their place as bourgeois colonists in New South Wales.

In some editions of the novel, Ready's greater authority than Seagrave's is enhanced through illustration, as with John Rae's depiction on the cover frontispiece of the 1928 Harper and Brothers edition (see Figure 5), which emphasizes the contrast between the two characters. The illustration places both men in a boat, traditionally Ready's domain, surrounded with the accouterments of his nautical profession (tangled ropes, tackles, tarpaulins). While Ready expertly holds a telescope to his eye, perhaps sighting their island for the first time, Seagrave stands a little behind him, his hand resting on what looks to be the helmet to a diving suit, looking hesitant but prepared to assist the capable, older man. The picture's composition, which places Seagrave slightly below Ready and makes him take up less space in the frame, emphasizes Seagrave's insecurity in that situation and his subordination. These compositional factors, sociologist Erving Goffman explains in *Gender Advertisements*, work to establish "relative size" (28), signaling Seagrave's lesser importance and status and coding that the working-class seaman Ready is the *true* patriarch of the story, the man upon whom everyone else relies.

FIGURE 5. Illustration of Masterman Ready and Mr. Seagrave by John Rae, in
Frederick Marryat, *Masterman Ready* (New York: Harper and Brothers, 1928),
frontispiece.

Interestingly, this illustration and Marryat's creation of Ready as a working-class castaway hero indicate an important modulation in castaway ideology. As imperial expansion grew to depend on the participation of ordinary citizens as well as wealthy investors or adventurers, texts decreased their reliance on nobility as a marker of masculinity so that unlike Prospero, most seventeenth- and eighteenth-century castaway colonists, like Crusoe and Ready, come from merchant or seafaring professions. Whereas Prospero's control comes from his ability to control the labor of others through his class privilege and magic, these men command their island through their ingenuity and labor.

Along with class privilege, absolute individualism also declines as a necessary component of masculinity between the early and high imperial periods. The island fantasy continues to be centered on a single strong, ingenious, white man commanding an island, but nineteenth-century narratives don't strand that man alone. (The entire Robinson and Seagrave families are cast away in *The Swiss Family Robinson* and *Masterman Ready,* as are the three boys in *The Coral Island* and the five companions in *The Mysterious Island.*) It is interesting to note that John Rae's illustration, which also suggests that on the island, social and economic rewards come from abilities, not inheritance, was published just two years after the 1926 Imperial Conference, where the British made verbal gestures toward an equality of Commonwealth nations. So, even if British society didn't always live up to that ideology, we can see this idea of rank based on worth instead of (or in addition to) birth circulating in and influencing both fiction and policy.

Examination of such scenes "between men" (borrowing Eve Kosofsky Sedgwick's language) and reflection on readers' reactions to those scenes is the focus of this chapter. It examines typical moments of masculine interaction in island narratives in order to interrogate interrelationships between fantasies of masculine discipline, island ownership, and real-world empire. In pursuit of that goal, this chapter investigates three gendered characteristics of the narratives, first exploring how island texts present the rewards of authority over colonizable land (symbolized by the island) as resulting from self-disciplining the body, an act achieved only by *certain* white men. Then, the chapter analyzes how texts frequently present that disciplined man as a literal or symbolic father in order to recodify cultural lessons about good imperial behavior through the naturalizing rubric of the father and the family. The chapter ends by looking at how the rule of "the father" over the fictional island ("the law of the father") becomes translated into written law, which shores up fantasies of colonial laws as natural phenomena. Let us begin by more closely examining the concepts of masculinity and discipline.

Island Self-Discipline and the Deserving Colonist

A castaway's masculine discipline earns him his island ownership. That is, he is able to incorporate the island and act as its owner because he apparently deserves it. Like *Masterman Ready,* Verne's *The Mysterious Island* provides an example of the disciplined, deserving colonizer in Cyrus Harding, whose rise to the top of his castaway group (literally rising to the top in Wyeth's illustration, Figure 2) comes from his intellectual prowess combined with his extraordinary ability to discipline his mind, body, and environment, capabilities demonstrated again and again in the text, both through his actions and through the other characters' confidence in and dependence on him. I remarked in chapter 1 on the despair of four of Verne's five castaways upon learning that Harding, "the man who was to be their guide, their leading spirit," had become separated from them during their crash landing (15). Though, in fact, they survive quite capably on their own, the four castaways' despair at Harding's loss attests to their belief in his superiority over them. Pencroft expresses, a bit later in the narrative, the depth of the group's psychological dependence on Harding: "The engineer was to them a microcosm, a compound of every science, a possessor of all human knowledge. It was better to be with Cyrus in a desert island, than without him in the most flourishing town in the United States. With him they could want nothing; with him they would never despair" (57). Cyrus Harding, like Ready, exemplifies the natural and unchallenged leader, the man possessing the knowledge and discipline necessary for survival in that island environment ("with him they could want nothing"), and more importantly, the man whose guidance helps the other castaways manage their emotions ("with him they would never despair") (57). As the man most in control of his own body, mind, and feelings, Harding is also the man best able to subconsciously correlate the island with his body, both of which earn him, the deserving colonizer, command of the island and the other castaways.

Throughout island tales, the actions of deserving colonizers, like Ready and Harding, demonstrate their command of their bodies—their ability to manage materials moving between their bodies' exterior and interior (food, beverages, air, objects), control their biological drives (eating, sleeping, procreating), and direct the movements of their body (work, play).[3] These qualities of bodily command, which make a "good" man, and which traditionally are associated with a certain type of masculinity (heteronormative, white, hegemonic), not coincidentally are the same qualities that the books show make a good imperialist. Yet such connections between masculinity, empire, and discipline presented in these island narratives were neither static nor novel. In most cases, the authors borrowed from and conformed to prevailing gender norms of their publication era. Prospero's seventeenth-century noble masculinity, which reflects ideals of the Renaissance and the fantasies of the gentleman explorer, differs from Crusoe's eighteenth-century, bourgeois, masculine entrepreneur, reflecting the ideals of the enlightenment; both diverge from the *Coral Island* boys' Victorian masculine pluck, embodying a post–Indian Rebellion panic for control. The ideology of masculine self-discipline that permeates the corpus of island narratives changes in response to the varying demands of empire, just as shifting demands of masculinity in part drove the transmogrification of empire.

Historian of masculinity R. W. Connell links masculinity and empire in *Masculinities,* arguing that through empire, certain forms of masculinity were brought into being (in the colonial frontier, for instance), while others were diminished, transformed, or eradicated (including masculinities in Confucian China, Polynesia, and Aboriginal Australia). As well, Connell remarks on links between race, masculinity, and empire: "'Race' was—and to a large extent still is—understood as a hierarchy of bodies, and this has become inextricably mixed with the hierarchy of masculinities" (*The Men and the Boys,* 61). The most important of Connell's arguments, for this chapter's purposes, though, are the theories about hegemonic masculinities—as put forth in *Masculinities,* that is, masculinities as necessarily defined against femininity and competing nondominant masculinities, which must constantly struggle to maintain dominance. To maintain such hegemony, real-world men must—regardless of time and place—constantly perform according to the codes of hegemonic masculinity lest they lose whatever privilege comes to men of their race, gender, and social class. As I will explain, island narratives both articulate and participate in those performances while attempting to mask them in their efforts to paint island imperial hegemony as natural.

Though masculinity does change chronologically over the island narrative corpus in response to sociohistorical changes in presentations of gender, we can also chart striking consistencies in the way masculinity is presented and in the type of masculinity the narratives reward with ownership. Perhaps because the majority of the narratives are modern, they reflect modern ideals of body and mind self-discipline, which are consistently linked to masculinity. As discussed in my introduction and first chapter, social theorists have tracked how a number of cultural movements coincided with the early-modern transition: increasing perceptions of the body as privatized, growing production and popularity of island narratives, and a developing capitalist-based economy in the West. Alongside these social developments emerged ideologies of body discipline as source of power. Klaus Theweleit, for one, argues that this ideology of individualism is particularly modern and masculine. Building on the insights of Norbert Elias about transitions from medieval to modern fantasies of a privatized self, Theweleit remarks that "the new human being who emerges from that [civilizing] process is, first and foremost, a new *man*" (*Male Fantasies, Volume 1*, 300; emphasis original). Theweleit separates this masculine individuality from the feminine, which he sees as "mere appendages of the development in question" (301) because the fantasy that a controlled body would earn rights of ownership over land depended on the notion of being able to own both property and body, societal benefits not historically available to women.

Likewise, Michel Foucault argues in *Discipline and Punish* that such ideologies of regulating the body underlie European modernity, and, I would add to his formulation, modern masculinity. Though Foucault prefaces his discussion with recognition of the ubiquity of body discipline ("in every society," he says, "the body was in the grip of very strict powers, which imposed on it constraints, prohibitions or obligations" [136]), he also locates the development of body discipline as part of the transition from a feudal to a modern capitalist economy between the seventeenth and eighteenth centuries, at the same time (not coincidentally) the island narrative began to flourish as a subgenre. Moreover, Foucault chooses male-centered examples for his discussion (the military, the monastery, the prison), suggesting that the cultural practices he explores as non-gendered are perhaps encoded practices of masculinity. The expansion of European colonization and the sociocultural anxieties it entailed resulted in a "particular need," he says, that mandated the adoption of "a new political anatomy" (138). Thus, that fantasy of masculine bodily discipline already existing in the cultural imaginary was available to male European imperialists for self-assurance of their control of and superiority over their Others. Fantasies of "civilized" (white, masculine, disciplined) bodies provided a handy contrast for "uncivilized" native (nonwhite, feminized, undisciplined) bodies. As Connell remarks in *The Men and the Boys,*

In many parts of the colonized world, indigenous men were called 'boys', and in other parts they were defined as unmasculine because they were thought weak or untrustworthy. But other groups of colonized men could be seen as hypermasculine, especially when involved in violence—e.g. the Sikhs in India, the Zulu in South Africa, the Sioux in North America. (61)

The popular island narrative, which dramatized those fantasies of contrasting gendered bodies, recodified fears of threatened or unstable imperialism onto the circumspect, safe island and further into the well-managed body of the male castaway at the center of that island.

We can best understand the importance of island narratives as ideological tools of empire by investigating how they responded to imperial anxieties (a task continued in the next chapter). Historically, ideologies of the disciplined male body increased in strength during times of perceived crisis to masculinity. A range of cultural critics have charted similar drives for bodily self-control among men in response to stresses from shifting gender roles, an evolving capitalist economy, and increasing competition from immigrant labor. This *counterphobic* fantasy of the self-disciplined male body, says Michael Kimmel, allowed white, heterosexual nineteenth-century U.S. males, for example, the illusion that they commanded a world they felt was menaced by developing democratic capitalism. The American self-made man of the 1880s who realized that he could, as Kimmel explains, "rise as high as he aspired" also had to demonstrate his masculinity constantly in a society full of equals and competitors, for he could fall as easily as he rose. These men responded to this threat by imagining their bodies as bounded, by psychically endeavoring "to build themselves into powerful, impervious machines, capable of victory in any competition" (44).

Theweleit's investigation of the German military human-machine, the Freicorps, similarly traces men responding to perceived crises by reimagining their bodies as closed, bounded, and disciplined. Theweleit argues that those soldiers responded to fears of communism (which they perceived as a feminine "Red Flood") with fantasies of bodily inviolability, which they described as "freez[ing] up . . . becom[ing] icicles"—rigid, cold, inflexible and phallic (*Male Fantasies, Vol 1,* 244). Through this imagined reconfiguration of the male body, the soldier, as Theweleit says, "holds himself together as an entity, a body with fixed boundaries," relieving his anxieties over threats to heterosexual, white, capitalist, masculine privilege by imagining his body as "stiffen[ed]," as a segregated "discrete entity" (244). One Freicorpsman explicitly connects this fantasy of isolation and inviolability to the geographical formation of the island, aptly describing these impregnable soldier bodies as "islands of Germanness, above the raging Polish flood!" (245).

Like Kimmel and Theweleit, David Rosen in *The Changing Fictions of Masculinity* views this fantasy of the armored and disciplined body as found in literature as responding to ideologies of threatened masculinity. Rosen's examination of 1500 years of British literature, from *Beowolf* to *Sons and Lovers*, charts each epoch's attempts to "create a new definition of masculinity" (xiii). Within that discussion, Rosen notes the continuity of some masculine ideals: "older masculine ideals inhabit spaces in new ones, although they are transmuted by their new residence" (xiii). The most clearly transcendent masculine ideology Rosen studies involves self/body discipline. Rosen begins by exploring medieval European masculinity, wherein "the ideal male . . . is a drawer of boundaries—boundaries that must be defended" (5). Yet, this "psychical armor" that Rosen finds as an important coping mechanism in *Beowulf* also, he argues, affects *Gawain and the Green Knight*, for "in Gawain's world a man must be hard, inside and out, should he wish to endure" (30). This same masculine drive for hardened psychical body boundaries manifests itself in *Hamlet*, in which "a man exercises self-control, subdues passion, ignores the knocks of the world at the door of his mind" (64); in *Paradise Lost*, where "men of Anglo-European culture long[ed] to experience their bodies, minds, and world as controllable" (123); and one hundred years later in *Hard Times*, wherein "a masculine order of seeking control and a feminine one of seeking relationships becomes a major theme in the work" (155). Rosen's final examination text, *Sons and Lovers*, explores fears of emasculation and subsequent attempts to recover "what was believed to be the essential, buried, primitive man" (185). Nevertheless, even in *Sons and Lovers* the doctrine of self-control and fantasy of inviolate bodily boundaries participate in the masculinity that haunts feminized twentieth-century men, who, like Paul Morel, used those traditional ideals to measure their own manhood.

This same fantasy of discipline and bodily impermeability in response to crisis exists in British and European imperial cultures, in men haunted by fears of being influenced by their colonial "inferiors." As noted by both Mary Louise Pratt in her articulation of the "contact zone" and Homi Bhabha in his exploration of the "third space," colonial influence, despite its depiction in much colonial literature, was fluid and mutual. While the "center" obviously influenced the "margins," the margins also shaped the center, seen most easily in how quickly the metropole adopted and became dependent on certain colonial products, such as coffee, tea, chocolate, tobacco, china, and silks.[4] Such a two-way exchange of culture in "third space," as Bhabha explains, producing colonial hybrids instead of a series of replications of "pure" imperial culture stamped around the globe, had real ideological repercussions: "The margin of hybridity, where cultural differences 'contingently' and conflictually touch, becomes the moment of panic which reveals the borderline experience. It resists the binary opposition of racial and cultural groups, sipahis and sahibs, as homogeneous polarized political consciousnesses" (*Location of Culture*, 207).

We can see this "panic" over the idea of mutual influence at the "borderlines" in texts depicting the manly colonization of islands and in writers who chose the island as a site for their colonial stories because they perhaps found in its form a symbolic mirror of the body they subconsciously fantasized commanding. By depicting the protagonist as gaining control of the island by maintaining control of his body, these writers transferred desire for total, natural authority over the colonized territory onto the island and then further onto the fantasy self-disciplined borders of the masculine form. The loosening of this discipline, the texts foretell, leads to degeneration (a phobia I will trace in chapter 4) or, as with the sailors in *Masterman Ready*, death. The castaway, then, must resist "going native" by hardening his body's psychical and physical boundaries and disciplining both island and body, thereby enacting for readers the fantasy of secure, natural, inviolable control over island and empire. As vehicles for assuaging deep-seated imperial-cum-masculine fears of loss of control, island stories recodify larger cultural desires about empire and masculinity into the comforting story of one man's disciplined body and secure land ownership.

Social theorists working to tease out the psychology of gendered perceptions of the body can help us understand these enduring connections between fantasies of masculinity, fantasies of bodily self-discipline, and the choice of the island as literary setting. Joan Lidoff and T. Walter Herbert, for instance, argue that masculine and feminine perceptions of the body's boundaries are fundamentally opposite. According to Lidoff, a woman's experience of the Oedipal/Electral conflict, which doesn't encompass the distinct differentiation from the mother that boys endure, results in a female "sense of adult identity defined by more fluid ego boundaries" (399). Building on Lidoff's theories, literary critic T. Walter Herbert, argues that males perceive their "self" as psychologically enclosed: males "patrol the boundaries of the self more anxiously. Men possess a touchier psychic immune system that responds with vehement measures of exclusion when 'self' is infringed upon by 'not self'" (421). These articulations of an innate gendered identity could, of course, also be seen as responses to societal expectations of gender, since in many cultures, women, as caretakers and mothers, traditionally haven't been allowed to expect rights of privacy over their bodies. Children, husbands, and the state could intrude upon women's bodily boundaries without consent in issues of sexuality, labor, and childbirth. In fact, only heterosexual men of a certain race and class could be historically thought to possess the means and social permission to be psychologically enclosed.

Such arguments about the psychology of space and gender as reflected in conceptions of psychical boundaries can be useful for understanding why the island was chosen time and again as fictional site for fantasies of colonization. To translate these sociopsychological theories into literary terms, a male writer wishing to describe the desire to colonize or control open or unbounded space (like a portion of a continent) might, without exactly understanding why, choose as a metaphor a man conquering the (according to Lidoff) "fluid" bordered female, as both McClintock and Kolodny have so well demonstrated. Sir Walter Raleigh's description of Guyana as a female body and discussion of his desire to colonize "her" in terms of taking "her maidenhead" provides a good example of such a linguistic choice.[5] Conversely, a male writer wishing to describe the desire to colonize or command an *enclosed* space (like an island) might choose the topos of a man controlling himself or his own body, responding to subconscious perceptions of the male self as bounded, as writers I discuss in this chapter do. Further, this writer might show how this male character would strengthen these psychological boundaries by working to discipline his own body and "civilize" the island space. The psychical mechanism used by the text or colonizer, in this logic, correlates with the geographical formation being chosen for the imagined or real colonization: for open landscape, a female body; for an island or other closed geographical formation, a disciplined male.

Women of the Island

Often this overwhelming masculinity on the island means that women and the feminine are displaced or erased, a significant occurrence in light of the fact that two of the most powerful British imperial figures, Elizabeth and Victoria, were women. The island becomes a fantasy space where women and the feminine often appear only at the narrative margins to perform an interesting circumscribing purpose, as does Mrs. Crusoe in *The Farther Adventures of Robinson Crusoe*. Crusoe has married but can only return to "his" island once his wife has died. The absent Mrs. Crusoe hovers always figuratively on the edges of the island, never to set foot on its shores, only through her death sanctioning Crusoe's return to that homosocial environment.[6] By consigning women firmly to the margins of island and empire, island narratives show women as largely incidental to the island colonization, reflecting their political invisibility in real-world imperial society, thus helping to construct an ideological and social map of a fantasy empire in which women's labors (in both senses of that word, as I will explain, and in their complicities) are erased.

When island narratives do include women as castaways, the texts often just as firmly marginalize them from authority and narrative importance, as in *The Narrative of the Life and Astonishing Adventures of John Daniel*. I briefly summarized in chapter 1 that John Daniel, cast away on an island with a fellow sailor, "Thomas," discovers after a year's cohabitation (and seventy pages of narrative), that Thomas is a woman named Ruth. After suffering a near-mortal groin injury (a stick slipped and penetrated Ruth's virgin groin, thus symbolically making way for John Daniel's upcoming sexual penetration of her), Ruth is forced to reveal her true identity or die. In a meditation, John Daniel admits to having no suspicions about Ruth's sex (though he did earlier remark on her gender in noting her slight body size, and though the reader, from the book's long and explicit subtitle, knows before reading the book that Thomas is a woman and that they will together "people" the island). Through Ruth, then, a woman who could convincingly work as and pass for a man, the novel could destabilize ideologies of naturalized gender hegemony, an aim suggested by John Daniel's conclusion, "what we take things to be, that they certainly are, as to us . . . the distinction rather lies in our own true or false judgment, than in the objects themselves" (72). Yet the book counters its own efforts to remap gender since, before knowing Ruth/Thomas is female, John Daniel "instinctively" assumes leadership and treats Ruth as second in command, a role she unflinchingly accepts. As well, though Ruth accompanies John Daniel in all of his castaway adventures, she is omitted both from the book's title (the narrative is *only* John Daniel's) and the narrating act itself; John Daniel throughout speaks for her, often reporting her words instead of directly quoting her, and even more often folding her voice into the "we" with which much of the first part of the narrative is told. She is, in effect, incorporated into John Daniel's story and, later, into his person as she becomes the vehicle through which he produces his progeny. Though she shares with John Daniel the incorporative monarch-of-all-I-survey moment, she does not become leader of the island, but becomes John Daniel's follower, consumed as part of the island into his corpus, his skin ego.

I return to Anzieu's language intentionally here, since he, like Klein and Freud before him, sees a unique relationship between the developing child and the mother. Anzieu theorizes a maternal dyad, whereby the infant at first doesn't distinguish itself from the body that produced and nurtured it. Klein, too, speaks of the child's first incorporated object and hence its first experience with object relations, as being the mother's breast, towards which it has ambivalent feelings. According to Klein, then, all incorporative actions originate in the neonate's relationship with the breast. John Daniel's folding of Ruth into his narrative and narrative voice could be read, then, as an attempt to rejoin with the feminine, to incorporate that essence along with the island. This impulse might seem contradictory to other narrative efforts to marginalize the female or, as I will soon discuss, replace the mother. Yet all of these narrative lines and character behaviors could be seen as originating in the same desire to secure an always unstable masculine dominance through manipulation of the feminine.

A second variation on the way in which island narratives reinforce the masculine through the feminine comes in their use of women as foils, to reinforce the point that the body discipline necessary to owning the island is a trait available only to men. Castaway women are often weak physically and mentally, naturally incapable of commanding their own bodies, as is the case in both *Masterman Ready* and *The Swiss Family Robinson*, where the primary female characters contribute little to their families' survival or to the development of the island beyond some light cooking and sewing. Any act truly important to the survival of the family that requires ingenuity and labor, even if traditionally in the female sphere, is likely to be performed by men. Both *The Swiss*

Family Robinson and *Masterman Ready* attribute any demanding cooking to their male characters, especially those important acts whereby they ingeniously create delicacies out of what appeared to be inedibles. *The Swiss Family Robinson,* for example, describes in great detail the father's engineering and labor to make bread out of manioc root but glosses over the mother's daily cooking, which must have involved just as many feats of resourcefulness.

In fact, women drain the island's resources: men expend valuable energy protecting them physically and emotionally, as in *Masterman Ready* when Mrs. Seagrave's innate mental and physical frailty requires that she stay in her cabin during the storm and that the others labor both to protect her and to shield her from the gravity of their situation. Though the narrative calls the sickly woman "courageous" (56) and "amiable" (6), she is really a foil, necessary to highlight the strength and pluck of the men. In effect, as Michael Roper and John Tosh stress in their introduction to *Manful Assertions,* because "masculinity has always been defined in *relation* to 'the other'" (1, emphasis original), white disciplined masculinity depends on its Derridian supplement—the native, the feminine, or the undisciplined—for its existence.

Complicating the gendering of castaway narratives is that a few colonial-era island narratives do make a woman the *sole* castaway on the island and show that woman undergoing a similar transition from survivor to owner as the male castaway. In eras of corsets and compulsory marriage and motherhood, such stories of female ingenuity could have been quite progressive, though the texts show that the female characters have to become masculine and act manly in order to survive and must return to traditional female roles once rescued. It is typical in pre-twentieth-century female narratives to show the female castaway becoming temporarily masculinized and losing the trappings of femininity during her experience on the island, as if required to internalize all of the rules of self-discipline presented in male Robinsonades in order to enjoy patriarchal rewards. The most widely read of these early female Crusoe narratives, Charles Dibdin's *Hannah Hewitt, or The Female Crusoe* (1792), for instance, tells of a woman who successfully colonizes her own desert isle—making a domicile for herself, controlling her food supply, disciplining her mind and body—in short, acting in what the narratives depict as a masculine manner.[7] Yet Hannah is clearly presented as an exception to the rule of typical femininity (according to the text's full title, she is "of *uncommon* mental and personal accomplishments") (emphasis mine). Her successful colonization results not from innate attributes but from her transformation from being on the island—a transformation that is only temporary, since, when "rescued," and no longer island owner, she loses that masculinization and happily returns to her expected role of marital counterpart and subordinate helpmate.

The Female American (1767) offers a second variation on the counter-transgressive female castaway through its protagonist, Unca Eliza Winkfield (the author's pseudonym) who prospers as an island colonist only because she still has a man to rely upon. She discovers an equipped but abandoned cabin complete with the island's previous, male castaway's journal, which serves as a survival manual, telling her everything from which animals and plants are edible, to when to hide from the natives who annually visit the island. Despite making Unca quite intelligent and self-sufficient (much is made of her prowess with a bow and arrow, for instance), the novel casts doubt on whether a woman could be resourceful enough to survive without male assistance. In fact, perhaps for this reason (or perhaps because the tale had nowhere to go once Unca held all of the tools to island survival), the castaway narrative transmutes into a tale of Unca's Christian conversion of the adjacent island's natives, a more "acceptable" eighteenth-century feminine endeavor. She, like Hannah, must display traits of masculine discipline in order to be in command of her island, but in order to contain the threat that a woman assuming a traditionally "masculine" role might present, her endeavors must be constantly preceded and bolstered by a man.

These colonial-era novels do take the progressive step of changing the castaway's gender, but unlike postcolonial works such as J. M. Coetzee's *Foe* (1986) and Jean Giraudoux's *Suzanne and the Pacific* (1923), they don't challenge the underlying logic of the fantasy: they stress the similarities between their female protagonists and Crusoe as a way of showing the girl/woman's heroic potential.[8] For instance, the girl protagonist of Lucy Ford's *The Female Robinson Crusoe: A Tale of the American Wilderness* (1837), who becomes "stranded" in the wilderness for ten years, heartens herself by imagining herself as like Crusoe, for she "was destitute like him, although not upon a remote island, amid a vast ocean" (50). Another nineteenth-century text, Julia Dean's *The Wonderful Narrative of Miss Julia Dean, The Only Survivor of the Steamship "City of Boston," Lost at Sea, 1870* (1890) also tells of a young female island castaway who discovers her self-sufficiency and survives quite well on her deserted island for nine years, finding hope, she explains, as "the story of Robinson Crusoe came to my mind, and every detail of his wonderful narrative, which I had read when a very young girl, returned to me now with renewed interest" (53). In an ultimately counter-transgressive use of circular logic, the authors of such narratives use the Crusoe story to show the natural strength of the young women, while stressing that the young women only achieve that strength through their identification with Crusoe and during their time as castaways.

Food, Drink, Sex, and Soap: Demonstrating Masculine Discipline

Just as island narratives often use contrasts with women and the feminine to highlight castaways' masculine character, so they also rely upon scenes showcasing the male castaway performing actions that demonstrate self-discipline (if he is a deserving colonist) or lack of self-discipline (if he is a foil for the deserving colonist). Again, Connell's theory of hegemonic masculinities is significant here, since in the fictional realm, as well, fantasies of what makes a good man and a deserving colonizer (self-sacrifice, hard work, and most of all, self-control) require perpetual performance, both in the same tale and through books telling similar tales. Demonstration of the deserving castaway colonist's masculine fortitude includes showing him in constant command of his biological drives, particularly his consumption of food and drink, which symbolize his actual incorporation of the island.

As noted in chapter 1, instead of accepting the repast naturally available for them on the island, castaways typically labor exhaustively to seize control of their food supply. The castaways match their control over their food source with command of their intake of food, demonstrating their mastery of their drives and ability to deny themselves short-term pleasures in the service of long-term survival and colonization. Likewise, the novels condemn and dispossess characters not in control of their hunger or appetites, as does *Masterman Ready* with the Seagraves' youngest son, Tommy, who remains in trouble for eating when and what he shouldn't.

As with food, the narratives also repeatedly demonstrate discipline (or lack of same) through characters' temperance. Marryat's characters, for example, deny themselves the drinking of alcohol to the extent that, when Ready and Mr. Seagrave discover a cask of gin, they agree not to drink it except as medicine. Likewise, when Fritz in *The Swiss Family Robinson* learns that a flask of sugarcane juice has fermented into rum, his father similarly warns him "to exercise moderation" lest the drink "go to [his] head" (37). The consumption of alcohol allows narratives to create contrast between the disciplined castaway and *un*disciplined white men (like the drunken Trinculo and Stephano in *The Tempest* and Montgomery in *The Island of Dr. Moreau*), who are therefore deservedly denied full participation in the island colonialist enterprise. Other characters disenfranchised because lacking the will to govern their bodies and minds include the sailors in *Masterman Ready* who never even reach the island, the lazy Jack in *The Swiss Family Robinson,* the lustful pirates and nonwhite cannibals in *Robinson Crusoe,* and the spoiled Tommy in *Masterman Ready.*

Of course, there are real-world corollaries to such notions of susceptibility to alcohol as used to justify denial of land-ownership and enfranchisement within the colonial system. For hundreds of years, settler imperialists, most notably in the United States and Australia, used alcohol and alcoholism for social control in indigenous communities and as justification for imperial and neo-imperial policies. As reported in the *Reconciliation and Social Justice Library of the Indigenous Law Resources,* a variety of Australian laws, such as the Northern Territory "two-kilometer" law, address Aboriginal alcoholic behavior, mandating, for instance, that alcohol not be consumed in public places or, in some states, not sold to Aboriginal people. Because public drinking laws in particular discriminate against people not in possession of a private space in town for drinking or welcomed in town bars, they seem to be aimed at apprehending Aboriginal people. While neglecting the social problems leading to alcoholism, such laws neither provide rehabilitation services nor recognize the gross overrepresentation of Aboriginal people in apprehensions for public drunkenness. Such laws aimed at controlling drinking in the colonies, which provide colonizers a further tool for social control, are certainly not recent, as David Hardiman explains in his examination of British laws controlling the drinking of alcoholic beverages in colonial India. The drinking of toddy (locally distilled from palm sap) was an important element of local custom in the religion and health of South Gujarat, Hardiman tells, yet the British Raj banned local manufacture of toddy and taxed it, both to control Indians' drinking and to raise revenue. Such laws stem from a bifurcated disciplinary logic: on the one hand, since Indians can't control their drinking, the Raj should tax the toddy to deter the Indians' destructive behaviors. On the other hand, since the Raj will have to suffer the consequences for the Indian's lack of self-control, the British should recoup their losses through taxation.

Accompanying such scenes of attempts to discipline the *body* are incidents of castaway colonists attempting to tame their *emotions*—clamping down loneliness, fear, and despair, providing readers with fictional models of imperial stoicism and the British "stiff upper lip."[9] For instance, the explanation of *The Swiss Family Robinson* father that he "never ceased contriving fresh improvements, being fully aware of the importance of constant employment as a means of strengthening and maintaining the health of mind and body" (243) raises the question of whose despair he works so diligently to overcome—his family's or his own? Perhaps Mr. Robinson's efforts to "strengthen" his sons through constant employment of their bodies in the name of "improving" their island and lives, in an endless cycle of work, worship, and occasionally restrained celebration, also function to distract himself, to help him reign in his own emotions, and to convince himself of the truth of his performed contentment. Not surprisingly, descriptions of work fill island narratives, as characters out of control of their circumstances (tossed about by storm, stranded by shipwreck) try to assert command through the labors of their minds and bodies. Like Verne's castaways, who need Cyrus Harding to feel they can survive, or the eighteenth- and nineteenth-century female Crusoes, who hearten themselves by imagining their plight as like Crusoe's, the struggle to keep the emotions in check and to not go mad (which I will discuss more in later chapters) is crucial to survival and to the story's imperial message: even when life seems to be unbearable, either because of colonial duties as part of the "white man's burden" or because of the violent upheavals of empire, one must stiffen the upper lip and fulfill one's duty.

This disciplining of the emotions and the body also requires strict command of sexual drives, for characters need to keep their bodies and minds busily employed to sublimate their sexuality as well as to forget despair. Many of the stories concern adolescent boys (*The Coral Island, Masterman Ready, The Swiss Family Robinson*) who enter into manhood and sexual awakening with no female object except possibly their mother or sister, who are forbidden under the incest taboo, or native women, like Juno in *Masterman Ready* and Avatea in *The Coral Island*, who are eliminated by the miscegenation taboo. Single adult males, too, must police their sexual drives lest they become tempted into incest (a threat in *The Tempest*), homosexuality (a threat in *Robinson Crusoe*), autoeroticism (possible in all of the texts), or bestiality (a particular threat in *The Island of Dr. Moreau*). Of course, these unsanctioned sexual outlets existed in real-world empire, with rape of indigenous women an all-too-frequent result of colonial contact. Island narratives—functioning as mechanisms to whitewash reality—would show colonial adventurers restraining their impulses.

As part of this recasting of colonial sexual discipline, narratives show mothers and especially fathers carefully monitoring young people's premarital sexual behaviors, illustrating how "civilized" parenting fosters and reproduces self-restraint. Prospero carefully checks the romance between Miranda and Ferdinand; even after the youths are engaged, he threatens harm to Ferdinand if he "breaks" Miranda's "virgin knot" (4.1.15). The Robinson parents similarly orchestrate the romance between their eldest son, Ernest, and the girl they find cast away on a nearby island, Jennie. In both stories, though the youths may develop romantic feelings, their parents oversee their bodies to keep them from acting on their impulses. The Robinsons first forestall all of their sons' sexual instincts by disguising Jennie as a boy, creating a homoerotic undertone to the boys' interest in her. After Jenny's boy disguise fails, the parents designate her as the boys' new sister, thus still keeping sexual behaviors in check by invoking the incest taboo. This incest taboo proves fluid, however, for after rescue, when sexual outlets exist for the other sons, the Robinson parents reclassify Jennie from sister to family friend to enable Ernest to court her. Yet, still, the parents monitor Jenny and Ernest's sexuality, only allowing it to bloom when officially sanctioned under both fathers' consent. The Jenny/Ernest union, then, demonstrates the rewards of self-control while reproducing (literally through their offspring) their fathers' power over their bodies.

The sex drive cannot always be so easily denied, though island narratives often attempt to redirect it into the service of empire. As cultural historian Jonathan Rutherford explains in his investigation of similar imperial fantasies in terms of masculine autoerotic narcissism, "narcissism was central to the psychopathology of imperialism. It was characterised by an asceticism, an affective immaturity and a tendency towards the denial of desire and instinctual life" (32). This imperial narcissism leads men in island narratives to redirect or repudiate their sexual instincts, for "the body and its sexualities" according to Rutherford "were indeed the source of the imperial Englishman's shame" (32). As a sort of precursor of *The Little Rascals'* boyhood fantasy "he-man-woman-hater's-club," the island narrative provides a male homosocial retreat from the erotic body and often from women, both for the male character and reader, while transferring sexual energy (as Rutherford notes, both characters' and readers') into the service of empire. "Imperialism became a divinity, an autoerotic pleasure offering itself as an object of love," Rutherford explains. "This transfer of ego-subordination from the mother to an imperial mission cultivated a demand for individual sacrifice and a tantalizing culture of the will to power" (34). Many of the typical castaway's behaviors of sexual discipline demonstrate this sublimation of the sex drive, as autoerotocism becomes transferred into the castaway's nurturing of the island, which has already been incorporated into his body image. His love for and obsession with his island-body provides the same visceral pleasure as the stroking of his own body, providing a lesson for readers about "acceptable" objects of desire. Meanwhile, his selfless service for the island recodifies the real-world sacrifice of men's lives and loves in the service of imperialism.

Island narratives also code characters' maintenance of masculine bodily discipline through the cleanliness of their body and immediate environment.[10] The tales alleviate anxieties of control by transferring them onto the body where masculine, disciplined characters can repudiate the island's influence on their bodies by ritual bathing (according to the standard of their time) and dressing in European clothing, even when impractical or improbable. Again and again, characters are described and illustrated with their bodies immaculately encased in "civilized" European clothing even after weeks of hard work and rough living on the island. Crusoe's fashioning of European-styled, goatskin clothes (a jacket, hat, breeches, tool belts, and umbrella) instead of wearing a native-styled, more practical covering, demonstrates this need for control of the body. Though Crusoe does need to shield himself from the sun (hence the umbrella and hat), heavy goatskin clothing (fur intact) fashioned after that worn in a much colder climate could not have been comfortable or practical in a semitropical environment. Crusoe even mentions his lack of need of heavy clothes, remarking at one point that he has "not Clothes to cover me" but that he is "in a hot Climate, where if I had Clothes I could hardly wear them" (49). Later in the novel, he remarks that "tho' it is true, that the Weather was so violent hot, that there was no need of Cloaths, yet I could not go quite naked; no, tho' I had been inclin'd to it, which I was not, nor could not abide the thoughts of it, tho' I was all alone" (98). He could not go naked, he says, because

FIGURE 6. Scenes of Crusoe at work by T. H. Nicholson, from Daniel Defoe, *The Life and Adventures of Robinson Crusoe* (London: Ward, Lock, and Company, 1879). By permission of the British Library, 12611.i.4.

he needed the protection from the sun's rays. But his not being able to "abide the thoughts of it" comes from his cultural training in civilized behavior and control of the body, which means separating the body from nature through clothing. With Friday's arrival, Crusoe creates a similar though less elaborate costume to symbolize Friday's near-civilized status, making him, as Crusoe says "*almost* as well cloath'd as his Master" (150, emphasis mine), or as Bhabha would say, "almost the same but not quite . . . almost the same but not white" ("Of Mimicry and Man," 238).

Another method texts employ to mark the castaway colonist's masculine self-discipline involves the management of space and time. Castaways order *space* by building multiple European-styled homes, enclosing and planting fields, diverting rivers, transforming caves, and most importantly, mapping their island landscape, behaviors discussed as rituals of possession in chapter 1. Though such acts of order and domestication could be thought antithetical to white masculinity, the domestication exhibited in these narratives in fact illustrates the epitome of imperial manhood, since maintaining a secure, well-ordered home and indoctrinating offspring were in many imperial cultures integral to demonstrating one's masculinity. As John Tosh observes in *A Man's Place,* his analysis of Victorian masculinity and domesticity, "the domestic sphere, then, is integral to masculinity. To establish a home, to protect it, to provide for it, to control it, and to train its young aspirants to manhood, have usually been essential to a man's good standing with his peers" (4). When stripped of those manifestations of masculinity because of shipwreck, male characters labor intensively to redomesticate (reorder) their surroundings. The island's enclosed shape enhances this fantasy of ordered space, for as Foucault observes, "discipline sometimes requires *enclosure,* the specification of a place heterogeneous to all others and closed in upon itself. It is the protected place of disciplinary monotony" (*Discipline and Punish,* 141, emphasis original). Following routines and schedules assumes a particular importance for castaway colonists, who order time by marking the Sabbath, tracking their stay on the island, and maintaining a semblance of a "civilized" schedule in their island home. Crusoe, for instance, constructs a calendar out of a stick he plants on the beach and marks with the passing weeks.

One illustration, from an 1879 Ward, Lock, and Company edition of *Robinson Crusoe,* (see Figure 6) juxtaposes Crusoe's ordering of time (his building of his calendar) and space (his construction of a tent and driving of posts for a fence) with his management of his food (he catches the wild pigeon for domestication) and his body (his sleeping in a tree protects it, as his neat dress orders it). This drawing handily encapsulates the primary performances of Crusoe's masculine discipline all on one page, allowing the reader to marvel at his work ethic. As well, this illustration creates a thumbnail of the narrative that emphasizes Crusoe's individuality, since excepting animals, he is always alone, and four of the six captions repeat simple declarative statements with the subject "I." Instead of narrating other series of events (his religious conversion, for instance, or interactions with Friday), this late nineteenth-century edition chose to emphasize Crusoe's continual work and remarkable self-discipline, both integral to establishing his masculinity (with, at that point in the narrative, no foil for contrast) and his deserved island command. By showing him age (he has a beard and looks older in the bottom two scenes), the illustrations stress that the older Crusoe continues to work just as hard as the younger. Significantly, each illustrated scene contains a caption to identify the type of work for the reader and paste together the individual moments into a symbolic representation of the novel, which, it seems, concerns self-discipline and order in the service of empire. Such a message of earned imperial control would have been significant for justifying an expanding British empire, which, for instance, in 1879, during the publication of this particular edition of *Robinson Crusoe,* invaded an independent Zulu kingdom, beginning the Anglo-Zulu war. In the wake of the Zulu's fierce resistance, such ideologies of the discipline and invincibility of the manly empire would have been even more needed to soothe fears of the viability of African self-rule.

The temporal order of the illustration signifies Crusoe's discipline and mirrors his national imperial ideology, for the notion of temporal order (found in its extreme in early twentieth-century efficiency movements, or "Taylorism," popularized by Frederick Winslow Taylor) was integral to Europe's ideals of discipline. As Foucault recognizes, "the Principle that underlay the time-table in its traditional form was essentially negative; it was the principle of non-idleness: it was forbidden to waste time" (*Discipline and Punish,* 154). Yet, as historian Frederick Cooper explains, attempts to institute European linear time measurements in the colonies often conflicted with a differing (not less motivated or less efficient) indigenous perception of time, discipline, and work, which he calls "task time": "When something had to be done, it was, and so effort varied seasonally and in other ways, while work rhythms were integrated into patterns of social life" (210). This "task time" conflicts with imperial notions of "clock time," which Cooper says "were not natural characteristics of a particular culture, but historical developments, consequences of the rise of wage labor and the imposition of discipline from above" (210). The work of island protagonists to order time, then, aims both at their own bodies and at the island's "nature" whose time they must transform. In the ultimate service of imperial capitalism, they must maintain their clock time (even without clocks or calendars) and resist the island's seductive task time, which leads down the slippery slope to "going native." By extension, the novel as a tool of imperial and capitalistic enculturation works to spread ideologies of clock time as natural, as part of imperial efforts to remake the colonized culture in the image of empire.

The island narrative as piece of writing also metaphorically participates in this demonstration of ordered time and space, for the book itself often fulfills the drive for discipline by opening with a list of chapters that provides a chronological overview of the plot (the ordering of time) and with a map of the island (the ordering of space). Like the frontispiece maps discussed in chapter 1, the two types of chart intersect: both the plot overview (which forecasts events in space and time) and the map (through its layered registering of the narrative's chronological and spatial events) chart the movement of characters across space and time, ordering both for the reader. Further, as post–*Robinson Crusoe* island narratives reconstruct order simply by following that familiar plot pattern (the island palimpsest), they participate in *reconstruction* of European order, control, and discipline.

Island Fatherhood and Manly Reproduction

As is the case in Marryat's novel, the deserving castaway, that is, he who displays the manly discipline necessary to earn the right to act as island owner, often is a biological or symbolic father. Biological fathers, like the almost-omniscient Mr. Robinson in *The Swiss Family Robinson* and Prospero in *The Tempest,* maintain strict control over the bodies of their offspring while passing on knowledge and self-discipline to them. As well as teaching his sons about science, nature, engineering, cooking, botany, geography, and a host of other topics, Mr. Robinson, for instance, instills into them his doctrine of masculine discipline, in one instance, chiding his son Ernest for napping instead of watching their herds. When Ernest explains that he blocked a bridge so that their animals could not pass and were thus contained, his father, though he "could not help laughing at the ingenious device by which the boy had spared himself all trouble," also cannot help scolding him for his lax work ethic, "at the same time [observing] that it is wrong to waste the precious moments in sleep when duty has to be performed" (106).

If the text doesn't contain an actual family, then it often depicts relationships between men so that one man acts as "father" to another. The illustration mentioned in the beginning of this chapter from the cover and frontispiece of *Masterman Ready* (see Figure 5) tells such a story of *symbolic* fatherhood in its depiction of Ready and Mr. Seagrave as "father" and "son." In fact, often we see that the most disciplined man, the man who commands the island in these books, serves as a literal patriarch to the other castaways. By drawing upon the supposedly innate hierarchy of the family, island texts labor to depict the systems of power on the island as natural, which, of course, by extension makes power hierarchies in the larger imperial system seem natural, even familial. This story line presents a metanarrative of a father (imperial colonist), as natural leader of a family (colony), who labors for his family out of concern for their goodwill and out of the natural wish to reproduce what is good in himself in others, not for selfish capitalist gain. Of course, as McClintock details in *Imperial Leather,* such ideals of innate family dynamics were widely used in imperial discourse, including the use of evolutionary "family trees" to justify racism and colonialism.

Verne's *The Mysterious Island* resurrects Captain Nemo from *20,000 Leagues Under the Sea* to serve as island patriarch. Throughout the novel, a mysterious force protects Verne's five main castaways from harm (including rescuing them from a dangerous sea monster, providing them with life-saving medicines, and warning them of the island's impending destruction). At novel's end, Verne reveals that a man has been engineering these mysterious events: the dying Captain Nemo. Nemo's command over the island and the others supercedes Harding's, perhaps since he enjoys a more long-standing and literally a deeper connection to the island. With his submarine wedged in a subterranean island cave (the Freudian symbolism hardly needs noting), Nemo exists inside the island while the others, though also living in a cave, are closer to and more often on the surface. Because of his control over the island, Nemo acts as "father" to the adult Harding (just as Ready does to Seagrave), while Harding also plays father to Herbert, the boy castaway (as Seagrave does to his sons) and to the other castaways. Through such layering of fatherhood and "sonhood," the narrative recodifies the multilayered hierarchy of power in the imperial system and in the European class structure through the naturalizing rubric of the family. One might be father (superior) to one man while son (inferior) to another, just as a powerful imperial governor ("father" to some) is subject to his king, who is subject to God.

Nemo's status as powerful patriarch is in some editions reinforced through image, as in a Wyeth illustration from the 1920 Scribner edition (see Figure 7). Despite the book's repeated assertion that he is dying (which leads to his decision to remain on the island when it explodes), in this depiction Nemo embodies omnipotence and fatherly wisdom, though perhaps a bit haggard. Instead of showing Nemo's authority by juxtaposing him to other characters, Wyeth indicates Nemo's power through elements of classical iconography. Wyeth shows Nemo sitting on a throne in a white robe in front of a stunning peacock wall covering (not mentioned in the text), which demonstrates the opulence of the submarine palace, symbolizes male vanity and royalty, and suggests Nemo's messianic immortality despite his age. As James Hall's *The Dictionary of Subjects and Symbols in Art* explains, the peacock was often included in depictions of Christ because in myth, its flesh never decays.

Nemo's penetrating blue eyes, which mesmerize both characters and reader, assert his white privilege and dominance, as do his white-on-white complexion, clothing, and voluptuous beard. Wyeth's portrayal of Nemo's extreme whiteness, in fact, is a bit ironic, since Nemo reveals that he is an Indian prince (Prince Dakkar) who fought on the Indian side of the rebellion of 1857. With the colonists "forgiving" Nemo for his past sins, including taking up arms against the British, the scene ends on a note of redemption and forgiveness, thus providing another important lesson of imperial behavior. Composed during postwar prosperity when the impending dissolution of empire could perhaps be ignored, this 1920 image of Nemo (like the 1928 image of Masterman Ready, and like typical portrayals of Prospero) holds on to a fantasy of a great white father—great in command, white in ethnicity and appearance, fatherly in relationship. Moreover, in all three stories, the father "dies" before the sons leave the island—Ready killed by cannibals while saving the Seagraves, Nemo dying of an unnamed sickness, and Prospero metaphorically dying when he surrenders his books and breaks his staff. As Freud explains in *Totem and Taboo*, the son must kill the father in order to take his place. In these stories, the book seems to do that work for the son,

FIGURE 7. *Captain Nemo* by N. C. Wyeth, from Jules Verne, *The Mysterious Island* (New York: Scribner, 1920), 454.

killing off the father and releasing the son (and the reader) to take up his imperial duties.

Such depictions of the white father (Nemo, Ready, and Prospero) read like textual reproductions of that most omniscient of fathers, the Christian God, most famously depicted by Michelangelo on the ceiling of the Sistine Chapel as on an island, imparting life and knowledge to Adam. The similarities between the literary island fathers and Michelangelo's God are striking, from the classical dress, to the white beard, to the absolute command over environment, including the bodies of others. The writers of these island narratives or their illustrators, if not imitating Michelangelo's painting directly, at least drew upon the same cultural trope of the white patriarch as did Michelangelo and other artists of biblical material. Such a connection with the Christian God would certainly increase the fantasy of the white imperial father as an omniscient Father with command over others' bodies and the natural world. Though the Christian God appears only to a chosen few and in very specific instances, while the castaway fathers are present on the island, like Michelangelo's God, who imparts the power of life to Adam, island fathers fulfill the narcissistic fantasy of reproducing oneself and one's power in the body of the "fruit" of the male loins.

Of course, with imperial "fathers" come "children," whose stories show how to be good imperial subjects. Ordinary colonial readers, even if not imperial pioneers or investors, could participate in empire as obedient "children" of their white imperial "fathers." Like *The Mysterious Island*'s colonists, who survive and prosper because they are wise enough to follow their "fathers" (Cyrus Harding and later, Nemo), ordinary imperial citizens and colonized people, so say these stories, could thrive if they are obedient and self-disciplined and adequately learn the lessons of self-discipline from their "father." The works teach these lessons of profitable imperial subjecthood through the behavior of good offspring, like Friday, and by contrasting good children with bad, like Caliban. Ironically, *Robinson Crusoe* combines its good and bad offspring in the figure of Crusoe, who, as a bad son, flees England and the life his father would have for him, but who discovers how to be a good son (both to his father and to God, the Father) and a good "father" (to Friday) only when stranded on the island, literally out of range of influence. *The Tempest*, as well, contrasts Miranda with Caliban, the disappointing child, who refuses the self-discipline Prospero tried to instill in him and attempts to rape Miranda (not only symbolic incest but also loss of body self-discipline). Caliban's constant bodily torment at the hands of Prospero (physical pain and disturbing visions) illustrates what happens to "children" (colonized people) who try to refuse the "benefits" of colonization.

Masterman Ready creates a similar contrast between a good, self-disciplined son, William, and a bad, undisciplined son, Tommy, a boy who remains in trouble for gluttony and disobedience. At different points in the narrative, Tommy loses his mother's thimble (crucial for her sewing) in a pot of soup he disobediently samples, becomes locked in a hen house while stealing eggs, is kicked by a goat after he kicks it first, and is knocked down by the recoil of a gun he was not supposed to shoot. The novel even makes Tommy, as the bad son, responsible for the death of Ready, his symbolic father (ergo patricide), for it is his undisciplined behavior that leads to Ready's self-sacrifice (though the novel's postscript reveals that Tommy did learn to discipline himself and grew up to be a major in the British army). William, on the other hand, makes the perfect pupil for Ready, soaking in all of the old man's wisdom and internalizing all of his lessons about obedience and discipline. Ready teaches William to fish, raise turtles, hunt, pilot a boat, and generally survive on his wits, allowing the childless Ready to fulfill a fantasy of reproducing himself in another male, a fantasy that also works to naturalize an ideology of imperial indoctrination. Such a fantasy of the transference of ideologies of self-discipline from the man who controls the island to his literal or symbolic offspring is in essence a fantasy of masculine reproduction, which also works to assuage desires for unidirectional colonial influence. Fathers in these stories "naturally" teach their children and reproduce themselves in them (playing out fantasies of colonial mimicry); their children do not teach them (which could result in threatening colonial hybridity).

Island Progeny and Fantasies of Masculine Reproduction

Several island narratives dramatize this fantasy of masculine reproduction through plots of a male castaway who peoples his island solely with his progeny, as does Henry Neville's *The Island of Pines* (1668). In Neville's story, one man (George Pine) becomes island-stranded with four women, all of whom agree to become his "wives" and through whom he populates his island. Similarly, in Morris's *Adventures of John Daniel* (1751), John Daniel reproduces himself through/with Ruth. They have children together and by marrying those children to each other, fulfill the fantasy of peopling a world with the pure products of one's body, with the patriarch in control of all. In such stories of exponential masculine reproduction, we can see a recodified desire for reproduction of the imperial culture in the colonies—in resistance to real-world fears of hybridity (about which, more will be said in following chapters). Such stories, we should remember, also allegorize real fears of paternity, which were not insignificant in imperial British culture in the familial, national, or cultural realms. Since, as David Miller reminds in "The Father's Witness: Patriarchal Images of Boys," paternity is always less certain than maternity; the father looks to his son's imitation of him for evidence of his fatherhood, thus making the child "into a symbolic object whose body signifies paternity" (121). Moreover, as Marie Hélène Huet remarks in *Monstrous Imagination*, seventeenth- and eighteenth-century anatomical debates perpetuated fantasies of what Huet calls "parental singularity" (41). Early-modern anatomists argued over whether children were the sole reproduction of the father or the mother, often with the "evidence" coming down on the father's side. In "Womb Envy," Eve Feder Kittay also notes that in the seventeenth and eighteenth centuries, scientists theorized reproduction so that men were the agents of procreation, with women merely the vessel. Though in the late nineteenth century, scientists did finally concede that women and men equally participate in reproduction, the scientific community continues to describe the woman's role as the more passive, as in the now-questioned theory of the active sperm fighting to get to the passive egg (recodifying social constructions of "natural" sexual behavior). Some scientists now theorize that the egg chemically *attracts* the sperm, making their joining the result of mutual work and agency.

At their most extreme, desires for unidirectional imperial influence culminate in a fantasy of "pure" reproduction, in stories of male parthenogenesis that omit women from propagation altogether. *The Tempest,* for instance, which strands Prospero with the young Miranda, also erases Miranda's mother, making Prospero, the single parent, into Prospero the single source of Miranda. The only mention in the play of Miranda's mother comes to insinuate Prospero's paternity—to remind of *his* role in Miranda's genesis. When Miranda questions him about her mother, Prospero answers "Thy mother was a piece of virtue, and/She said thou wast my daughter" (1.2.55-56), after which Miranda admits only remembering "four or five woman once that tended [her]," not her mother.

Moreover, as Stephen Orgel remarks in "Prospero's Wife" and in his introduction to the Oxford edition of the play, Prospero describes his and Miranda's voyage and landing on the island (the process by which he gained sole control of her) in terms of a single, male metaphoric childbirth. When first cast out to sea, Prospero narrates, when he "under [his] burden groaned," then Miranda's smiles heartened him, "rais[ing] in [him]/An undergoing stomach to bear up/Against what should ensue" (1.2.156–58). Shakespeare's use of language evocative of childbirth to describe Prospero's bond with Miranda, turns the event of their coming to the island into a story of Prospero's symbolic birthing of her, a fantasy of his reproducing himself in Miranda without the corruption of woman, as Zeus reproduced himself in the masculine war goddess, Athena. The play, however, does not present Caliban as the product of male asexual reproduction as it does Miranda. Instead of erasing Caliban's mother, Prospero persistently *invokes* Sycorax to remind Caliban of his demonic and woman-corrupted genesis. Again contrasting characters to make a point, the narratives show that masculine, asexual reproduction results in the successful reproduction of the father in the good child (Miranda), while sexual reproduction, especially outside of marriage, results in Calibans.

Klaus Theweleit also discusses fantasies of masculine reproduction, but he finds them expressed in war. Men, he says, partially fulfill their birthing fantasy (both the fantasy of reproducing themselves in others and the fantasy of their own pure birth) through war: "Men are re-born by killing. They always stand up, re-erect out of something that dies around them. You have to deal with that logic of metamorphosis when dealing with war. WAR ranks high among the male ways of giving birth" ("The Bomb's Womb," 284, emphasis original). Imperial expansion on one level is a continuous war—a war to take land, a war to maintain control of that land, a war to transform the uncivilized into the civilized. On yet another level, we could also examine Shakespeare's (and other writers') acts of literary creation as parthenogenesis—as acts of masculine self-reproduction, where these writers/fathers "labor" to reproduce themselves and their vision of masculinity in their characters/readers/sons.

As well as transferring imperial insecurities about colonial influence, such stories could recodify masculine insecurities about and longing for female power. Again, psychoanalysis provides theories useful for analyzing stories of masculine reproduction as metanarratives on femininity as well as masculinity, especially Eve Feder Kittay's arguments about womb envy. As Kittay explains, coexisting with Freud's penis envy is womb envy. Like girl children who, when discovering their lack of a penis supposedly come to envy the male who does possess a penis, boys learning that they lack the biological equipment to produce babies become envious of females. But both envies, as Kittay explains, stem from *identification* with the object of envy. Envy would only, Kittay says, develop from the perception that the lack of the envied penis or womb is arbitrary (as would small children with limited abilities to conceptualize sexual difference). If we perceive the object of envy as completely different from us (for instance, as birds are different from humans), we do not imagine our lack (of wings, for example, or the ability to fly naturally) as arbitrary. But if we imagine the object of envy as *like* us (identifying with it) then possession or nonpossession of the desired trait seems arbitrary, eliciting envy. A small-statured human male might thus envy a tall human male, since the possession or lack of height seems random and perhaps unfair. Recognition that longings for masculine reproduction result from identification forces reconsideration of the imperial disavowals of the feminine.

Moreover, as Kittay notes, both penis and womb envy are necessarily linked to and complicated by the Western, modern, sociopolitical environments that produced them. Just as penis envy *embodies* a girl's learned awareness of her lack of cultural and economic power (perhaps more aptly called "phallus envy"), a boy/man's womb envy stems from his indoctrination into the fantasy world of hegemonic white masculinity, whether or not his class/caste or race allows him to fully enjoy its privileges. Womb envy, then, results from the boy's residual sadness at being forced by the modern, Western, patriarchal culture to separate from his mother, his primary object of identification, his anger upon learning of his disenfranchisement from the miracle of childbirth, and his dependence on a woman to fulfill legal inheritance. As Kittay summarizes, in order to deal with these feelings of lack or envy, men enlist a variety of defensive measures, including devaluation of the mother role or of the woman's role in childbirth (as modern medicine often places the male or scientifically masculinized doctor in control over the passive, pathologized, pregnant woman). A second culturally sanctioned method of managing subconscious womb envy involves imagined *appropriation* of the female role in birth, as found in mythopoetic male initiation rituals, in which men assert that though woman can create a male child, a man can only be "born" from other men.

Island narratives employ both measures, devaluing women through the repeated characterization of women as weak and inferior to men, and appropriating the power of the womb in stories of male childbirth. Prospero's recasting of coming to the island in terms of male childbirth, for instance, both erases Miranda's first birth (devaluing her mother) and appropriates the power of reproduction for himself. Neville's *The Island of Pines* provides another example. Neville's castaway, George Pines, is stranded with four women (three white and one African American), all of whom he takes as wives and frequently impregnates. In Neville's story, the male contains agency in reproduction, since it is he who *grants* babies to the women. After six months on the island, for instance, after Pine has had sex with the three white women and impregnated two of them, the sole African-American woman, who "seeing what we did, longed also for her share" (232), coerces Pine into also sharing his magical seed with her. In this fantasy, Pine repeatedly impregnates all four women so that the island fills with his offspring. The narrative records the island's population at the time of Pine's death at nearly two thousand beings (and despite lack of genetic diversity, at ten thousand, when a ship eventually discovers the island and brings forth the narrative for publication)—all issued from Pine's loins.

Through stories like Pine's, white, masculine control of colonies becomes naturalized through a fantasy of male birth. The island colony (representing the imperial system) acts as a *masculine* womb from which the most bodily disciplined man (or men) can literally (and literarily) *issue* his superior culture. When Pine, for instance explains his coupling with the black woman (miscegenation), he stresses that the act was only at her behest (another imperial fantasy) and that he refrains from having sex with her except to get her pregnant, which occurs each time he has sex with her "in the night and not else" (233). He lowers himself into that sex act as the giver of children, and he defensively insists that their children are white and "as comely as any of the rest" (233), corresponding to seventeenth-century perceptions of the male "seed" reproducing the father in the vessel of the mother. Both the story and the language used portray these children as coming from *his* body and *his* island/womb, both of which have the power to whiten biracial children. Through such stories, readers could participate in fantasies of the empire as male womb for the reproduction of masculine, imperial power in the bodies of Others, who might be whitened/civilized by virtue of the male womb, but who, as "children" would remain subservient to the white father.

In some narratives, this masculine reproduction is more clearly cultural. *Robinson Crusoe,* for instance, shows a fantasy of cultural reproduction of the self in Crusoe's efforts to duplicate himself in the physically adult (though childlike) native we know as "Friday," whom he remakes in his own image and even renames after Friday's day of symbolic (re)birth. Significantly, even when Friday's biological father does reappear, Friday remains Crusoe's loyal "son." Crusoe has no interest in Friday's previous life and, in fact, endeavors to erase his native culture, forcing Friday to renounce cannibalism and his indigenous name, to adopt Christianity, to dress in European clothes, to be his servant, to call him master, and to learn English, though the text presents all of these actions as the sensible self-made decisions of the loyal offspring Friday. Crusoe first "adopts" Friday because he sees in Friday a reflection of himself, as suggested by his description of Friday upon their first meeting as masculine (he had "something very manly in his Face"), light skinned ("the Colour of his Skin was not quite black, but very tawny"), with Caucasian features ("he had all the Sweetness and Softness of an *European* in his Countenance too, especially when he smil'd") (148–49, emphasis original).[11] Of course, despite having European traits, Friday is *not* white (in the words of Bhabha, "almost the same but not quite . . . almost the same but not white"), which means that he could always only provide a reassuring mirror for an ambivalent Crusoe and reader ("Of Mimicry and Man," 238). As Gregory Woods notes, Crusoe's description of Friday invokes the always present fear of the savage by listing the characteristics Friday does not have: Friday is "not too large," having "not a fierce and surly Aspect," with hair "not curl'd like Wool," skin "not quite black," and a nose "not flat like the Negroes" (148–49). As Woods says, "The interesting thing about these resounding negatives—and others which are left implicit in the text . . . is that they conjure up a phantom savage at Friday's side, more impressive because more frightening than he" (135). Even as Crusoe's progeny and imperial reflection, Friday can never escape his savage essence, just as British colonies, no matter how thoroughly acculturated, would always be marginal.

Manly Islands and Homosocial Bonds

Over and over in island narratives, accompanying the responsibilities of fatherhood are its many pleasures. In *The Swiss Family Robinson* and *Masterman Ready,* for instance, on the island the father has motivation and

time (freed from the demands of typical capitalist labor) to spend quality time with his boys, recovering his own sense of boyhood adventure
in the process. Thus, we can see in these highly narcissistic fantasies of
male asexual reproduction, as well as desires of cultural reproduction
through empire, also nostalgia for the male imperialist's lost boyhood,
that is the fantasy of freedom *from* responsibility and freedom *to* relate
to other males. On the island, men and boys work and play together in a
remarkably noncompetitive manner, bonding over a hard day's labor of
building, exploring, farming, or fighting (typically cannibals or pirates,
not each other) and enjoying the fruits of a job well done.

According to some theorists, like Eve Kosofsky Sedgwick in *Between
Men: English Literature and Male Homosocial Desire* and Jonathan Rutherford in *Forever England: Reflections on Race, Masculinity and Empire,* this
masculine "homosocial" fantasy results from pressures of modern capitalism and a culturewide repudiation of motherhood. Rutherford reminds that Freud analyzed modern, primarily male, bourgeois, Western
subjects to postulate that the two primary objects of desire for pre-oedi-
pal children are the mother and the self. In Victorian England, Rutherford argues, where boys were discouraged from identifying with their
mother (with the future leaders of the empire even being sent off to
school to learn stoic British masculinity), this lack of identification with
mothering resulted in a culturewide male narcissism, played out in the
adult world as homoerotic nostalgia for the lost innocence and possibilities of boyhood, epitomized in the homosocial island society of J. M. Barrie's *Peter Pan* Never-Never Land and in R. M. Ballantyne's boy-utopia in
The Coral Island (1868). "Imperial manliness," Rutherford remarks, "in
its production of emotionally repressed, sexually confused, mother fix-
ated, women fearing men, fostered in them a morbid nostalgia for 'the
brave bright days of his boyhood'" (26). Rutherford's analysis helps to
explain how island fantasies, where the frustrating and disappointing
realities of imperial manhood could be dropped to pursue adventure
with youths on coral islands, could provide the means for readers to temporarily scratch such a subconscious nostalgic itch, while reinforcing
images of imperial usurpation as innocuous, innocent, good, clean fun
and images of imperial adventure as noncompetitive. Graham Dawson
likewise explores the masculine homosociality of empire in *Soldier Heroes: British Adventure, Empire and the Imagining of Masculinities.* Though
imperialism is predicated on capitalism, as Sedgwick and others have
argued, white men do not always find the competition that capitalism

demands or the mundanity of imperial administration to be rewarding. Thus, as Dawson notes in his exploration of the adventure hero, these men looked to the imperial project to provide the brotherhood, sense of purpose and excitement they longed for. Because these men found their ambitions disappointed in the capitalistic, imperial world to which they flocked, they looked to fiction for bonding and fraternalism, often to the secluded, anticapitalistic, fraternal world of the island narrative.

Similar to the masculine homosocial fantasies of boy castaways are those island narratives with adult male castaways, in which one man naturally emerges as leader because of his superior self-discipline, and other male castaways naturally follow, as in *The Mysterious Island* and in *Masterman Ready*. In this fantasy, because all parties equally benefit from this innate hierarchy, overt competition between men for power is minimal; each man cheerfully cooperates, performing his duties with skill and pleasure. Though this plot characteristic, on one level, recodifies real-world hegemonies of imperial power between the colonized and their colonizers into a willing and mutually beneficial friendship, it also often deflects conflicts between European men of different social classes, between those men most clearly benefiting from empire and the privileges of white masculinity, and those merely laboring in its name. At times this deflection means that class hierarchies are temporarily reshuffled, as in *Masterman Ready*, to be restored once the characters leave the island. It is this temporary reshuffling of hierarchies that Barrie lampoons in his 1918 castaway play *The Admirable Crichton*, which tells of a working-class man (a butler) whose natural leadership abilities and ingenuity make him rise to the top of society when stranded on an island with his social "betters," though upon rescue the previous class order is restored, with everyone working hard to forget that it was ever disrupted. Again, the question arises of how the island setting and the illusion of controlling the island through the disciplined male body would participate in this multivalenced male fantasy. In order to respond to that question, we need to turn back to Sedgwick's theories in *Between Men*.

Male homosocial bonding, says Sedgwick, often stems from men's romantic rivalry, as they bond with each other over the body of a woman. In island narratives, which are typically less about men's relationships with women than about their relationships with an island, male castaways relate with each other through a bond with the island. The island, in effect, replaces the woman as the third point of the homosocial triangle.

As Sedgwick further remarks, male homosocial rivalries/relationships need not *only* be over women, for "any relation of rivalry is structured by the same play of emulation and identification, whether the entities occupying the corners of the triangle be heroes, heroines, gods, books, or whatever" (23). It is not surprising then, that in island narratives lacking women (such as *The Mysterious Island*), male characters relate homosocially with each other *because* of their relationship with the island: the men are all cast away together, with all of the physical and emotional problems that isolation brings, relating to each other as they fight for survival, first working together to survive the wreck, then to make a fire, then collaborating to build a shelter, then a *better* shelter, next fighting savages, and finally rescuing themselves from the island.

Reading stories of male bonding on the island through Sedgwick's model highlights the underdiscussed psychological identification inherent in the homosocial relationship, for the island that the men relate through is, on one level, *themselves* (they incorporated the island into their bodies and psychically identified with it after projecting themselves onto it). We should remember that in Freud's model, the oedipal boy both identifies with his rival father and with the object of his father's affection, his mother, who is also his rival as well as his love object. We might similarly find, then, that a similar dynamic exists in the traditional homosocial triangle: the male rivals bond with each other through the beloved woman because they simultaneously psychically identify with her, allowing the rivals to fantasize about a noncompetitive subjectivity (being pursued instead of pursuing) while not having to risk their masculinity by enacting it. Likewise, on the island, male castaways bond through the island because they psychically identify with it (though curiously, one man—the group's leader—would enjoy a more secure or complete identification with the island because of his superior discipline). Interestingly, such homosocial bonding through the body of the island (self) would also maintain a narcissistic desire for purity and discipline of the male body, for, like the fantasy of asexual reproduction, this type of homosocial masculinity lacks the taint of contact with femininity, and by de-emphasizing male *rivalry*, island narratives insist on the purity of the masculine imperial bond, rerouting competition through the family system into a safer, more controllable, more "natural" economy. And this economy then becomes reified into colonial law.

Law of the Father

After discussing masculine discipline and fatherhood, we come to our third significant component of gender in island tales, which involves how, in narrative after narrative, the "father" or patriarch's command over the island and the others on it becomes codified into a form of island colonial law.[12] In *The Swiss Family Robinson,* for instance, the Robinson father's wishes serve as law in every aspect of island life, from work routines, to settlement procedures, to command of animals, to family holidays. Nearly every scene contains his directions and pronouncements to his sons and wife, all of which carry the weight and penalty of law. Similarly, in *Robinson Crusoe,* Crusoe's word becomes law on his island, first for Friday and later for the island's colonists (the mutinous sailors who settle on the island at the end of the volume 1). At several points in the narrative, Crusoe must directly assert his authority as island lawmaker and enforcer, first when remaking Friday (telling Friday what he can eat, wear, and do) and later when rescuing the captain from the mutinous sailors. Crusoe responds to that potential threat of competing authority by, before agreeing to help the captain, making him concur: "That while you stay on this Island with me, you will not pretend to any Authority here; and if I put Arms into your Hands, you will upon all Occasions give them up to me, and do no Prejudice to me or mine, upon this Island, and in the mean time be govern'd by my Orders" (184). In volume 2, when Crusoe comes back to the island as its governor, his unofficial "law" becomes sanctioned by his official government, making him both source and enforcer of colonial law for the island's nascent society. These island texts, as do others, routinely labor to pave over the cracks between patriarchal authority and colonial law—a process we can better grasp by reading the behaviors of fathers and sons through the lens of the theoretical "law of the father."

As Freud describes it, patriarchal law originates in the incest taboo of the oedipal triangle, when the male child's desire for its mother is blocked by his rival father (or father figure), representing the threat of castration. Instead of competing with his father and risking castration, Freud argues, the boy learns to repress (discipline) his bodily desires and identify with his father, thereby learning the "reality principle" (to replace the earlier ungoverned "pleasure principle"), later termed by Lacan the "father's law." For young girls, the "Electra complex" (counterpart to the male-centered Oedipus complex) ends with girls identifying with their mother but also desiring/fearing their father. This fear of the father for both children leads to the development of a limiting super-ego and assumes the power of law, which, Lacan and Freud say, they internalize partially as self-discipline and bodily management. The child's earlier repressed desires never entirely disappear but remain in the unconscious, always governed by the superego and the law of the father, whether or not the actual father remains present. Thus, the law of the father becomes not just the fear of the actual father or the threat of castration but the internalization of all the written and unwritten cultural rules of the patriarchal (literally "father ruled") cultural system into which we are all born and interpellated. Just as Freud in *Totem and Taboo* observes the societal fears of incest transferred into elaborate cultural marriage and courtship rituals in what he calls "primitive" (i.e., *colonized*) societies, so colonial island narratives recodify imperial cultural desires for natural colonization into fantasies of self-discipline governed through the family dynamic.

Lacan builds on Freud's theorization to explain the law of the father as recognized in the moment that the child enters the symbolic order. This entry is traumatic because of the child's awareness that the father has priority and is prior in access to the mother, resulting in the Oedipus complex. In fact, the child's very existence reminds of the father's prior access to the mother and remarks that the child needs to learn to accept a restricted desire for access to her. Because this trauma is coincident to and inseparable from the child's encounter with language and the verbalization of prohibition, for the child the law is codeterminate with language. Like Freud, Lacan also remarks on how rituals and rules create culture. The symbolic order, then, which both regulates social behavior and is intersubjective in structure, invents that which it regulates, for there is no need for the law if there is nothing to regulate. We see this notion of fatherly priority worked out in island narratives like *The Mysterious Island*, in which Nemo's status as father figure stems as much from his prior status on the island, which gives him a closer, embodied relationship to it, as his prowess with commanding his own and the bodies of the others. But only a certain type of priority would be respected. An indigenous person visiting the island would not, for instance, typically have rights of law over the castaway, as the cannibals who habitually visited Crusoe's island weren't treated by him or the novel as having rights based on priority.

Significantly this "law of the father" endures on the island even when the "father" is absent, as in Ballantyne's *The Coral Island,* in which the three young men maintain the discipline of good imperialists without direct coercion from parents or parental figures. When Ralph, Peterkin, and Jack first land on the island, they share a fantasy of island colonization that demonstrates their internalization of the law of the father. Instead of imagining a new world outside of the imperial dynamic, one free from societal constraints, they reproduce the European symbolic in their mythical island kingdom. As Peterkin explains, "We've got an island all to ourselves. We'll take possession in the name of the king; we'll go and enter the service of its black inhabitants. Of course we'll rise, naturally, to the top of affairs. White men always do in savage countries" (25). The young men interestingly declare willingness to earn their rewards in the service of indigenous people (a promise they don't keep) while, in the same breath, declaring their natural privilege. In their fantasies, the young men reproduce the internalized law of the father (here, the king, in whose name they will colonize and work) with the effect of making the imperial economy appear as logical and natural as their "natural" and inevitable rise "to the top of affairs." As good imperialists-in-training, who enact society's edicts without a parent enforcing them, the young men discipline their bodies and repress their biological drives (including their budding sexuality) through hard work and clean play (mostly swimming, which also keeps their bodies clean and orderly).

It is this fantasy of seamlessly maintained discipline and order in *The Coral Island* that famously spurred William Golding to rewrite the story in *Lord of the Flies.* Golding shows how "real boys" would react without their father's presence and law, which means that they quickly forget and learn to ignore the father's prohibitions against killing, revert to a state of lawlessness, and enact violent savagery. Early in the novel, Ralph, Simon, and Jack (Golding's counterparts to Ballantyne's boy castaways) climb the island's mountain to enact the "monarch-of-all-I-survey" moment, but it doesn't take long for that first incorporative impulse to spread beyond the landscape to the bodies on it, both animal and human. As Carl Niemeyer remarks, "the blood lust once aroused demands nothing less than human blood" (244). The British navy, however, rescues the boys soon after they kill Piggy and before they complete their hunt of Ralph, a hunt headed toward cannibalism. One could argue that adult British men taught proper imperial discipline would have been able to keep the power of incorporation in check. As the officer says, "I should have thought that a pack of British boys—you're all British,

aren't you?—would have been able to put up a better show than that"
(186). But, then, as Golding himself remarks in a 1962 interview with
James Keating, he ended the novel with the officer turning away from
the island to look at his ship, a cruiser, "and of course the cruiser, the
adult thing, is doing exactly what the hunters do—that is, hunting down
and destroying the enemy" (194).

In *The Coral Island*, the boys' discipline of their bodies and minds
includes their relationship with each other, for as the book stresses, they
cooperate perfectly in their island labor and feel only pure and platonic
affection for one another. Ralph, when speaking of their "agreeable tri-
umvirate," explains that "there was, indeed, no note of discord whatever
in the symphony we played together on that sweet Coral Island; and I
am now persuaded that this was owing to our having been all tuned to
the same key, namely, that of *love!* Yes, we loved one another with much
fervency, while we lived on that island" (111). The pubescent young men
work, bathe, and sleep together, but the novel includes no hint of any
sexual tension or homoerotic longing, only homosocial desire. In fact,
not surprisingly for the intended audience, the novel ignores the subject
of homosexuality completely, even in reference to the pirates who capture one of the boys later in the novel (which I discuss further in chapter
3). In disciplining themselves and repressing their biological drives, Ballantyne's young men enact a willing submission to the (moral) law and
derive a paradoxical pleasure at the pain of knowing they have been obedient. Their love, which binds them in a nonsexual fraternity, becomes
the face of the father's law and the foundation of colonial law.

Regardless of the rumored tradition of homosexual love in British
boys schools and in other male institutions (such as the navy), these
young men, well trained in the law of the father, restrain their sexual
drives even when a heterosexual object presents itself in the light-skinned
and beautiful young native woman, Avatea. Though native, Avatea represents the helpless "white" woman (she is so light-skinned that Ralph
speculates that "she must be of a different race" from the other natives),
allowing the young men to display their imperial masculine prowess
(152). Yet she is also untouchable, both as a native and as engaged to
a Christianized native from another island, allowing the young men to
homosocially relate through their protection of her. Since she is conveniently unavailable for romantic interest, and since no serious rivalry exists over her, Avatea provides an excuse for an adventure but no threat
to the purity of the masculine retreat. Thus when the boys risk their lives

to save her, it is in the service of the law of the father, not lust, which is an ironic plotline when read against the historical frequency of rape of colonized women. As well, in Avatea's light skin the boys find evidence that another white man has been on the island before these boys. Avatea of the light skin, like the mother in the Lacanian model for the child's entry into the symbolic order, also reminds that the father has priority and that the child/son has to restrict his desire for access to the mother figure. The boys' restraint with her, like the child's learned restraint with its mother, forms the very basis of their re-creation of imperial law on the island.

Some late nineteenth- and twentieth-century island narratives show a quite different approach to law, partially because these later islands are frequently described/imagined as already inhabited. In later island narratives, the island becomes a space imagined as free of the inhibitions and taboos of European law instead of a space to immediately re-create European law (which would inevitably come later). The Tahiti of Gaugan and the mutinous Bounty crew, and the Marquesans of Melville provide space for the castaway colonist (who, in these narratives is frequently a visitor, instead of stranded) to temporarily escape European law and embrace a different law—a native law with different taboos and fewer sexual inhibitions than European law. The colonist also frequently perceives himself as embracing and melding into the native culture instead of "civilizing" it, playing the role of Memmi's colonizer who refuses. As Memmi notes, the colonist still holds essential racialist and colonialist ideals; he still sees himself as superior to the native because of his whiteness and "civilization" (and benefits from the privileges of these categories), though he is attracted to the feminized and erotic elements of the island culture. The island in these later narratives is still a commodity, but now its inhabitants are included, as well.

It is important that we look at how law and masculinity are linked in island tales because, of course, in the real world, empire was erected on the scaffolds of laws and legal self-justification. As explained in chapter 1, elaborate rituals of possession were enacted to demonstrate that a land was legally colonized, and a range of "legal" decrees was used to demonstrate lines of possession. One of the earliest of these was the Borgia Pope, Alexander VI's, 1493 papal bull dividing the colonizable world into two spheres of plunder for the Portuguese and Spanish. Through that bull, the Pope, that great white father, attempted to lay down law governing future colonization. Later white fathers would also endeavor to legally divide up land they desired, on the "legal" supposition that the people already living there did not have any legal rights to it, such as with the 1884 Berlin Conference, the meeting of European colonial powers that has become more famously known as "the scramble for Africa," and also with the Treaty of Versailles and with U.N. mandates about rights to Palestine and Papua New Guinea. The legal notion of *terra nullius* is still being debated in post-settler nations, such as Australia and Canada.[13] Law wasn't only employed by kings and popes for self-justification. Examination of Columbus's diary and Cortez's letters reveals that both were quite aware of how their positioning within a legal system gave them maneuverability as explorers.[14] Cortez in particular knew when to interpret royal decree to justify circumventing the legal rights of the governor for his desires for unsolicited exploration.

Analysis of how island narratives labor to present law as natural and familial helps us to see fissures in colonial law in nonfictional situations. One of the most important of these nonfictional, legal colonial situations involves the re-creation of law in the colonies. In the fictional realm of the island narrative, the uninhabited island as tabula rasa has no laws except those that its inhabitants perpetuate or create. Because isolated, the island's castaways escape the threat of outside law. Yet instead of re-laxing imperial law, inhibitions, and taboos, early island narratives confirm and naturalize imperial laws by showing characters who *choose* to uphold the European imperial symbolic even while far removed from its threats. Men discipline their bodies, the logic goes, not because their cultural morés dictate and reward such discipline (as a function of "habitus," as Bourdieu calls it) but because it is universal and natural to do so. Let us, for a moment, compare that fantasy of colonial island law to a real-world example of law on a colonized island, Papua New Guinea, under Australia's colonial rule.

In 1921, after World War I, the League of Nations made British-controlled Papua New Guinea a territory under Australian rule, with the mandate to "civilize" the space and its people, meaning to impose a Western economic structure and British system of laws on the indigenous people.[15] As part of these "civilizing" maneuvers, the Australian government through patrol officers, called "KIAPS," broke down the remarkably diverse Papua New Guinean tribal structures by bringing an administrative presence into the "undeveloped" island interior, by building roads, and by negating tribal leadership hierarchies. In Papua New Guinea, the Australian KIAPS imposed themselves as judge, jury, and executioner for legal situations formerly handled by tribal leaders, which (as depicted in postcolonial novels, such as Chinua Achebe's *Things Fall Apart*) often resulted in irreparable violence to indigenous social and legal systems. Colonizing governments representing indigenous law as inherently dangerous (based on warfare) and illogical, mandated indigenous law null and void. Then, after imposing systems of government more amenable to the colonizing mission, which typically mirrored Western systems (thus assuring colonizers that Western-styled systems of representative democracy were natural and superior), the colonizers trained people how to vote and take part in the new law, with the stated eventual aim of restoring native autonomy. Ironically, native autonomy, the goal of that colonial intervention, was the situation in Papua New Guinea before the Australians got there. It is situations like that of the Australian intervention in Papua New Guinea that show the importance of island narratives in depicting law as natural, as coming from the white father's disciplined body. Colonial powers were not only inventing law to justify their own rule (*à la* Cortez and many others), they were forcing colonies to take on Western law, replacing "flawed" indigenous law with "natural" colonial law. But in these island fantasies, of course, the castaway typically imposes law on an empty island, with no natives to rule (except Friday).

Bad Fathers and Animal Children

These literary portrayals of fathers who enact patriarchal law through their innate authority show imperial law as natural and inviolate. But not all narratives show that law as fair and benevolent. *The Island of Dr. Moreau,* for instance, which both critiques and constructs imperial ideology, illustrates a complex interaction between fathers and children and the ideology of imperial masculine discipline as concretized in law.[16] *The Island of Dr. Moreau* raises the issue of what happens when that law is abused or when the governed don't willingly consent. As in other island narratives (those more like Defoe's in plot), Wells's Dr. Moreau earns control of his island through his white, male, disciplined body, but in Moreau's case his "discipline," his devotion to science, as well as providing the source of his strength, becomes a tragic flaw. Moreau's mania for control of the bodies on his island leads him to practice vivisection on animals (which are, as Cyndy Hendershot notes, overdetermined indigenous bodies) (124), as he attempts to mold their bodies into human shape and discipline their minds and animal natures into a semblance of humanity. Moreau rules over his animals as a colonial governor might over colonized natives, maintaining his command through a set of laws born of patriarchal authority, ritual, and fear. As the colonizer who attempts to "civilize" their bodies, Moreau doesn't feel that his animals have rights or purpose except as raw material for his aims. Prendick, the narrator, upon encountering the semi-humanized animals in the forest, learns that the animals self-discipline their instincts through memorizing, frequently chanting and blindly following a system of laws implanted by Moreau's hypnotism and mutated by religious rituals and their own desire to discipline their bodies into being more human. As the Sayer of the Law explains to Prendick, the laws for each humanized animal come from its own fears of its animal appetites, or "For every one the want that is bad . . . Some want to follow things that move, to watch and slink and wait and spring, to kill and bite, bite deep and rich, sucking the blood. . . . It is bad" (86–87). The Sayer then breaks into his nightly nocturnal chant of the laws, punctuated by the restraining reminder that the animals strive to be men: "'Not to chase other Men; that is the Law. *Are we not Men?* Not to eat Flesh nor Fish; that is the Law. *Are we not men?*'" (87, emphasis original). The "are we not men?" refrain forms the central quandary of the island narrative, as characters have to assert both their humanity and their masculinity to counter the threat of their imperial Other. This chant, however, is ironic as well and the law it upholds baseless, for they are *not* men; they are the Other (animal and undisciplined) against which the white, Western men on the island define themselves.

Wells's novel illustrates two intersecting lines of law, discipline, and masculinity. First, Moreau's masculine discipline (his science) leads to his disciplining (making human) the animal bodies and requiring that they self-discipline their animal drives. Like the colonial law it allegorizes, these multiple disciplines then are pasted together into a law of the island. Secondly, events in the narrative demonstrate that this law emanates *from* the masculine, disciplined patriarchal body of Moreau and works *on* the animal body. The punishment for breaking these laws governing bodily behavior is, not coincidentally, bodily pain. The animals fear Moreau as their maker and their destroyer, chanting "*His* is the House of Pain. *His* is the hand that makes. *His* is the hand that wounds. *His* is the Hand that heals" (84, emphasis original). They discipline their own bodies because they have internalized Moreau's disciplinary law

and further reified it into ritual (similar to the "primitive" rituals denying incest that Freud outlines at length in *Totem and Taboo*). Prendick describes their ritual: "The voice in the dark began intoning a mad litany,
line by line, and I and the rest to repeat it. As they did so, they swayed
from side to side, and beat their hands upon their knees, and I followed
their example" (83). Through this ritual performance of the law, the
animals literally embody it. This craving for a human body leads the
animals to designate their "undisciplined" animal natures "taboo"—at
once sacred, terrifying, and denied—and to set up a hierarchy in their
society based on the approximation of the animal's body to the human
body. Like good children, they want to please their father (Moreau) by
becoming like him.

The novel's ambiguous ending provides another important lesson,
perhaps of what happens to colonial fathers who lose their discipline or
abuse their power and what happens to children who don't follow the
law of the father. Moreau's precarious command over the island and
his transformed animals breaks down, beginning with his inability to
control Montgomery's abuse of alcohol and eating of meat (breaking
the vegetarian rule—which signals further loss of control over consumption). After Montgomery breaks the island's laws of bodily discipline as
established by Moreau, the animals also begin to lose their imposed self-
discipline and begin to eat meat. Eating meat codes the animals' loss of
control over their biological drives and the beginning of their eventual
reversion to their "native" state. If all law isn't obeyed, so says this lesson,
anarchy results. When the law completely breaks down, the animals re-
claim their island and the natural law of their bodies, burning down the
"house of pain," killing Moreau and Montgomery, "cannibalizing" them,
and burning their remains. The animals revert to their instinctive behavior, which in the novel seems both exhilarating (for the liberated carni-
vores) and terrifying (for Prendick and the weaker animals). Moreau's
terrible order, the novel suggests, countered the order of the law of the
jungle. Thus, the novel could also be read both as warning against the
bad colonial father who can't maintain discipline (not a warning against
"good" colonization), and as a cautionary tale of what happens to colonial hybrids (which by their very existence threaten the purity of imperial reproduction) or to colonies that revolt. Colonies that dare to
reclaim their own rule, the novel seems to say, risk losing the "civilization" that the colonizer brought to them to end up in savage chaos. We
should remember that the commercial processes described in Wells's

novel and in other island narratives is not so far off from the reality of colonialism. Imperial governments did transubstantiate their ideologies of bodily discipline into law, as with the drinking laws mentioned earlier. Like Moreau's torture in the name of science, these laws and others like them reveal a simultaneous condescending paternalism and disdainful objectification, as empire demanded that the colonized be represented as both incapable and somewhat capable of governing themselves.

Also as in Wells's novel, indigenous people often internalize colonial laws into a form of Foucaultian self-discipline and self-definition. Frantz Fanon's experience of the third space as described in *Black Skin, White Masks* provides a famous example of the colonized internalization of imperial ideology and law into self-definition and perception of one's body. In that traumatic but enlightening train-bound moment when Fanon encounters a startled young boy who says to his mother (while looking at Fanon) "Look, a negro," Fanon realizes his third space—his view of himself he has internalized from the colonial stereotypes and laws he daily encounters (109–13). The insurmountable gaps between who he has been told to be by the colonial culture, what he tries to achieve, and how others see him lead Fanon to the same momentary self-loathing Wells allegorized with his animals. Fanon's recodification of hegemonic ideologies of acceptable behavior onto his individual body reflects Wells's recodification of larger issues of imperial decorum and acceptable treatment of colonized people onto the story of Moreau and his animals.

That these narratives place such emphasis on a specific kind of masculinity suggests the importance of such masculinity to the functioning of imperialism. Imperialism, which encouraged and rewarded certain models of white, heterosexual masculinity and provided a method for proving one's manhood to oneself and one's peers, functioned better because of this specific hue of manhood, which encouraged hard work, staying in one's innate class (caste) and following the orders of one's natural superiors (fathers). These island narratives provide important insights into imperial psychology as predicated on discourses of masculinity and discipline and, as this chapter argued, predicated on a psychical correlation between the island and the colonist's body. The next chapter will show how the portrayal of cannibals and pirates in colonial island narratives provides scholars of colonial psychology a glimpse into the deep terror of loss of control, of native revolution, of being consumed instead of doing the consuming.

3. Voracious Cannibals, Rapacious Pirates, and Threats of Counterincorporation

TIME and again, in tale after tale, the castaway feels forced to defend his island from an invader. Typically the invader is an intruding native (a cannibal) or treacherous white man (a pirate), and frequently, as in *Robinson Crusoe,* the castaway repeatedly and successfully defends against both the cannibal's feast and the pirate's foray. The ubiquity of these attempted invasions raises several questions, the first being: Why would writers of island narratives bring the pirate and cannibal so repeatedly into their plots? Since, as argued in the last chapter, the manly castaway commands the island through his disciplined body, what, we might ask, is the symbolic purpose of these potential invaders of his island, who (not coincidentally) are also men and who also threaten to invade his body? Or perhaps we should pose these questions in a slightly different manner: what anxieties or desires of empire must the cannibal and pirate stories index and help readers of island narratives manage? Answers to such questions can be found in analysis of the similar portrayals of cannibals and pirates and through exploration of their symbolic significance. To begin this analysis, I turn to Crusoe's first encounter with a trespasser, or at least with a trespassing footprint.

To Crusoe, the footprint he discovers on his pristine shore stands for much more than a foot. Instead of heralding a possible friend, the footprint to him always only signals an invader, a possible violator of his island sanctity. After first guessing that the owner of the footprint must be the devil, for "how was it possible a Man should come there?" (112), Crusoe reaches the ghastly realization that the footprint must have been made by "some of the Savages of the main Land over against" him (113). Crusoe's "terrible Thoughts" then turn to what could happen if the savages learned of his existence, a fantasy ending in his own gruesome cannibalization, for as he predicts, "I should certainly have them come again in greater Numbers, and devour me" (113). Crusoe also imagines an equally dire episode, in which the savages would, as he says, "find my

Enclosure, destroy all my Corn, carry away all my Flock of tame Goats, and I should perish at last for meer Want" (113).[1] In both scenarios, Crusoe transfers fears about his command over his island into paranoid fantasies about his body (cannibalism or slow starvation), thus drawing upon the same subconscious psychological mechanisms of incorporation he did when imagining gaining command of the island. Instead of finding in the footprint a potential companion, Crusoe only imagines threatening invaders who would either "devour" him or his food in a reversal of the incorporative process through which he gained his own authority over the island. It is significant that he reacts to fears of invasion of his island by resolving to tighten his control over his literal island incorporation, his food consumption. He reproaches himself for not having enough control over his food supply (for only planting enough to meet his immediate needs) and "resolv'd for the future to have two or three Years Corn beforehand, so that whatever might come, I might not perish for want of Bread" (113). Moreover, as Diane Armstrong points out, even before he sees the footprint, Crusoe already perceives "cannibalism in all its forms" as "the force which threatens to engulf the life he has painstakingly created on the island" (214), for he also battles the island's animals (hares and birds) as if they were cannibals threatening to "devour all [his] hopes" (85).

Two years after seeing the prophetic footprint, Crusoe's fears of infiltration are realized when he discovers the remains of a cannibal feast on his island shore. Again he reacts with horror and, again, responds to this transgression of his island inviolability through an interesting inversion of the subconscious incorporation through which he first imagined his island command. As he explains, upon seeing the remains, "my stomach grew sick, and I was just at the Point of Fainting, when Nature discharg'd the Disorder from my Stomach, and having vomited with an uncommon Violence, I was a little relieved" (120). Crusoe's language and his visceral reaction suggest that as well as fearing cannibalism as a threat to his body, he fears its "disorder," its ability to jeopardize the order and island/body discipline he labors so intensively to maintain. Such moments in the narrative, in which Crusoe briefly loses his self-imposed mental discipline and panics, provide glimpses into his subconscious, into his conflation of his command of his island space—his colony—with command of his body. When incorporation seems hazardous (when he fears being its victim), Crusoe reacts by reversing that consumption: he vomits, violently. Though his fears about the impending invasion of the boundaries of his island prove true, not so the invasion of his *body*. When the cannibals come again, instead of being incorporated by them, he is able to successfully defend his body and his island from them, chasing them off and instead "incorporating" what they would consume: their prisoner/dinner, Friday.

After battling his own fears of the footprint and then actual cannibals, Crusoe confronts a potential threat to his island a third time in the novel, and again he psychically processes this third threat—this time from pirates—through the management of his body.[2] When he sights a ship off the coast, as upon seeing the footprint, Crusoe reacts with ready suspicion. His surprise quickly turns into "secret Doubts" that the ship must be visiting the island "upon no good Design" (180). As men from the ship come ashore, Crusoe learns that that there has been a mutiny and that some of the mutineers intend to kill their overthrown captain and turn to piracy. Just as he saved Friday, Crusoe uses his wits and discipline to thwart the pirates' scheme and save the captain, who, like Friday, becomes Crusoe's loyal, lifelong "servant."

Only Friday recognizes the similarities between the cannibal and pirate threats. While Crusoe and Friday watch the landing and unloading of three bound and unarmed men, Friday observes the likeness between that scene and the earlier one with the cannibals and calls out "O Master! *You see* English *Mans eat Prisoner as well as Savage Mans*" (181, emphasis original). Attempting to distinguish between white men (even lawless ones) and savages, Crusoe hastily corrects Friday, assuring him that though the pirates may "murther" [sic] the other men, "*you may be sure they will not eat them*" (181, emphasis original). Yet as Friday perceives, the cannibal and pirate threats are similar; they both imperil Crusoe's control of his island and body, for both aim to "incorporate" him and the space. These parallels are not coincidental; both literary invasions enact fears of what I call "counterincorporation," meaning that they dramatize a potential reversal of the process of psychical incorporation through which the castaway colonist gained control of the island. In such fantasies of counterincorporation, cannibals attempt literally to incorporate (consume) the castaway colonist, while pirates try metaphorically to incorporate him by engulfing him into their lawless society. Instead of the castaway achieving control of body and space through his own acts of incorporation, in stories of *counter*incorporation, someone else (pirate or cannibal) tries to "consume" his island and his body, leaving him terrifyingly powerless or dead.

Despite the routine co-existence of pirates and cannibals in the same island text, critics don't often analyze them together.[3] Reading the two figures alongside one another, however, not only allows us to analyze their similar counterincorporative work but also to investigate why they show up so often together in colonial literature.[4] With both pirates and cannibals, the castaway faces loss of command of his island and body in stories that recodify real-world fears of loss of colonial control: cannibal encounters symbolize the imperial anxiety of loss of control of the colonies to indigenous inhabitants, and pirate encounters symbolize loss of control of colonies to a competing colonizer. Typically, however, the disciplined and manly colonist resists that counterincorporation, as does Crusoe, who repels both cannibal and pirate. The story dramatized, then, is one of the *preservation* of the island/empire despite challenges, a comforting myth that needed frequent recounting, and which at least partially explains colonial literature's fixation on cannibals and pirates.

This chapter focuses on these dramas of the castaway's battle with fierce cannibals and shifty pirates. Building on my first and second chapters' exploration of the disciplined male body as metaphor of *natural* control of the island (standing for the larger empire), this chapter analyzes how pirates and cannibals participate, by negation, in such fantasies of naturalized colonization. Here I examine fears of *loss* of that imperial power as played out in dramas of counterincorporation of both island and body, beginning by drawing upon the psychoanalytic theory of abjection to explain how pirates and cannibals fit into the empire/island/body metaphor. I argue that by reading stories of cannibals and pirates alongside of (instead of in isolation from) one another, we can see how they work together to mark the boundaries of both body and empire. Then, to aid our comprehension of the colonial desire for release from responsibility and for masculine homosocial union, the chapter analyzes another common plot element, wherein the castaway is "forced" to become a cannibal or a pirate himself.

The Abject Pirate and Cannibal

In order to understand how and why pirate and cannibal stories perform similar functions in island narratives, we first need to examine their place in the psychological drama of the body, a task aided by Julia Kristeva's and Mary Douglas's theories of the "abject." Drawing upon Douglas's anthropological work in *Purity and Danger*, Kristeva articulates the

"abject" as that which human beings on a subconscious level psychologically reject because it traverses our corporeal boundaries. Materials that
pass through or exist on the body's borders (such as dirt, feces, mucus,
menstrual blood, sweat, and vomit), Kristeva explains, call into question
one's sense of bodily unity and ability to control the body. It is this threat
to the deep, psychological need to imagine ourselves in command of
our bodies, Kristeva says, that makes human beings process those objects
as emotionally and psychologically repulsive. We must psychically expel
those objects in order to maintain our sense of self and bodily wholeness. Yet because this act of rejection helps to maintain one's sense of
bodily wholeness, through their disputing of bodily boundaries, abject
objects can also be said to *confirm* bodily boundaries. Anne McClintock
in *Imperial Leather* calls this double function "the paradox of abjection"
(72) and explains that "the abject is everything the subject seeks to ex-
punge in order to become social; it is also a symptom of the failure of
this ambition" (71).

Critics have expanded this notion of abject objects into the larger
cultural realm to explain why certain *people* and *jobs* associated with
those bodily products are also perceived as threatening and repulsive—
as abject—and thus equally repudiated by society. McClintock, focusing
on modern Western, imperial cultures in particular, argues that those
societies tend to reject people considered on the social boundaries of
empire because they work with abject objects (like coal miners, scullery
maids, and chimney sweeps) or violate the morés of "acceptable" behavior (homosexuals, slaves, prostitutes, and the insane). By rejecting those
"abjected groups" as she calls them, imperial societies assert their own
purity and mark their social boundaries. In this paradox of abjection,
the dominant culture relies upon the abject to define itself, to define
what remains solidly within the communal body and what society deems
acceptable, for as McClintock explains, "abjection traces the silhouette
of society on the unsteady edges of the self" (*Imperial Leather,* 71). Expanding this theory a bit, we can also understand inhabitants of the *geographical* "boundaries" of empire, the colonized, through this paradox
of abjection. Colonized people, by living on the social and geographical
edges of empire, both challenge and confirm imperial boundaries. The
so-called imperial center, then, needs the abject, its colonized people,
in order to establish itself.

As denizens of the imperial geographical and social borderlands,
literary pirates and cannibals likewise help to mark the boundaries of

empire. Although, as William Arens notes, debates rage as to the veracity of some claims of cannibalism, both pirates and cannibals did exist in the real world. Anthropologists have studied cannibalistic behavior in a variety of historical cultures, and pirates did historically frequent the high seas, especially in the Caribbean region around the "new world" from the fifteenth to the twentieth centuries. Their "golden age," from 1650–1730, according to Lizabeth Paravisini-Gebert, spanned the Spanish War of Succession, "whose end," she explains, "left the soldiers from disbanded armies looking for ways to survive" as "piracy became one of the few job options" (72). Complicating these realities, however, were textual and cultural representations of pirates and cannibals, which showed them as simultaneously fascinating and inherently abject, as hovering on empire's social and physical boundaries. Beginning with Columbus, imperialists depicted cannibals as either located in the Caribbean region or in Africa, both on the so-called geographical margins of empire. By denoting cannibals as "uncivilized" (or "uncivilizable") savages, these same imperialists marginalized them socially, as well, making of them signs of the contours of acceptable behavior.

Pirates, too, were considered and represented as socially and geographically marginal. As Nina Gerassi-Navarro explains, the real-world pirate was, in fact, *defined by* his spatial and social liminality: "So long as he does not confine himself to a fixed place," she remarks, "the pirate's identity remains intact" (9). Supposedly killing at will and taking what they want, pirates defy the constraints of Western law, society, and capitalism. Yet as Barbara Fuchs notes, the label "pirate" was a slippery one, primarily used to define nautical men participating in any enterprise unfavorable to empire. So, a "pirate" could be a member of one's own nationality who was attacking ships without governmental sanction, while another man performing the same behavior but with a writ of mandate would be labeled a "privateer" and possibly a hero, as was Sir Francis Drake, a "privateer" knighted for his efforts (45). Fuchs also remarks on Elizabethan England's attempts to conscript pirates into an imperial navy (economically consuming them) by allowing them to declare themselves "reformed" from their formerly illegal behavior. Anne Perotin-Dumon similarly observes that labels of piracy were often used in struggles between competing European imperialists for control of the seas and of potential colonies; one colonizer's "exploration" was often considered by another as piracy. Pirates and cannibals, then, like colonized people, participate in "the paradox of abjection" for European imperial cultures, functioning as both interrogator and assurer of colonial boundaries, a role we see reflected in the constant tension in narratives of colonization between embracing them and thrusting them away.

Perhaps responding to this bifurcated need for questioner and confirmer, island narratives often split their representation of cannibals and pirates. As Hulme remarks in *Colonial Encounters,* this split began with the first colonizer, Columbus, who felt compelled in *The Four Voyages* to denote a split between good "savages" (passive and welcoming) and bad "cannibals" (resistant to colonial aggression), so that the idea "cannibal" from its inception, whatever its relationship to reality, signified the undesirable Other toward whom aggression was justified. Colonial texts similarly split pirates. The first type, *irredeemable* cannibals and pirates perform abject behaviors, lack command of their bodies, and refuse to learn proper manners from contact with the castaway. These pirates and cannibals threaten the castaway's masculine discipline (meaning his ability to control what enters or exits the boundaries of his island and body) through their attempts to tear his skin, to enter his body's interior with their knives and teeth, to swarm over the interior of his island, or to kidnap and force him to participate in illegal actions. Texts show those in the second category, *reformed* cannibals and pirates, as having repudiated their former abject actions after mastering enough bodily control to bring them within acceptable social parameters. Though these "reformed" characters condone imperial conduct by adopting it, they never lose the taint of their formerly abject behavior and status, never gaining the complete trust or status of the castaway colonist, though they may be elevated above the abject. Crusoe, for instance, despite "disciplining" Friday not to eat human flesh, never seems to believe that Friday could entirely renounce cannibalism, at one point fearing, with "no doubt . . . that if Friday could get back to his own Nation again, he would not only forget all his Religion, but all his Obligation to me and would . . . come back perhaps with a hundred or two of [his countrymen], and make a Feast upon me" (162). Though he recants that thought soon afterward, Crusoe's lingering suspicion of Friday's loyalties suggests that he sees cannibalism as deeply rooted in, even innate to, the savage soul.

Typically, the castaway colonist reacts to both sets of characters according to his (and his culture's) psychological need for them: he rejects "irredeemable" cannibals and pirates, who confirm imperial social boundaries through their resistance to colonial order, refusal of colonial culture, and reification of an unacceptable alternative lifestyle; and he embraces "reformed" cannibals and pirates, who also confirm imperial boundaries through their attempts to mimic imperial culture. As Bhabha notes in "Of Mimicry and Man," such efforts at colonial mimicry, which would always be imperfect, would bolster the fiction of the superiority of imperial culture. This split portrayal of and reaction to the cannibal and pirate again metaphorically enacts the castaway's subconscious efforts to incorporate what he desires; the colonist (and his imperial culture and reader) spits out the irredeemable but consumes the reformed. Crusoe, for instance, ejects from his island some cannibals (those he doesn't kill) while absorbing others into his community (Friday and his father), and he reacts in a similarly split manner toward the pirates, accepting some (allowing them to repent and join his community) but rejecting others.

But how is it that the literary castaway colonist can symbolically consume some abject cannibals and pirates but not others? Kristeva's theory of abject objects helps to explain the psychology behind the split. Human beings, she says, will not consume abject objects (will not, for instance, consume vomit, blood, or mucus) *unless* that abject object has first undergone a process of purification. If the abject object is transformed into an acceptable form (a medicine, for instance) through a process that gives psychical mastery over the abjection, the abject object can be consumed. Such socially sanctioned "consumption" after purification of the abject emerges in some anthropological explanations of second burial rituals, as well, in which, as Michelle Stephen explains, a body is buried, then exhumed and "cleaned of any remaining flesh and moved to a final resting place, usually amidst celebration of various kinds, and mourning for the deceased is officially brought to an end" (1175). As Stephen further explains, "the deceased, who begins by being a polluting and horrific corpse, and usually a malignant ghost, is, by the end of the second phase of the mortuary rituals, converted into a benign ancestral force, often installed in a household or community shrine where it becomes an object of worship along with the other ancestral shades" (1175). The community, it would seem, can only incorporate the dead body of the departed (the abject) after a ritual of purification or transformation.

We can see a similar process of purification or transformation in the course of reformation of some literary pirates or cannibals and in the literary colonist's acceptance of them. To purify and prepare a cannibal or pirate for "incorporation" into his island community, the colonist engages in a process of projective identification similar to that through which he imagines himself in command of his island. He first projects himself onto the cannibals or pirates he desires to incorporate, "reforming" them and making them enough like himself to be taken in. Before Crusoe incorporates both Friday and the ship's captain, for instance, he projects himself onto them by forcing them to swear to follow certain rules of behavior to which he subscribes (renouncing cannibalism, converting to Christianity, forfeiting claim to his island). When they have agreed to behave according to his desires, the no-longer-abject men become "consumable" for Crusoe, and he brings them into the bowels of his island. He "incorporates" them into his society by bringing them from the island shore (where they would exist as abject) into its interior, symbolically swallowing them into his island/body. When bringing the captain into his castle, for instance, Crusoe describes the castle as protected by the grove of trees he planted when first on the island, which had "become a little Wood, and so thick, that it was unpassable in any Part of it, but at the one Side, where I had reserv'd my little winding Passage into it" (186). With its own protective skin (the wood) and throat/intestine (the passage through the wood), Crusoe's enclosed fort resembles a stomach within his island body. By consuming the captain and Friday, Crusoe gains authority over them and, by countering their claim, confirms his ownership of his island and his selfhood.

Such literary splits of the reformed native/pirate off from the abject also, of course, help island narratives to justify real-world colonial policies toward natives and other colonizers. While literary depictions of abject natives (cannibals) and abject competing colonizers (pirates) justify the killing, carrying of arms, and violence inherent in colonization, literary portrayals of "reformed" natives or beneficial competing colonizers (merchants or traders) show that people as well as places can be colonized or can cooperate in the colonial enterprise, thus proving the worth of the "civilizing mission." Often the texts attribute the desirable behavior of reformed natives and pirates to their having been "tamed" by education or Christianity, thus justifying colonization through missionaries. Adrian Paul's *Willis the Pilot* (the 1857 sequel to *The Swiss Family Robinson,* originally published in French), for instance, contains a conversation about being able to correct cannibalism through education. Willis speculates to the Robinson son, Jack, that cannibals, though they have "flesh and bone, arms, legs, hands and teeth like [white men]" are not "possessed of souls and hearts." Jack replies "The chances are that they possess both, Willis; only neither the one nor the other has been

FIGURE 8. Scene of Crusoe rescuing Friday from cannibals, engraving after T. Stothard from Daniel Defoe, *The Life and Adventures of Robinson Crusoe* (London: J. Stockdale, 1804). By permission of the Hubbard Imaginary Voyages Collection, Special Collections Library, University of Michigan.

trained to regard the things of this world in a proper light. Their notions as to diet [cannibalism], for example, arise from ignorance as to what substances are fit and proper for human food" (270). Cannibalism, in Jack's eyes, is a behavior correctable with "proper" training (most likely by a missionary or, later a colonial school). Echoing the notion of cannibalism as correctable by missionaries, the reformed pirate Bill likewise explains to the boy castaway Ralph in *The Coral Island* that "the South Sea islanders are such incarnate fiends that they are the better of being tamed, and the missionaries are the only men who can do it" (182). As part of his reformation from piracy, Bill himself also becomes further "tamed" by Christianity upon his deathbed, illustrating that Christianity can make good men of both abject groups, and providing further justification for colonial intrusion in the name of mission work.

In their efforts to portray reformed cannibals and pirates as different from their irredeemable counterparts, island narratives often return to the familiar symbolic system of gender.[5] As discussed in the last chapter, the texts suture gender to body discipline. One could chart these representations along a continuum of gradations of gendered discipline, with undisciplined (what Geoffrey Sanborne calls "hypermasculine") cannibals/pirates on one extreme; undisciplined, feminized reformed cannibals/pirates on the other; and the perfectly disciplined, precisely masculine castaway in the middle. This gendering of the colonial Other into the feminized and the too-masculine allows colonizer, writer, and reader to fantasize about being "just right": masculine and disciplined, the perfect imperialist.

I deliberately use the term "feminized" instead of "feminine" in reference to reformed pirates and cannibals because, whereas texts only sometimes make reformed characters female, they consistently place them in the "feminized" position of object of the colonist's desire or control, as no longer in complete command of their bodies.[6] *Robinson Crusoe*, for instance, enhances the notion of Friday as reformed by showing him as feminized in pictures as well as in text. Illustrated editions of the novel typically include several drawings of Friday and Crusoe, often reproducing the scene of Friday placing Crusoe's foot upon his head in a demonstration of his willing subjugation and objectification. As well, texts frequently illustrate the scene of Crusoe rescuing Friday from cannibals. For instance, one 1804 edition depicts that scene of Crusoe rescuing Friday with a remarkably feminized (and marginalized) Friday (see Figure 8). Friday cowers behind the manly (and centered) Crusoe, who straddles one cannibal he has just slain while aiming his (phallic) gun at another. In contrast, Friday, in a posture of what Erving Goffman in *Gender Advertisements* calls "licensed withdrawal" (a typically feminine response to conflict that leaves the figure dependent on others) (57), turns his body away from the cannibal as if to flee or embrace the small tree within his grasp, looking timidly over one shoulder, eyes large, lips parted in fear. The illustrator, Stothard, constructs Friday's body in a typical feminized posture, his shapely right shoulder raised in a gesture of fear (to protect his neck), his right arm bent close to his body (as if protecting his breasts), and his right hand, wrist cocked, fingers spread, in a feminine pose. As well, Stothard portrays Friday's acceptance of his subordination through placing him in what Goffman calls a "canting posture" (46), indicated by his bent knee and neck and his head position as lower than Crusoe's. His spare loin cloth and body placement (turned so that most of his body is visible) makes him the available object of the reader's and Crusoe's desiring gaze, in contrast with Crusoe's fully clothed figure, posed in profile only. This early nineteenth-century illustration of Crusoe protecting Friday could be said to reflect one argument used in colonial competition, which concerns the differences between good and bad colonizers. Published just a year before the Battle of Trafalgar during an intense period of British-French struggle over American territory, this illustration shows the powerful British colonist as committed to both civilizing and "protecting" the vulnerable American Indian natives, from other "bad" natives and (later in the story) from "bad" Europeans (the pirates).

Texts similarly use verbal description to equate pirate and cannibal gender with lack of command over their bodily drives. Often the narratives depict irredeemable cannibals' craving for human flesh and pirates' for bloody deeds as coming from unrestrained and undeniable lusts, from (as discussed in chapter 2) undisciplined masculinity; likewise the texts represent reformed pirate or cannibals' inabilities to adequately self-govern, to manage their own economy, or to control their own armed forces—in short, their inability to exist without the rule of the colonizer—as stemming from a feminine lack of discipline. Often coexisting in the same text, both hypermasculinity and femininity equal lack of discipline.

We can see this gendered logic at work in *The Coral Island* from the boys' first sighting of natives in two canoes racing toward their island. As Ralph narrates, the first canoe "contained a few women and children, as well as men—perhaps forty souls altogether; while the canoe which pursued it contained only men" (149). The text immediately genders the people in the two canoes to better contrast the first group of natives, whom the boys will aid and reform, with the second group of irredeemable cannibals, whom the boys will kill. As the two canoes reach the shore, the gendered split becomes more apparent, when after a fierce battle, Ralph, Jack, and Peterkin must rescue the desperate women and men of the first canoe from the violent and hypermasculine cannibals of the second canoe. The act of placing themselves under the boys' power confirms the natives' powerlessness and status as feminized objects. The boys aid the natives of the first canoe in fighting off and slaying the cannibals, but before becoming their permanent allies (socially "incorporating" them), Jack must first reform them (transform them from being abject) by teaching them that cannibalism is wrong. When after the battle, one of those natives cuts a slice of flesh from a dead enemy to ingest, Jack seizes the man, makes him bury the serving with the rest of the body, and communicates through signs to him and to the other natives the evils of cannibalism. Though the whole tribe listens to that lesson in "civilized" behavior, the person who most seems to learn the lesson is the lovely maiden, Avatea, who comes to symbolize the newly "educated" (reformed) natives, and who becomes the agent of reform of others. When several members of her tribe later stubbornly refuse to behave according to the rules of imperial decorum (including her father, who threatens to kill her instead of marrying her to the Christian native of her choice), it is Avatea who in the end brings about their conversion to Christianity, their taming, reformation, and feminization, which ultimately results in their imperial subjugation. Given the civilizing ideologies around Christianity and their connections to gender, it is not surprising that a woman is chosen to civilize her tribe; white women have the same charge. And once begun, it would seem, reform naturally self-perpetuates.

This same gendered split exists in portrayals of reformed and irredeemable pirates. The split between honest trader and pirate often hinges on whether the mutiny that typically begins the switch to piracy was justified. Both *The Narrative of Arthur Gordon Pym* and *Robinson Crusoe* present the mutinies in their pages as unjustified, with the captain, the lawful ruler of the ship, as the victim of criminal mutineers, which makes pirates of the mutineers. Yet many depictions of the infamous Bounty mutiny, including the first one by Mary Russell Mitford (and Byron's poem "The Island or Christian and his Comrades"), and much of the public discourse about the mutiny, present that mutiny as jus-tified—as resistance to cruelty and tyranny. Such works cast the mu-tineers as heroes, not pirates, though Bill Pearson's account of their cruelty to the natives on Pitcairn Island suggests otherwise. *The Coral Island* provides a useful example of the split representation of pirates, for it contrasts its hypermasculine, undisciplined pirates with Bill, the re-formed pirate, who befriends Ralph and then prevents his captain and other bad pirates from murdering a village of natives.[7] The novel codes Bill's feminization through his advanced age, his ultimate powerless-ness against the other pirates (he is mortally wounded in battle against them), and, as I will soon discuss, his homoerotic attraction to the boy, Ralph. Contrastingly, the novel marks the pirate *captain's* hypermascu-linity by representing him as overly aggressive, as too concerned with denial of any tender emotions (kindness, fairness, generosity), and as lacking the discipline that makes a male into a man. As with the split of natives into reformed or cannibal, imperial fantasies require reformed pirates like Bill to reassure their readers that white men had some level of humanity even when soured by the act of piracy. Readers might have been aware of real cases of "reformed" pirates, such as Sir Henry Mor-gan, who after years of piracy in the Caribbean, was "reformed" by the English government, knighted, and made governor of Jamaica in the 1680s. As well, some readers might have been aware that the British Em-pire was in part built on the labor of "pirates" such as Sir Francis Drake and Captain Morgan, whose behavior was sanctioned by the Queen. As Trevor Lloyd remarks in *Empire: The History of the British Empire*, Eliza-beth not only financed Drake's expeditions, she supported other plun-dering operations as well, for "by providing support she encouraged private individuals to spend their own money building up little navies. . . . Drake's example suggested that it was perfectly possible to fight the Spaniards and make a profit" (4).

Yet the texts also need bad pirates, like *The Coral Island*'s pirate cap-tain, to justify real-world violent persecution of outlaws and competing colonizers and to blame for native aggression. *The Coral Island* voices this second point of rationalization when Bill explains to Ralph that much of the hostility and duplicity with which the island natives greet them stems from a legacy of past contact with cheating, murdering pirates, like their captain. It was such recalcitrant behavior that eventually led to real piracy being labeled outlaw, abject, and even subhuman, as notes the unknown author of *The General History of the Pyrates*, who claims that piracy, that "Course of Life, that so much debases human Nature," lowers white men to the "Level with the wild Beasts of the Forest, who live and prey upon their weaker Fellow Creatures" (114). Defiant of the rules of fair capitalism and imperial discipline, pirates were declared "Hostis humani generis," which Baer explains as "a common Enemy, with whom neither Faith nor Oath is to be kept" (7). The undisciplined behavior of the pirate makes him *legally* abject, as Baer remarks "beyond the pale of civilized society and hence the lawful prey of any who could destroy him by foul means or fair" (7).

As well as showing cannibals and pirates as "abject" by their geographical position on the boundaries of island and empire, and by depictions of their undisciplined lawlessness and impurity, island texts mark them as abject by marking their bodies, in effect racializing the pirate/cannibal skin and exoticizing their body coverings to demonstrate their marginality within a culture of imperial white privilege. In reference to cannibals, Peter Hulme remarks in his introduction to Barker, Hulme, and Iverson's *Cannibalism and the Colonial World* that "the racial dimension of the discourse of cannibalism was never far from the surface during the colonial period: the tendency was to associate cannibalistic practice with darkness of skin" (30). *The Coral Island* provides a rich example of such racial markers in Ralph's description of the cannibal chief:

His hair was frizzed out to an enormous extent, so that it resembled a large turban. It was of a light-yellow hue, which surprised me much, for the man's body was as black as coal, and I felt convinced that the hair must have been dyed. He was tattooed from head to foot; and his face, besides being tattooed, was besmeared with red paint, and streaked with white. Altogether with his yellow turban-like hair, his Herculean black frame, his glittering eyes and white teeth, he seemed the most terrible monster I ever beheld. (150)

While being fascinated by the man (as evident by his length and detail of the description), Ralph's diction (he describes the chief as "besmeared" as if with feces instead of "decorated" or "designed") also suggests coexistent feelings of repulsion; he calls him a "monster." Ralph's description, as well, both emphasizes and confuses the man's racial identity by amalgamating signs associated with multiple "races" (hair like a Middle-Eastern "turban," skin "black as coal" like an African, copious tattoos like a South Pacific islander, face paint like an American Indian). The man is both all Other races and specifically none of them. Moreover, Ralph repeatedly comments on the artificiality of the cannibal's look, describing the man's wild blond hair as "dyed" and "frizzed" and his skin as

FIGURE 9. "A Heavy Hand Grasped My Shoulder and Held It as If in a Vice" from R. M. Ballantyne, *The Coral Island* (London: Dean and Son, 1958), frontispiece.

"tattooed," emphasizing that he *chooses* the look that reflects and contributes to his abjection, thus further blaming the cannibal for his own colonial victimhood. Such descriptions, when contrasted with those of the assimilated "reformed" natives, work toward a scenario in which the irredeemable cannibal has rejected the benefits of "civilization," which makes violence against him and those like him that much easier for the colonial reader to stomach.

Ralph's description of the irredeemable pirates, as with their cannibal corollaries, intimates that they purposefully display their abjection through their assumption of darkened skins and exotic costumes. The explanation Ralph gives for pirates' dark skins, that the men are "deeply bronzed" "from long exposure to the weather" (168), suggests that they choose their darker skin just as they choose their uncivilized behavior. Ralph describes the pirate captain as dressed exotically, with a "Greek skull-cap" and "a broad shawl of the richest silk round his waist" in which were housed "two pairs of pistols and a heavy cutlass" (168). The pirate crew, Ralph describes as "a ferocious set of men, with shaggy beards and scowling brows," who "were armed with cutlasses and pistols," with clothing that "with trifling variations, [was] similar to that of the captain" (169). As with the cannibals, Ralph's description of pirate clothing both enhances their alterity to the Euro-American protagonist and stresses their deliberate display of their abject lifestyle.

Illustrated editions of island narratives almost always include pictures of pirates, just as they do cannibals. Seemingly fascinated with the image of the pirate, the books use illustrations to enhance the verbal description and heighten the reader's sense of experiencing danger from safe distance. The typical characteristics of pirates as shown in these illustrations, when added together, create a visual code for piracy that is as recognizable as the "Jolly Roger" flag, the symbol that often alerts the castaway colonists to the coming danger. As do the verbal descriptions, such illustrations, like this frontispiece illustration from a 1958 Dean and Son edition of *The Coral Island* (see Figure 9), frequently contrast pirates with the colonists by stressing the pirates' exotic costuming, their close, cloth head coverings (to which Ralph refers as a "Greek skull cap"), their gold hoop earrings, their plentiful and unruly facial hair, and their sharp (phallic) cutlasses. As well as contrasting the pirate from Ralph through their differing clothing, this drawing makes the pirate darker in complexion, more aggressively masculine, and larger than Ralph in every detail (including the pirate's big black boots, muscular build, powerful stance, and large sword). The picture also establishes the pirate's menace through his proximity to Ralph. He grasps Ralph's shoulder, which, despite already violating the island boundaries, is the first of the pirates' challenges to what Edward Hall calls Ralph's "invisible body boundaries." Since they are non-intimates, this act of touch serves as an act of aggression. Because the illustrator draws Ralph to mirror the book's intended reader (young, white males) and positions him facing the reader (with the pirate in profile), he seems to be inviting readers to identify with Ralph, to become emotionally involved in his plight instead of the pirate's.

Against the powerful but unruly pirate, the unarmed Ralph seems vulnerable but also civilized, especially when read against the narrative that portrays him as clever and resourceful. Yet the image paints the pirate as the more compelling figure, betraying ambivalence about (attraction to) piracy. Like the feminized Friday, the illustration shows Ralph in the canting stance (as Goffman says, lower head position and bent knee) (46), suggesting his youthful inferiority, heightened by his fearful facial expression and protomasculinity, contrasting with the pirate's frightening hypermasculinity. Even while we fear for Ralph, our eye is drawn to the pirate, who takes up more space (using Goffman's language, "relative size" [28]) and is the more visually compelling figure (a notion I will explore momentarily).

It is significant that we see such portrayals of piracy as dangerously attractive in an edition, like this one, published as late as 1958, while much of the world was seeing significant decline in the old European empires (in contrast to the expanding Soviet and American empires) and escalating Cold War tensions. It is true that pirates are fascinating and frightening to children, the primary audience of the book, but perhaps at that time, as much as (or more than) during periods of greater imperial security, one might feel a need to invoke the abject cannibal and pirate to aid in marking the quickly fading social and geographical boundaries of the British and other European empires, separating the familiar, civilized, and "white" from the foreign, savage, and "ethnic."

Fantasies of Counterincorporation

As do images of the pirate/cannibal, narratives of encounter between the castaway and the pirate/cannibal provide insight into how texts work to process readers' anxieties of empire. Island tales summon the real historical figures of the cannibal and pirate to dramatize fears of losing control of colonies to indigenous inhabitants or to other European imperialists, fears which were very much based in reality. Historical investigation shows that acts of colonization did often, in fact, induce indigenous resistance, from battles with the "cannibals" Columbus encountered (most likely the Caribs who, as Hulme reminds in *Colonial Encounters,* probably earned their fierce reputation from their initial resistance), to the 1857–58 Indian rebellion, to the Algerian and Irish struggles for independence in the twentieth century. Recodifying historical incidents of indigenous resistance into tales of repelled cannibal invasion possibly helped some imperial readers to contain the fears of violent rebellion engendered by those incidents. Likewise, stories of piracy in colonial island narratives could have helped readers to process real-world fears of colonial competition, for, as with the colonization of the Americas and the Caribbean and what is now called "the scramble for Africa," competition between colonizers for land was often intense. In fact, England fought many a war (including the French and Indian War, the Boer War, the Crimean War, and the War of American Independence) to protect or secure its colonies, not counting the countless campaigns and skirmishes between "legitimate" British trading vessels and other nations' "pirates." In order to reassure the reading public of the security of the empire, texts recodified indigenous resistance and colonial competition into tales of the cannibal and pirate, thus transferring the messiness of imperial expansion into a simplified story of a man successfully defending his legitimately earned space.

Mirroring this real-world competition between European nations for colonies, island narratives often designate pirates as of a competing colonial nationality. Philip Ashton's English Robinsonade, *Ashton's Memorial* (1725), quite clearly uses national designations to distinguish the lawful from the unlawful. The narrator often refers to the threatening pirates as "Spaniards," and they refer to Ashton (as they pursue him) as "O Englishman" (35). As the narrative proceeds, Ashton vacillates between referring to the threatening men by the national designation "Spaniards" and the legal designation "pirates," as if the two terms were in his mind interchangeable. At one point, the narrative creates a distinction between pirates and Spaniards, ironically with the suggestion that pirates considered Spaniards to be more dangerous. When Ashton and some newly castaway companions encounter some strangers while out in a canoe, the strangers tell Ashton that "they were Pirates, and not

Spaniards," which is meant to communicate that the Englishman "need not fear" (41). Ashton, however, considers pirates the more dangerous at that moment thinking "But they could not have mentioned any thing worse to discourage me from having any thing to do with them, for I had the utmost dread of a Pirate" (41). Yet, meanwhile, other narratives, like *Robinson Crusoe,* define piracy as an abject set of behaviors largely divorced from nationality. The pirates in *Robinson Crusoe* are English, and as reinforced in *The Farther Adventures of Robinson Crusoe* (1719), Spanish men can be loyal, honest, gentlemen. As Crusoe attests, "let the accounts of *Spanish* cruelty in *Mexico* and *Peru* be what they will, I never met with seventeen men, of any nation . . . who were so universally modest, temperate, virtuous, so very good-humor'd, and so courteous as these *Spaniards*" (82).

As well as providing reassuring fantasies of imperial triumph over counterincorporation, scenes in which the colonist clashes with and overcomes pirates and cannibals also provide means for fantasizing about *being* incorporated. Story lines of the castaway being threatened with incorporation create avenues for readers to flirt with taboo—perhaps subconscious—desires to be incorporated, all the while knowing that the book's heroes would resist the threat. This vehicle for the "safe" experience of being incorporated suggests one reason for the pirate's and cannibal's popularity with the colonial reading public. Psychoanalysts explain that fantasies of being incorporated often supplement fantasies of being an incorporator. Alex Blumstein, for instance, in his work linking masochism to what he calls "fantasies and acts of self-preparation for being incorporated," explains that, whereas the fantasy of *performing* incorporation can give one a sense of power over an object, the fear/desire of *being incorporated* combines the subconscious desire to relinquish responsibility to another, "an omnipotent figure," with the seductive fiction of being bodily conjoined with another (292). We can see this desire, as well, as it is channeled into sanctioned imperial fantasies of being consumed into a larger entity (the empire), and of relinquishing authority to an "omnipotent" figure with a larger mission (perhaps the Christian or national mission).

This desire for being incorporated combined with the fear of being incorporated exists in a range of island narratives with cannibals and pirates, but we can see this dichotomy particularly clearly in Melville's cannibal narrative *Typee.* As well as being terrified at the idea of cannibalism, as Caleb Crain explains, Tommo, Melville's semiautobiographical protagonist, fantasizes about being the victim of cannibals because he "desperately wants to lose his self" (34). It is this attraction to cannibalism that makes Tommo linger in the Typee village, the exciting cannibal danger zone. The novel, in fact, largely derives its interest from tension between the titillating evidence suggestive of cannibalism and Tommo's (and the reader's) disbelief and attraction to the exotic natives. Because Tommo psychically identifies with his cannibal captors, being especially enamored of the lovely and light-skinned Fayaway, his fantasy of being cannibalized becomes complicated with a fantasy of *being* a cannibal. But once Tommo discovers evidence of Typee cannibalism (as is usual, in the aftermath of a feast), he must reject his cannibal friends and flee the island. Crain argues that Melville purposefully interrupts the reader's identification with the Typees at the end of the novel when Tommo, in attempting to escape the then-revealed cannibals, throws a boathook at a Typee man pursuing him. That act, Crain posits, "breaks a threateningly attractive sense of identity with the cannibals" as "the Typees relapse into a fierce but reassuring otherness. Tommo is not a cannibal," Crain explains. "He is a man who kills cannibals" (33). Tommo's rejection of the Typees and denial of his desire to be consumed culturally and bodily marks a predictable but necessary finale to such a drama; colonial readers needed to be shown the danger of romantic fantasies of being consumed into a native culture or "going native" (and the attendant redemption from those fantasies), lest the empire lose control of its subjects in a nonviolent but equally harmful cultural revolution. The *fear* of consumption must be restored in order for the novel to ultimately reinforce a fear of insurgency. A similar moment occurs in *Robinson Crusoe* when Crusoe decides that he does not, in fact, identify with his island's cannibals. Crusoe undergoes a period of attempted understanding of the cannibal culture, but upon finding the remains of a cannibal meal, delineates the differences between himself and the cannibals as he gives "God Thanks that had cast my first Lot in a Part of the World, where I was distinguish'd from such dreadful Creatures as these" (120). As Hulme explains in his analysis of this moment, "As the text conjures up the 'reality' of cannibalism, so the tentative ego is strengthened in its knowledge of itself. It may not be too sure what it is, but it knows it is not a cannibal. It is at this moment that Crusoe becomes the fully-fledged colonial adventurer, self-composed, ready for action" (*Colonial Encounters*, 198).

Moreover, in the heteronormative world of empire, any desire to be consumed must be denied/subverted/transferred since the fantasized act of being cannibalized, if between two men, could mimic male homosexual sex, that taboo taking of another into one's body through anal intercourse or fellatio. Crain, in fact, connects the popularity of cannibal lore in the nineteenth century to the allure of homosexuality, for both "violate the distinctions between identity and desire; between self and other; between what we want, what we want to be, and what we are" (34). As he speculates, for those reasons both cannibalism and homosexuality are attractive, which "is why the nineteenth-century American man is horrified to discover that they [both cannibalism and homosexuality] appeal to him" (34). This fantasy of holding another within one's body through consumption could also fulfill fantasies of male reproduction, as discussed in chapter 2. During cannibalism, a male body encompasses another male body much as a pregnant woman's holds a fetus, and the cannibal even metaphorically "births" the cannibalized body through excretion. As Freud notes (in his famous discussion of Little Hans) the fantasy of children being born through excretion is a common one for little boys, who want to imagine that they can birth children, as well.[8]

Pirate stories play out a similar fantasy of being incorporated, only that "incorporation" is into the pirates' lawless but egalitarian/homosocial (and potentially homoerotic) society. In *The Coral Island,* for instance, pirates invade the island, kidnap Ralph, take him aboard their ship, and force him to participate in illegal behavior. Instead of being threatened with having his body consumed in pieces, the pirates threaten Ralph with having his body "consumed" as a whole and with being compelled to use his body to perform acts that he detests (robbery, murder, rape), which plays out a horror of loss of command of one's body. Although at first enraged by his capture and powerlessness, Ralph comes to enjoy the homosocial, manly environment and, though still repulsed by their rough behavior, grows pleased to be consumed into the corpus of their masculine community. When Ralph is first aboard ship, the pirate captain sees him crying and humiliates him in front of the others, calling him "weak," a "whelp," and a "water-eyed puppy." In retribution, Ralph tosses a keg of powder overboard to be washed ashore to Jack and Peterkin on the island, who are in need of gunpowder. When the captain again rages at him, Ralph replies that he is "made of such stuff as the likes of you shall never tame, though you should do your worst" (172–73).

Paradoxically, it is this resistance that earns Ralph the captain's and other pirates' admiration. They exclaim "Well done, lad! You're a brick, and I have no doubt will turn out a rare cove" (which is, itself a suggestive yonic metaphor, since a cove provides a hollow into which the pirate ship would insert itself) (173). In an act of symbolic communion (which is itself symbolic cannibalism), the pirates offer Ralph beer and meat to welcome him into their society. But Ralph's pleasure at this homosocial communion is tempered by abhorrence at the pirate behavior. As he explains, "I must add that the zest with which I ate my meal was much abated in consequence of the frightful oaths and terrible language that flowed from the lips of these godless men, even in the midst of their hilarity and good humour" (173). Though Ralph is pleased to participate in their communion (to act as both pirate and cannibal), his need to keep resisting the pirates' attraction demands that he not enjoy himself *too* much.

It is the pirates' forecast that Ralph will learn to enjoy these detested acts that truly horrifies him, reproducing the same anxieties of loss of psychological control as "going native" (which I will discuss at greater length in the next chapter). As Ralph recognizes his growing indifference to violence, he becomes sickened: "I began to find that such constant exposure to scenes of blood was having a slight effect upon myself," he explains "and I shuddered when I came to think that I too was becoming callous" (204). Ralph's kidnapping and incorporation by the pirates, which costs him the power to command his own actions, also threatens his ability to resist, and risks his status as a civilized imperialist. Such juxtapositions of the undisciplined, dishonest, and cruel pirate with the island colonist, while demonstrating pirate abjection, also function to define the boundaries of "acceptable" behavior for white, male, imperial capitalists.

The male bonds of these pirate dramas, like those in fantasies of cannibalism, can also be highly homoerotic, for the fantasy of being consumed into the "body" of such a male-dominated community, where behavioral inhibitions are loosened as one's allegiance to the law of the land are suspended, carries within it the same masochistic, sexually charged pleasure of being incorporated or of having one's bodily boundaries sexually penetrated. B. R. Burg, in fact, calls pre-nineteenth-century pirates "one of the most unusual homosexually oriented groups in history" (xvi). Burg also reminds that "sexual encounters involving sailors are a part of maritime lore, and fo'c's'le humor abounds with stories of below deck encounters in which salty bosuns initiate tender cabin

boys into the arcana of the sea" (xvii). The relationship between Bill
(the "salty bosun") and Ralph (the kidnapped "tender cabin boy") in
The Coral Island plays out just such a story of pirate homoeroticism. The
bond that Bill and Ralph develop aboard ship strengthens during their
escape from the other pirates, and they exhibit tenderness and affection
toward each other. Despite his painful mortal wound, for instance, Bill
allows Ralph to sleep while he pilots their escape craft because, as he explains "you seemed to sleep so sweetly, Ralph, that I didn't like to disturb
you" (216). Like Will and Ready in *Masterman Ready*, Ralph responds by
devotedly caring for the older man until his death, finally tenderly reassuring him that even he (an ex-pirate) can go to heaven (an acceptable
incorporation).

As I remarked in chapter 2, *The Coral Island* throughout ignores any
potential homoeroticism in its male relationships, instead emphasizing
homosociality and acceptable demonstrations of platonic manly love. In
Ralph's relationship with Bill, as well, the text denies the intensity of their
relationship at key moments, such as in Bill's death scene. The interaction between desperate, lonely man and boy in what could be a highly
emotionally charged moment is astonishingly devoid of direct connection, except that redirected through the acceptable terms of Christianity.
Instead of expressing any deathbed appreciation or affection, Bill and
Ralph discuss Christianity (for the first time in the novel, except in the
context of natives and missionaries) and how one progresses to heaven.
Yet, if one reads the scene, as Jonathan Goldberg suggests, *relationally*,
for what is repressed, silenced, or eliminated, one finds hovering on the
edges of that sanitized scene the one that would have completed their
developing relationship and fulfilled the reader's expectations, wherein
man and boy express affection, perhaps love, and perhaps acknowledge
homoerotic desire and regret.

Playing Pirate, Becoming Cannibal

As well as marking the boundaries of imperial society/behavior/land,
the drama of the cannibal/pirate encounter serves other sociopsychological needs of expanding European empires, especially during the
nineteenth century. As observers from Michel Montaigne to Caleb Crain
note, employing cannibalism as a signifier of savagery entailed a certain
amount of denial and projection on the part of the European imperialists, for European disciplinary practices themselves involved a great

deal of violence to the body, often involving the body's fragmentation or dismemberment, either through drawing and quartering or beheading. One could argue, then, that part of the colonial fascination with potential cannibal or pirate victimhood stems from seeing one's own actions and desires projected onto the colonial Other, and that these island narratives help to project the enactment of and desire for violence on the real victims of colonial violence, the native and the working-class European sailor. As Ted Motohashi remarks, "in describing the Other's transgressive behavior, the colonisers in fact expressed their own fantasised desires (and actual behavior): treachery, rape, murder, misogyny, sexual deviance—they themselves were hybrid, transgressing entities" (90). As well, this projection allows the colonizer to paint himself as innocent: instead of taking land from natives or other European would-be-imperialists, whom he often kills directly or indirectly, the colonizer in this version becomes the defender of his legitimately and naturally gained land from violent and murderous Others. Perhaps yet another attraction of this projection stems from masochistic needs to be punished or forgiven for certain behaviors. Punishing or persecuting Others for one's own behaviors could allow a sort of cleansing of the colonial conscience similar to the ancient scapegoat ritual or the Christian belief in Christ being persecuted for the sins of others.

Playing Cannibal

Though island narratives do most often project incorporation onto the Other so that the colonizer becomes the innocent victim of cannibalism and denies his own incorporative fantasies, occasionally the texts include story lines in which colonizers themselves turn cannibal. As Marina Warner (in "Fee Fie Fo Fum") and Gananath Obeyesekere note, cannibalism was part of the cultural imaginary of the European colonizer, who as children, would have been immersed in a mythology of cannibalistic witches, ghosts, and pirates, stories that would have fed both adult fear and fantasy. Bertram D. Lewin links childhood fears and fantasies of cannibalism to fears of castration or "in regressive oral terms a fear of retributive castration for sexual wishes toward the mother and castrative wishes toward the father" (130). Lewin also remarks on the cultural commonplace of children being referred to by names of edible objects ("honey," "cookie") and of adults "playfully threaten[ing]" them with "eating them up." As he remarks, "Children evidently can attribute to food a pleasurable wish to be eaten; they are able phenomenologists and seem readily to appreciate how the cookie and sugar-pie feel" (131). In fantasies of *being* an incorporator (like fantasies of consuming the island) colonist and reader could find a sense of control through the fantasied assimilating of desirable aspects of another, a fact anthropologists have recognized in real-world studies of cannibalism. Eli Sagan explains that a family that consumes the body of a departed loved one gains the sense that they control death, just as a warrior who consumes the body of his slain enemy imagines that he obtains the enemy's strength, incorporating within him the desirable aspects of the enemy while expunging the undesirable ones. The story of the island castaway as cannibal/pirate similarly perpetrates the fantasy of gaining another's strength, which is uncannily analogous to the reality of colonizers who, by plundering the resources (raw materials, labor, national treasures) of the colonies they controlled, consumed, and fought over, strengthened their own economies.[9]

But why is it that cannibalism makes such an attractive and convenient myth for describing relationships with the Other? Some twentieth-century psychoanalytic theorists place cannibalism into the realm of "normal" human object-relations, seeing it as a natural and integral part of the earliest relations a child has with its first Other, the mother (or as Lacan would say, the " (m)Other"). The "oral sadistic" theories of Karl Abraham and Melanie Klein, for instance, describe babies as innately wanting to devour the mother, whom they fear wants to consume them. Of course, before Klein and Abraham's comments on object relations, Freud's analysis of cannibalistic practices in *Totem and Taboo* had already placed cannibalism within the domain of the "natural" development of societies. It is through (perhaps symbolic) murder and cannibalism, Freud explains, that sons enact the ritual of the oedipal drama, incorporating the father's power and law by actually consuming his body.

What these theorists treat as a universal experience, however, others understand as a psychocultural phenomenon reflecting Western capitalism. These theorists argue that it is no coincidence that the Kleinian model of object relations, a defensive model of a world organized around the economy of "eat or be eaten," mirrors economies of capitalism and imperial expansion. Crystal Bartolovich, for one, sees as one of the primary attractions of cannibalism as a system of representation its ability to provide a cultural metaphor for capitalistic appetites. Similarly Maggie Kilgour connects Klein's oral sadistic stage with consumer-oriented imperialism. Just as "the infant's fear of being devoured by the parent is a reaction against its own desire to assimilate and possess what is external to the self," she says, "recent studies of imperialism and 'colonial discourse' have indicated how a society's desire to appropriate other cultures can be disguised through the projection of that impulse onto the other" (*From Communion to Cannibalism*, 5).

Kilgour also links imperialism, consumption, and fears of incorporation to the discipline of psychoanalysis, which, she says, concerns "increasing internalization, a movement toward a world in which everything is imagined as being 'inside'" (*From Communion to Cannibalism*, 226–27). Accordingly, we could explain cannibalism's popularity as a metaphor for fantasies of imperial expansion and natural control as resulting from modern, Western subconscious envisioning of relationships with Others in the family and societal system through the capitalistic lens of consumption. In island narratives, the drama of capitalist empire and consumption becomes recodified into the fictional castaway colonizer, who, in a projection of their writers' and readers' most basic desires, is forced to "consume" (assimilate or eradicate) the Other (mother, pirate, or cannibal) whom they fear wants to incorporate them.

Typically, the story of the castaway colonist who cannibalizes tells of a man being *forced* into that extreme, often called "survival cannibalism." Usually on a raft or other floating craft after a storm or wreck with neither food nor water, the castaway would be compelled by his situation and allegiance to the greater good to consume human flesh and blood lest he die. In most of the stories of survival cannibalism, as in Poe's *The Narrative of Arthur Gordon Pym*, the group of survivors chooses to sacrifice one individual for the good of the greater number, often choosing the victim by lot. That the books rarely show colonists turning on each other or order breaking down suggests that such stories of cannibalism contribute to the fantasy of imperial body discipline. If order does break down, as it does in the cannibalistic scene in *The Island of Dr. Moreau* when the two sailors attack each other, the disorderly men die for their transgression. Though narratives depict scenes of natives sacrificing one of their own as barbaric and uncivilized, as when the natives in *The Coral Island* sacrifice one of their children to their god for the community's greater good or when Melville's Tommo discovers the Typee cannibalism, the tales often present the act of colonizers sacrificing one of their own as horrible but reasonable.

Such fictional tales of survival cannibalism drew upon rare, sensationalized accounts of white cannibalism, as A. W. Brian Simpson remarks in *Cannibalism and the Common Law: The Story of the Tragic Last Voyage of the Mignonette and the Strange Legal Proceedings to Which It Gave Rise*. In these journalistic tales, as in island narratives, acts of survival cannibalism by white, Euro-Americans are portrayed quite differently from native cannibalism: native cannibals, who supposedly eat human flesh out of lack of discipline or inferior morality are doomed postcannibalism to a life of craving human flesh, whereas survival cannibals, because forced to consume human flesh by necessity, are released from the guilt and savagery associated with The Deed. Texts present white cannibals as able thereafter to maintain their discipline and resist the lust for human meat, which again upholds the fantasy of the colonizer who would never—even when forced into cannibalism—"go native." Book 2 of Byron's *Don Juan* contains a wry comment on this logic, for when Don Juan's companions draw lots and are forced to eat his tutor, everyone who consumes the flesh dies. Only Don Juan, who has the bodily self-discipline to ignore his hunger and not eat survives.

We find such an instance of survival cannibalism in Edgar Allan Poe's *The Narrative of Arthur Gordon Pym* (1831), in Pym's ability to defy the longing for human flesh after consuming it. Stranded with three others on a storm-wounded ship with no access to food, Poe's characters cast lots in a tense scene to see who will die and be consumed. Interestingly, Poe narrates the drawing of the lots, the choosing of who would be cannibalized, as more horrific than the actual cannibalism (two meaty paragraphs describe the drawing of lots but the cannibalism itself gets two sentences), perhaps because during that scene the narrator is still potentially the cannibalized instead of the cannibal. Pym/Poe describes the drawing of the lots as being so horrific that he can't forget it, but neither does he want to describe it: "It is with extreme reluctance that I dwell upon the appalling scene which ensued; a scene which, with its minutist details, no after-events have been able to efface in the slightest degree from my memory, and whose stern recollection will embitter every future moment of my existence" (*Complete Stories and Poems*, 675). After Pym lingers over the drama of the drawing of lots, he promises to gloss over the details of the cannibal meal. Yet he narrates that,

Such things may be imagined, but words have no power to impress the mind with the exquisite horror of their reality. Let it suffice to say that, having in some measure appeased the raging thirst which consumed us by the blood of the victim, and having by common consent taken off the hands, feet, and head, throwing them together with the entrails into the sea, we devoured the rest of the body, piecemeal, during the four ever memorable days. (*Complete Stories and Poems,* 677)

In addition to a terrible pun (on "piecemeal"), Pym, while claiming to spare readers from the horrors of the deed, gives enough gory details to stimulate their imaginations and be "ever memorable." That titillation, however, is only part of the function of such scenes, for through scenes of white, survival cannibalism, colonial readers could *identify* with cannibals, enacting the abject deed with the protagonist, also without suffering its savage consequences, except perhaps feeling a bit disgusted. Like the successful repelling of the threat of cannibalism, this demonstration of the colonizer's (and reader's) impenetrability to the savage effects of cannibalism enhances the myth of imperial fortitude. This man, the logic goes, maintains control of his body in situations in which natives (and possibly undisciplined Europeans) would develop uncontrollable blood-lust.

Sixty years after the publication of *Pym,* H. G. Wells's *The Island of Dr. Moreau* (1896) begins with a similar tale of survival cannibalism, though this time aborted, as if thus to establish Wells's protagonist's (Prendick's) discipline. When Prendick, Wells's protagonist, survives the shipwreck that begins the novel, he becomes stranded with scarce provisions on a boat with two other men. The sixth day, the castaways discuss cannibalism. Prendick, like Pym, "stood out against [the proposition] with all [his] might," opting instead for "scuttling the boat and perishing together among the sharks that followed us" (9). But though he at first refuses to draw lots with the other men, he finally relents and, like Pym, escapes being chosen for consumption. As did Poe, Wells titillates his readers with a dramatic scene of drawing lots but then spares (or denies) them the grisly cannibal scene by having Prendick's two companions fall overboard while grappling for the knife. Though Wells's novel does not complete that act of cannibalism (except for the animals' ultimate "cannibalizing" of Moreau and Montgomery), it still provides a vehicle for its audience to flirt with the thrill of incorporating another while demonstrating the superior self-discipline of the colonizer. In fact, it is Prendick's self-discipline that enables him to overcome the extreme thirst that brings his companions to the brink of cannibalism. Unlike scenes of native cannibalism, which the books describe in some detail, the texts demurely avert their readers' eyes when white men turn cannibal,

FIGURE 10. Scene of cannibalism by Gerry Hoover, from Edgar Allan Poe, *The Narrative of Arthur Gordon Pym* (Boston: D. R. Godine, 1973).

perhaps because detail in white cannibal scenes would spoil the reader's stomach for the vicarious and safe experience.

Despite Wells's and Poe's half-hearted attempts to gloss over the gory details of white cannibalism, one recent illustrator of *The Narrative of Arthur Gordon Pym* fills in the blanks in Poe's story for the reader, demonstrating at least one postcolonial reader's ability to mentally construct the scene from Poe's sparse but sufficient details (see Figure 10). The 1973 David R. Godine edition of the novel, as if to challenge Poe's pretense at aversion, graphically depicts the cannibal incident, drawing the three men's intertwined bodies so that it is disturbingly difficult to discern cannibal from cannibalized. The illustrator, Gerry Hoover, depicts both eater and meal as similarly horribly thin, naked, and cadaverous, particularly the skull-like bald head of the cannibal on the picture's bottom. The surprisingly bloodless corpse lacks its head, hands, and feet, as the story stipulates, though, in contrast to Poe's description, it is not disemboweled. All three bodies are contorted, with the bald cannibal tenderly cradling the leg into which he hungrily bites, all teeth, with a look of visceral satisfaction.

The cannibal at the drawing's top, which based on other illustrations seems to be Pym, stares defiantly at the reader, with what the cultural historians Gunther Kress and Theo Van Leeuwen in their work on visual representations call a look of "direct address," which they explain "demands that the viewer enter into some kind of imaginary relation with" the pictured (122). Pym's "direct address," presented while he gnaws a forearm (or sucks its blood), *demands* that the reader participate in the cannibalism with him, as if challenging us to deny that we wouldn't resort to the same extreme, that we don't fantasize about committing that same act, and that we wouldn't similarly enjoy it. The illustration forces the reader to confront what the tales obliquely suggest, which is the human desire to experience the taboo act of cannibalism. Even in an age of slasher films and bloody video games, the illustration is disturbing.

It is interesting to note that colonial island narratives that dramatize moments of white cannibalism typically cast those impulses as starvation-driven necessity. But two postcolonial twentieth-century revisionary island tales show white cannibalism in a different vein (so to speak), bringing to the light of day the full horrors of the deed. In these stories, the same incorporative hunger that gives colonizers control over the island becomes magnified so that they descend to its unavoidable but horrible extreme—cannibalism. The most widely read of these tales of uncontrollable incorporation, Golding's The *Lord of the Flies,* famously rewrites Ballantyne's *The Coral Island* to show a different version of how young boys would react to island isolation. Instead of enacting what imperial ideology would say was the "natural" discipline of their race and behaving as perfect gentleman adventurers, Golding's boys discover the savages in themselves. *John Dollar* (1989), Marianne Wiggins's revision of Golding's revision, also presents cannibalism as a natural progression of colonial incorporation, but Wiggins's novel focuses on girls, who become stranded on their island with their teacher, Charlotte Lewes, as part of a group of Anglo-Indian colonists claiming and renaming a local island in the king's name in honor of his birthday. After a tidal wave tragically disrupts their plans, kills many of them, and strands the remaining few on the island, the surviving girls witness their fathers being cannibalized by natives. The traumatized girls, instead of rejecting the cannibalism they saw, discover the same incorporative impulses in themselves, impulses the novel portrays as depraved. The girls cannibalize alive the only surviving adult and symbolic parent (to their knowledge), the paralyzed John Dollar, former boat captain and Charlotte's lover. Yet the girls' actions are much more horrific than the cannibalism they witnessed, for the girls eat Dollar piece by piece while he is still alive. Though he is somewhat sedated, he is aware of the gradual and painful consumption of his body. The girls both exceed the cannibal behavior they witnessed and literalize the incorporation of the colonial system into which they were born. As Stephen Connor notes, "Deprived of fathers and their law, the girls are in a sense forced to become the authors of themselves, but, without any clearly-formed sense of identity, their acts of self-authorship are parasitic upon the absent law of the father" (89). They literally suck dry the only father they have left. Graphic dystopian stories like Golding's and Wiggins's, and the illustration of the scene from *Pym,* force contemporary readers to confront and reevaluate the delusion that white survival cannibalism is almost civilized.

Performing Piracy

As with cannibalism, the replayed story of the pirate threat also plays out the supplementary fantasy of *becoming* a pirate, which means being allowed to enact aggressive fantasies, to ignore the laws prohibiting theft and violence, to incorporate what one desires with no repercussions, and to live within an entirely masculine community. Unlike the masculine homosocial fantasy described in chapter 2, in which the colonist reproduces the law of the father on the island, the pirate fantasy dramatizes the fantasy of living *outside* of the law, and, moreover, of enjoying that taboo lifestyle *guilt-free*. In the fictional realm, because pirates forcibly conscript the castaway into their community and because the castaway continues to resist, he is absolved of guilt for his behavior, just as texts spare the survival cannibal who was also forced into that abject behavior from "going native." Interestingly, Barbara Fuchs reports that this desire to enact the deed without suffering the guilt or punishment affected real-world practices of piracy. As she reports, the "reformed pirate" Henry Mainwaring admits "staging false kidnappings to allow respectable folk to join him in piracy; should they later wish to return to respectability, they could point to their forced captivity as an excuse" (48). As Hans Turley also remarks in *Rum, Sodomy, and the Lash: Piracy, Sexuality, and Masculine Identity,* piracy held a very real attraction for seamen, whose endurance of terrible working and living conditions for little financial compensation made piracy, which promised the offer of better pay under better conditions with less harsh discipline, seem attractive. In island narratives, however, though the pirate society may "consume" the castaway colonist and force him to act as a pirate, it is important to the story that he continue to resist, thereby demonstrating his continued self-discipline. Typically, the colonist does eventually successfully free himself from the pirate gang, so those stories further bolster the myth of the colonist (and empire) who can defy attempts of counterincorporation. But the castaway colonist's freedom comes only after he (and vicariously, his reader) first participates in a few forbidden but rousing piratical adventures.

The best of these fantasies of attraction to piracy come from the pen of Robert Louis Stevenson, whose novels *Kidnapped* (1886) and *Treasure Island* (1883) both involve the conscription of island-bound young men into a band of pirates. In *Kidnapped,* pirates abduct young David Balfour and make him their cabin boy at the behest of his uncle, who wants to prevent his claiming an inheritance. In *Treasure Island,* young Jim Hawkins encounters pirates while he searches for treasure on a deserted island. Though *Treasure Island* is not a typical castaway narrative, it plays out a similar story of incorporation in its pages, for the treasure map that all the characters seek (with its enabling of the superior gaze and incorporation) grants ownership of the island and the treasure to its holder. The book's protagonists (Jim, the local doctor, and squire)

FIGURE 11. Scene of pirate invasion by N. C. Wyeth, from Robert Louis Stevenson, *Treasure Island* (New York: Scribner, 1911).

sail to the island with the belief that they can legitimately harvest its treasure, though they find when they get there that they must first battle pirates who want to steal the map and claim the island and treasure. As in other island narratives, the protagonists prevail over the pirates and win command of the island, but unlike those other tales, their ownership is temporary and their reward the right to *leave* the island with the treasure.

Because both pirates and "colonists" are already on the island, the fight for map/island/treasure in *Treasure Island* is conducted in an already-built enclosure in the center of the island, the island stockade. When Jim and his friends reach the island, their largely piratical crew mutinies, forcing Jim, the doctor, the squire, the ship's captain, and a couple of loyal seamen to abandon the ship and move into the stockade. If only for a few days, the men become island castaway colonists, and they proclaim their incorporation of the island by defiantly flying the imperial Union Jack above the stockade, clearly a ritual of possession as discussed in chapter 1. Like other castaways, they must defend their island from its piratical invaders, an action that becomes symbolized in battling over the stockade, which (like Crusoe's "fort") symbolizes their incorporative bodies. N. C. Wyeth's illustration of that scene in the 1911 Scribner edition captures the terror of the pirate invasion of the stockade (see Figure 11).

Wyeth portrays three pirates (as usual, signified by their cloth head wraps, gold earrings, and large mustaches) just at the moment they clamber over the boundary separating the civilized/colonized stockade from the pirate terror. Like the abject men they are, Wyeth's pirates violate the colonist's boundaries, threatening to overtake the stockade's inner sanctum and to transgress the line between the body's inner and outer space. In fact, this invasion as depicted seems to be of the island itself, since the drawing shows no land outside of the stockade's walls, only showing a couple of tree tops against a small backdrop of sea and an expansive and gorgeously painted pink and orange twilit sky. Wyeth's depiction stresses the pirates' battle-readiness—their drawn swords, the knives carried unsheathed in their feral, bared teeth, their guns pointed at the stockade interior. Yet, despite the ferocity of the attack, the colonists by virtue of their superior position on the inside of the ramparts (the colonial center) are able to fight off the pirates, killing those that invade the stockade, and temporarily scaring off those outside. In this edition of *Treasure Island* published in 1911 during the escalation of international tensions that led to World War I, Wyeth's depiction of a horrifying twilight invasion of a stockade/island by unruly white men may have resonated with British readers fearful of invasion of their own island at what might have seemed to be their own twilight.

Treasure Island, like many colonial island narratives, shows piracy as both feared and magnetic. In fact, Jim's mixed attraction to/revulsion at piracy becomes evident when he leaves the safety of the stockade and is captured by the pirates, who (as with Ralph in *The Coral Island*) force him into their community, both as hostage and helper in finding the treasure. Though he continues to resist, Jim becomes ever more drawn to the charming but duplicitous Long John Silver, the original one-legged pirate with shoulder-perched talking parrot, until finally Jim agrees to secretly collaborate with Silver. Jim and Silver make a desperate deal that they will help each other survive the other pirates, a deal that Jim knows the self-serving and murderous old pirate will only keep if to Silver's advantage. Yet, despite Silver's transparently evil nature, Jim is fascinated with him (as evidenced by his angry feelings of betrayal at Silver's attentions to another young sea man), and Silver is equally taken with Jim. When threatening the other pirates if they hurt Jim, Silver says "I like that boy, now; I never seen a better boy than that. He's more a man than any pair of rats of you in this here house, and what I say is this: let me see him that'll lay a hand on him" (173). Unlike the relationship between Ralph and Bill in *The Coral Island,* Jim knows that Silver will *never* reform, that he remains an untrustworthy pirate at heart. Jim's (and the novel's) preoccupation with the old pirate, homosocial or homoerotic though it may be, then, instead of showing the desire for reform, shows a fascination with the abject—a love of piracy—an infatuation that neither character, nor reader, nor culture could fully admit.

Such is the high price of colonization for the colonizer, for the struggle to maintain an exploitative system was never without tensions and anxieties, conflicting desires and fears. As shown in chapter 1's analysis of psychical incorporation and mapping and chapter 2's investigation of masculinity and discipline, stories of counterincorporation, as well, helped the anxious imperial culture manage its fears, though in this case fears of losing command of their colonies to native rebellion or colonial conflict. Here the text plays out the fear of loss of control through the threatened fragmentation and consumption of one's body in the body or society of an abhorrent other. The next segment of this developing discussion continues this exploration of how the island nar-

rative aided the management of the anxiety about extra-colonial influence. Chapter 4 focuses on stories of the threatened transformation of
the colonist's body through being marked (tattooed or pierced) or being transformed into something monstrous or animal. The fear I focus
on there is the horror of "going native."

4. "Falling to the Lowest Degree of Brutishness"
Wild Men, Monsters, and the Bestial Taint

WHEN in the last chapter I noted that Gideon Spilett, the leader of Verne's *Mysterious Island* castaways, warns his companions that they need to guard "against enemies from the interior as those from outside" (115), I promised to return to further examine that warning's rather significant phrasing. I was then in the midst of analyzing those enemies "from outside" the island and empire, invading cannibals and pirates. I argued that a fantasy of disciplined body boundaries enables castaway and reader to imagine guarding against those "outside" foes. But I now ask, what about the "enemies from the interior" that Spilett feared? It is likely that Spilett means to refer to the island's own potential (but nonexistent) indigenous people. Yet, keeping in mind that by that point in the narrative Spilett mentally processes his colonization of the island through command of his body, could it be that this fear he voices of "enemies from the interior" also reveals his subconscious fears that his *own body* might betray him? Could it be that Spilett's castaway's extensive efforts to "civilize" the island in fact help to forestall fears (and perhaps fantasies) of being transformed to be more like the island, instead of transforming it to be more like them? Does he (and other castaways) live in terror of "going native"? Suggesting that he does indeed live in terror of "going native" are the castaway's often phobic reactions to other white men who have "gone native" and to the island's nonhuman indigenes, two plot points frequently found in island narratives and the two themes traced in this chapter.

The Mysterious Island provides a strong example of this panic over "going native," for when Verne's castaways (long after Spilett's warning) encounter Ayerton, a tattered and wild-eyed castaway on a nearby islet, they behave as if terrified that they might similarly "go native." They immediately react (perhaps to assuage their alarm) by denying the wild man's humanity; they tell themselves that he is "a savage being, apparently a gigantic ape" and a "monster" in whose "terrible yells . . . there was nothing human" (277).[1] Though upon closer inspection they admit his humanity, they instead rationalize his savagery as resulting from degeneration, which, as Sander Gilman and J. Edward Chamberlin explain in *Degeneration: The Dark Side of Progress* means "to lose the properties of the genus, to decline to a lower type," a less civilized, intelligent, evolved form (ix). Reflecting this notion, Verne's protagonists describe the wild man as "a savage in all the horrible acceptation of the word, and so much the more frightful that he seemed *fallen* to the lowest degree of brutishness!" (278) [emphasis mine]. Reluctant to recognize the wild man as like them, the castaways continue to refer to him as "it" and wonder if he still has a soul or if "the brute instinct alone survived in it" (278).

Before hearing explanations that the wild man (whose name we then learn is Ayerton) gives of his criminal past and descent into despair when cast away on the island, the colonists settle upon the idea that "after having arrived there [on the island] a rational being[,] solitude had reduced him to this condition," an explanation conveniently comforting to castaways stranded as a group (279). Later, the castaways discover other reassuring differences between Ayerton and themselves—differences that, to them, help to explain why he (but not they) could "go native." Primarily they learn of his past criminality, which at that time was thought to result from an embodied depravity resulting in a "criminal stain" which, as Robert Hughes notes in *The Fatal Shore,* was thought to be biologically passed through generations.[2] Supported by studies of craniology (the study of the shape and form of the head) fears of embodied criminality endured well into the twentieth century, and (based on the practice of "racial profiling" in the United States) into the twenty-first century, as well. Ayerton's criminal past, the castaway's think, explains why he lacked the necessary moral fiber to maintain discipline without supervision.

A second possible rationale for why Ayerton would "go native," while the other castaway would not, exists in how he was cast away. Instead of being stranded by an act of God or nature, Ayerton (like the real castaway Selkirk) was purposefully marooned on the island after committing a transgression against his community; he attempted mutiny. Perhaps since his island solitude resulted from crimes against the community instead of from providence bestowing him with an island colony, Ayerton was less able to guard himself against going native. When stranded alone, Ayerton lost the mental and bodily self-discipline necessary to be "civilized," letting his boundaries—both mind and body—become

FIGURE 12. *The Wild Man of Tabor Island* by N. C. Wyeth, from Jules Verne, *The Mysterious Island* (New York: Scribner, 1920), 279.

permeable and letting what the other castaways call the island's "brut-ishness" affect him. Instead of civilizing the island as would a properly disciplined imperial man, that potential colonist/former criminal al-lowed his own degeneration into a savage; Ayerton's corporeal connec-tion to and attempted incorporation of the island, instead of taming it, made him wild.

The notion that Ayerton's degeneration results from an unhealthy relationship with the wild landscape is a colonialist phobia which, as I will show, endured until the twentieth century. This explanation for the wild man's degeneration is underscored in N.C. Wyeth's 1920 Scribner edition illustration of Ayerton, which suggests that the wild man is bod-ily connected to the island (see Figure 12). In the scene, the four adult castaways, upon searching for Herbert, from whom they have become separated while exploring a nearby islet, find him trapped in the wild man's grasp.

As Wyeth illustrates the episode, the man crouches over Herbert, one long-nailed hand covering the boy's face and another pinning down his arm. Though the man's hair looks unkempt, Wyeth depicts him as relatively clean and white in contrast to the book's description of him as having "skin the color of mahogany" (278). Instead of making the wild man's skin dark, Wyeth suggests the man's savagery using another tech-nique—by making him resemble one of the island's natural entities: the large, strong, dark, wild (perhaps mahogany) island tree. By juxtaposing the man's protruding muscles and unkempt hair with the similar fea-tures and composition of the backgrounded tree, Wyeth shows him as not the *color* of mahogany but *like* the mahogany tree, suggesting that the resemblance is more than skin deep. The tree's two main gnarled roots sprawled over a white rock resemble in shape the wild man's muscle-knotted arms and gnarled hands enfolding Herbert's white-shirted body and face. The lines of the tree's gently curving green foliage similarly du-plicate the lines of the wild man's tangled locks, and while the man looks off to the picture's left, the spots of filtered sunlight on the tree form a face-like image on its trunk that also seems to look left. In Wyeth's illus-tration, which enhances the implied bond between the wild man, wild tree, and ultimately wild island, early twentieth-century readers could find visual confirmation of the castaways' theory of degeneration. Be-cause too connected to the island, the wild man has *devolved* into an-other of the island's wild denizens.

Colonial island literature contains other similar stories of a man who has for a time "gone native" (also called "gone primitive," or in Australia "gone tropo" for "gone tropical"), including old Ben Gunn from *Treasure Island* and Prendick at the end of *The Island of Dr. Moreau*. Such tales warn colonial readers against loosening self-discipline of the mind and flesh, which, as the stories show, results in devastating loss of imperial control. This chapter focuses on such plots in order to explore yet another method by which island narratives process imperial fears of loss of colonial authority. Like the last, this chapter explores how island narratives dramatize a castaway repelling threats to his body and speculates that such plots perhaps helped readers to process fears inherent in colonization. Yet here, rather than pirates or cannibals, I examine stories of "going native," which locate this threat *inside* the colonist's incorporative domain, coming internally (from the island and its indigenes) instead of externally (from invaders and outsiders). In such tales, the colonist fears *being transformed* into something wild, like the island and its native, instead of being able to transform Others into being civilized, like him. The connection between his body and the island, the same bond that enables the castaway to transform the island, potentially provides a means for the landscape's "brutishness" to seep into his body if he does not sufficiently discipline body and mind. The beautiful, bountiful island has a feral side, a side that, as this chapter will show, must be tamed, contained, or eradicated, lest it spread to the castaway colonist.

This chapter's analysis divides into three sections, each reading the colonist's interaction with a type of *body:* first the island's "body," next, with the body of what Terry Goldie calls the "indigene," and finally with the colonizer's own body. The chapter begins with exploration of how texts depict "going native" as resulting from a type of infection, of which the island "body" forms the primary source of contagion. Next I examine the colonizer's interaction with the indigenous island native and animal, showing, specifically, how texts represent both as already-infected (and transformed) dangerous carriers (and embodiments) of the island's pathogenic brutishness. The chapter ends with analysis of the castaway's relationship with his own body, examining how he employs the discourse of science to protect his body from degeneration while exploring his own hidden savage desires. Overall, the chapter aims to trace how real-world ambivalence about empire becomes recodified into the fictional colonist's fear and desire for the island, its indigene, and his own body.

"Going Native" and the Infectious Island

Literary accounts of going native have real-world corollaries in cases of "white" men and women who became so attracted to the culture they colonized that they preferred it to their own. These people were regarded as renegades, for as I. C. Campbell explains in *"Gone Native" in Polynesia*, "to have 'gone native' was the mark of degeneration, an act of a man who turned his back on progress, enlightenment, civilization, order, law, and morality and preferred a life of savagery, immorality, paganism, and lawlessness" (4). As Ella Shohat and Robert Stam remark in *Unthinking Eurocentrism*, "going native" "was not in fact an infrequent occurrence during the first centuries of conquest" (72). Shohat and Stam and James Axtell note that the American colonial farmer, Hector de Crevecoeur, in his autobiographical letters described "white Indians," that is, European colonizers who "went native" in such large numbers that laws against "Indianizing" were passed in some American colonies. With the frequency and notoriety of cases of—to pull out a few other terms—South Sea island "beachcombers," North American "Indian traders," or Australian "white black-fellas," it is likely that readers of island narratives had heard some account of the phenomenon, at least with European men.

More unusual would have been the highly publicized case of the Russian *woman*, Isabel Eberhardt, who in 1900 (in)famously deserted colonial society to live the rest of her short life with indigenous Algerians as a native, even over the objections of the French colonial regime. Fluent in Arabic, the controversial Eberhardt converted to Islam, becoming such a devotee that she fought in armed anticolonialist struggles, and lived much of her time in Algeria disguised as a young, male Tunisian scholar, disliked as much by some Muslim Algerians for her gender transgression as she was abhorred by the French colonials for her cultural transgression.[3] In fact, as Annette Kobak remarks, it was Eberhardt's public writing requesting leniency for an Algerian man who tried to assassinate her that brought her to fame as a colonial who had "gone native" and earned her the title "Amazon of the Sahara" (11).

Readers who missed the story of Eberhardt had likely heard another tale of "going native" in the story of the infamous mutiny on the HMS Bounty, one of the most popular and widely discussed island adventures available to readers in a range of print sources, including newspaper stories, Captain William Bligh's own popular accounts, Byron's poem "The Island, or Christian and His Comrades," and dozens of eighteenth- and nineteenth-century retellings. The Bounty's mutinous sailors who "went native" were in the exotic South Seas on a mission to collect breadfruit plants to be transplanted in the West Indies as cheap food for the slaves when they (in)famously rebelled against Bligh's strictures and European law, deciding to live on a South Sea island with native women consorts and without the comforts of the civilization they eschewed. Debates continue as to the causes of the mutiny, but popular opinion holds that, in part, it was triggered by the attractions of Tahitian culture compounded by the distressing proposition of the voyage back to Britain under Captain Bligh. Perhaps to oppose rumors of his cruelty inciting the mutiny, Bligh, in a letter from Batavia of October 13, 1789, following his open boat voyage from Tonga, where he and some of those loyal to him were set adrift by the mutineers, attributes the mutiny to the allure of native Tahitian culture: "I can only conjecture that they [the mutineers] have ideally assured themselves of a more happy life among the Otaheiteans [*sic*] than they could possibly have had in England, which, joined to female connections, has most likely been the leading cause of the whole business" (Robert Langdon, 29).

Also significant is the Crown's reaction to the Bounty crew, for the tribunal disdained as much the mutineers' choice to live as island natives as their actual mutiny. As Caroline Alexander observes in *Bounty: The True Story of the Mutiny on the Bounty,* the Crown tried several sailors who didn't participate in the mutiny but who joined the Bounty crew's island community because there wasn't enough room on Bligh's boats. Though eventually acquitted, their mere habitation in the island community and the fact that, as stated by the presiding counsel, Lord Hood, they "did not surrender themselves [to the officers of the Pandora, the ship that has been sent to capture them] until compelled from necessity" (219) made them suspect. In short, they were court-martialed for not being excited about being brought back to England.[4] In "going native," I. C. Campbell reminds, the men offered "an affront and a challenge to the ethos of Western society, which assumed and asserted a moral and existential superiority over savagery or life in the 'state of nature'" (4). Treason, in this case, would seem to be defined as challenging the notion of the superiority of "civilization" as much as transgressing the Crown's actual authority.

In each of these historical cases, the behaviors of someone *choosing* to go native calls into question the supposed superiority of European cultures, which explains the characteristically ambivalent (or condemning) attitude of nonfictional and fictional texts about people like Eberhardt, the Bounty's sailors, and the men who inspired Kurtz in Joseph Conrad's *Heart of Darkness*. Adam Hochschild in *King Leopold's Ghost* speculates that Conrad based Kurtz, "perhaps the twentieth century's most famous literary villain," on one of several noteworthy real-world colonial administrators who had "gone native" (144). Among these probable Kurtz prototypes Hochschild includes George Antoine Klein, "a French agent for an ivory-gathering firm at Stanley Falls"; Major Edmund Barttelot, "the man whom Stanley left in charge of the rear column on the Emin Pasha expedition" who "went mad, began biting, whipping, and killing people, and was finally murdered"; and Arthur Hodister "famed for his harem of African women and for gathering huge amounts of ivory" (144–45). Yet, Hochschild's bet for the primary inspiration for Kurtz is on Captain Léon Rom, who, like Kurtz, decorated the border of his garden with African heads on stakes (145).

Accounts of those romantic figures who choose to go native also often depicted them as mad, degenerate, and geographically or socially beyond the pale of colonial civilization. Contrasting with such accounts would be cases of European men able to don and slough off "native" guise at will and in the service of empire, such as Sir Richard Burton, who disguised himself as a Sunni Muslim doctor to visit and write about the forbidden city of Mecca in *Personal Narrative of a Pilgrimage to al-Madinah & Meccah,* or T. E. Lawrence, aka "Lawrence of Arabia." Although he was passionately committed to the Arab cause—even unsuccessfully pleading the cause of Arabian independence at the Versailles conference—Lawrence's Egyptian military intelligence work in World War I, his postwar position as adviser on Arab affairs to the British Colonial Office, and his notoriety as a European who could live out the fantasy of going native at will, make him, as well, a "cross-dresser" working in the service of empire. Other "acceptable" instances of Europeans donning native disguise, as Michael Silvestri reminds in "The Thrill of 'Simply Dressing Up'" came in police undercover work and data collection (both thought important to successful rule). The officers' admission that they found dressing in native costume enjoyable, however, was disturbing to imperial decorum.[5]

Paradoxically, stories of degeneration, of "going native" *not* by choice, which often involve being stranded outside civilization, were equally threatening to imperial ideologies. Like Verne's wild man, some solitary castaways, when stranded in nature, lost the tools and markers of civilization, such as language, cultivated dress, and civilized management of the body. Alexander Selkirk, the presumed inspiration for *Robinson Crusoe*, for instance, provides a well-publicized example of the dangers of "degeneration." When rescued from his deserted island after only four years and four months alone (not Crusoe's twenty-eight years), the scruffy Selkirk had nearly lost his power of language. Woodes Rogers, one of Selkirk's rescuers and his first chronicler, described Selkirk upon rescue as "a Man cloth'd in Goat-Skins, who look'd wilder that the first Owners of them" who had "so much forgot his Language for want of Use, that we could scarce understand him" (Megroz, 92, 96). Such stories of men *forgetting* how to be civilized might jeopardize imperial culture because they portray civilization as a veneer quickly worn away if not maintained by a vigilant society, even for white men. Reassuringly countering those cases of degeneration were stories that present being civilized as natural and embodied, as in Edgar Rice Burroughs's character, Tarzan, whose European heritage and bloodline transcend even his simian rearing: Tarzan/Lord Greystoke, after being stranded alone as a child in the African jungle, spontaneously teaches himself to read and displays an innate sense of European honor and justice.[6] Being "civilized" in Burroughs's fantasy is an innate quality that natives could never really acquire but that disciplined white men could never really lose, a fantasy bolstered by doctrines of the chain of being and pseudoscientific arguments of evolutionary racial family trees. That such fictional stories of a white man resisting going native could have soothed nagging fears about the security of imperial power, about influence from the colonized, and about the possibility that white men could degenerate, partially explains the frequency of these stories in colonial literature, including in island fiction.

While reflecting fears about colonial influence, stories of castaways resisting "going native" equally suggest an ambivalence about the underlying colonial civilizing mission, an ambivalence also found in the castaway's behaviors toward and descriptions of his island. From the moment of his acquaintance with it, the castaway both desires and fears the island's possibilities, wanting to own it yet fearing becoming consumed by it. When Crusoe, for instance, first realizes he is on an island, he sees the island's potential consumability (it is "uninhabited" and ripe for colonization) as well as its potential to consume him (he admits being "afraid to lie down on the Ground, not knowing but some wild Beast might *devour* me") (40, emphasis added). As well, later, just after completing a

wall he had worked hard to construct, Crusoe experiences three separate shocks of an earthquake, each one making him increasingly more
terrified, as he puts it, of being "swallow'd up alive" by the island (61). Yet
his feelings remain mixed; his evolving descriptions of the island from
"horrid isle" to "little kingdom" indicate his affection and desire for it.
Despite this fondness and sense of ownership, however, Crusoe continues to neurotically labor to build enclosures and defenses and to civilize
the space and himself, behaving as if the island, if he does not maintain
sufficient control of the space and of himself, is potentially perilous,
not just to his body but to his mind. Like other fictional island castaways, Crusoe's obsessive behavior hints that he fears the island could
transform him into being wild, instead of allowing him to "civilize" it. In
short, he, like other castaways, seems to fear being *infected* by the island
into savagery or madness, a fear enhanced by lack of a European community to help reinforce his psychical ego boundaries, his "civilized"
habitus.[7] Like Ayerton, part of the threat of degeneration Crusoe must
fight comes from solitude.

Crusoe's fears of degeneration were not so different from those
documented and explained in *nonfictional* scientific and medical texts.
Fears of going native and of degeneration would have been exacerbated
by reoccurring debates on the moral decline of the colonial-era European. Lawrence James notes one such debate, which was sparked by the
publication of John Brown's *An Estimate of the Manners and Principles of
the Times* (1757), which "directly attributed the nation's misfortunes to
interior moral weaknesses, in particular among the ruling classes" (74).
As James explains in his discussion of the British Empire, this fear was in
part based on European imperial successes, on the fear of an inevitable
descent from their colonial apogee: "If, as was commonly believed, human development passed through phases of growth, fruition and decay,
then Britain might be approaching the last state" (74). Mrinalini Sinha
notes similar pseudoscientific theories of the "decline and degeneracy"
of the Bengali race into what was seen as its nineteenth-century "effemi-
nacy," a decline that could equally affect the British. In stories of a man
resisting "going native," then, exist fantasies of resistance against the inevitable decline of the so-called center.

Also recodifying fears of colonial degeneration were eighteenth- and
nineteenth-century medical studies focused on describing the dangers
of white colonizers living in "tropical" climates (which was often defined
to include most non-European colonial spaces, including the Americas).

As Warwick Anderson notes, "until the end of the [nineteenth] century, medical experts on the tropics argued that the European's struggle to adapt to the humid, equatorial regions, so unlike those in which the race had evolved, was an impossible one" (511). Hence, as Anderson quips, "the 'white man's grave' was at least as real as the 'white man's burden'" (511). This belief in the menace of colonized lands centered on notions that they transmit disease, an idea which, David Arnold notes, ignored realities of Europe's own epidemiological battles with cholera, smallpox, and plague. "Disease became part of the wider condemnation of African and Asian 'backwardness,'" Arnold remarks, "just as medicine became a hallmark of the racial pride and technological assurance that underpinned the 'new imperialism' of the late nineteenth century" (7).

As well as pathogenic, tropical climates were thought to be dangerous to the mental health and intellect of colonizers. Medical experts considered the landscape itself to be threatening to Europeans because of the heat and intensity of its sun, which was thought to cause lethargy, sickness, and even mental or racial degeneration.[8] These climatic symptoms were thought to explain both the "natural" regressiveness of indigenous people and the dangers to the not-sufficiently disciplined colonizer. In his analysis of early anthropological debates that link degeneration to environment, Brian Street quotes from a relevant discussion held in the first issue of the *Anthropology Review,* where one anthropologist remarked that "cattle taken to America become so stupid that they lose the instinct of self-preservation and the trains on the American railways are obliged to be provided with cattle catchers, as the animals will not get out of the way" (97). Street explains the logic of this inference: "If animals deteriorate because of the American climate, so too do human beings" (97). Such fears over real-world "dangerous" colonized climates both contributed to and mirror the fears of degeneration that island narratives recodify.

Fears of degeneration, Helen Tiffin has shown, were also linked to malaria. In "Metaphor and Mortality," quoting W. H. S. Jones's *Malaria, A Neglected Factor in the History of Greece and Rome* (1907), Tiffin points out that in Greece and Rome, European imperialists found two clear examples of how the tropics could lead white men to degenerate and commit atrocities, resulting eventually in a diseased society. Malaria, so thought Jones and other nineteenth-century specialists in tropical medicine, could leave a "moral taint" in one's blood that could be passed on and "catalyse an atavistic febrility or savagery" (49). Early twentieth-century scientists codified an amorphous fear of the Other and of invasion in a malady called *horror autotoxicus,* a then-newly discovered autoimmune disease, which, Tiffin explains, involved "the attack on the self by one's own system" (50). Through *horror autotoxicus* and theories of malaria, medicine participated in, in Tiffin's words, creating "a (European) history of conquest and colonisation that was ironically reversed" (50), since, as Alfred Crosby has remarked, Europeans and European disease (influenza and smallpox especially) were far more deadly to indigenous people than the reverse. Especially significant to my argument is that, as Tiffin explains, one method of guarding against malaria and *horror auto-toxicus* involved policing "race and colonialist boundaries" and enforcing "the individualist concept of the self, of the body as finitely bounded" (53). In malaria, then, we find a particularly cogent expression of fears of going native, of degeneration, and of colonial contact.

A few fictional island narratives build on this ideology of contagion as expressed in colonial-era scientific discourse, denoting threats of degeneration as an *infection* a white man could catch from contact with a savage landscape, or with savages themselves. H. G. Wells, for instance, uses the notion of contagion to explain Prendick's terror of "going native" in *The Island of Dr. Moreau.* At first, Prendick misconstrues the animals Moreau has tried to humanize as men who have degenerated because of Moreau's scientific experiments, of which Prendick suspects he is the next subject. Of course, in that case, ironically, Moreau and his assistant, Montgomery, would be the "savage" source of infection. When Prendick challenges Moreau and Montgomery to admit to their experiments, he uses a language of infection to explain the degeneration he thinks he's witnessed: "Who are these creatures?" Prendick asks and then himself indignantly answers, "They were men—men like yourselves, whom you have *infected with some bestial taint,* men whom you have enslaved, and whom you still fear" (95, emphasis mine). In his paranoia, Prendick is sure that Montgomery and Moreau mean to equally infect him. He fears that "these sickening scoundrels had merely intended to keep me back, to fool me with their display of confidence, and presently to fall upon me with a fate more horrible than death, with torture, and after torture the most hideous degradation it was possible to conceive—to send me off, a lost soul, a beast, to the rest of their Comus rout" (73–74). Prendick's fears of "the most hideous degradation it was possible to conceive" and "a fate more horrible than death" include panic over loss of control of the body, infection, and perhaps sexual violation.

Prendick's employment of a metaphor of contagion, of "going native" resulting from being "infected . . . with some bestial taint," is significant to understanding his behavior in the last part of the novel when he "goes native" himself. For the ten months after Moreau and Montgomery's deaths until he is rescued from the island, Prendick lives with the animals, as an animal, "an intimate of the these half-humanized brutes, . . . one among the Beast People in the Island of Dr. Moreau" (176, 172). He never seems to fully recover from his period of "going native" and ends the novel back in England but withdrawn from "the confusion of cities and multitudes" (197). He projects fears of his own degeneration onto others, always, he explains, fearing that "the animal was surging up through them [the people he met]; and presently the degradation of the Islanders will be played over again on a larger scale" (190). It is significant that at the novel's end he continues to refer to the process Moreau sees as uplifting the animals to humanity in terms of "the degradation of the islanders," despite knowing that there were no islanders who were degraded—unless he calls being made half human "degrading," a label that the rest of his behavior contradicts. Perhaps what Prendick's language betrays is a need to maintain that fantasy to explain his own conversion to a wild man, to blame someone else for his degeneration and not own up to his own flaws. Since he was never "infected" by Moreau but only by association with the island and animals, for the reader, Prendick's conversion to a wild man suggests that (in accordance with the studies Anderson quotes on the effects of the tropics) degeneration could result simply from being in the island's savage space.

Such significantly recurring language of sanitation and infection used in colonial fiction and nonfiction can be best understood when read against the work of the anthropologist Mary Douglas, who, in her groundbreaking study, *Purity and Danger,* analyzes other instances of the employment of logics of purity and pollution to maintain cultural boundaries. Douglas observes that cultures worldwide create a sense of order by constructing rituals of cleanliness and that societies often manage perceived threats or societal transgressors by labeling them "impure." Beliefs of cleanliness and infection often thinly mask elements of cultural ideology, for, as Douglas theorizes, "some pollutions are used as analogies for expressing a general view of the social order" (3). We see such analogies in island stories, as well, where plots of the castaway risking but resisting infection from "a bestial taint" mask a fear of *cultural* contamination. Fictional tales of infection of the castaway's body stand in for anxieties of "infection" of the island, which represents the larger empire. In other words, stories of potential contamination with elements that could lead to degeneration recodify real-world fears of mutual colonial influence, or hybridity—literally, taking on the culture or even the blood of the colonized. Homi Bhabha and other postcolonial critics often theorize hybridity in terms of a beneficial "third space," a space of free exchange and synergy. Yet because it disturbs fixed racial, ethnic, and national categories, hybridity can also be perceived as personally frightening or culturally threatening (a fact of which we in our supposedly postcolonial world are, unfortunately, reminded all too often). As Leonard Cassuto explains in his analysis of "the grotesque," hybridity disrupts the human need to categorize the world. "The organization that [categories] provide lies at the heart of order," he says, "for without categories the essential distinctions (e.g., good and evil, us and them)—the ones that give rise to further divisions—would not be possible" (8). Stories focused on the castaway's controlled body and his ability to resist going native or infection by the island's brutishness often dramatize fears of hybridity or of cultural contamination. In such tales, the possibility of mutual cultural exchange becomes a type of contagion that must be contained, resisted, or inoculated against in order to maintain the strength of the empire and the purity of the colonizing "race." Just as the stories of the successful repelling of cannibalism and piracy bolster the myth of an impervious empire, these tales of the man who does *not* go native or become infected with the savagery of the island solidify that myth of unidirectional influence. But first, the castaway has to defend himself against the sources of that potential infection, both the island and its natives and animals.

The Infectious Indigene

Island texts presenting the castaway's battle with dangerous contagion often represent indigenous inhabitants as embodiments of the island's (in Verne's words) "brutishness" and as potentially threatening *carriers* of that contagion. Again, this fictional trend reflects sociopsychological ideas found recorded in scientific discourse, specifically perceptions of indigenous people as contagious. Warwick Anderson, for instance, has remarked on cases of real-world fears of infection becoming transferred in the early twentieth century from anxiety over the landscape to suspicion of the colonized body, as medical communities began to examine native *bodies,* as well as the environment, as carriers of disease. Though Anderson's work focuses on early twentieth-century medical discourse, we can see the same type of shift of anxiety from threatening landscape to infected colonized body in fiction long before his twentieth-century nonfictional examples. When they do include indigenous islanders, eighteenth- and nineteenth-century narratives often depict colonized bodies as "contagious," as carriers of degeneration, just like the island that transformed/infected those bodies.

Typically, island texts present a world where castaway colonists can resist infection from the island, but where indigenous islanders have not or *cannot* withstand degeneration, perhaps because of their long exposure to the island, but surely, as well, because of their lack of body discipline. Before the castaway arrives and the drama begins, the indigene has already been infected by the island's savagery and has already had his body mutated as a result of the contamination, an a priori situation the island texts reflect through the indigene's savage demeanor. In short, the texts show the colonist as having the ability to close his body boundaries to exclude dangerous elements, just as he has the ability to bring the objects he desires within those boundaries, yet the indigene, who lacks such discipline and command over his body boundaries, also lacks this ability to resist infection from the island.

Such a notion of the indigene as "open" to infection and transformation by the island, while the disciplined colonist is "closed" are reflected in typical depictions of bodies in the stories. Though not directly discussing colonial literature, Mikhail Bakhtin's explanations of literary portrayals of open and closed bodies in *Rabelais and His World* are useful for clarifying these concepts and how they relate to colonial fantasies of naturalized control, despite the fact that Rabelais was writing in the early- to mid-sixteenth century, slightly before the increase in island narrative production (after More's *Utopia,* but 60 years before *The Tempest* and 160 years before *Robinson Crusoe*). In his analysis, Bakhtin distinguishes between what he calls "grotesque" bodies common in medieval literature and modern, closed bodies. The latter parallel perceptions of the body I have been discussing as masculine and self-disciplined. As Bakhtin explains, textual depictions of grotesque bodies stress their openness, with gaping orifices (mouth, nose, eyes, genitals) and protruding parts (belly, nose, buttocks, mouth, phallus, breasts, tongue, teeth)—as he says, "that which protrudes from the body, all that seeks to go out beyond the body's confines" (226). Texts often portray grotesque bodies' boundaries (including boundaries between the body and the outer natural world, and between the body's inner and outer spaces) as more fluid than those of the "Modern" body. The grotesque body's surface, he says, naturally *reflects* its interior, blurring distinctions between inner cavities and outer surfaces, as "outward and inward features are often merged into one" (227). Similar portrayals of indigenous bodies fill island narratives, which often represent such bodies as open and grotesque (like those Bakhtin analyzes) and, as I will momentarily show, animalistic or monstrous. These stories show indigenes as indiscriminate in what they eat and of voracious appetite, with open mouths and naturally permeable inside and outside boundaries. Their open and undisciplined bodies make them vulnerable to the island's infectious savagery. Moreover, the corporeal openness that makes island indigenes potentially infectious also places the culpability for their infection *on them*, which further reassures readers that the colonizer's closed, disciplined body ensures his (and their own) safety from going native.

Illustrating this idea of the "open" indigenous body is Tommo's description of the native women boarding the ship in Melville's *Typee* as naked, innocent, and ignorant of the danger from the "bachelor sailors" (117), receptive to the male colonizer, and completely without boundaries: "Not the feeblest barrier was interposed between the unholy passions of the crew and their unlimited gratification" (118). Tommo sees their bodies as open to infection, which he sees, ironically, as coming *from the colonizers*, an attitude not atypical in colonial literature critical of colonial competition. He exclaims,

Alas for the poor savages when exposed to the influence of these *polluting* examples! Unsophisticated and confiding, they are easily led into every vice, and humanity weeps over the ruin thus remorselessly inflicted upon them by their European civilizers. Thrice happy are they who, inhabiting some yet undiscovered island in the midst of the ocean, have never been brought into *contaminating* contact with the white man. (118, emphasis added)

Tommo at first sees "European civilizers" (excepting himself, of course, as an American) as the source of the pollution and the island as benign, but as the novel progresses and he becomes more and more entranced with the Typees, he risks "going native" himself. To counter that possibility, the novel transfers the source of contagion from the colonizer to the island and transmutes the threat to Tommo from the seductive Typee woman to the violent cannibal man, allowing the novel to remove Tommo from the threat of "going native" by a simple physical escape from the Typees. With the threat reconfigured, the danger of Tommo longing for the Typee culture disappears; he can safely and completely return (physically and emotionally) to European civilization, secure in his identity. Of course, such textual depictions of indigenes' bodies as nonthreatening and open—demonstrated by their lack of clothing, their lack of defenses and armor, their lack of civilized body discipline— enhance the fantasy of their being naturally open to positive "civilizing" colonial influence, as well.

Not all island texts narrate a castaway's contact with indigenous peo- ple, but nearly all do include an encounter between the castaway and some sort of animal. And an island's *animals* (according to these stories) can embody or carry an island's infectious savagery just as a human can. Island texts typically present both native and animal as always/already "infected"; they don't *degenerate* because, as island denizens, they are *al- ready* savage or animalistic before the narrative commences. In *The Mys- terious Island,* for instance, when Gideon Spilett cautions his comrades that they need to defend against threats from within and without, Pen- croft replies that they will also need to "fortify ourselves against savages with two legs as well as against savages with four," a comment reflecting tendencies of that narrative and others to amalgamate an island's na- tives and its animals (115). Through such statements and, as I will show, castaways' similar behavior toward animals and natives alike, island nar- ratives depict island animals and natives as equally indigenous, as shar- ing savagery and a mutual innate relationship to the island (a portrayal I foreground by referring to both indigenous human and animal island- ers as "indigenes"). Just as island narratives symbolize the colonizer's compulsion for control of the island through his ability to discipline his own body, they recodify the colonist's ambivalence about the island and colonial mission into the body of the indigene.

Stressing similarities between animals and natives, island narratives depict both indigenes as sharing an embodied savagery and assert the physiological differences of both from colonizers, even further reassur- ing the colonist of his innate protection from degeneration. As Robert J. C. Young's *Colonial Desire* notes, this logic is related to the many eigh- teenth- and nineteenth-century discussions of the colonizing European white man as being of a different *species* from the colonized. According to Young, proponents of this position, such as Morton, argued that the off- spring of the union between the "white" and "black" races would be less vigorous, just as the offspring between a donkey and a horse (two different species) results in the sterile mule. This logic, again, naturalizes cultural and economic distinctions. Depicting natives and animals as kindred allows the text an even greater fantasy of control over the indigene's body (the natural hierarchy of man over beast), making the possibility of going native—of being seduced by the indigene—less threatening. Examples of texts transposing animals and natives fill island narratives, most obviously in *The Island of Dr. Moreau,* in Prendick's labeling of the animals as natives and in Wells's use of animals to play out what is essentially a colonial story. Such a correlation between natives and animals, of course, would reinforce popular and well-documented colonial-era misperceptions of race, evident in pseudoscientific racial family trees that show black Africans and aboriginal Australians as existing on a developmental continuum with simians and protohumans. "Savage" and "civilized" thus become code for race, for some found in the publication of Darwin's *The Origin of Species* in 1859 confirmation of a naturally ordered social hierarchy, with adult white male humans at the apex of the tree.

We also see such transposition in castaway tales, such as *The Mysterious Island,* that create clear connections between animals and humans through their *descriptions* of both. In *The Mysterious Island,* Jup, the wild ape that the castaways capture as he defends their cave from other invading and pointlessly destructive apes, plays a role that in other imperial narratives is played by indigenous humans.[9] The novel never explains Jup's motives for defending the castaways' cave, but nevertheless, by fighting his own kind (apes) to help the humans, Jup corresponds to the collaborating colonized, the "colon" or "brown bourgeoisie," that is the indigenous person who works with the colonizers against his own people. After helping the castaways, Jup becomes elevated from jungle ape to almost-human house slave, a plot device transparently allegorizing the enslavement of African people, the fiction of "civilizing" the colonized, and the trope of the African as simian. The novel, in fact, employs a discourse of eugenics to compare Jup to Africans and Australian Aborigines from its first description of him as "belong[ing] to the family of anthropoid apes, of which the facial angle is not much inferior to that of the Australians and Hottentots. . . . It is to this family of the anthropoid apes that so many characteristics belong which prove them to be possessed of an almost human intelligence" (215). The novel also consistently compares Jup to its one character of color, Neb, the African-American servant who comes to the island when loyally following his former owner, Cyrus Harding. The novel frequently refers to Jup as Neb's (but not the "white" characters') "friend" and equal, playing out scenes where both ape and black man serve as house servants for their white masters. By animalizing Neb and humanizing Jup, the novel *naturalizes* the servitude of both indigene and black man, showing them both as willing servants who are (or seem to be) biologically distinct from/inferior to the white men. Though Neb, as "indigene," is not actually an island native, his African heritage and race seem to serve the same purpose for the novel of establishing his previous savage infection and degeneration.

Such textual efforts to animalize indigenous people contribute to the naturalizing of colonial control by reinforcing the fantasy that one can *see* savagery, a fantasy playing into the colonizer's desire for protection from savage contagion. Simply, the texts show internal attributes (i.e., presence or absence of body discipline and "civilized" culture) manifest on the exterior of the body. The tactic of creating a fictional character's visage to mirror his morality is common in fiction, but I argue that here the logic goes deeper, literally, in that these texts portray characters' very bodies as constructed by a priori infection from savagery; the same infection that threatens to transform the fictional colonizer's body has already transformed the indigene and also governs the relationship of both with the island. Whereas the castaway colonist can command and incorporate the island, the indigene is commanded and incorporated by it.

Though indigenes are savage in these stories, they are not always unattractive. Just as island texts split their portrayals of pirates and cannibals into reformed and irredeemable characters, they split their depictions of indigenes to resemble what Rousseau famously termed the "noble savage" (innocent, beautiful, and good) and the "ignoble" savage (ugly, depraved, and bad).[10] We can see a fine example of the split between the noble and ignoble indigene in Jonathan Swift's parody of the island genre, *Gulliver's Travels*. Perhaps to lampoon the island narrative genre's habit of linking native and animal indigenes, Swift makes his noble indigenes literally animals (the beautiful, gentle, and intelligent Houyhnhnms) and his ignoble indigenes human (the ugly, violent, and incorrigible Yahoos). In his efforts to psychically distinguish himself from the Yahoos, Gulliver ironically draws upon that same logic, depicting the Yahoos as irredeemable animals, calling them "animals," "beasts," and "monsters" and describing their beards as "like a goat's," their climbing as like a squirrel's, calling their nails "claws," their arms "fore feet," hands "forepaws," and breasts "dugs." And whereas in typical colonial island narratives, the castaway feels himself superior to the animal/animalized indigene, Gulliver longs to mimic and be accepted by the superior equine Houyhnhnms, thus inverting tropes of the closed, disciplined, and noble human form. Swift's reversal, as well as parodying this literary trope, also attests to its vigor and might.

One of the most important functions of noble and ignoble indigenes in island narratives comes from their furnishing a body with which the castaway (and vicariously, the reader) can interact. We can understand the indigene as an "imago" of the island, that is, as a filter for the castaway's expectations and unconscious fantasies about the island and his relationship to it. The noble indigene provides a form for the castaway to literally embrace (allowing him to enact his/the reader's longing), while the ignoble indigene provides a form for him to discard or harm (allowing him to relieve his/the reader's apprehension). By embodying the island and the colonizer's fears and desires in the indigene, narratives can better demonstrate the fictional colonizer managing those fears. As well as controlling his own body and thus protecting himself from savagery, he can handle (consume or kill) the body of an Other to inoculate against another potential source of infection and, thus, completely protect himself, his body, and his culture from going native. Yet because the island that becomes embodied through this fantasy is also sutured to the castaway's own body (through the processes of incorporation discussed in chapter 1), his complicated interaction with the indigene is on one level an interaction with the ghosts (demons and angels) of his own psyche.

The purpose of each character is manifest in its exterior beauty or monstrosity, so noble indigenes are typically beautiful, as is the case in Robert Paltock's often-overlooked castaway tale *The Life and Adventures of Peter Wilkins* (1749). Stranded on an island, Peter Wilkins encounters the beautiful Glumms and Gawreys, a cultured but troubled race of graceful and classically dressed winged beings, who, despite their extraordinary flying abilities, are technologically and socially less "evolved" than the eighteenth-century England that Paltock left behind. Impressed by his knowledge of technology and believing him to be the leader forecast in an ancient prophesy, the noble Glumms and Gawreys decide that Wilkins should lead their society, whereupon he resolves their societal conflicts and begins a civilizing mission. In this version of the castaway tale, the castaway marries one of the noble indigenes, and then by "divine right," (forecast in their religion) justifiably consumes/colonizes their entire society, an imperial fantasy indeed.

Philip Quarll and Beaufidell.

Also beautiful and desirable are noble *animal* indigenes, like the monkey Beaufidell in Peter Longueville's castaway tale *The Hermit* (1727). Beaufidell (whom Quarll names for his *beauty* and *fidel*ity) provides the perfect companion for Quarll, "a Companion far exceeding any ever he had . . . a beautiful Monkey of the finest kind and the most compleat of the Sort, as tho' made to manifest the unparallel'd Skill of Nature" and "sent him by Providence to dissipate his Melancholy" (248). It is significant that Quarll describes Beaufidell as "sent by Providence," implying that nature or God blesses and encourages their relationship and that Beaufidell exists for his pleasure, to be used (symbolically consumed) as Quarll wishes.

Beaufidell's great beauty combined with his superior companionship, "far exceeding" the three duplicitous wives Quarll had before being shipwrecked, places him in the role of supplementary companion (wife) and creates in him the embodiment of Quarll's desire for the island.[11] Yet, the novel eliminates the possibility of the ultimate consummation of Quarll and Beaufidell's affection by killing off the monkey, though Quarll's chaste affection endures and Beaufidell's death haunts Quarll for the rest of the narrative. In Beaufidell, Quarll has a creature of the island with which he can interact, creating a vehicle and object for his desire. That the novel places Beaufidell, an animal, in this role hints at an underlying cultural ambivalence about the island and suggests fears of being seduced by the indigene into going native; an animal, presumably, would be less likely to seduce Quarll into going native than a human indigene, and Beaufidell, as an animal, would exist naturally under Quarll's human authority, just another of the island's "resources" to exploit. Yet in its need to remove temptation even further by transforming Beaufidell from flesh to memory, the novel attests to the slippage between human and animal indigenes that can make animals, in their symbolic role, also dangerously seductive.

Quarll's description of Beaufidell as noble indigene and consumable helpmate is enhanced by a frontispiece illustration of Quarll and Beaufidell from the 1786 Harrison and Co. edition (see Figure 13). The illustration presents a closely framed scene of domestic harmony and castaway authority, important in an edition published soon after the

FIGURE 13. *Opposite,* "Philip Quarll and Beaufidell" from Peter Lonqueville, *The Hermit* (London: N. Merridew, 1727), frontispiece. By permission of the Hubbard Imaginary Voyages Collection, Special Collections Library, University of Michigan.

British loss of its American colonies and coinciding with British colonial expansion into a new colonial island, Australia. The similarly posed man and monkey both carry wood to their home, but Beaufidell plays the role of the loyal mate, walking on dainty paws to follow Quarll and demurely carrying his burden of wood like an offering to his master. Quarll carries the phallic ax, marking his superior status as civilized human male and his power over Beaufidell.

The mirrored posture of man and simian serves two purposes, first emphasizing what Erving Goffman refers to as the figures' relative size (28), meaning that the picture demonstrates Quarll's domination of Beaufidell by his superior size in the picture as well as by his human masculinity contrasted with the feminized simian. Secondly, the upright stance, unnatural for a monkey, attests to Beaufidell's training and suitability as helpmate. But like the colonized person he stands for, his attempts to mimic the colonizer only reaffirm his "natural" inferiority through his failure to *be* human. As well, the drawing showcases other results of Quarll's labor, devoting nearly half its frame to his orderly settlement and other domesticated animals amidst the lush island background. The framing of the image by the borders of the drawing and the trees at either side, the leaves across the top, and the shadow across the bottom, offers a packaged image of domestic harmony to the reader, one easily "consumed" in a glance, like the island in the monarch-of-all-I-survey moment.

The figures' direction of gaze enhances the fantasy that the illustration presents, for while Beaufidell looks at Quarll, Quarll looks at the reader in (borrowing Kress and Van Leeuwen's term) direct address (122), allowing the reader to identify with Quarll (but not with Beaufidell), imagining ourselves as the owners/incorporators of that fine colonial display and of that desirable, obedient, and exploitable animal. Such illustrations would provide a vehicle for fantasies of the family, perhaps a lesson for the good English patriarch reading the book to his family in the parlor by the fire.

In contrast with the noble indigene, the ignoble indigene provides a body for the castaway colonizer to interact with his *fear* of the island (and of going native). Like the noble indigene, the ignoble indigene's body manifests his previous savage infection, so that his internal threat becomes visible externally, often through violently animalistic behavior, body marking, or monstrous traits. These texts display ignoble indigenes' unsuitability for becoming civilized on the surface of their bodies; they could never be "almost but not quite, almost but not white" because the natural differences between the ignoble indigene and the colonizer are insurmountable. Island texts often depict the ignoble indigene as incorrigibly animalistic, as voluntarily and excessively marked, and as monstrous.

As they do with cannibals and pirates, island narratives frequently depict ignoble indigenes with body marking, such as tattooing and body painting, which colors, darkens, or racializes their skin. As discussed in chapter 3, in addition to enhancing their nonwhiteness and marking their readiness for warfare with the castaway, body painting in these texts can suggest characters' resemblance to animals, monsters, or demons. In *The Coral Island,* for instance, Ralph compares the war-painted natives to demons:

> They wore grotesque warcaps made of various substances and decorated with feathers. Their faces and bodies were painted as to make them look as frightful as possible; and as they brandished their massive clubs, leaped, shouted, yelled, and dashed each other to the ground, I thought I had never seen men look so like demons before. (249)

Body painting here externalizes the corruption of the native soul—sometimes monstrous as well as savage.

Tattooing provides a crucial method of characterization in *Typee* as well, for the more threatening a Typee person is, the more tattooing Tommo describes him/her as having, while those he admires most he describes as hardly marked. As Leonard Cassuto asserts, tattooing in real-world encounters was thought to mark savagery, for early naturalists "saw tattooing as 'the ultimate sign of primitiveness'" and atavism (191). In *Typee,* though, tattooing and body painting come to be such overdetermined symbols of the fears that are placed onto the indigene that the markings *themselves* seem to threaten transformation into savagery. In an oft-analyzed scene Tommo quickly becomes aware that a Typee tattoo artist wants to tattoo his face.[12] Tommo reacts with panic, as if the tattooing, which represents his fear, could actually infect him with the taint of savagery. "Horrified at the bare thought of being rendered hideous for life if the wretch were to execute his purpose upon me" he says, "I struggled to get away from him" (346). When the tattoo artist touches Tommo's face to indicate where the marks might go, Tommo flees the scene "half wild with terror and indignation" (346), for the Typee tattooing (and perhaps the man's touch) represents not just racialized disfigurement but potential degeneration. The tattooing, which involves injecting plant dye under the skin, could infect Tommo with a "bestial taint," making him into a "savage" if for no other reason than that he would be henceforth rejected by civilized society. As he explains his panic, he admits "I now felt convinced that in some luckless hour I should be disfigured in such a manner as never more to have the *face* to return to my countrymen" (347, emphasis original). Not only would the Typees' savagery taint him, but like the indigene, his savagery would be externally visible. He would, in short, become monstrous.

Here Be Monsters

Some island texts even more clearly code characters' ignobility by making the indigene an actual monster (making the figurative literal), thus naturalizing distinctions between colonizer/colonized and noble/ignoble indigene into distinctions between human and monster, earthly and supernatural. Monsters provide a comforting fantasy that would make colonial readers feel even more secure from devolving into that type of native.[13] Monsters, of course, have been present in literature of exploration as long as it has existed. The travel tales of Pliny, Aethicus, Solinus, Marco Polo, and Herodotus all contain accounts of monsters. Herodotus's, for example, contains accounts of gold-digging ants and dog-headed men. The widest array of monsters perhaps comes in the travel narrative of Sir John Mandeville, who in a one-page gloss of monstrous island people, tells of giant Cyclops, headless creatures with eyes in their shoulders and mouths in their chests, headless people with eyes and mouths in their backs, mouthless pygmies, giant-eared people, horse-footed people, hermaphrodites, one-giant-footed beings, and people who consume nourishment by smelling instead of eating (137). These tales and others of their ilk create a tradition of describing alterity in terms of monstrosity, a tradition island narratives continue and draw upon in their own portrayal of alterity. Typically, castaways encountering a monster indigene respond to him as a perversion of nature, as an embodied evil and embodied savagery. These monstrous island indigenes are portrayed as always/already "infected" by the island's most sinister and savage aspects, thus recodifying the imperial fear of the unknown into the body of the monstrous indigene and allegorizing conflicts between colonizer and colonized as battles between man and monster, good and evil. We see this dichotomy at work most famously in *The Tempest*. At the play's first mention of Caliban, Prospero calls him "not honoured with/ A human shape" (1.2.283–84) and, though the play several times describes him in animalistic terms ("tortoise" [1.2.316], "fish" [2.2.24], "mooncalf" [2.2.102]), it most often describes him as monstrous. In act 2 scene 2 alone, Trinculo and Stephano refer to Caliban as a monster ten times, making of the word "monster" a sort of mantra, reinforcing the reader/viewer's mental conception of Caliban as monstrous, unnatural, and evil, as if to contradict perceptions of the human actor playing him. The play links Caliban's grotesque external form to his internal evil by explaining his monstrosity as resulting from his hybridity, for Caliban was "got by the devil himself" (1.2.319–20) and a witch, which makes him a "demi-devil" (5.1.272). Caliban's demonic parentage and monstrosity, as well as representing his ignobility, form his hybridity, which, in colonial culture, was dangerous.

Other monstrous hybrids exist in colonial island narratives, including *The Life and Astonishing Adventures of John Daniel,* which dramatizes one colonizer's discovery that exterior monstrous forms code internal savagery and dangerous hybridity. As I explained in chapters 1 and 2, after John Daniel "discovers" that his fellow castaway, "Thomas," is a woman, Ruth, they marry and have a family. One of their sons, Jacob, builds a flying machine that accidentally takes him and his father off of the island into global adventure. On one of these excursions, they crash on another island and encounter a family of humanoid sea monster indigenes. As John Daniel describes them:

They bore the exact resemblance of the human species in their erect posture and limbs, save their mouths were as broad as their whole faces, and had very little chins; their arms seemed all bone, and very thin, their hands had very long fingers, and webbed between with long claws on them, and their feet were just the same, with very little heel; their legs and thighs long, and straight, with strong scales on them, and the other parts of their bodies were exactly human but covered with the same hair as a seal. (Morris, 190)

The illustrations accompanying the description, one reprinted here from a 1926 R. Holden edition, which was also in the original 1751 edition (see Figure 14), embellish this description, allowing the reader to see the sea monster's alterity. The book includes separate pictures of the male and female adult sea monsters, not enacting a scene from the story but merely offered as illustration of a specimen for the prurient, much like anatomical drawings in books of natural history or anthropological accounts, which were gaining popularity in the mid-eighteenth century when this narrative was first published. The monster's stance—naked

in a one-quarter pose, providing a complete view of his anatomy while still modestly concealing his genitalia—mirrors other illustrations of indigenous people or animals in volumes of natural history. Yet his very nakedness attests to his alterity, for it is unlikely that any nineteenth-century novel would include a picture of a naked, white, human male in its pages. Following the textual description closely, including scaly skin, wide mouth, and elongated limbs, the illustration positions the monstrous figure with hands aloft and fingers spread so that we can note their webbing, as we can in his feet. The rocky background and foreground of the picture that frames the figure also plays a part in this colonialist tableau, giving the impression that the reader observes the sea monster from a hidden vantage point behind the rocks, as if the reader were an anthropologist in the field observing a particularly interesting new specimen of "primitive" colonized or colonizable natives.

Much of the encounter between John Daniel and the sea monsters in the text revolves around speculations as to the cause of the monsters' strange form. The male sea monster explains that the monstrous shapes of himself and his sister (who is also his wife) result from their mother being scared by a sea monster while pregnant. John Daniel soon discovers, however, the true (but unknown to the monsters) origin of their monstrosity when he finds their mother's diary, where she, who calls herself "a child of hell, and companion of demons" confesses that she "embrace[d] a sea monster" (223). As she explains, "I cast off my love to my husband, that dear husband, and entered into criminal commerce with this brute, this beast, this devil, this monster; nay, nor could I be satisfied without a daily repetition of my crime, till I became fruitful by him" (223–24). The novel, thus, explains how it is that the monsters' form reveals their internal depravity by genetic association, for like Caliban, this man-monster and his sister-wife are monster-human hybrids, resulting from the deviant sex of their mother. As well, the man-monster and his sister-wife are further depraved, since they create other monstrous hybrids (their children) through their own incestuous union. In their hybridity, the novel recodifies colonial fears of miscegenation and "unnatural" love (bestiality and incest) as well as fears of cultural influence and degeneration, all so threatening to colonial order that they become

FIGURE 14. *Opposite,* illustration of the male sea monster by Mr. Boitard, from Ralph Morris, *A Narrative of the Life and Astonishing Adventures of John Daniel* (London: R. Holden, 1926), 191. By permission of the Hubbard Imaginary Voyages Collection, Special Collections Library, University of Michigan.

textually symbolized as monstrosities. In order to uphold the fiction of mutually exclusive colonizing and colonized cultures, true hybrids (not just those who could "pass"), as transgressors of cultural boundaries, must be represented as monstrous.

Moreover, because the monsters issue from the female libido that can't be satisfied, they also evoke patriarchal fears of ambiguous paternity. As Marie Hélène Huet explains in *Monstrous Imagination,* this fear is typical in stories of monstrosity, for "instead of reproducing the father's image, as nature commands, the monstrous child bore witness to the violent desires that moved the mother at the time of conception or during pregnancy . . . the monster thus erased paternity and proclaimed the dangerous power of the female imagination" (1). David Williams also notes in *Deformed Discourse* that the Bible's explanation of monsters links them to unnatural sexuality, since they supposedly resulted from Cain's sexual contact with the beasts that lived east of Eden. From this union, Williams reminds, "there arose a race of beings of mixed natures, human and animal. This story is crucial in the Western tradition of monstrosity, for it identifies the moment and the act by which monsters come into physical being in the world" (116–17). In the notion of monsters resulting from contact with the biological and religious Other could be read warnings against miscegenation with the colonial Other. Of course, these stories could have also merely provided justification for disavowing the offspring of forbidden unions.

Interestingly, the tale precedes John Daniel's discovery of the monster's origins with what at first seems to *question* the notion that one's outside accurately reflects one's internal characteristics. Before John Daniel hears the true story of the sea monster's parentage, he at length reassures the sea monster of his humanity. In pity, John Daniel tells the monster "to look upon himself as one of the most reasonable creatures in the creation, but somewhat only diversified in parts from others of them" (Morris, 213) and even enters into a ruse with the sea monster to act before the monstrous children as if their form were superior to John Daniel's human one, though this scene, instead, serves to showcase John Daniel's compassion before his ultimate repudiation of the monsters. Despite the brief pretense, by so clearly linking the sea monsters' forms to their demonic parentage, the tale ultimately reinforces the fantasy that exterior monstrosity reveals some sort of internal depravity and that the colonizer is biologically and morally distinct from the colonized. Complicating this notion, however, is the fact that the sea monsters throughout behave nobly, not suddenly exhibiting threatening behavior (like the Typees) before the protagonist's repudiation of them. Nevertheless, by connecting monstrosity to island indigeneity, the tale implies that native bodies (presented so often as naturally different from the colonizer's) externalize internal corruption, further justifying the colonist's mistreatment of indigenous people and providing additional reassurance against the colonist ever going native. To reinforce the novel's use of the monsters to code depravity, John Daniel, once he knows about the sea monster's demonic parentage, alters his reactions to him, as evident in his references to the creature, which change from the friendly and tolerant "my host" or "my companion" to the repudiative "the monster." Significantly, the tale's assertion of biological distinctions separating John Daniel from the sea monster is actually undercut by his subsequent refusal to associate with him, for to protect himself from going native, it seems that biological distinction must be reinforced by physical and social separation (just as in the colonies, housing communities and colonial social clubs enabled the segregation of colonial officers and their families from indigenous societies). Like Tommo, who had to ultimately leave the Typees, John Daniel and Jacob must ultimately declare the monstrous indigenes abhorrent, not appealing, and must leave the island and the lonely sea monsters behind.

As suggested in John Daniel's initial and dangerous attraction for the sea monster family, stories of the ignoble indigene are fraught with moments of ambivalence, for as with pirates and cannibals, the colonist also *desires* the exotic, dangerous, and exciting *ignoble* indigene, whether in the form of cannibals, animals, monsters, or tattooed warriors.[14] As well as providing moments of passion and action in the narrative, ignoble indigenes can transgress the boundaries that the colonizer can't and, so can become figures for imaginatively acting out transgressive desires. Thus, the Calibans of the island are often the most vivid, interesting, and (to modern audiences, at least) appealing of the island figures. As Jeffrey Cohen explains, "the same creatures who terrify and interdict can evoke potent escapist fantasies; the linking of monstrosity with the forbidden makes the monster all the more appealing as a temporary egress from constraint" (16–17). Like the stories of white cannibalism and forced piracy, stories of the ignoble savage allow the reader to momentarily experience what the novels present as the raw thrill of the colonial encounter.

Like the cannibal, the pirate, and the wild man, the monster represents confusion of the boundaries of the imperial self with its Other and embodies the uncomfortable admission of the mystical unknown, just as in the cartographic phrase "Here be monsters," marking the limits of charted, thus knowable, territory. The monster, thus, provides another figure to be blamed and rejected, the ultimate overdetermined symbol for a variety of fears and phobias of empire. It is interesting to note, as well, that in at least two island narratives, *The Tempest* and *The Life and Astonishing Adventures of John Daniel*, the castaway doesn't kill the monster but instead leaves it behind on the island, perhaps prefiguring the colonial use of the island as prison (like Robbin Island, Van Dieman's Land, Norfolk Island, and Alcatraz) for the worst transgressors of empire.

The Ambivalent Colonizer: Savage Play and Reestablishment of Order

Matching the fictional colonist's vacillation about the savagery of the natives and animals he encounters is his ambivalence about the savagery in himself. He (like Dr. Jekyll) is fascinated by his own "savage" aspects as much as he wants to tame them and is equally attracted to the savage side of the island. This allure of the savage exists in nonfictional imperial adventure, too, for in the real world, the thrill of the safari, the tiger hunt, or the colonial commission comes in its promise of adventure and danger combined with the challenge to conquer, tame, or kill the uncivilized. Likewise, though part of the fun for readers of island narratives lies in seeing the colonist prove his worth and display his cleverness when faced with the challenges of the uncivilized world, an equal source of appeal comes from experiencing the uncivilized and savage in safety, that is, through acts of reading. Colonial readers, through castaway narratives, could fantasize about testing themselves against nature and experiencing their own savage alter egos. Yet, paradoxically, the texts must ultimately promote the superiority of and return to civilization; colonist and reader can *play* native but certainly not *go* native. Recognizing this permeable and delicate boundary between playing and going native helps to explain why narratives at some points blur partitions between native/civilized, animal/man and at other points redraw those lines with, as I will soon demonstrate, the quill of masculine science.

Defoe's creation of Crusoe's goatskin clothes, for instance, relates to such a desire to safely experience savagery. As I argue in chapter 2, Crusoe feels compelled to clothe himself in order to maintain his status as a civilized man, for clothing affirms strong and controlled corporeal boundaries. Yet by taking the skin and fur of an animal onto his body, especially to make clothes he describes as "of a barbarous shape," Crusoe can experiment with his own savage side, can play an elaborate game of dress-up as native or animal. Three hundred years of illustrated interpretations of the novel emphasize Crusoe's animality, showing a greatly be-whiskered Crusoe (possessing "Scissars and Razors sufficient" Crusoe chooses to grow his whiskers long, as he describes as "of a Length and Shape monstrous enough . . . [that] in England would have pass'd for frightful") in a very furry goatskin costume (despite the tropical climate, he leaves the fur on the skins) (109). It is while dressed in animal skins, looking like an animal, that Crusoe performs his "civilized" tasks—sowing seeds, shooting his gun, recoiling in horror from cannibalism—as if to remind readers that characters (and readers) can experiment with their natural or uncivilized side as long as they behave in such a manner as to maintain the discipline that guards against savage infection.[15] The novel's repeated visual and literary connection between Crusoe and goats expresses the castaway's and the culture's mixed feelings toward "savagery," for while the worst fate was *going* native, *playing* native provided a most thrilling experience.

In fact, throughout the novel, Defoe continually juxtaposes the human Crusoe with animals, with the effect of both asserting and questioning human/animal distinctions. Two encounters stand out among the others as moments when Crusoe feels especially kindred with animals, the first being when the castaway Crusoe is stunned to hear a voice calling out *"Robin Crusoe*, poor *Robin Crusoe*, where are you *Robin Crusoe?* Where are you? Where have you been?"* (104). The voice turns out to be that of his parrot, Poll, but Crusoe's initial shock turns to identification and affection, as he feels related to the only other creature on the island (at that point) able to speak. Crusoe's second encounter comes after he has seen both the footprint and the remains of cannibalism (but not the cannibals). He discovers a new cave, and entering it, sees "two broad shining Eyes of some Creature, whether Devil or Man I knew not," hears "a very loud Sigh, like that of a Man in some Pain," and becomes terrified, "struck with such a Surprize, that it put me into a cold Sweat" (128,129). This human-like animal turns out to be a dying old he-goat, which Crusoe, in a moment of compassion, tries to help get out of the cave. Crusoe finally buries the old goat in the cave, which he then claims as one of his new homes. Though he explains his efforts to bury the goat

"IT WOULD HAVE MADE A STOIC SMILE TO HAVE SEEN ME AND MY FAMILY
SIT DOWN TO DINNER."

FIGURE 15. "It Would Have Made a Stoic Smile to Have Seen Me and My Family Sit Down to Dinner" by E. Nister, from Daniel Defoe, *The Life and Adventures of Robinson Crusoe* (London: Dutton, 1895), 61. By permission of the Hubbard Imaginary Voyages Collection, Special Collections Library, University of Michigan.

as being "to prevent the Offence to my Nose," Crusoe could have also been motivated by an empathy with the old goat, once he recognizes that he, too, might die alone in a cave (dressed in goatskins, a metaphoric "old he-goat") and need some sympathetic soul to bury his body.

Those incidents are among many other encounters Defoe creates between Crusoe and animals. As well as being afraid of wild beasts and constantly vexed by the island's wild cats and birds, Crusoe forms several important relationships on the island with animals, including his dog, whom book illustrations show accompanying him everywhere; his domesticated cats and goats, who become important sources of companionship; and, of course, his parrot. In fact, Crusoe refers to this island menagerie as his "family." Illustrated editions of the novel often depict Crusoe in a domestic scene with one or more members of his family; the 1895 Dutton edition paints a family mealtime, which, if the animals were children, could have come out of an illustrated Victorian book of manners also popular at the time of this edition (see Figure 15). The picture's caption reads "It would have made a stoic smile to have seen me and my family sit down to dinner." The illustrator, E. Nister, composes the scene, in fact, in a manner suggesting a filial relationship between Crusoe and the animals. The texture and color of Crusoe's fur outfit make him resemble the cats on his table and the dog on his lap; in fact, it is difficult to distinguish the dog's fur from Crusoe's. By posing the bearded Crusoe and dog both in profile, Nister highlights their similar features; and the green shading to Crusoe's fur makes him resemble the parrot at his left shoulder. Despite these similarities, though, Nister still depicts Crusoe as the animals' master, reminding of Crusoe's ultimate humanity despite the savage play. Crusoe touches the animals but does so in a paternalistic manner, and Nister reminds of Crusoe's control of the family food supply by showing the cats' and parrot's food dishes. Moreover, Nister places the "civilizing" tool—the knife-like eating implement—on the table at Crusoe's hand (just as Quarll carries his ax in his hand), as if to emphasize his human authority, for the use of tools was, at that time, thought to separate man from beast. As Crusoe expresses in the passage accompanying the picture, "I had the Lives of all my Subjects [the animals] at my absolute Command" (108).

The image suggests that Crusoe's animal family fulfills many of the needs a human family would, both providing companionship and allowing him to assert his masculine authority. Most importantly, like other indigene types, animals also present objects for the affection Crusoe holds for his island and additional outlets for the desire he also lavishes upon his island/body.

We see castaways other than Crusoe experiencing and enjoying the "savage" sides to their personalities while on their islands, including the protagonists of the *Swiss Family Robinson, The Mysterious Island,* and *The Island of Dr. Moreau,* all of whom develop close bonds with indigenous animals and act, at some point, as if at least partially enjoying their escape from the constraints of "civilization." Though such colonizers might find their bestial impulses attractive, narratives also consistently show them resisting that desire and even compulsively enacting certain defensive, counterphobic maneuvers that protect their bodies from savage infection. They often respond to threats of going native by imaginatively resecuring the boundaries of the self through which they gained control of the island in the first place. They do so by employing their intellect, since control of the mind supposedly separates man from beast, civilized from savage. More specifically, the castaway relies on his reason, knowledge, and scientific prowess to reinforce distinctions between his body and others, to keep the cultural influence flowing *from* him (and his culture) and not *into* him (and his culture). So, for instance, castaway colonists' obsession with science and natural phenomenon, such as plant life, animal behavior, geological formations, astrological patterns, and meteorological trends, as found in *The Swiss Family Robinson, Masterman Ready, The Mysterious Island,* and *The Coral Island,* function as a way of asserting their command over nature, the island, and ultimately the colonial encounter.

Scientific discourse functions similarly for readers of the novel, educating and reassuring them of their nation's intellectual and technological prowess and of its secure control over its empire in the face of challenges. Foucault asserts throughout his work, but particularly in *Power/Knowledge* that knowledge in the modern, Western world equals power, just as power determines what is considered knowledge, which explains why indigenous understanding of nature, because disempowered, would not be considered "knowledge." Because Western science supports a certain type of understanding of the natural world, displays of scientific "knowledge" further *naturalize* the colonist's power over of the island and, by analogy, naturalize European imperial power. As well, science, as a marker of "evolution" and "progress" distinguishes the civilized from the savage.

Such attempts to use scientific discourse as defense against going native permeate island texts such as *Typee, The Narrative of Arthur Gordon Pym,* and *The Island of Dr. Moreau.* In *The Narrative of Arthur Gordon Pym,* for instance, Pym employs scientific language when he feels most in need of reasserting his status as a civilized man: after he has turned cannibal. Poe's narrative is, as Andrew Horn notes, famously full of digressions, but the text's many lengthy detours on natural and nautical life, particularly those following Pym's cannibalism, serve to reestablish his control over his environment. Even though, as explained in chapter 3, texts somewhat excuse turning cannibal under dire circumstances, Pym must still afterwards protect himself against turning native by relying upon the power of reassuring, Western, "civilized" science to solidify the boundaries of his psychical body. So, for instance, neither Pym nor the others express regret for what turns out to have been a hasty action, not even when Pym, shortly after the cannibal meal, suddenly remembers the existence of an ax that they then use to break into the ship's storeroom—an act of remembrance that could have saved the cannibalized man had it occurred a day earlier. Instead of expressing horror at his unnecessary cannibalism when they bring up an edible turtle from the storeroom, Pym educates the reader about giant tortoises, a brief but significantly placed digression of Western scientific knowledge. When a passing ship later rescues Pym and his shipmate, providing another chance for reflection on his premature cannibalism, Pym instead meditates at length on island topography, flora, and fauna, leading into a lengthy digression on the albatross. Perhaps we can see Pym attempting to recognize or process his feelings of remorse through this meditation on an albatross, an allusion to Coleridge's trope of shame and guilt in his seafaring adventure, *The Rime of the Ancient Mariner* (1798), published just forty years before *Pym.* Earlier in the story—pre-cannibalism, before the threat of going native—Pym didn't include such gratuitous details in his narrative, suggesting that he increasingly perceives the natural world through the lens of Western science to keep it within his scientific gaze and intellectual control, allowing him to keep his mental and bodily boundaries safe during his time of crisis. Pym's counterphobic use of science, in fact, seems to erase the horrific event from his consciousness, for though he proclaims that the "stern recollection [of the cannibalism] will embitter every future moment of my existence" (*Complete Stories,* 675) the story never again mentions cannibalism, either his or anyone else's. And as we know from Poe's poem "To Science" (1829), this depiction of science as working to quell emotion and reestablish reason jibed with his general approach to science as a discipline that "alterest all things with . . . peering eyes," that cools or destroys the passions.

As with so many other elements of these fictional island narratives, nonfictional texts of the day contained and perpetuated similar ideologies. Cultural critics and historians have noted that real-world colonial scientists and naturalists, like their fictional counterparts, used science as a lens to filter, classify, and control the natural world, including their colonial Others. As Elleke Boehmer explains in *Colonial and Postcolonial Literature,* indigenous cultures encountered through colonial contact became "*objects of study,* bodies of knowledge to assemble and to bring into shape" (72, emphasis original). Such protoanthropological studies focused on the native and native culture, an aim that fictional texts mirror in their study of the island world with the same intention: to reassert the colonizer's scientific gaze and control over his environment, a control emanating from his disciplined body. Mary Louise Pratt, among others, has remarked on how the Linnaean system of classifying nature allowed just such a myth of scientific control by encouraging the fantasy that all the world could be classified using one European-produced, superior, and centralized system—that the world could be dissected, understood, and consumed by breaking it down into its parts and studying it using the "rational," European-produced scientific method. Linnaeus's system answered fears of the world's instability and dangerous hybridity by creating a method for living and dead bodies and space to be objectified, classified, and managed. Such moments of scientific explanation and classification found in island narratives allow both protagonist and reader to participate in that fantasy of control and in the myth of the incommensurability of colonizing and colonized bodies. The colonizer "disciplines" his island and its inhabitants in both senses of the word, dissecting the indigene with the scientific blade that he creates and wields.

Such fictional and real-world defensive uses of science and knowledge, however, often merely mask the imperial frailties they supposedly fortify. Thomas Richards suggests as much in his argument in *The Imperial Archive* that the British Empire in the nineteenth century (though I would argue that this trend was building during the seventeenth and eighteenth centuries, as well) was obsessed with the accumulation and control of knowledge, in part, because that collection of facts enhanced the fantasy of a uniformly controlled and secure empire, whereas the reality was closer to a collection of tenuously controlled territories. As Richards explains,

The work of the Foreign Office was often done by any educated person, however unqualified, working in whatever department, stationed wherever, who felt he had to do it simply because he happened to be British. These people were painfully aware of the gaps in their knowledge and did their best to fill them in. The filler they liked best was information. From all over the globe the British collected information about the countries they were adding to their map. They surveyed and they mapped. They took censuses, produced statistics. They made vast lists of birds. Then they shoved the data they had collected into a shifting series of classifications. In fact they often could do little other than collect and collate information, for any exact civil control, of the kind possible in England, was out of the question. The Empire was too far away, and the bureaucrats of Empire had to be content to shuffle papers. (3)

As Crusoe's diary, Prospero's books, and Moreau's experiments demonstrate, this same compulsion to control information resides in these island texts (and Rukmini Bhaya Nair adds in *Lying on the Postcolonial Couch*, in the postcolony, as well). Within the realm of the novel, it is the castaway colonist who collects data about the island and benefits from that sense of control, but in the real world, the collector and beneficiary is the colonial reader, whose sense of the empire's security gains strength from passive participation in the fact-gathering, information-wielding adventure.

As well as collecting facts within their pages, island narratives also metaphorically collect objects; they collect descriptions, pictures, analyses of objects, serving much the same purpose as the museum that the castaway colonist occasionally constructs on his island: to collect and inform. Critics exploring the role of eighteenth- and nineteenth-century museums in securing the fiction of empire note that imperial museums, in fact, functioned as sponsors of collecting projects, as repositories and display mechanisms for those collections, and as vehicles for the education of the public as to the value of empire.[16] As Tim Barringer explains in "The South Kensington Museum and the Colonial Project," the didactic museum "open[ed] up economic and cultural possibilities of empire to a general public" (15). Moreover, as a reification of the power and control of the empire, the museum "functions as a metonym of the state itself" (17). Tracing the practice of collecting curiosities back to the early days of empire, Peter Mason notes that early imperial adventurers collected artifacts (tools, jewelry, religious statues, objects of precious metals, household articles, clothing) and specimens (preserved plants and animals, drawings and descriptions of plants and animals, entire human bodies, live or dead) in what were called Curiosity

Cabinets or Wonder Closets to allow those who could not travel to the new world to taste the experience. As he explains, "fragmentary though they inevitably were, such partial glimpses of America, their legitimacy shored up by the presence of eyewitnesses who had been there to collect them, might be reassembled to form a recreation of the American continent by the totalization from part to whole that is generally known as *synecdoche*" (64). This mania for collecting of curiosities co-evolved with expansions of European empires in the New World, shifts to a modern sensibility (including perceptions of a privatized body and the spread of imperial capitalism), and the rise in popularity of the island narrative. And we should remember that, rather than simply a product of the colonial project, such hunger for the new and exotic actually created a political economy that *drove* the expansion of empire. I would, in fact, equate this obsession for collecting curiosities from the New World with the incorporative fantasy played out in island narratives.

Museums in island narratives serve a function similar to that of the real-world imperial museum, providing for colonizing characters and European readers a method of psychically incorporating—and thereby controlling—a threatening environment. But, as Gyan Prakash notes in "Science 'Gone Native' in Colonial India," the imperial museum in India had the second purpose of "educating" Indian people, reminding them of their subjugation through the display of the colonial incorporation of their culture and themselves. The museums constructed by fictional island colonists are far less grand than those of empire, typically consisting of a collection of the island's natural products and valued possessions from home stored in the island cave or hut. In *The Swiss Family Robinson,* for instance, the family creates a museum by stuffing and displaying specimens of island fauna in their cave. The family's one encounter with a giant boa constrictor, for instance, ends with the snake's death, taxidermy, and display in their cave museum. As the father explains, "We took great pains to coil it round a pole in the museum, arranging the head with the jaws wide open, so as to look as alarming as possible, and contriving to make eyes and tongue sufficiently well to represent nature. In fact, our dogs never passed the monster without growling and must have wondered at our taste in keeping such a pet" (270–71). By incorporating the boa into their cave and transforming the "monster" into a "pet" displayed in a manner as threatening as it was in life, the Robinsons symbolize their mastery over the potentially threatening indigene and, ultimately, their own resistance against going native. No doubt, we are meant to imagine the undescribed stuffing and display of the boa as yet another educational experience for the Robinson boys, an experience the reader shares through reading Mr. Robinson's lessons on the boa. In fact, in a metaphoric way of viewing it, the entire novel could be called a sort of museum since it provides a contained space for an extended educational experience for the reader, a display of the empire's prowess, a repository of knowledge, and a vehicle for the reader's incorporation of the island empire.

Novels that don't narrate the construction of a museum of natural history still often assert the colonial command of the natural world through a figure who wields scientific knowledge, the castaway scientist. Most of these fictional male island colonists, if not scientists before they were stranded, seem to develop a taste for natural history while on the island. Yet, though the novels teem with scientific explanation and wonder, they often distinguish between practical scientific knowledge and a purely intellectual, abstract science, suggesting conflicting feelings about the role of science in empire and colonial culture.[17] Practical science protects the colonist from going native; abstract science doesn't. *Masterman Ready* and *The Swiss Family Robinson*, for instance, don't declare the family fathers to be professional scientists, but the good colonists' vast and impressive command of the scientific disciplines of engineering, agriculture, medicine, taxidermy, biology, and botany could nonetheless qualify them as scientific professionals. Mr. Seagrave in *Masterman Ready*, "a very well-informed, clever man," though not a professional naturalist, gives a two-page detailed explanation of the formation of coral islands to his son that could have come from the pages of a nineteenth-century science textbook (6). Similarly, Verne in *The Mysterious Island* emphasizes practical knowledge when describing Cyrus Harding, another colonist who seems to possess every skill and bit of information necessary for island prosperity. Harding is "learned, clear-headed and practical" (9), an engineer, but the kind of engineer "who began by handling the hammer and pickax, like generals who first act as common soldiers" (8). Verne also stresses Harding's command of his body, explaining that "besides mental power, he also possessed great manual dexterity," and calling Harding "a man of action as well as a man of thought" (8). These scientists are not simply intellectuals; they are sensible, handy, disciplined, and moral men who use their skills for the improvement of humanity—or, at least, for the white, colonizing, male portion of humanity. By stressing their practicality, these authors ensure that their colonists' intellectual prowess doesn't feminize them. As *manly* scientists, the colonists control nature, and their closed, disciplined bodies protect them from degeneration, whereas, pure intellectuals risk being feminized, being controlled by nature, and being "infected."

The only island novel considered here that does include professional scientists among its characters, *The Island of Dr. Moreau,* also prefers practical scientists but does so by interrogating its professional scientists for their *lack* of practicality, for their obsessive and impractical pursuit of scientific truths, which perhaps lead to violation of unwritten imperial rules of decorum, ethics, and scientific responsibility. R. D. Haynes in "The Unholy Alliance of Science in *The Island of Dr. Moreau*" examines the novel's three scientists, concluding that all three give negative examples of scientists, presenting "a trenchant satire on the cult of research for its own sake" (24). One scientist, Moreau, unfeelingly performs his torturous experiments on animals and continues work the European scientific community considered so awful that they forced his exile, providing, Haynes says, a prototype of the "mad scientist." The second of Wells's scientists, Montgomery, had to abandon a brilliant scientific career in England to come to the island after what he describes as a minor indiscretion (which critics often interpret as either a homosexual experience or a drunken botched operation). Though complicit in Moreau's awful experiments, Montgomery acts less as scientist and more as game warden over Moreau's animals and policeman of the beast people. As Haynes explains, the novel presents its third scientist, Prendick, as a dilettante naturalist, who took "to natural history as a relief from the dulness [*sic*] of my comfortable independence," a gentleman scientist uninterested in publishing his findings, which means that his work ultimately provides no benefit to mankind (Wells, 14). These three professional scientists, unlike the well-rounded colonist, engage in impractical work and are proud of it. In fact, at one point in the novel, when Moreau justifies not using anesthesia in his operations, he explains that he is "differently constituted" on a "different platform" from the "materialist" Prendick (Wells, 104). Prendick, an equally impractical scientist, takes being called a "materialist" as an insult, which he "hotly" denies (Wells, 104). The novel shows these scientists as having removed themselves from the bounds of imperial discipline, for a good scientist would use his skills to remove pain (not cause it), to ease the burdens of daily life (not increase them), and to improve humanity (not to endanger the purity of the species).

Because Moreau, Montgomery, and even Prendick practice this eso-teric kind of science, their knowledge does not protect them from going native. By the novel's conclusion, we see each of the three infected by the island's savagery. Montgomery's degeneration is confirmed by his (per-haps sexual) relationship with the beast people and alcoholism (dip-somania). As Prendick remarks, Montgomery's "long separation from humanity, his secret vice of drunkenness, his evident sympathy with the Beast people, tainted him to me. Several times I let him go alone among them. I avoided intercourse with them [the animals] in every possible way" (139). Despite this claim, Prendick, too, degenerates when forced to live with the beast people, only somewhat reassuming his humanity when rejoined with English society at the novel's end. Finally, the novel illustrates Moreau's deterioration through the nature of his obsessive ex-periments, which, instead of working for the improvement and greater purity of the human species, taint humanity with animality. Science un-dertaken for unnatural reasons and divorced from imperial discipline, warns the novel, won't protect man from degenerating into beast. The men who would practice such science, unlike practical colonists, are bad imperialists as well as bad scientists.

In their efforts to paste over the holes in the fantasy through science, island narratives remind of a consistent panic of loss of imperial control. The texts summon the island's bodies—its indigene, its colonizer, and itself—to enact the cultural anxieties poured into its pages, betraying more ambivalence and guilty desire than noble intentions. This particu-lar fantasy of natural imperial control, as I have argued, built upon a va-riety of psychological impulses—drives of incorporation and consump-tion, desires to command the body, and anxieties over controlling what enters and leaves the body's boundaries. In this chapter, I have traced how island narratives dramatize, through stories of wild men and go-ing native, fears of a decaying or threatened empire. Island narratives recodify such fears into threats coming both from the island and its ani-mal, monster, and human indigenes, threats that can be partially man-aged by securing the psychical boundaries of the self with science. This chapter and its predecessors have demonstrated that maintaining the imperial island myth required hard work and constant vigilance. The next chapter will argue that coexisting with these tales that repeat the island fantasy were other texts challenging that fantasy, texts that often took dramatic form and employed humor.

5. Island Parodies and Crusoe Pantomimes

Resistance from Within

Every joke is a tiny revolution.
George Orwell

OUR examination of how island castaway narratives contributed to empire has so far only hinted at a range of tales that were produced alongside those narratives and also parodied them. Centuries before the twentieth-century revisions of the island story with which I opened this book—like Coetzee's *Foe* and Walcott's *Pantomime*—came novels like Jonathan Swift's *Gulliver's Travels* and dramas like Gilbert and Sullivan's operetta *Utopia Limited* and Thomas Duffett's *The Mock Tempest*, which take as their comedic subject the castaway island story, mocking and in some cases subverting that foundational myth of British imperialism. Some of these texts, such as Geoffrey Thorne's play *Grand Christmas Pantomime Entitled Robinson Crusoe, or Harlequin Man Friday, Who Kept the House Tidy, and Polly of Liverpool Town* (1895), for example, poke fun at the so-called benevolent motives behind imperialism. When Thorne's Crusoe and his companions first come to the island on which they are stranded, for instance, one of its natives (not in Defoe's version) protests "How dare you come to my country without being asked," to which the play's villain, Will Atkins, quips in a moment of humorous honesty, "We're English, you know, we always do that" (40). Later in the play, after the natives have decided to eat the encroaching castaways, and English imperial sailors arrive just in time to save them, a grateful Crusoe asks the sailors why they came to the island. They candidly answer, "Sighting this island we came ashore to annex it—a pleasant little way we English have, you know" (52). In other scenes, Thorne's pantomime of *Robinson Crusoe* challenges imperial propaganda by lampooning the unjust results of colonization for the colonized. After their prevention of the cannibal feast, for instance, the English sailors "make peace" and promise to "teach [the natives] civilization." But when a confused cannibal asks, "What's dat swivelization?," an English sailor wryly replies "Gunpowder and rum" (53). At another point in the play, after Crusoe explains the process of a treaty to the cannibal king as: "the Government undertakes to take your land, and undertakes to take you to England, and take you about a bit; and then you undertake to take yourself off," the cannibal king astutely observes, "Golly! dere's a good deal ob de undertaker about dat. I might as well be dead" (59). The humor in these exchanges results from their bald admission of the self-serving motives and detrimental results of imperial expansion—realities the island narratives that this study has so far examined have typically worked to mask.

The existence—indeed the *abundance*—of narratives such as Thorne's coevolving with colonial castaway tales raises a range of questions important for continuing our examination of the role of island narratives within empire.[1] Though the plays do have these moments of questioning empire, they aren't simply anti-imperial. In fact they are quite patriotic in some spots, such as in George Conquest and Henry Spry's Crusoe pantomime of 1885, in which Crusoe reminds a cannibal of "our soldiers in the sad Soudan/ They fought like lions, attacked within their den, / Or, better still, they fought like Englishmen" (28), a statement as interesting for its claiming of indigeneity for the British (by symbolizing British soldiers in Africa as creatures attacked on their own soil) as for the statement that Englishmen are more fierce than lions. Such moments of jingoism make the bits of imperial satire stand out even more. What should we make of such narratives, written during the development and expansion of the European empires of the fifteenth through twentieth centuries, which poke fun at some of the most deeply rooted elements of imperial ideology? And how might these parodies, which have existed as long as/alongside of island narratives, affect the sociopsychological effectiveness of island narratives? If, as I have argued, island narratives (in their nonparodic form) participate in the maintenance of empire by helping the culture to process colonial anxieties and manage imperial desires, do these parodies play a sociopsychological role, as well, perhaps helping to dissipate ambivalence over colonial deed and imperial policy or instead helping to mobilize such ambivalence into a more active resistance? Finally, why are so many of these texts that offer resistance to the island fantasy dramatic in form, when so many of the island narratives themselves were novelistic?

This chapter will investigate these questions, hypothesizing that these island parodies interact with imperial ideology in a complex manner. Based on a reading of the plays themselves and their reception, I will argue that they both dissipate and concretize popular ambivalence toward empire for different audiences at different times. Without recorded historical responses to these island parodies from readers and audience members (which, since we are primarily analyzing subconscious responses would be suspect, anyway), it is difficult to pin down which texts produced which response at which time and in whom. But, examination of these works (particularly when the works were produced contemporaneously with repetitions of imperial myths) *can* provide clues as to their interaction with their consumers' views on empire and can further our understanding of the complexities of imperial culture and the ambivalence inherent in colonial island fantasies. Aiming to investigate what these modifications of the island fantasy reveal about the internal stresses of imperial culture, this chapter will focus on such parodies, reading Thomas Duffett's *Mock Tempest*, Swift's *Gulliver's Travels*, J. M. Barrie's *Peter Pan*, and Gilbert and Sullivan's *Utopia Limited*, alongside several pantomimes of *Robinson Crusoe*. After first discussing how several island parodies reflect opposition to empire from within the so-called imperial center, the chapter investigates how they might work to dissipate that opposition through carnivalesque performance, finally speculating on how they could, while providing an outlet for revolutionary energies, still contribute to fomenting latent dissatisfaction with empire. This chapter's analysis of colonial-era pantomimes and plays that rewrite the island fantasy builds on previous work focusing on postcolonial rewritings of the island castaway trope that are more explicit and direct in their challenges than the texts examined here. It is my hope that by focusing on those less familiar island parodies and pantomimes, we can explore the ambivalences of empire from a slightly different angle—from within imperial culture—which helps us more fully understand the complexities of resistance and better appreciate those postcolonial revisions.

Opposition to Empire and the Mock Island Fantasy

When looking at how island parodies express deep ambivalence over empire, we should remember, as we have seen before, that their fictional plots often mirror real-world psychological conflicts over imperial actions and ideologies. A range of historical events—slave revolts, militarized rebellions, anticolonial struggles—bear ample witness to anticolonial movements occurring on *colonized* soil.[2] But, as Robert Young points out in *Postcolonialism: An Historical Introduction,* though often ignored by contemporary theorists, anticolonial movements always existed within the colonizing cultures *themselves,* that is, in the metropole as well as in the colony, a centripetal as well as centrifugal force. Young lays out a range of humanitarian, economic, and legal objections to empire that were raised in debates in metropolitan governments, churches, and homes. Trevor Lloyd's history of empire also notes imperial opposition in the so-called center in debates over the political or economic wisdom of colonial spread, especially during debates over expansion into India. As first documented by the sixteenth-century Spanish priest Bartolomé de Las Casas and later by others, colonizing cultures frequently debated a range of imperial issues, including the morality, practice, and legal justification of colonial slavery, colonization, and much later, the treatment of convict colonists.[3] Organized internal opposition to slavery eventually led the British to the outlawing of the colonial practice of slave trading in 1807 and of all slavery in 1833, despite their continuing efforts to colonize what they saw as unclaimed spaces of the world. Historian Lawrence James remarks in *The Rise and Fall of the British Empire* on one particularly striking moment of internal questioning of the imperial mission in "the Eyre debates," which centered on the reactions of Jamaican colonial governor, Edward Eyre, to an insurrection in Morant Bay in 1865. Fearing a situation like the Indian Rebellion of eight years earlier, James explains, Eyre reacted to the Caribbean uprising with a mortal violence toward both guilty and innocent Jamaicans of color that shocked portions of the English society into calling for his prosecution for murder. The outcry over his cruelty for a time divided English public opinion about empire, coinciding with what James calls "a wider political controversy over the empire's future" (194). Yet such resistance from within the "center" was often limited. The urgency and insistence born of being the one prostrate before the conqueror, his foot upon your head (*a la* Friday and Crusoe), is typically absent from such historical events. The incentive is not as clear, for those at the center, in Albert Memmi's words the "colonizers who refuse," stand to benefit from colonization, whether they find it personally repugnant or not.

Though recent postcolonial scholarship has begun to pay more attention to such instances of debate over empire "at home" and to corresponding fictional works expressing anticolonialism, we often don't pay enough attention to less overt expressions of opposition coming from the so-called imperial center. As John Carlos Rowe suggests,

At the moment, too many of our interpretations of literature merely judge a text as resistant to or complicit with the dominant ideology. We need subtler, more varied standards of political, and thus aesthetic judgment, if we are to respect the complexity of literature's "action" in an historical moment, especially when such a moment is defined by crisis and conflict. (257)

Like Rowe, I see a need to examine more closely that dissatisfaction with empire (or at least an incomplete support of it), which I suggest was more pervasive than many contemporary scholars assume. As evidence for the popularity of this dissatisfaction with empire we have the island parodies themselves. Based on the long-term and widespread existence and popularity of these texts challenging imperial dogma, I surmise that each well-documented and studied instance of resistance existed amidst a much more pervasive but passive unease over imperial practice coming from citizens who were otherwise generally complicit with colonial policy. The production of these island parodies suggests that this widespread dissatisfaction existed *dura* colonialism. Excepting an unusual and isolated response to the Yahoos in Swift's *Gulliver's Travels* (which I discuss later in this chapter), there are few traces of direct audience objection to these potentially controversial narratives challenging actions of church and state. In fact, many of these texts were quite popular among middle and working class Britons, and the pantomimes (as I will discuss) were performed year after year with updated political commentary.

Also suggesting the presence of dissatisfaction with empire among their audience is the fact that these texts were meant to be *funny*. Comic expressions typically evoke laughter, but laughter is complex and ambivalent, arising from a variety of impulses.[4] The laughter might be nervous (because the audience is uncomfortable with what is being expressed), social (the audience wishes to share in the sentiment of others), guilty (the audience recognizes some truth in the expressed idea but knows the idea is transgressive), or genuine (the voiced idea strikes the audience as funny). Though the sources of a joke's humor differ, in all of these cases the audience recognizes the existence or truth of a joke's subject, even if unconscious of that thought before, or they wouldn't "get it." As Freud theorized in *Jokes and Their Relation to the Unconscious,* jokes can function like dreams in that they can express desires, feelings, or aggression of which one is unconscious but that when vocalized, cause laughter. The examples beginning this chapter are funny, I argue, because both audience and author recognize elements of veracity in the barbs, and because both share—or at least acknowledge—a sublimated opposition to empire that, when held to the light, is humorous perhaps because taboo or transgressive. For example, Crusoe's definition of a treaty in terms of its potential for abuse and usurpation would result in humor only if the audience identifies reality in that statement, though perhaps that audience was never conscious of that thought before or never verbalized that criticism themselves. As Gregor Benton explains in his study "The Origins of the Political Joke," "political jokes are not a form of confrontation. People will only tell them when they are confident that their listeners will respond in fun" (36). These island texts, I argue, created laughter and made money by recognizing and verbalizing, in a nonconfrontational manner, their audience's dis-ease with England's imperial actions, which means that the authors and producers of those island parodies (in their search of joke fodder) tapped into a subtle, perhaps unrealized, ambivalence about empire.

We can only guess at the intentions of these parodies' creators. Yet, even if they lacked revolutionary intentions, by distorting the island fantasy, these writers contributed to its disruption, perhaps stirring their audience's dissatisfaction with empire or making them aware of the downside of colonialism for the first time. It is entirely possible that in the act of providing humor for their audience, the parodies (unintentionally?) passed on messages of opposition. Perhaps some members of Thorne's audience, for instance, after hearing Crusoe voice duplicitous aims of empire, could no longer view a treaty as a straightforward and honest agreement between equals, though not conscious of that thought before.[5] Such heightened awareness of imperial flaws might not incite active resistance, but Thorne's audience could have understood and found humor in its government's shortcomings while remaining politically acquiescent. By paying attention to moments of sublimated or subtle opposition, we can better appreciate the complexities of colonial society and more completely understand how island parodies both expressed and vented the public's discomfort.

Thomas Duffett's *The Mock-Tempest* (1675), an early island parody, demonstrates just how effectively comedy can be employed to deride the supposed humanitarian motives of empire, a move that could have proven offensive if audience members didn't at least partially share suspicion of those motives. Duffett's bawdy play subverts myths of the ideal colonist and benevolent civilizing mission by portraying one prototypical male colonist, Prospero, as a selfish and paltry criminal instead of noble father of empire. Duffett's play provides a fitting starting point for this investigation, as well, for two additional reasons: first because it was written so early in the era of the castaway narrative—in 1675, merely sixty years after Shakespeare's death and *The Tempest*'s assumed publication date; and secondly because, when viewed against its *Tempest* predecessors, *The Mock-Tempest* shows how parodies arose from the island myth simultaneously with serious treatments, highlighting the fallacy of a unified public support of imperial ideology. The same characteristics that made the castaway story an effective tool of imperial ideology, it seems, made it an attractive (and perhaps necessary) target for opposition.[6]

Duffett's parody followed close on the heels of two other noncomedic revisions of Shakespeare's play, the first revision, *The Tempest, or The Enchanted Island,* resulting from collaboration between John Dryden and William Davenant in the early 1660s.[7] As Dryden explains in his introduction to their play, he and Davenant "revised" *The Tempest* with an eye toward improving (not parodying) it, yet as contemporary critics often remark, this "improvement" results in a greatly simplified version of Shakespeare's multifaceted colonial allegory. For one, Dryden and Davenant actually narrowed the original story's focus from revenge and romance to just romance, removing the play's political elements, and making it a tale of innocent and successful colonization.[8] Instead of having to forgive his former countrymen and duplicitous brother (as does Shakespeare's Prospero), Dryden and Davenant's Prospero only has to forgive Caliban, who in this version deserves mercy even less than Shakespeare's Caliban.[9] Though Dryden and Davenant give Caliban more agency, they also make him more simplistically evil and less deserving of the audience's compassion. According to Stephano, Caliban commits incest with Sycorax (who in their version, is his sister) as well as trading on her sexuality as commodity, which would simplify viewers' sympathies and channel their affections toward the colonizers. This revision (lacking most of the play's ambiguity about island ownership and complexity of colonial relationships) nonetheless was an enormous commercial success. In 1673, this version was further adapted by Thomas Shadwell into an operetta, which was as much of a financial success as the Dryden-Davenant revision, with even more spectacle, color, costuming, and of course song. Though as Gerard Longbaine explains, it was the operetta's immense popularity that spurred Duffett to write *The Mock-Tempest* in 1675, Ronald DiLorenzo argues that Duffett's play ruthlessly and successfully satirizes all of the previous *Tempests*—the opera, the Dryden-Davenant play, and the Shakespearean original.[10]

Duffett's carnivalesque *Tempest* chips away at many of the elements of the developing island fantasy as presented in Shakespeare's play and re-presented in its Dryden-Davenant and operatic revisions, including the fantasy of the disciplined and righteous colonist. Unlike Shakespeare's original, Dryden and Davenant's revision, or Shadwell's opera, Duffett's parody undercuts Prospero's authority and character, making him a petty gangster not a powerful magician or a good colonist. Duffett makes his Prospero the head prison keeper of Bridewell, a workhouse turned prison, and turns Ariel into his henchman, whose "magical" powers are "to lye, swear, steal, pick pockets, or creep in at Windows" (1.2.75).[11] Shakespeare's exotic, enchanted island in Duffett's hands becomes a prison, jokingly called within the play an "enchanted castle," a space as insular as an island but less pleasantly so. Duffett satirizes Prospero's power by making the world he commands "the underworld" and the "elements" he controls "criminal elements." As well, Duffett subverts Prospero's appeal for audience members by juxtaposing him with Stephania, the surprisingly sympathetic Madame of a brothel Prospero orders his men to attack, whose humor, strength, and character while incarcerated make her rival Prospero for the role of the strong leader if not ideal colonist. Changing Prospero's position and pursuits from noble to ignoble parodies the fantasy of the powerful white father colonist as upheld by Shakespeare's character and the notion of an island colony as a space of freedom and prosperity. The law-giving and law-upholding colonist becomes a thief; the island becomes a prison. These changes would, of course, only seem funny to an audience ready to doubt colonization's motives, at least subconsciously suspicious that civilizing and rescuing missions were often instead stealing and exploiting ones.

Duffett further subverts the appeal of Prospero by mocking the tempest that earlier playwrights used to demonstrate his magical control over the elements. Duffett's mock tempest is an assault on a brothel ordered by Prospero, who commands Ariel to incite several apprentices to "storm" it. Duffett's choice of a brothel for the site of his tempest is significant, for, as Anne McClintock's recent work argues, a brothel could be seen as one place where man is *not* in ownership, where women wield the power of *self*-commodification.[12] Duffett's version, then, could be read as offering an ironic comment on the imperial fantasy of the male controlled female landscape. Instead of the male colonizer naturally taking control of the virgin female space that offers itself freely, in Duffett's play Ariel, Prospero, and their lackeys—all men—have to seize that female embodied space for themselves and endure active and violent resistance from women during the assault on the whorehouse, which as Gonzolo says, makes "more noyse and terrour then a Tempest at Sea" (1.1.67). The prostitutes battle to "save the ship" (emptying chamber pots and urinating out of windows on the intruders, shooting them with the corks of bottles of cheap wine, and blockading the doors); but still the henchmen "break in like a full sea" upon them (1.2.225), after which Ariel brings the prostitutes and their customers to Bridewell to be under Prospero's eye.

By changing Prospero from wise imperial father to mob boss, Duffett offers his audience both a counternarrative and a rival production—Duffett was, after all, attempting to lure viewers from other theaters to his. As well, it's possible that Duffett's play could have offered some members of its audience the chance to see colonization from the standpoint of the colonized. By making the captors (Prospero/Ariel) despicable and the captives (Stephania, the whores) likable, Duffett's play possibly encouraged his viewers to identify with the captives.[13] Instead of being a space of liberation, a space where a man could make his own world and remake himself, Duffett's "island" (for all of the characters but Prospero) becomes a space of confinement and oppression. Duffett fashions his island/prison, Bridewell, as a space where, instead of gaining control through one's body, one's body becomes the object of another's panoptic gaze and control, thus providing a vehicle for an inversion of the island fantasy and a chance for his audience to exchange imperial roles and fantasize about being the captured instead of the colonizer. By parodying the Dryden-Davenant and operatic Tempests, as well as satirizing the imperial obsession with islands and the role that *The Tempest* played in that imperial fantasy, Duffett chides the public that so readily consumed that fantasy and offered an "improved" version for a more savvy audience. One could read his play, then, as didactic, with the aim of pointing out to the public the pablum it had so enthusiastically consumed, waking them up from their willing absorption in that fantasy.

The Carnivalesque Island and Pantomimed Gender and Race

Like Duffett's play, other island fantasies provided a space for an audience to experience an inversion of the norms and orthodoxies of imperial culture, however fleetingly. The well-known theories of the Russian theorist Mikhail Bakhtin on what he calls the "carnivalesque" help to explain the complicated relationship between island parodies, island narratives, and empire, and it aids our understanding of how island parodies can recognize but also dissipate opposition. In *Rabelais and His World,* Bakhtin analyzes elements of medieval and early-modern carnivals as potentially anti-authoritarian, as subversive of cultural establishments of religion, social class, or state. In their temporal and geographical space of freedom of statement, of inversion of power, of the world turned upside down, Bakhtin argues, carnivals (and the carnivalesque) potentially encourage resistance and foment revolution. Yet as Bakhtin's critics astutely argue, carnival can also help to *maintain* social order by creating a controlled safety valve for the aggression, sexual energies, and frustrations resulting from social and economic inequalities, as well as (or instead of) a mobilization of these subversive tendencies. As social anthropologist Max Gluckman explains in analysis of Frazer's *The Golden Bough,* "rites of reversal" could also reinforce hegemony, since, despite appearances, they are "intended to preserve and even to strengthen the established order" (109). When channeled into the excesses of carnival, would-be revolutionary forces would not erupt into revolution, or as Roger Sales explains, through carnival, "they [medieval and early-modern authorities] removed the stopper to stop the bottle being smashed altogether" (169).

We can find a range of fine examples of carnivalesque texts in the British dramatic form of the pantomime (not to be confused with the contemporary pantomime genre of silent performance, though both evolved from the same source). Pantomimes, like the one with which this chapter began, are carnivalesque in their use of song, dance, extravagant costuming and expensive scenery. As Dawn Lewcock explains, the pantomime form—or "panto" as it came to be popularly known—evolved from medieval stylized, silent sketches focused on the antics of Harlequin and Columbine into the elaborate burlesque, musical dramatization of a fairy tale or myth that reached its zenith in popularity in the nineteenth and early twentieth centuries. Pantos are still performed sporadically today in England and former Commonwealth countries (as indicated by Derek Walcott's parody of the pantomime tradition in his 1978 play *Pantomime*). Most often presented seasonally at Christmas time, pantos have predictable plots, which replay stories familiar to their audience (including Cinderella, Dick Whittington, Aladdin and, the focus for this study, *Robinson Crusoe*), altering them into pantomime form, which means including stock characters (the hero, the love interest, the rival, the dame, etc.), brief songs, dance, physical humor, bad puns, sections of verse, and all available stagecraft of the day (including sliding shutters, flying trapezes, stage traps, explosions, and smoke to enable quick scene changes). The comedies typically ended with an elaborate noncomical scene known as the "harloquinade" or "grand transformation scene," showcasing, in one instance, a historical parade in full regalia of all of the kings and queens of England, a feat involving complex stage machinery, flamboyant costuming, and vivid scenery—all evocative of carnival.[14] In addition to their sensational production characteristics, pantos are carnivalesque in their production schedule; they *participate* in carnival, as well, by being performed primarily during the Christmas season, a holiday that evolved from a carnivalesque pagan celebration and which is the closest modern England gets to the cultural freedom and excesses of medieval carnival.

Carnivalesque Crusoe pantomimes and other parodies of the island myth could have, as Gluckman argues, functioned both as agents of social control and vehicles for social protest for the same audience, venting frustrations with empire while recognizing and concretizing them in language, for in pantomimes we see the inversion of power that Bakhtin describes, not so much in class or race but in gender. Pantomimes of *Robinson Crusoe* follow the conventions of pantomime in casting and plot, which means that they alter Defoe's original castaway story, as is typical of the panto frame story, into a battle between good and evil forces over Crusoe's fate. Crusoe pantomimes often begin with one or more male, supernatural character ("Hurricanos, Demon of the Storm and Darkness," "King Shark," and Neptune, to name a few) revealing to the audience designs to harm Crusoe by wrecking his ship. A supernatural, female, good character (often a fairy, as in "Chrystalline, the Fairy Genius of Sweetness and Light," and "The Spirit of Good Luck," but in one case designated "Britannia") quickly reveals her plans to foil the evil force and save Crusoe by putting him on an island. Though the play provides little justification for either the good or evil characters' actions, having the plot controlled by two such deus ex machina makes neither Crusoe's hardships nor his successes result from his own efforts or from those of imperial society. All seem to be the will of God.

Also, since the early nineteenth century, productions typically cast women in the pantomime's male title role, called the "principal boy" and in other powerful male roles, including pirates and sometimes cannibals. As well, a white male comedian would typically play the stock

older female character, called "the Dame." Though the roles were cast
cross-gender, the characters were supposed to be of the traditional gender, which means that other characters respond to the female-acted Crusoe on stage as male, despite the character's feminine costuming, and
treat the male-acted Dame as female, despite her comically masculine
appearance.[15]

But at least one production, George Conquest and Henry Spry's
*Robinson Crusoe, The Lad Rather Loose O' and the Black Man Called Fri-
day, Who Kept his House Tidy* (1885), does call attention to Crusoe's gender through bad puns about Crusoe's lack of manliness. Will Atkins re-
buts Crusoe's threats by calling him a "beardless boy" and forecasting
"From me you cannot save her." Crusoe answers "Beardless boy, indeed"
to which Will puns "Well, young shaver, You'll get in a horrid scrape."
Crusoe ends with an even worse pun. "Too funny by half," he says. "You
think by your shaver perhaps to rasor laugh/But I'll have a brush and
lather you" (13). This badly punned moment links the female actor's
beardlessness to lack of masculine power (as a boy or woman). Though
the audience would know that in the expected outcome of the play Crusoe would be able to save Polly from Will Atkins, Atkins's threat reminds
them for an instant of the "natural" order of the universe of white male
privilege. Ironically, it takes Crusoe's threat of violence, a typically "masculine" response, to restore the play's carnivalesque challenge to the
"natural" order. Likewise, the casting of a male actor in drag as Crusoe's mother would have held up imperial gender structures to scrutiny,
for the play often involves Mrs. Crusoe in a love plot, creating quasi-
homoerotic love scenes between two male actors, one being the humorously mannish Mrs. Crusoe.

Though such cross-gender casting is not unique to pantomimes of
the Crusoe tale (as opposed to pantomimes of other stories), it likely *affected* the public's perception of the colonial island fantasy. The carnivalesque practice of casting a woman as the principal boy in these Crusoe
pantomimes would shape reception of the castaway fantasy, which centers on notions of masculine self-discipline and order. In the last chapter,
I speculated that by blurring and reinforcing the lines separating the
categories "human" and "animal," island texts enabled the character,
author, and reader to safely experience the thrill of transgression, of
playing native while not *going* native. We see a similar dynamic at work
in these island parodies, in their use of humans to play animals (such as
the cat in *Puss in Boots* or in *Dick Whittington*) and through their blurring

of the lines between masculine and feminine, male and female. As Lewcock remarks in reference to the human/animal interchange but also reflective of the cross-gender casting: "The audiences expected and expect this as part of the topsy-turvy world where nothing is quite what it seems to be and/or unexpectedly changes into something else. The inbuilt ambiguities confirmed and confirm the audience in the certainties of their own existence while allowing a delicious thrill of fantasy" (134).

The island parodies achieve this complication of gender boundaries by showing gender as both performed and natural. On the one hand, casting a woman in the role of Crusoe shows gender as a set of identifiable and duplicatable behaviors, thus calling attention to Crusoe's masculine discipline as *performance* rather than as natural. The female-acted Crusoe could adopt certain signs to be coded as manly, including, for instance, carrying her body in a masculine manner (taking up more space with her walk and body gestures), perhaps talking with a deeper voice, and certainly behaving aggressively toward other males on stage. The pantomime Crusoe would, for instance, engage in hand-to-hand combat with Will Atkins, cannibals, or pirates to protect his rights to their shared love interest, Polly.[16] Similarly, battle scenes would be staged between Crusoe (female actor) and Will Atkins (male actor) or Crusoe and cannibals or pirates (sometimes played by female actors), with Crusoe triumphing over male and female actors, alike. Having Crusoe's feats of swordsmanship performed by a woman dressed in skimpy costuming *acting* like a man would have subverted notions that those skills and behaviors were sutured to the biological state of maleness. The plays' transgendered love scenes would also—at first glance—seem to additionally demonstrate gender as performance, since love scenes between Crusoe and Polly, enacted between two female actors, and thus titillating or humorous to nineteenth-century audiences, would seem to show masculinity and the right to court women as gained by right of behavior and not biology.

But how much subversive power could cross-gendered casting weild? Perhaps we can find insight in Peter Stallybrass and Allon White's analysis of the carnivalesque: "For long periods carnival may be a stable and cyclical ritual with no noticeable politically transformative effects," they say, but "given the presence of sharpened political antagonism, it may often act as *catalyst* and *site of actual and symbolic struggle*" (14, emphasis original). Thus, even though each instance of challenging the gendered logic of the imperial island fantasy might not have resulted in subversive

thought or action, at the right time and to the right audience, such performances could have catalyzed and participated in colonial struggle,
thus contributing in small ways to the eventual breakdown of empire.

Upholding Gender Traditions on the Balcony

While recognizing the strong subversive potential of these plays, I don't
want to overstate their consequences. These plays do seemingly show
the cracks in imperial ideology by asserting a disconnection between
biology and gender through their casting, but through their costuming
and makeup, they also qualify their own subversive potential, suggesting
an ambivalence about their own oppositional project as strong as their
ambivalence about imperial ideology. These performances assert the
notion that masculinity and femininity are marked by certain socially
recognizable behaviors. Yet, as a photograph of Clarkson Rose from a
1930 production makes obvious (see Figure 16), the costumer and actor playing the Dame emphasize the actor's masculine traits for comic
effect. They find humor in the actor's attempt and failure to adequately
perform femininity, including appropriate feminine dress. As Lewcock
explains, "Part of her [the Dame's] appeal is that she is often dressed
in an extravagant parody of current fashion" (139). The male actor, as
the "Dame," wouldn't act like a woman very convincingly, which would
mean that the play, while superficially subverting biological underpin-
nings of gender, at a deeper level reinforces those same conservative
imperial ideologies. For Rose's 1930s depression-era British audience,
faced with a crumbling financial system and shaky empire, such bolster-
ing of imperial norms might have, in fact, been quite comforting. The
feminine details of Mrs. Crusoe's baggy clothing (bows, lace, small gar-
ish hat) and ill-fitting, frizzy wig make the character look silly and mannish instead of womanly.

Moreover, instead of softening the actor's masculine features, the
makeup artist appears to have accentuated his bushy eyebrows, the bags
under his eyes, and the creases on his forehead. It would seem that despite the cross-gendered casting, the play does not allow the male actor
to *realistically* portray a woman. To do so would risk bringing homosexuality and transgendering into the play in too overt a manner for the
play's *safe* transgression. Eric Gilder and John Crocker in the production
notes to their 1972 Crusoe pantomime explain why the Dame should
always be played by a male actor: "audiences will laugh more readily at

FIGURE 16. Clarkson Rose as Mrs. Crusoe in a 1930 production at the Lyceum Theatre, reprinted in Raymond Mander and Joe Mitchenson, *Pantomime: A Story in Pictures* (New York: Taplinger, 1973), Figure 219.

a man impersonating a woman involved in the mock cruelties of slapstick than at a real woman" (3). And in their acting directions for the Dame, they remark that "an actor playing a dame should never quite let us forget he is a man, while giving a sincere character performance of a woman; further, he can be as feminine as he likes but never effeminate" (3). The makeup, costuming, acting, and pantomime conventions, then, undermine any real subversion of imperial gender, revealing a doubled agenda of presenting masculinity/femininity as performance while on another level reinforcing gender as tied to biological sex difference. Like playing with notions of going native, then, these texts enable a *safe* experience of gender transgression.

The practice of costuming Crusoe in revealing outfits similarly reveals ambivalence over imperial gender roles. Instead of playing Crusoe as a male imperial hero who, because he learns to discipline his body, is able to psychically incorporate his island into that body, pantomimes typically costume Crusoe in a form-fitting outfit that presents his/her body for display. Illustrations and photographs from pantomimes show how the costuming shockingly (for the time) revealed and emphasized the feminine figure instead of modestly concealing it. As A. E. Wilson explains, the scantily clad principal boy evolved in proportion to nineteenth-century fashions: "Principal boys, it may be noted, were discretely skirted to the knees during the 'sixties [1860s] and it was not until the more advanced 'seventies [1870s] that trunks were worn, the amplitude of thighs was daringly revealed and the major portion of a bare arm audaciously shown" (*Pantomime Pageant,* 117). A photograph of one nineteenth-century Crusoe played by Lydia Thompson (see Figure 17) gives an interesting example of how Crusoe's standard costuming was transformed on the pantomime stage in order to reveal feminine flesh. Crusoe's goatskin umbrella becomes in Thompson's costume a stylish parasol, his gun now an elegant walking stick, his parrot a smart shoulder ornament—all practical details made decorative. The robust dog that kept Crusoe company on his island is here replaced by toy poodles, ladies' companions and useless for hunting (except perhaps for ratting). The rugged fur clothing Defoe describes becomes sexy on Thompson, for the fur skirt allows the costume to both barely conceal and teasingly reveal the female thigh. Ironically, the play's costumer could show more of Crusoe's skin than of the female characters because Crusoe was coded as masculine on stage; in an age of corsets, bustles, and floor-length hems, the pantomime Crusoe could wear short skirts and low necklines

FIGURE 17. Lydia Thompson as Robinson Crusoe, reprinted in Gerald Frow, *"Oh, Yes It Is!": A History of Pantomime* (London: BBC, 1985), vii.

because (ironically) he/she was male. The production cast a woman to play the male role of Crusoe, but production conventions undermined that performance of masculinity. Even if Crusoe could convincingly perform masculinity, his/her costuming would emphasize the female actor underneath, making sure that she could not completely pass and playing to the desires of titillated audience members.

At this point I would like to return to a question I posed at the outset of this chapter, which is: Why were so many of the challenges to island narratives dramatic in form, when the parodied narratives were typically novelistic? What does the *performance* aspect add to these texts' abilities to both disturb and tidy imperial ideologies, and how would the panto tradition have affected audience response to the performances, since, as Dawn Lewcock remarks, "The English Christmas Pantomime is the quintessential entertainment involving the audience and encouraging their active participation in the happenings on stage" (133)?

Again, Bakhtin's theory of the carnivalesque offers provocative explanations, for it includes analysis of the social function of the balcony, the architectural feature that allowed the elite to surveil and visually incorporate the poor during carnival. By watching from the balcony, he explains, the privileged could vicariously participate in the transgressions of carnival, an action that actually reinscribed their (literal and figurative) hegemonic position. Similarly, the audience from their seats (perhaps literally in the balcony) could observe, perhaps participate in the carnivalesque transgressions of the island parody on stage and flirt with the carnivalesque inversions acted there without having to participate or risk themselves psychologically or jeopardize their own precarious social identities. By watching the play and identifying and consuming, the audience could toy with gender inversion, and, as Marjorie Garber suggests in her study of transvestitism, *Vested Interests: Cross-Dressing and Cultural Anxiety* (1992), they could temporarily escape the demands of masculine hegemony. Moreover, such observers of the staged island parody could visually incorporate the objects on stage, ironically making the island castaway into an object of incorporation instead of the incorporator. It is this exchange between the audience and performers—not just allowed but encouraged by forms like the panto—that would make the stage an attractive venue for parodies of imperial ideology, and once some parodies were successful (perhaps because of the interaction between audience and actor) imitators would follow. Of course, one could argue that the island castaway was always available for visual incorporation through

Here Crusoe courts sweet sleep, without a doubt here, | The only thing he had to court about here.

FIGURE 18. "Here Crusoe Courts Sweet Sleep, Without a Doubt Here, / The Only Thing He Had to Court About Here" from J. F. McArdle and Frank Green, *Mr. Edward Saker's Grand Comic Christmas Pantomime Entitled Robinson Crusoe; or Friday and His Funny Family* (London: Daily Post and Journal Offices, 1878). By permission of the British Library, 11785.C.27.

book illustrations and through being a creation of text, which is, after all, consumed through the eye. Yet these theatrical performances contain a self-awareness of the gaze that complicates the notion of incorporation as a mechanism of power, more so than illustration or text, since, *all* of the characters on stage (not just Crusoe) are presented to be observed, to be simultaneously consumed as it were, by the gaze of the audience in the Bakhtinian balcony and since the actors can see the audience looking at them.

Furthermore, scrutiny of the gendered politics of the gaze in Crusoe pantomimes allows us to speculate on the source of the principal boy's attraction and the Dame's humor. Because of the cross-gendered casting, male and female audience members alike could identify with (imagine themselves in the place of) and desire (as a sexual object) the appealing principal boy, which partially explains the character's charm for the audience. Similarly, because the Dame was both male and female, he/she could be imagined as *neither* male nor female, which meant that both male and female audience members could find the Dame's unattractive excesses to be funny and not threatening to their gender identity.

A drawing included in the program for J. F. McArdle and Frank Green's *Mr. Edward Saker's Grand Comic Christmas Pantomime Entitled Robinson Crusoe, or Friday and His Funny Family* (1878) (see Figure 18) suggests the cross-gendered appeal of the principal boy, Crusoe.[17] In this drawing of a scene from the production, a nineteenth-century she-Crusoe seductively stretches out on a hammock looking dreamily off into space (a pose Goffman identifies as traditionally associated with femininity [64]) evidently dreaming of Polly, an acceptably heterosexual union only if Crusoe is male. Meanwhile, Friday gazes at Crusoe longingly, an acceptably heterosexual union only if Crusoe is female. Crusoe in this drawing is both male and female, desired by both genders. Moreover, the illustration shows Crusoe as the object of every *thing*'s desire, since most of the animals also gaze lovingly at Crusoe (except for the monkey and parrot, who look at each other). The universal object of gaze and yearning, Crusoe only desires Polly, who is out of the range of his literal gaze but viewed in his imagination.

The drawing's caption highlights this gendered conundrum: "Here Crusoe courts sweet sleep, without a doubt here, / The only thing he had to court about here" (59). The caption reinforces Crusoe's heterosexual desire for the absent Polly and not for Friday or the animals (who are unacceptable mates for reasons of race and species) and emphasizes his role as sexual agent, which counters the picture's portrayal of him as sexual object. This role as sexual agent is a real-life role reversal for the female actor within the narrative, but as a performer she is reinscribed as the object of the audience's gaze. All could consume Crusoe and identify with his imperial ambitions, which in this and in most other pantos, surprisingly were more concerned with defending his already acquired territory (Polly) than colonizing the island.

It is significant that instead of working to claim territory for himself and his nation, panto Crusoes labor to defend something that is already theirs: Polly. The pirates and cannibals that in noncomic island narratives threaten Crusoe's island, here threaten only Polly—or Crusoe's rights to Polly. Surprisingly, the pantomime Crusoe doesn't show much interest in the island. He sometimes claims ownership of the island, as in Conquest and Spry's *Robinson Crusoe,* when he declares that "for a long and weary time/ I've lived alone/ Upon this island /Which I call my own" (22). But he ultimately displays little interest in staying on the island or creating a colony, always happily leaving the island at the play's end to return to England. The island, in fact, plays a relatively minor part in the story, usually only one act of three, with the other two being set in England or on shipboard. Instead of being interested in creating an island colony, this Crusoe simply wants to marry his girl. Conveniently, the possessed object (Polly) also has "agency" to assert her need to be owned. Polly's role in the play is to repeatedly choose Crusoe over all of the other men interested in her. Crusoe likewise aims to protect his right to Polly from Will Atkins or other characters who want to take her from him, playing out an imperial fantasy of protecting one's already-acquired property instead of gathering new possessions.

Peter Pan, and the Perils of White Masculinity

We see the same ambivalence about the fantasy of imperial masculinity in another famous island parody, J. M. Barrie's *Peter Pan, or The Boy Who Would Not Grow Up* (1904). As Marjorie Garber discusses at length in *Vested Interests,* productions of *Peter Pan,* like pantomimes, typically challenge the notion of imperial masculinity by casting a woman in the role of Peter, the island castaway hero.[18] Yet, unlike the Crusoe pantomimes, *Peter Pan*'s questioning of imperial masculinity goes deeper than staging, going into plot, as well. Peter Pan, originally ran away, he tells Wendy, to avoid becoming a man, though as a white male in a society full of economic opportunity, with the future right to vote, own land, or pursue a trade or profession, Peter might have enjoyed what some would see as a life of relative privilege. Yet Peter ran away, he explains, when he "heard father and mother talking of what I was to be when I became a man" (32). And it's no wonder that he fled from that fate, for the play presents white adult manhood as dismal, blaming Mr. Darling's petulance and bullying of his family on his entrapment in the monotonous world of middle-class hegemonic white manhood. Barrie, in fact, introduces Mr. Darling in terms of a masculine machine, as "a good man as breadwinners go . . . In the city where he sits on a stool all day, as fixed as a postage stamp, he is so like all the others on stools that you recognise him not by his face but by his stool, but at home the way to gratify him is to say that he has a distinct personality" (11). As Garber notes, Barrie's first title for the play was "The Great White Father," which perhaps remarks on what Barrie saw as the play's central topic: hegemonic white masculinity. Moreover, the fact that the role of Mr. Darling was sometimes doubled with that of Captain Hook, with one actor playing both parts, must have also affected the play's criticism of masculinity. Mr. Darling becomes a much more likable character by the play's end, after having spent some time in Nana's doghouse and after his counterpart, Captain Hook, has been symbolically castrated by the alligator (which, as Garber says, functions as an "ambulatory vagina dentata"[178]).

It is this type of repressive manhood from which Peter and his lost boys flee. Instead of learning to be fathers, breadwinners, and white-collar automatons, the boys choose to spend their days fighting impotent pirates and harmless Indians in a safe, playful version of imperial adventure on their homosocial imaginary island, while successfully avoiding adult manly responsibilities. When the boys play family in Never Land, for instance, Peter reluctantly plays father to Wendy's mother, but she has to reassure him frequently that he isn't really a father. Any sort of real obligation (even providing real instead of pretend food) is too much for Peter. Yet, though Peter avoids adulthood, he doesn't reject masculinity; he is not a feminine hero, despite being played by female actors. In fact, Tiger Lily, Wendy, and Tinker Bell all seem to have romantic designs on Peter, which, in true boyish fashion, he refuses to recognize, much less reciprocate. After all, to develop into true men, colonial boys had to repudiate the feminine.

We should remember that *Peter Pan* offers a critique of a *certain kind* of masculinity, a kind that, as Martin Crotty argues, some early twentieth-century British people blamed for the loss of the Boer War of 1899–1902. We can see evidence of this perceived crisis of masculinity in Baden-Powell's (himself a hero of the Boer War) developing of the boy scouting movement and, on another front, as Gail Bederman points out, G. Stanley Hall's effort to produce a U.S. educational system that allowed boys to act wild, like savages. A great deal of intellectual and cultural energy in the early twentieth-century went into developing plans and programs to train boys into rugged men. And, though Barrie's lost boys end the play by deserting their masculine island commune for the English middle-class parlor, Mr. Darling ends the play a changed man, no longer the middle-class automaton but ready to assume a more active, vibrant, boyish masculinity.

While disparaging adult, white masculinity, however, the play in other ways upholds it (like the pantomimes), thus subverting its own ability to be subversive. The play's ending provides one clear example of how the play undermines its own opposition to imperial, white masculinity. In the beginning of the play, we are introduced to the lost boys, all of whom have rejected adult masculinity, but by play's end they all (excepting Peter) decide to return to boyhood and to the manhood that will inevitably follow. They all decide that they prefer being mothered by Wendy and Mrs. Darling to being led by Peter, choosing heteronormative reality over homosocial fantasy.

Interestingly, also like the Crusoe pantomimes, Barrie's play undermines the conquest element of the island fantasy by changing the fantasy's trajectory from the acquisition of new land to returning home to enjoy what one already has. The play ends with Wendy, Michael, and John returning to the Darling nursery to be welcomed by their worried parents, who adopt all of the lost boys whom Wendy has brought home with her. Because the fortunate characters at the play's conclusion seem to be those who have returned to or found a home, the story privileges returning from the island adventure over embarking on one. As in the Crusoe pantomimes, the island story here becomes not one of conquering new lands and creating new homes there but of returning to the already-possessed but left home. The play ends with a feeling of nostalgia for the lost Never Land, perhaps akin to (or a precursor of) the imperialist nostalgia Renato Rosaldo describes in late twentieth-century texts. The point, it seems, just as with the museum, is to bring the best of the colony (in this case, a wild masculine spirit of unfettered boyhood) back to the homeland.

Peter Pan undermines its own oppositional ability as well, by stressing its own existence as myth. Though the play reproduces the island adventure story, it subverts the myth's usefulness for psychological self-justification by stressing its fantastical nature and by presenting the story as a *children's* fantasy. As I argued earlier in this study, island narratives often worked to legitimize imperialism by depicting colonization as a natural process of the disciplined male body. The typical castaway story's effectiveness, in part, comes from its realism, from its ability to convince its reader that it could be true, that a man could survive on an empty island, make his own perfect colony, and gain control of a space through his body. Like other island parodies, Barrie's play disrupts the island fantasy's potency as a psychical mechanism of imperial self-justification by halting that pretense of realism. As Martin Green remarks, though *Peter Pan* "uses all the devices of the boys' adventure story, the Indians, the hollow tree, the underground house, the lost boys, the pirates, it treats them all as conscious fantasy, and so denies their connection with the real world, a connection which is the life line of any energizing myth" (*Dreams of Adventure, Deeds of Empire*, 229). Though Barrie contends that white masculinity is dismal, he insists that the only way to escape it is through fantasy on the make-believe island of "Never-Land," a place existing only in the space between being awake and sleep, a space "you have often half seen . . . before, or even three-quarters, after the night lights were lit, and you might then have beached your coracle on it if you had not always at the great moment fallen asleep" (48). Neverland, for all its attractiveness, doesn't present a real alternative to or escape from imperial manhood, but only another space for imperial nostalgia.

Subversions of Race and the Colonial Other

As pantos and *Peter Pan* do with gender, island parodies (especially pantos) are often carnivalesque in their potential (if unrealized) transgression of authority based on race, calling into question ideologies of natural difference and embodied control. Pantomimes often adapted characters of color to fit the racial politics of the particular audience, so that the indigenous islanders in versions shown in Australia, as in W. M. Akhurst's *Harlequin Robinson Friday or The Nimble Naiad, The Lonely Squatter and the Lively Aboriginal* (1868), became recast in the title as Aboriginal people and the white characters as settlers, though little in the actual play changed to reflect this adaptation.[19] But whoever may be the colonial Other, a typical plot element of these pantomimes involves an interracial romance, which, though white actors in blackface would play the black characters, could have been risqué for simply dramatizing miscegenation. These interracial romances frequently involve a native island princess (often daughter of the cannibal king) or an African woman who falls in love with one of the English characters, as Princess Tamborini does with Azbestos, the pirate king, in McArdle and Green's *Grand Comic Christmas Pantomime* and as Princess Piccaninni does with Crusoe's brother, Billy, in Thorne's *Grand Annual Christmas Pantomime*.[20] At least one version, though, reverses the gender so that it is Mrs. Crusoe who becomes involved in an interracial love plot with a cannibal king (though the transvestite casting might have, in fact, made that relationship more humorous than scandalous). One wonders if such a plot would have been acceptable had the performer been an actual woman rather than a man obviously in drag. The English character who romances a native partner typically brings her back to England at play's end with no mention of racial differences or of the difficulties a racially mixed relationship would encounter in eighteenth-, nineteenth-, or twentieth-century England.

Though definitely unrealistic, one could argue that these plotlines provide early revolutionary (though comical) models of a postcolonial community, of nonviolent intimacy between colonizer and colonized, of a fantasy of peaceful assimilation, in contrast with the fear of infection played out in other contemporaneous island narratives. These mixed marriage endings are even more remarkable when compared with interracial love plots in their contemporary colonial novels, such as H. Rider Haggard's *King Solomon's Mines,* which might contain miscegenistic romances in their pages, but typically kill off the native love interest before consummation, removing the possibility of marriage and racial "contamination." As well as undermining imperial ideology, these Crusoe pantomimes could, then, as Said (quoting Benedict Anderson in *Culture and Imperialism*) says, help to "imagining a new national community," which he sees as one of culture's roles in devolution (200). Yet, by showing a completed interracial romance, these plots could also be criticized for simply reinscribing a colonial relationship into a heteronormative one, for typically the colonial hero brings his colonized partner back to England, which would mean the native woman taking on his culture instead of the other way around. Perhaps because he will "civilize" her in England, the colonist does not need to fear that association with an indigenous person will "infect" him and make him "go native" as we see in serious treatments of the island fantasy, or perhaps the native princess is not infectious, is acceptable to marry, because of her royal blood, which makes this model reliant upon stereotypes of class and caste as well as race.

Yet, these same pantomimes show race, like gender, both as performance and as natural, as if unable to sustain their own oppositional impulses. A photograph from a 1930 performance in Liverpool, England (see Figure 19), shows a scene from a Crusoe pantomime with a white actor in blackface playing Friday (shown here kneeling in an Al-Jolson-singing-"Mammy" pose) and a white woman playing Crusoe (here ironically bestowing upon a grateful Friday the phallic power of the gun, the same power she earlier wielded to save him). Despite the casting conventions, obviously neither costume masks the realities of the actor underneath. In fact, the white circle around Friday's lips would prevent audience members from being able to forget the actor's whiteness, just as Crusoe's feminine dress would constantly remind of Crusoe's femininity.[21] Such casting inversions complicate the play's portrayal of both race and gender, for the biological form typical of the imperial adventurer (a white male) performs the colonial Other, while the biological form typical of the engendered Other (a woman) plays the island colonizer. Yet, again the costuming does not support the oppositional possibilities of the casting inversions. The white actor playing Friday (based on lines from the play and the costuming) could never get beneath the stereotype represented by his costume to really experience being (or to pass as) Other any more than the female Crusoe was allowed or able to experience being (or pass as) a man. It seems that these nineteenth- and twentieth-century producers, actors, and audiences were not ready for that level of power inversion or for its potential transgressive outcomes.

Comparable to the treatment of the colonial Other in Crusoe pantomimes is the much earlier island parody, *Gulliver's Travels,* which followed *Robinson Crusoe* in publication by only seven years. Martin Green argues in *Dreams of Adventure, Deeds of Empire* that *Gulliver's Travels* took off from *Robinson Crusoe,* despite deviating in that Gulliver's islands are never deserted but are always inhabited by an exotic population of "natives" he is destined to encounter, which means that he lacks the opportunity for the moment of incorporation typical of the island fantasy. In *Gulliver,* Swift caricatures adventurers like Crusoe, men unable to

FIGURE 19. Dorothy Ward and Arthur Conquest as Robinson Crusoe and Man Friday in a production at the Empire Theatre, Liverpool, in 1930; reprinted in Raymond Mander and Joe Mitchenson, *Pantomime: A Story in Pictures* (New York: Taplinger, 1973), Figure 215.

restrain their wanderlust even though each voyage lands them in a precarious situation on yet another island.

As noted in the last chapter, Swift inverts stereotypes of the noble/ignoble savage and the civilized colonizer, thus creating a carnivalesque island world where invalidated expectations subvert the fantasy of the ideal colonized person as biologically incommensurable with the imperial adventurer. As well, Swift parodies the stereotype of the fantasy colonized person as dangerous savage, a being justifiably colonized, controlled, or eradicated because of its inhumanity. The most savage beings Gulliver encounters, book 4's Yahoos, he ultimately discovers to be human and (ironically) biologically similar to himself (which Ronald Knowles reports disturbed many of Swift's eighteenth-century readers to "near hysteria"[32]). Upon first seeing the Yahoos, Gulliver is as disgusted by their dirtiness and uncivilized behavior as he is enamored of the civilized and refined equine Houyhnhnms. Of course, the tale's irony comes from Gulliver's discovery that it is the savage, animalistic Yahoos whom he resembles in body and not the intelligent, cultured Houyhnhnms. As with the white circle around the pantomime Friday's mouth, Swift constantly reminds that the Other is like the colonizer. Here, the savage beings (qua indigenous colonized people) are naturally like the castaway, while the civilized beings (qua colonizers) are naturally different, an inversion that undermines the typical fantasy of embodied colonial status.[22] As well, like the colonized people in much colonial literature, Gulliver ironically but unsuccessfully tries to hide his true form and to mimic the Houyhnhnms, who eventually, to his dismay, reject him, making him (the white, male, adventurer), to borrow Bhabha's phrase, "almost the same but not quite ... almost the same but not white" ("Of Mimicry and Man," 238).

Utopia Limited and Ridiculing Colonial Mimicry

Other island parodies besides Swift's take up the task of ridiculing the practice and notion of colonial mimicry, preeminent among them Gilbert and Sullivan's fin de siècle operetta *Utopia Limited* (1893). Gilbert and Sullivan focus their clever satire on England's cultural and economic colonization of the fictional South Sea island of Utopia, an island ruled by King Paramount, who begins the play awaiting the return of his eldest daughter, Zara, from England, "the greatest, the most powerful, the wisest country in the world," where he had sent her to gain "a complete mastery over all the elements that have tended to raise that glorious country to her present pre-eminent position among civilized nations" (586). Zara returns with the six "flowers of progress," which are, as she explains, "six Representatives of the principle causes that have tended to make England the powerful, happy, and blameless country which the consensus of European civilization has declared it to be" (615). Zara begins this cultural exchange by reminding the Utopians of English superiority: "Attend to me, Utopian populace," she says, "Ye South Pacific Island viviparians; / All, in the abstract, types of courtly grace, / Yet when compared with Britain's glorious race, / But little better than half-clothed barbarians!" (616). Agreeing with her, the Utopian populace responds "Yes! Contrasted when/ With Englishmen, / Are little better than half-clothed barbarians!" (616). The humor in this scene combined with the success of the play tells us something about the audience's attitude toward their empire. The humor in this scene of Princess Zara and the Utopians in the role of the gratefully colonized comes from its irony, which means that it would have been funny only if the audience did not take at face value the Utopian excesses of enthusiasm over England's greatness. If the audience couldn't recognize that England was not the perfect place the Utopians proclaim it to be, then the scene would not be funny to them. On the other hand, if the audience found the idea of mimicry to be threatening, if they feared that the colonial mimics might, for instance, provide future competition for jobs, then, again, they would not find Utopian attempts to be like the English so humorous. The play's great success suggests that many audience members (at least the white, middle-class theatergoing crowd) could recognize Gilbert and Sullivan's irony and find the ability to laugh at their culture's pretensions, and the fantasy of the rest of the world wanting to be just like them.

The play satirizes the notion of England's natural superiority in its ending, as well, in which the Utopians surpass the English in their "Englishness"—first in their use of the economic and legal concept of limited liability, and then in their military domination of the region and enactment of social reforms. The Utopians, for example, improve on the English practice of holding "drawing-rooms," moving them from afternoon (as is the English custom) to evening, because, as Zara explains, "we all look so much better by candle-light!" (627). As Carolyn Williams notes in her reading of the play as political satire, another "improvement" that the Utopians made to the English drawing room was providing a "cup of tea and . . . plate of mixed biscuits," which was, ironically enough, a practice then taken up by the nonfictional British royal family and integrated into their drawing room customs after the play (Williams, 232). Amazingly, the fictional colonized Utopians, then, influenced the real-world colonizers; their performance of mimicked Britishness became "real" Britishness. By demonstrating the Utopian ability to surpass the English in their adoption of English cultural practices, the operetta undermines the imperial myth of the "natural" superiority of the English. Englishness becomes a set of behaviors that can be *performed,* and moreover that could be performed *better* by others. As Williams remarks, "the Gilbert and Sullivan operas seem to entertain the notion that national identity is something that may be 'put on' (like a costume) and 'taken-off' (like a burlesque parody)" (226). And the Utopians do learn to perform Englishness better than the English. Instead of being "almost the same but not quite . . . almost the same but not white," the Utopians become "better than," which could prove quite threatening to the colonial psyche—that is, if not coming from a wholly imaginary colony.

Yet while showing Britishness as a set of behaviors that can be adapted and surpassed, the play in other ways presents the Utopians as *unable* to emulate the English. Many Utopian attempts at mimicry are humorous because of their misapprehension of English culture, which leads to an ironic juxtaposition of characters' sense of the colonial culture versus the audience's self-knowledge. As Edward Galligan explains in *The Comic Vision in Literature,* "comedy consistently calls for double vision, for the ability to see this and that at the same time and to see both accurately . . . Comedy derides clods and pedants who are able to see only one thing at a time" (34). In contrast with English theatergoers, who would expect irony from Gilbert and Sullivan and would be rewarded for their "double vision" of England, the Utopian and English *characters* can only see England as superior to Utopia, which must have been presented as a source of humor for the audience. In one scene, for instance, King Paramount announces that his other two daughters, whom he has had "'finished' by an English Lady," will "daily be exhibited in public, / That all may learn what, from the English standpoint, / Is looked upon as maidenly perfection" (593). The girls are to be models for the Utopian populace of proper English femininity, especially English discipline of the body and emotions. As the girls explain, "Although of native maids the cream, / We're brought up on the English scheme— / The best of all / For great and small / Who modesty adore. / For English girls are good as gold, / Extremely modest (so we're told), / Demurely coy—divinely cold— / And we are that—and more" (594). The girls' demonstration of proper English ladylike behavior is humorous because, in their attempts to mimic the English, the girls take their performance of English stiffness, reservation, and politeness to a comical extreme. In fact, the play ends with a deconstruction of this exaggerated performance, as two English soldiers attempt to woo the girls by singing them a song about what "real" English girls are like—warm, athletic, bold, large of stature, physically healthy, pure, frank, fearless, and bright—not cold and distant like the Utopian mimic maids. The Utopian girls find themselves in a conundrum: they either take on a new, more "accurate" performance of Britishness or continue the inadequate performance they had already mastered. Of course, this "new" version of English womanhood merely provides the Utopians with a new model (perhaps a working-class model) to emulate, not any "truth" about "real" Englishness, especially not license to be themselves or to invent their own version of femininity. In this moment of the play, only the English can define or accurately perform Britishness, which seems to reinforce an essential link between behavior and nationality or ethnicity instead of undermining it.

As well as mimicking colonial mimicry, Gilbert and Sullivan's play is potentially revolutionary in its meditation on the idea of drama's potential to incite revolutionary tendencies. Utopia has only one vehicle for expressing criticism of their autocratic king, a newspaper, *The Palace Peeper*, which is both produced by the state itself and consumed only by the state. In other words, the palace buys up all copies of the paper it produces itself so that no one else ever sees it, thereby controlling both the publication and consumption of all resistance to official state policy. Even more interesting is the fact that Utopia's King Paramount himself composes the majority of the paper's attacks on him and of the other "public" criticism of the crown, even writing his own self-parodying carnivalesque opera, called "King Tuppence, or A Good Deal Less than Half a Sovereign." Despite having written the opera, he must rely on one of his advisors to explain its purpose to him:

During the day thousands tremble at your frown, during the night (from 8 to 11) thousands roar at it. During the day your most arbitrary pronouncements are received by your subjects with abject submission—during the night, they shout with joy at your most terrible decrees. It's not every monarch who enjoys the privilege of undoing by night all the despotic absurdities he's committed during the day. (600)

By encouraging an inversion of power on stage, King Paramount's self-parody creates a carnivalesque environment. His subjects have no voice in political affairs, but his play encourages them to vent feelings of frustration at night, which, conversely, keeps them docile during the day.

As they often do, Gilbert and Sullivan add an ironic twist to the situation, making King Paramount a puppet king controlled by his two advisors with the power to execute him at will and to force him, as he says, "to write libels on my own moral character" (602). So, *The Palace Peeper* and the King's opera both work to maintain existing power structures in two ways: by giving the Utopian populace space to expel frustrations and by helping to keep the king under the thumb of his advisors. Yet, at the same time, Gilbert and Sullivan suggest that the King's advisors might be using his opera to foment real opposition to him and cement their power over him, which belies one advisor's claim that the King's parodies only work to vent frustration. Because being made a fool on stage really *does* subvert the King's authority, *Utopia Limited*'s questioning of the power of opposition also implies that dramatic forms do carry the real potential to foment opposition.

This layering of opposition is compounded by the fact that King Paramount's opera is a play within Gilbert and Sullivan's play, *Utopia Limited,* which also has the ability to both voice and vent dissatisfaction with English imperialism through humor. Gilbert and Sullivan's commentary doesn't end with the audience of King Paramount's play but extends to *their* audience, as well. They present a brilliant satire on the notion of colonial mimicry, perhaps presented with the aim of pointing out the absurdity of that fantasy to their British audience. In the Utopian desire to be like the British, Gilbert and Sullivan hold up to scrutiny various beliefs and stereotypes about the ideal colonized person. That ideal colonized person, as presented in earlier serious revisions of the island fantasy, would be like Defoe's Friday, who expresses his gratitude and submission in that famous gesture of lying on the ground and placing Crusoe's foot on his head. That ideal colonized person would be willing and grateful for being colonized, and for having the island castaway teach him the rudiments of civilization, even if he could never hope to reach the same level of sophistication. The ideal colonized person would, like Friday, be an acceptable mimic who could pick up enough of the mechanics of "civilized" behavior to reinforce the superiority of the colonized culture but not enough to threaten passing. Gilbert and Sullivan, however, reveal ambivalence over this fantasy of the colonized person by deriving much of their play's humor from the ironic juxtaposition of the Utopian expectations of England with the audience's knowledge of its flaws. Having stereotypes mocked before one's eyes could make one reconsider those beliefs, could perhaps undermine the very imperial propaganda that those beliefs help to support.

To end this chapter, I want to return to *Gulliver's Travels*, to a famous passage near its end wherein Swift lays aside all pretenses and describes colonization in a baldly harsh manner offering an ironic description of the imperial adventure and creation of a colony:

A Crew of Pyrates are Driven by a Storm they know not whither; at length a Boy discovers Land from the Top-mast; they go on Shore to rob and plunder; they see an harmless People, are entertained with Kindness, they give the Country a new Name, they take formal Possession of it for the King, they set up a rotten Plank or a Stone for a Memorial, they murder two or three dozen of the Natives, bring away a Couple more by Force for a Sample, return home, and get their Pardon. Here commences a new Dominion acquired with a Title by Divine Right. Ships are sent with the first Opportunity; the Natives driven out or destroyed, their Princes tortured to discover their Gold; a free License given to all Acts of Inhumanity and Lust; the Earth reeking with the Blood of its Inhabitants: And this execrable Crew of Butchers employed in so pious an Expedition, is a modern Colony sent to convert and civilize an idolatrous and barbarous People. (356)

This version of the violent and immoral birth of a colony offers quite a contrast to the innocent and natural one presented by writers of imperial island narratives like Defoe. Swift's motivations for writing his parody were undoubtedly complex, perhaps including professional rivalry with Defoe or his firsthand experience as a native of Ireland, the first of Britain's colonized islands.[23] As I suggest with Duffett's motivations, one aim of Swift's could have been to educate his audience to the flaws of the imperial island fantasy. The passage above suggests such an aim. Though that passage might narrate what Swift takes to be the realities of imperial adventure, that is not the story he tells in *Gulliver's Travels*. *Gulliver's Travels* presents a tale of one man's innocent imperial escapades, an adventuring that does not result in colonies and that is not an example of imperial violence. Perhaps Swift is more realistic about what a single man can do on consistently inhabited islands, or perhaps Gulliver's nonviolence results from the fact that the cultures Gulliver finds are already rather Western-like. Ironically for Swift, much of his audience missed his satirical aim. Despite his intentions to undercut Defoe's story, as Green explains, *Gulliver's Travels* "was read as yet another traveler's tale. . . . It was Defoe who triumphed, and Swift was carried along in his wake" (*Dreams of Adventure, Deeds of Empire*, 92). So, instead of subverting the power of the island narrative, the public's misreading could mean that his work instead participated in the strengthening of the genre. Also like the pantomimes, for some readers his carnivalesque parody could have provided a space for the venting of imperial oppositions, which perhaps worked against their mobilization.

These island parodies, it would seem, recognize, appeal to, and perhaps vent an existing dissatisfaction with empire, but could such texts simultaneously contribute to the dissolution of empire? Could they forward an already existing momentum or actually highlight fissures in the colonial façade instead of, as did the earlier narratives, working to paste over those fissures? Perhaps. Edward Said's discussion of a growing disillusionment with imperial ideology, which he terms "exhaustion with empire," suggests that literary texts, like these island parodies, might indeed partially act as catalyst by making way psychologically for imperial dissolution. As Said explains in *Culture and Imperialism*,

Just as culture may predispose and actively prepare one society for the overseas domination of another, it may also prepare that society to relinquish or modify *the idea of overseas domination.* These changes cannot occur without the willingness of men and women to resist the pressures of colonial rule, to take up arms, to project ideas of liberation, and to imagine (as Benedict Anderson has it) a new national community, to take the final plunge. *Nor can they occur unless either economic or political exhaustion with empire sets in at home,* unless the idea of empire and the cost of colonial rule are challenged publicly, unless the representations of imperialism begin to lose their justification and legitimacy. . . . (200, emphasis added)

Here Said eloquently expresses what history suggests: that challenges to imperial ideology eventually contributing to devolution must come from within the imperial machine as well as without. By making fun of imperial propaganda and destabilizing one of the founding myths of empire (that of "natural" control and the deserving, manly colonist), parodies of the island story worked from inside the imperial machine to "modify the idea" of empire, reminding us of the complicated forms resistance can take. The works in this chapter have shown some of the ambivalence and contradictions involved in writing from the imperial center about colonization. Where some writers like Defoe and Wyss, or even Shakespeare, weave tales that ease the colonial conscience by rationalizing island conquest, other writers, such as those from this chapter, who parody colonial island texts, show the messiness and dissent that always accompanies empire. And still other writers, especially, as the next chapter will show, of television and film, recast the castaway tale into a vehicle for twentieth-century neo-imperial fantasy.

6. The U.S. Island Fantasy, or Cast Away with Gilligan

That's the tale of the castaways.
They're here for a long, long time.
They'll have to make the best of it.
It's an uphill climb.

from the closing theme to *Gilligan's Island,* 1970s U.S.
television show about a group of American island castaways

I WOULD like to close this book by circling back to the questions with which it began. In my introduction I asked what was so powerful about the colonial island story that postcolonial writers felt compelled to rewrite it and colonial authors to repeat it. The power of the island and its story, I have argued, comes from its ability to sustain a fantasy of natural bodily command of space, a fantasy important to legitimizing colonial expansion both at home and with the newly colonized peoples. The second question with which I opened this study asked how those stories of island colonization affected the way people (both of the colonizing and colonized cultures) thought and felt about real-world empire. By looking at how the texts evolve and remain constant, at who read them, and at how they so often mirrored codeterminate realities of colonization, I have argued that island narratives made a range of people feel better about empire, either by giving them a comfortable fantasy to ease doubts, by giving them a space to express opposition in a manner fairly unthreatening to sociocultural standing, or by giving those anxious for resistance (postcolonial writers and reader) space for dissension. Now comes the time to skip ahead chronologically to the twentieth and early twenty-first centuries and to examine how and why the island fantasy remains current. This final chapter, then, takes as its topic a third related question, which is: Why are island narratives still being so widely produced in our supposedly postcolonial world?

Instead of rehashing discussions about the power of literature to

"write back," though, here I would like to change our focus slightly, to examine a range of contemporary film or television revisions of the island
castaway story produced primarily in or by the United States. A number
of such castaway stories have been produced by Hollywood in recent decades, a group impressive in number if not in quality.[1] To give just a partial
list, in the last five years the U.S. film industry has yielded *Six Days, Seven
Nights* (1998), in which Harrison Ford and Ann Heche find love as castaways; *The Beach* (2000) (adapting Alex Garland's 1996 novel), where
Leonardo DiCaprio's Gen-X tourist, Richard, joins an international island commune on a deserted South Sea island; *Cast Away* (2000), where
Tom Hanks's Chuck Noland becomes stranded on an island with only a
volleyball for a companion; and Madonna's latest acting attempt, *Swept
Away* (2002) (a remake of Lina Wertmüller's 1974 film) another castaway tale where mismatched castaways find love. In the mid-nineties,
a remake of *The Island of Dr. Moreau* (1996), with Marlon Brando and
Val Kilmer, also graced film screens, as did a remake of *Robinson Crusoe*
(1996) starring Pierce Brosnan. Before that, 1980s Hollywood produced
a number of versions of the *Blue Lagoon* (1980), in which a nubile Brooke
Shields and Christopher Atkins learn about "nature" on their deserted
island, and *Crusoe* (1988), another filmed adaptation of *Robinson Crusoe*
starring Aidan Quinn. As well, recent television has brought the *Survivor* series, the first of which in 2000 and the most recent 2003 version
were constructed as island castaway dramas. Preceding *Survivor* were
the 1970s show *Gilligan's Island,* in which, to quote its theme song, the
characters were stranded on an "uncharted desert isle," with "no phone,
no lights, no motorcars / not a single luxury" and "like Robinson Crusoe" were "primitive as can be"; and the 1970s–'80s show *Fantasy Island,*
in which Ricardo Montalban's Mr. Rourke (like a modern-day Prospero)
magically fulfills his guest's fantasies just by broodingly looking into the
camera. More recently, television has also brought the popular *Temptation Island* reality series, *The Real Gilligan's Island* reality series, and *Lost,*
in which forty-eight men and women stranded on an island from a plane
crash battle deprivation, social conflict, and mysterious monsters.

As evident from this roster of films and shows, in recent decades the
United States has produced an inordinate number of updates of the
castaway theme. While recognizing that the United States is one of the
world's leading producers of all films and television, I still wonder, why
the continued U.S. interest in islands and castaways? Popular ideology
holds that the United States is the world's leading democracy, the type of

place that should be *un*-interested in an imperial fantasy of island coloni-zation. So why, if the island fantasy is a tool of colonial ideology, as I have argued throughout this study, does the contemporary U.S. television and film industry so often reiterate the castaway fantasy? What should we make of contemporary filmed or televised adaptations that don't seem to be challenging the castaway story to subvert its power (like the postco-lonial revisions mentioned in my introduction) so much as borrowing the genre for a related contemporary purpose?

By viewing *Cast Away,* one of the most recent and widely viewed of these U.S.–produced island tales, for how it reiterates and adapts the castaway story, we find several potential answers for such questions. In many respects, *Cast Away* (co-written by Tom Hanks and screenwriter Bill Broyles, creator of *China Beach* and co-writer of *Apollo 13*) follows a tra-ditional Robinsonade plot. After a horrific plane crash, Chuck Noland, appropriately played by the all-American Hanks, becomes stranded on an island, where he survives by utilizing the objects from Federal Express packages washed ashore from the crash, rather than from a wrecked ship as in Defoe's tale.[2] *Cast Away,* however, varies from colonial island stories in that, though Chuck adapts to island life, he never really *settles* his is-land in the sense that generations of other castaways did. He remains a perpetual visitor, not island owner—never, for instance, building a house (except for a temporary shelter out of his rubber raft and FedEx boxes), never constructing a bridge or defense measures, never assembling a sta-ble or pen to domesticate animals. After four years on the island, he still lives in a cave, though he has decorated its walls a bit with art. We see no evidence that he plants gardens, orchards, or crops or domesticates ani-mals; he seems to eat only fish, crabs, and coconuts. Yet, the film makes much of his intelligence, demonstrating, for example, that he can con-struct a calendar on the wall of his cave that follows the sun's seasonal rays and can quickly calculate complex algorithms to determine the dis-tance he crashed off course and the amount of rope needed to build a raft. Moreover, Chuck's engineering proficiency enables him to build with materials at hand, as shown by his construction of a seaworthy raft out of a recycled port-a-potty and by the ingenious uses to which he puts the objects he finds in the FedEx packages. Of course, such ingenuity has always provided one of the pleasures of castaway tales, as seen in the consistent jokes on *Gilligan's Island* about the elaborate machinery the Professor could construct out of coconut shells and string. Out of ob-jects in the FedEx packages that at first seem humorously useless, Chuck creates similarly ingenious implements: making an ax from ice skates, rope from video tapes, a fish net from a dress. An intelligent, industrious, impressive man, Chuck surely could have "civilized" his island in the four years he was there—had he wanted to.

That Chuck doesn't settle the island suggests that the film means to show him lacking feelings of ownership. As shown by his obsession with the pocket-watch picture of his girlfriend (Kelly, played by Helen Hunt), all of Chuck's emotional energies are turned toward his lost U.S. home. Chuck never psychically incorporates the island because, even though he lives there for four years, he is not invested in the space. He remains perpetual visitor, never owner. The island to him represents only potential hardship, danger, and death—the ultimate obstacle between him and his desires, not an object of desire itself. In fact, he risks a perilous voyage to leave the island because he fears dying there alone of accident or sickness; as he says, "I would rather take my chance out there on the ocean than to stay here and die on this shit hole island talking to a goddamned volleyball!" Chuck's story differs significantly from colonial island stories, in which the castaway initially longs for home but works through his despair to find real joy in island life, as does Crusoe, who begins to imagine what he first called a "barren" island as his "little kingdom" (40, 100). Chuck never performs those behaviors that reveal and cement a sense of ownership, never even naming the island. He does scratch on a rock "Chuck Noland was here 1500 days. Escaped to sea. Tell Kelly Frears, Memphis TN, I love her." But this message marks his fears of not surviving the hazardous sea voyage rather than feelings of island ownership. Unlike Crusoe, who can't wait to return to the island once in England; or the Swiss Robinsons, who decide to stay on the island even with the chance of rescue; or Verne's castaways, who dream of annexing their island as a U.S. colony, Chuck leaves the island, we suspect, for good. The ironically named Chuck Noland ("chuck no land") does just that.[3]

One of the most important of the film's demonstrations of Chuck's feelings of nonpossession come in its handling of its two monarch-of-all-I-survey moments. Instead of making way for his imagined ownership of the island, they amplify Chuck's sense of loss and his overwhelming desire to leave the island to return to the United States. These moments are of rejection, not possession. The first monarch-of-all-I-survey scene encompasses hope turned to grief. When Chuck sees the captain of his ill-fated flight floating below in the surf, he quickly abandons his island-top vista and races down to the shore to find further despair in discovery that the man is dead. Chuck's next trip to that spot comes with his attempt to hang himself from a tree at its summit, a moment that highlights his sense of dismay and powerlessness when he realizes, as he says, "I couldn't even kill myself the way I wanted to. I had control over nothing." After the attempted suicide, Chuck avoids the hilltop, only reluctantly going there to retrieve the rope he needs to escape the island. Chuck's first two monarch-of-all-I-survey moments are grief-filled instead of thrilling, and the third represents his determination to leave the island. By inverting this archetypal castaway moment, the film, like other U.S.–produced island stories, shows Chuck *rejecting* the island, refusing to make it into a home or colony.

Also significantly turned on its head is the motif of the castaway forming a "relationship" with a human/animal/monster island indigene as a way of asserting control over and interacting with the island he desires. In *Cast Away* Chuck does form a relationship, but instead of "befriending" an indigenous animal or human (as does Crusoe with Friday and his "animal family," John Daniel with his sea monsters, the Swiss Robinsons with their variety of animals, and others), Chuck finds companionship in an anthropomorphized object: Wilson, an inanimate volleyball, a commodified item of U.S. sport and one of Chuck's few reminders of home. Instead of taming birds or other small animals that could have provided companionship and interaction with the island environment, Chuck chooses a fantasy relationship with an object that symbolizes U.S. capitalistic sport and the world Chuck left behind. Wilson also symbolizes Chuck's despair, since Chuck "creates" him when he smears blood on the volleyball while throwing it in frustration over a failed attempt to start a fire. More importantly, instead of providing interaction with an Other, Wilson provides only a reflection of Chuck's profound loneliness, since Chuck's "conversations" with Wilson are really only projections of his own desires and anxieties. Ironically, Chuck's fixation on Wilson diminishes his one chance encounter with a potential animal companion, the whales he meets while drifting at sea after leaving the island. It is the whales that repeatedly save him, blowing water on him to cool him and waking him when he almost sleeps through his rescue ship, but his preoccupation with losing Wilson makes him miss that potential and perhaps heartening encounter with something new.

Other filmic castaways behave in much the same manner, with the island often providing only a vehicle for romantic relationships between two Westerners (as in *The Beach, Swept Away,* and *Six Days, Seven Nights*) instead of a relationship between the castaway and someone or something truly different. What does it mean that in these new, filmed tales, the island provides only a space for the castaway, by *rejecting* the island and *disregarding* its indigenes, to reaffirm (instead of test) his/her Western identity? Perhaps we can better understand the symbolic significance of this shift to the castaway rejecting (instead of embracing) the island and its indigenes by reading and analyzing them as, like their print forebears, reflections of and vehicles for cultural fantasies of the time and place in which they were created—the late twentieth-century United States.

U.$. Empire

We can explain the shift to the castaway rejecting the island and its indigenes in *Cast Away* and other recent U.S.–produced filmed island tales if we consider them as replicating a myth of *non*colonization especially popular in the contemporary United States. The films, it seems, portray a *neo*-imperial island fantasy, meaning that, instead of representing traditional fantasies of empire (as do classic island stories), these U.S. tales reflect recent behaviors of trading direct military and political colonization for a more indirect (sometimes covert) economic and cultural hegemony. These new island stories have been produced alongside a national mythology of global "development" and "democratic capitalism" that has permeated U.S. culture since the 1940s and become exacerbated in recent decades.[4] In this national ideology, the United States as *non*colonizer fights for global democracy and opposes imperialism (with communism as imperialism's traditional avatar). Edward Said, in fact, explains what he calls a "semi-official" narrative of U.S. international involvement: "The commonest sequence is the old one that America, a force for good in the world, regularly comes up against obstacles posed by foreign conspiracies, ontologically mischievous and 'against' America" (*Culture and Imperialism,* 324). Historically, U.S. foreign policy has, instead of resorting to occupation, provided unofficial support and installed "friendly" governments in places it deems crucial to its own national interests. As Said remarks, the United States' "foreign-policy elite has no long-standing tradition of direct rule overseas, as was the case with the British or the French, so American attention works in spurts; great masses of rhetoric and huge resources are lavished somewhere

(Vietnam, Libya, Iraq, Panama), followed by virtual silence" (*Culture and Imperialism*, 289).

Of course, as numerous postcolonial critics have noted, this fairy tale of U.S. anti-imperialism ignores facts about the origins of the United States (such as its legacy of land theft from American First Nation peoples, Mexican settlers, and native Hawaiians, and its history of enslavement of Africans), as well as ignoring policies aimed at domination in politics (through institutions such as NATO and occasionally the United Nations), military power (enforced by military bases in sixty-nine countries), and international economics (as practiced by U.S.–run institutions such as the International Monetary Fund and World Bank). "Despite the hauling down of colonial flags in the 1950s," as Anne McClintock reiterates, "revamped economic imperialism has ensured that the United States and former European colonial powers have become richer, while, with a tiny scattering of exceptions, their ex-colonies have become poorer" (*Imperial Leather*, 393). (McClintock also reminds that the president and managing director of the World Bank are *always* from the United States.) Most elusively, this fantasy of U.S. non-imperialism ignores the U.S. practice of *cultural* imperialism: its exporting of Western myths of capitalism, individualism, and "progress" through a variety of media (including television and film), its control of what passes for news through what Said calls the "New World Information Order," its sending the world McDonald's franchises and reruns of *Dallas* while allowing United States–based international business conglomerates to exploit other nations' labor pools so that Wal-Mart can continue to "roll back" prices.

Discussion of the United States as an empire (or as something resembling empire, but not quite) has been much in the news in the early 2000s. This debate is hardly a new one. Many of these essayists note that arguments about the United States as an imperial power go back at least to the early days of the United States and debates over what form the nation's relationship with the Philippines should take (a topic over which, as Jim Zwick notes, Mark Twain and Rudyard Kipling argued). Yet, this debate has received new life in the mainstream press from debate over international political events. As Leon Hadar explains, "Click 'American empire' on your Internet search engine and you'll be linked to hundreds of Web sites, newspaper columns, magazine articles and books that discuss and debate Washington's new imperial role around the globe" (15). Some of these columns bring up U.S. past "imperial" behaviors (its annexations of Hawaii, Cuba, Puerto Rico, Guam, and the Philippines, as well as its militarily enforced trade with Japan) and other more recent "imperial" actions (attacking Afghanistan, invading Iraq, denouncing the U.N.) as reasons to label the United States as an "empire," interestingly forecasting both good and bad consequences of this empire.[5]

Significantly, as many of these discussions declare the U.S. *not* an empire as those that do, a disavowal as provocative as the tangled webs of logic some authors employ to support that claim. Many compare the United States to empires of the past, particularly the Roman and British empires, reasoning that since the U.S. differs from those previous empires, it is not an empire per se but more world leader, akin to a term that seems to have gone out of fashion of late, "superpower," which also elides the devastating effects of such "leadership" on poorer, smaller countries.[6] Even George W. Bush felt prompted to answer charges of American empire during his 2000 presidential campaign, denying plans to engage in what he calls "nation building" and vowing an increase in isolation and "humility" in foreign affairs. Though his policy and actions since 9/11 belie those early promises, he still maintains his claims that the United States has "no territorial ambitions. We don't seek an empire. Our nation is committed to freedom for ourselves and for others" (Robert Bellah, 20). Such denial could be a new national pastime. As Michael Ignatieff commented in his January 5, 2003, piece in *The New York Times Magazine,* "A historian once remarked that Britain acquired its empire in 'a fit of absence of mind.' If Americans have an empire, they have acquired it in a state of deep denial" (22). Such expressions of ambivalence—this wish to *have* an empire (whatever one calls it) while denying *wanting* one—as expressed in these mainstream media debates are also echoed in these new, cinematic island tales, in their stories of *not* making a home on islands one is forced to colonize.

In the pattern of the castaway choosing *not* to express ownership of the island, while still being forced to live there, we can see reflected a culturewide fantasy of the United States as an anticolonial world power that simultaneously engages in neo-imperial foreign policy because forced to police the world. That these new, filmed island narratives offer a means for managing subconscious cultural desires about the place of the United States in the world, makes them as important to some contemporary Westerners' feelings of well-being as their literary castaway predecessors were to sixteenth- through early twentieth-century colonists. Significantly, as well as echoing those desires, the films also reflect *fears* about the global role of the United States, specifically fears of the loss of that same global hegemony.

Michael Hardt and Antonio Negri's controversial book, *Empire* (2000), which, as Timothy Brennan notes, revamps arguments in globalization theory, reintroduces a provocative thread to this tangled debate over the United States and empire that helps to explain this fear of declining U.S. hegemony. Taking a slightly different approach from those critics who see U.S. military and economic domination as straightforward neo-imperialism, Hardt and Negri perceive U.S. economic and political foreign policy as part of a larger globalizing, deterritorialized, supranational system of capital, information, and people. International flows of politics, money, information, culture, business, and people of the last forty-odd years—what many call "globalization"— Hardt and Negri theorize as part of what they call (capital "e") "Empire." More precisely, as Hardt and Negri explain, these flows of politics, money, information, culture, business, and people are *controlled* by Empire, that is, by a universal collective of primarily business and financial forces, which exists beyond the domain of the traditional nation-state and national boundaries, which supercedes any individual national authority in favor of a global dominion, and which answers primarily to the needs of international capitalism. Though suspicious of their claims of our postimperiality and of Empire's potential for eventually fomenting anticapitalistic revolution, I do find that some points of Hardt and Negri's involved and provocative arguments ring true to my ear, particularly their articulation of a deterritorialized empire. If we can suspend disbelief for a moment and think of international events in recent decades in terms of a growing deterritorialization, then perhaps we can understand cinematic island narratives' consistent insistence on plots of noncolonization in a new light—as mechanisms to also manage cultural fears of obsolescence.

The Island Cosmopolitan and Fear of Deterritorialization

Taking Hardt and Negri's argument about a deterritorialized Empire into account, we can understand these new filmed island narratives as both a reflection of U.S. desires for an anticolonial empire and a vehicle to manage fears of deterritorialized Empire, for in Empire the United States becomes just one of a host of increasingly obsolete nation-states. Such prophecies of potential irrelevance provide an immense challenge to a U.S. national identity built around notions of righteously earned economic, military, political, and cultural dominance. My argument is not that the United States has *lost* its hegemony—recent military and political actions belie that argument—but rather that the United States *fears* losing its hegemony through its own global capitalistic excesses, which partially explains the popularity of story lines in which castaways reject the island to return to the United States. These new tales reflect a perception of islands as commodified, as places to be visited (as tourists) or used but *not* to be settled, since, logically, they could never offer all of the cultural and economic advantages of the United States—which in this fantasy remains the center of everyone's desires.

In several of these films (*Six Days, Seven Nights; Swept Away;* and *The Beach*), the castaways are American tourists, cosmopolitan in their weariness with travel, who are initially ecstatic at island life but (like tourists sated with sun and sea, impatient to get home) come to realize the island's inherent flaws and the advantages of the United States. The island, as bountiful, beautiful, and inviting as it is, ultimately falls short of the home from which they came. Like Chuck Noland, these new castaways naturally pine for home, logically never really settling on the island. In another variation, tales such as *The Beach* show castaways who are at first elated at island life (like Tommo in *Typee*), but who come to realize the island's deficiencies and recognize the attractions of their underappreciated U.S. home. In *The Beach,* the island's defect is its native inhabitants (violent and suspicious marijuana farmers) who attack Richard's Euro-American commune with a murderous rage when more tourists in search of the perfect beach come to the island. Likewise, the newly formed couple in *Six Days, Seven Nights* (Anne Heche as Robin Monroe, and Harrison Ford as Quinn Harris) leaves their island after encountering violent drug smugglers, the modern-day equivalent of pirates. Of course, returning to any large city in the United States, the castaways could encounter a drug war just as violent, a fact that both films neglect. So, Richard, Robin, and Quinn gratefully return to the United States at the end of their respective films. In *Swept Away,* cruel capitalist Amber (played by Madonna) and communist fisherman Giuseppe (played by Adriano Giannini) learn to love the island where they find romance, but also choose to leave it to test the strength of their relationship in the "real world," a test they fail. Instead of violence, their island's flaw is its utopic nature, its very existence so outside of "reality" that it fosters a romance so groundless that it could survive nowhere else. The film ends with Amber, brokenhearted and softened, flying back to her New

York jet-set life with her millionaire husband, leaving behind her beautiful island and lover, which are likely to fade into bittersweet memories as
should any good vacation.

Though the films consistently and ultimately present the United
States as a preferable home to the island, they are not without brief moments of conflicted nostalgia, especially as the castaway leaves the island.
In *Cast Away*, Chuck gazes with apparent ambivalence at the island as
he sails away. Richard, in *The Beach*, looks with seeming regret at a photograph of his commune on the island, but then he turns to get on his
U.S.–bound plane, and Amber, looking out of her helicopter window,
weeps quietly as the island and Giuseppe recede below. But none of
these castaways turns back; none suggests that their attraction to the island means that the United States is less desirable. They all fly home. In
such endings we can see reflected a popular mythology of the United
States as metaphoric center of the world, the place one would never
willingly leave and to which the rest of the world flees in search of a better life. In such an ideology, governmental representatives, the military,
business people, or tourists may visit other spaces, but they always *return*
to the United States, where the water is cleaner, the technology more
available, and the streets safer.[7]

These new castaway films and their stories of U.S. centrality could
smooth the edges of such fears of lost desirability. Just as one could read
print castaway tales as diminishing *colonial* fears of unfair colonization
by depicting colonization as unavoidable and legitimate, castaway narratives in their most recent film incarnation could aid the management
of new fears of Empire, even if the narrative must be inverted so that
castaways *reject* the island in favor of their U.S. home to demonstrate
their own national superiority and deny their own fears of marginality. The popularity of these new stories of the brief island idyll can also
be partially explained by their timing, coming as they do during an era
of exponential growth of Internet and communications technologies
(making the notion of centrality itself suspect) and the collapse of the
Soviet Union. As well, the dissolution of the British and Russian empires
raises lingering anxieties about the remaining superpower suffering a
similar fate. (In fact, several of the aforementioned comparisons of the
United States with past empires take great pains to show how and why
the United States could and will enjoy a different outcome, bypassing
an inevitable fall.)

Cast Away is unique in that it directly engages this issue of international competition and failed empire. As in the other films, *Cast Away*'s Chuck is a world traveler, though for business instead of pleasure, with his cosmopolitan status demonstrated in his and Kelly's well-rehearsed pre-flight routine and in his flying on a FedEx private plane, where both flight attendant and captain know him by name. The film divides into three acts: Chuck before becoming cast away, Chuck on the island, and then Chuck after returning from his stay on the island. In the first act, we see Chuck as an efficiency expert for the shipping firm, Federal Express, a participant in globalization as much through its international offices as through its instant worldwide delivery of mail. The few scenes the film shows of Chuck at work for FedEx before becoming island-bound help to explain his preoccupation with U.S. cultural superiority. Chuck's work involves teaching FedEx employees in other nations (who, it seems, are incompetent and backward without his help) how to live up to the high standards of FedEx and U.S. business in general, and spreading ideologies of the superiority of Western time-management, technology, and self-discipline around the globe. In particular, the film shows Chuck fighting Russian inefficiency (supposedly carried over from communist days), training his employees to "live and die by the clock" and perpetuating the fantasy that the economic global empire of the United States benefits others by (and stems from) encouraging democracy, "progress," and free-market capitalism. It's no coincidence that the place we see Chuck work his magic is postcommunist Russia, which, by attempting conversion to a capitalist economy, continues to provide reassurance of U.S. cultural superiority and economic centrality. Moreover, by depicting Russia as inefficient, regressive, and pleasure-loving, *Cast Away* provides "evidence" of why the U.S. empire will *not* fall to the same fate as the Russian.

Psychologies of the Neo-castaway Narrative

So far this chapter has argued that castaway films serve a psychocultural function, that their consistent tales of noncolonization reflect fantasies of a seemingly anticolonial empire and disperse fears of national marginality. We can gain further understanding of the mechanics of how they do so by speculating a bit on *how* they involve viewers in their stories. Though several subsequent seasons have also used island sets, the first season of the reality series *Survivor* provides a good starting point for such investigation. During the summer of 2001, a large portion of the U.S. television audience was captivated by the day-to-day escapades of sixteen volunteers carefully chosen by television producers to be confined together for thirty-nine days on a South Sea island off Borneo that was "deserted"—except, that is, for the show's producers, crew, omnipresent cameramen, and indigenous people, who were not shown. That first *Survivor* series, which could be said to have launched the reality television trend that still has hold of U.S. television sets, was the most popular of its genre (including its sequels set in Australia, Africa, the Marquesas, Thailand, and the Amazon), captivating millions of viewers, netting the network millions of dollars in advertising revenue, and making its finalists into celebrities.

In some ways, *Survivor* presents the same version of the castaway fantasy as the castaway films, for *Survivor*'s castaways also reject their island. The reward for their discipline and performance is *not* staying on or possessing the island but winning the game to return to the United States wealthy and internationally recognized. It might seem that these reality TV castaways are merely playing out the truth behind the ideology of castaway stories, since even in fiction some castaways of old became wealthy from their island colonization. Crusoe, for instance, once rescued, finds himself a wealthy man, based on investments made before he was stranded and on his ownership of his island. But castaways of old, as well as becoming wealthy, maintained a responsibility to and relationship with the island and often its inhabitants. Crusoe, for example, remains "governor" and steward of his island for life, and takes care of Friday until his death. As a neo-imperial fantasy, however, *Survivor* carries none of the responsibilities for the island or for its indigenous inhabitants found in traditional castaway narratives. I am unaware of any indigenous inhabitants ever being interviewed, involved, or even shown as part of the first *Survivor* series, excepting perhaps in the opening credits, and I would bet that few (if any) indigenous islanders or the island ecology benefited from the island being appropriated as it was.

Yet *Survivor* differs from the films in its fairly direct staging of anxieties about marginality. The crisis *Survivor* dramatizes week after week involves being cast off the island, of not being allowed to play (and potentially dominate) the game of capitalist competition. Instead of the fears of loss of control present in traditional castaway novels (of falling victim to cannibals or pirates, of going mad or native), *Survivor*'s story of being expelled from the island reflects fears of loss of centrality—of being rejected instead of being the one doing the rejecting, of being relegated to the watchers instead of the actors. This plot of the horrors of being excluded from the game mirrors a deeply rooted fear of the United States within Empire, of being barred from sites of current political power, financial influence, and military authority—just as post-imperial British and Russians have been excluded from some former positions of power.

How the show involves its viewers in the dramatization of that cultural anxiety perhaps partially explains some of its popularity. Of course, the show responds to a certain voyeurism, with its lush island setting, thrilling competition, and scantily clothed bodies (even if those bodies aren't exactly traditionally attractive, as with Richard Hatch's paunchy nudism). But more than that, *Survivor* appeals because, as a reality television show, it involves its viewers in its tale in a way not quite achieved by films and scripted television, letting viewers, from the safety of their homes, vicariously join in the thrill of the castaway adventure. By reworking the fantasy of self-discipline seen in traditional castaway stories, the show allows viewers to marvel at players' endurance of physical hardships, particularly of diet, famously being fed in one early episode a meal of rat meat, though otherwise they tolerated only a monotonous regimen of all the plain rice and clean water they desired (a diet on which much of the world already relies). Viewers could also watch the castaways suffering not from isolation but from lack of contact with loved ones, growing thinner and grumpier as the weeks progress. Interestingly, as the shows progress, the suffering of the participants increases. On the African *Survivor* series, the participants had to boil all of the water they drank, for clean water was not available, and they suffered from poor nutrition (hair falling out, vomiting). In the seventh *Survivor* series, participants could no longer bring luxury items. Perhaps American viewers increasingly require more suffering to keep their interest, or perhaps the show's producers are attempting to more accurately simulate the daily hardships of third-world existence. In either case, I would argue that viewers would be aware of the fabrication of the events on the screen, for which participants volunteer and which happened months before being aired on TV. Exacerbating that realization is the fact that the haggard participant voted off each week regularly appears shiny and healthy on the morning talk shows immediately following *Survivor*'s airing.

In truth, contestants face little danger of actual starvation, injury, or solitude on that giant sound-stage island, but instead they confront competition, manipulation, betrayal, and self-serving alliances, as declared in the show's motto adorning its logo: "Outwit, Outplay, Outlast" (which could ironically fit any corporate raider). It is likely that many contemporary viewers understand those obstacles better than physical hardship, perhaps finding some respite from the routine or stresses of their own lives by vicariously experiencing controlled competition and a fantasy of life reduced to its basic elements. As well, one could read such dramatization of alliances and competition, of an enemy from within, as transferring fears about threats from within the United States and one's own community: the hidden terrorist cell, the neighbor who turns out to be an enemy. Though the first *Survivor* series preceded by a few months the events surrounding September 11, 2001, it followed the 1995 Oklahoma bombing and the 1996 arrest of the Unabomber.

Also important is how *Survivor,* as reality television, allows viewers to process fears of personal and national rejection. Though one of the players each week is expelled from the community, the viewer, significantly, is not, but is allowed to "play" through to the end. The viewer is never rejected like the players and retains the power to reject player after player from the comfort of the couch and television "island." In fact, the show's editing of footage often presents the person who will be ejected in that week's show in an unfavorable light, a maneuver too consistent to be accidental, indicating that the show in its narrative construction encourages viewers to dislike some players over others. The viewer's manipulated decision of whom to reject and the viewer's position as continuing player (not being rejected) are confirmed by each show's "tribal council." Just as the filmed castaway's rejection of the island confirms the superiority of the United States, *Survivor*'s positioning of viewers as rejectors but never rejected tackles fears of social and national marginality. *Survivor* offers viewers the chance to share in the castaway's experience, and leads them, while being attracted to the inviting island, to ultimately reject it, glad to return when the experience is over to the comfort and familiarity of home.

An investigation of the psychological effects of these new, filmed stories must also consider the impact of their being presented through the visual media of film and television. Film critics such as Laura Mulvey in her influential "Visual Pleasure and Narrative Cinema" (1975) have discussed psychological effects of watching films and the complex processes of projection and identification taking place in the theater or in front of the television. Postcolonial film critics, such as Ella Shohat and Robert Stam, have likewise speculated on the ideological effects of film and on the act of viewing maps, tropes of empire, and racial stereotypes on colonial, colonized, and neocolonial viewers. Filmmakers often take into consideration, perhaps rely upon, their audiences experiencing projection and identification with the images and characters of cinema, and these new island narratives (whether intentional or not) tap into that experience, as well. While recognizing that the film might, in fact, elicit more complex responses among viewers than its makers intend, we can still examine its story and construction to speculate on one predictable (perhaps intended) response from some of its viewers.

A good example of how film as a medium could affect the castaway tale's psychological effect can be found by returning to the monarch-of-all-I-survey scene in *Cast Away* to examine suggestive elements of its construction. As Michael Hiltzik explains in his analysis of Hollywood digital effects, the film's monarch-of-all-I-survey scenes were shot in a parking lot in front of a blue screen. After shooting the footage of Chuck looking down from the summit, computer graphic artists added in the island vista below in postproduction. The island as it naturally existed wasn't adequate for the fantasy the film needed to present, perhaps lacking a hill or mountain of sufficient height to film that archetypal castaway moment. But since that scene is crucial to the castaway tale, filmmakers had the task of creating it. In other scenes, nearby islands on the real Fijian island's horizon were digitally erased, and the real island's surf (which was lessened by its actual close proximity to other islands) was enhanced to explain why Chuck couldn't raft over the surf without a sail. The "creation" of the island is significant for more than allowing us yet again to marvel at the achievements of technology and careful filmmaking. Such efforts demonstrate the continued existence of a pervasive mental construct of what the island ought to be to function properly in such fantasies of island (non)colonization—an image that apparently doesn't exist in reality but that the filmmakers understood enough to create and project onto the film and screen. Viewers are led to access that mental image and perhaps recognize the centrality of that moment to begin, along with Chuck, to reject the island and progress with him to the third act of the film, his return to the United States.[8]

To understand this last point, we must look more closely at how the filmmakers position the viewer within the first monarch-of-all-I-survey moment in which Chuck overlooks the island before spying his drowned companion below. The scene is filmed so that for thirty seconds the camera performs a near 360° pan of the edges of the island, inviting the viewer to participate in that monarch-of-all-I-survey moment with (or instead of) Chuck, viewing the island's borders in the one sweeping shot, encompassing the entirety of the island in one's gaze. The camera tilts dizzyingly in an attempt to draw the viewer into the sickness that Chuck feels, too. Chuck becomes peripheral to the scene, often falling out of frame; it is the viewer's desperate sight of the island's impenetrable boundaries that is important. The camera is also positioned so that it shows the back of Chuck's head as he looks down, a shot that denies the viewer knowledge of Chuck's reaction to the sight of the island's circumscribing boundaries and the realization that he is stranded. It is only after the camera's pan that viewers see Chuck's stunned and terrified countenance, and then only for a moment before his face registers a faint glimmer of hope as he spies his friend's body below. Racing down to find him drowned, however, leaves Chuck sobbing in disgust and despair. The positioning of viewers so that they can participate in the monarch-of-all-I-survey scene, in effect, invites them to access the mental image of how the castaway narrative typically progresses and to experience that moment enough to recognize its centrality before seeing Chuck's reaction and sharing in his repudiation. This process of repudiation continues throughout the rest of the island sequence, as the film prepares viewers to anticipate Chuck's return to the United States.

The island sequence is divided into two sections four years apart. After the monarch-of-all-I-survey scene, viewers progress with Chuck through adaptation to island life, including momentary joy at making fire and fishing. But when the film returns to Chuck four years later, viewers find only loneliness and continuing despondency. Viewers' desires to see how Chuck "civilized" the island in that interlude are frustrated by his obvious refusal to do so and by his withdrawal and grief (the sequence begins with a feral, crouched, matted-haired, empty-eyed Chuck chewing on a raw fish). Viewers are thus led, like Chuck, to reject the island experience and hope for his return to the United States and reunion with Kelly, a hope fulfilled by the last third of the film. For nearly an hour during the island sequence, the film is virtually silent except for the background noise of the pounding surf, with the camera fairly static and focused nearly always only on Chuck. In its last act, however, the film both shocks and rewards viewers (as Chuck is shocked and rewarded) with return to the sounds, colors, and movement of civilization. Despite Chuck's momentary difficulty of readjustment to "civilization" (trouble sleeping in a bed, discomfort in crowds) and bittersweet reunion with

Kelly, Chuck's behavior leaves no doubt that he prefers his U.S. home to his island and to the other sites he visits in the course of the film. Returning to the island never seems to be an option. Whether or not viewers actually do prefer the last U.S. sequence over the island sequence, the film presents them with the opportunity to participate with Chuck and other castaways in a refusal of island settlement, in a return to modernity and the comforts of human contact, in a return to the refuge of home, nation, and the security of identity.

Being stranded on an island, one would think, would be a life-revolutionizing experience, but *Cast Away* suggests that though Chuck is more appreciative of the comforts of home (he marvels several times at ice), his worldview has not significantly altered. On the one hand, the film shows him laughing at the irony of his old FedEx motto as he repeats it to Wilson while languishing on the island: "Time is a relentless taskmaster. We live or die by time. And we must not commit the *sin* of turning our back on time." On the other hand, the film also shows that while on the island in his desperation to be rescued, Chuck grows even more haunted by notions of time and efficiency until his self-discipline pays off and he rescues himself. Indeed, his obsession with time provides the vehicle by which he is able to judge the weather enough to plan escape. And, the film is even ambiguous about Chuck's future plans, leaving open the possibility that he might return to work for FedEx, since he doesn't seem to blame them for calling him to work on Christmas, or for sending him on a flight into dangerous weather with mislabeled dangerous materials on board, which likely caused the deadly plane crash (perhaps because, in reality, FedEx had approval rights on the script). The film ends with a calmer, perhaps more thoughtful Chuck in the United States standing at the same crossroads where it began, choosing which of four directions to take for his new life. Ironically, *Cast Away* suggests that in this U.S. landscape Chuck rediscovers opportunity, freedom, and possibility, while he could only see constraint and limitation on the island (the space that could have really allowed him freedom from his obsessions with work and time). In the end, the island seems to only remind Chuck of an unpleasant episode in his life before returning to the United States.

What, in the end, should we make of this apparent inability to move beyond the confines of the island narrative, of our failure to escape the lure of the castaway tale, and of our need to remake the castaway story to bolster whatever image our culture needs of ourselves at the moment? Given the enduring popularity of the genre and its inevitable reiteration, perhaps we should simply accept the likelihood that it will continue to be employed for a variety of purposes and hope that one of those will be the promotion of social justice instead of the maintenance of first-world hegemony. We could perhaps lobby for publishers and creators of film and television to embrace the artistic motivations that moved so many postcolonial writers to refashion the traditional castaway narrative into a subversive vehicle, and we can support those books, films, and television shows and their makers should they appear. We have already seen a few instances of subversive castaway stories, as in Lina Wertmüller's original *Swept Away*, which was an anticapitalism treatise presented through a castaway film, a political aim that unfortunately got much diluted in the recent Madonna/Guy Ritchie version. Of course, film and television are expensive media, which means that through the process of having to drum up financing and distribution venues, radical works risk becoming watered down. Yet it is just this risk that shows the value of a globally familiar vehicle such as the castaway narrative, which financiers might be more likely to see as a sound investment. As well, we might find hope in independent film and cable television, which if not themselves generating more radical uses of the castaway story, might at least bring versions from other parts of the world and other film industries (such as Bollywood, India's film industry) to the United States to provide alternate film versions and alternate national fantasies to those discussed in this chapter and this book.

Acknowledgments

BECAUSE *Empire Islands* is the product of many years of work, the list of those to whom I owe gratitude is expansive. Without the guidance, unflagging support, and inspiration of those on this list, I could not have written this book.

I owe many thanks to those who provided mentorship over the course of this project. Chief among these people are the members of my dissertation committee (David Miller, Ellen Rosenman, Virginia Blum, Paula Bachetta, Anne McClintock, and especially Dana Nelson), and Gordon Hutner, from whom I learned about good writing and great publishing. I am also grateful for the guidance of members of the profession not on my committee who became unofficial mentors out of simple kindness, including O. R. Dathorne, Peter Hulme and the members of the University of Queensland Postcolonial Research Circle (which provided an intellectual community while I was revising this manuscript in Australia), especially Helen Gilbert, Helen Tiffin, and Leigh Dale. I also owe thanks to the University of Minnesota Press, especially to my editor Richard Morrison, with whom it has been my pleasure to work. I am grateful that the project caught his eye and for his patience and assistance reworking my manuscript into a much tighter book. I also owe many thanks to Laura Westlund, Renie Howard, and Daniel Ochsner for their tireless and excellent editorial work, which made my prose more precise and my arguments more persuasive. Finally, I am grateful for the help of my student assistants, Laura Hinshberger and Keaton Sondreal, who so ably assisted me with fact checking and indexing.

This project (and my writing skills, in general) greatly benefited from the assistance of kind colleagues and friends working with me in writing groups. From my time at the University of Kentucky, I thank my dear friends Katherine Ledford, Valerie Johnson, Jeannie Provost, Jeff Osbourne, and Kristy Branham. From my time at Michigan State, I thank Jane Holwerda and Kim Little, and from my time in Australia, again I thank the University of Queensland Postcolonial Research Circle. I owe many thanks to friends and colleagues in the Department of English at the University of North Dakota, especially to my writing group members Kathleen Dixon, Kim Donehower, and Elizabeth Hampsten, for their assistance with my introduction. I am also grateful for the comments of the anonymous readers for the University of Minnesota Press, who gave me the guidance to make that all-important final revision, when many of my arguments really came together. The person to whom I owe most thanks for writing and editing skills is Marcus Weaver-Hightower, who logged in so many hours reading and commenting on multiple drafts of this book and talking through ideas with me that we only half-jokingly talked about giving him coauthorship. Marcus's brilliance shows on every page of this manuscript, and I will never be able to adequately repay him for all that he has taught me about writing, scholarship, and intellectual work.

A project such as this could not have been completed without financial assistance, for which I continue to be grateful. The English department at the University of Kentucky and Jack Weaver both supported me (in more ways than one) during the majority of the writing of this project. The University of Kentucky Graduate School generously provided a fellowship year for writing and funding for several research trips to the British Library and for conference travel, all of which was invaluable to this book's development. The University of Kentucky Graduate School and the University of Kentucky Social Theory Collective both provided funding for a Visiting Distinguished Faculty Award, so that I could work with Anne McClintock. I am grateful to the English department of the University of North Dakota and Michigan State University's department of Writing, Rhetoric, and American Cultures for funding my work. Finally, I greatly appreciate the University of North Dakota's Office of Research and Grants, which funded the illustrations in this book and my student assistance.

My research required many long hours in libraries around the world, and I would be remiss if I didn't thank the staff members who generously assisted me with this work. I owe warm thanks to the staff of the British Library (who led me through analysis of scores of old castaway narratives and editions of *Robinson Crusoe*), the Interlibrary Loan Department at the University of Kentucky Library (which kindly ordered for me nearly every book ever written with "Island" in the title), the National Library of Australia, the University of Michigan Library Special Collections Department (especially Franki Hand), and the librarians at the University of North Dakota. I appreciate the publishers of the *Journal of Common-wealth and Postcolonial Studies* and the *Journal of Popular Culture*, who allowed me to reprint chapters (3 and 6, respectively) that appeared in altered form as essays in their pages.

Finally, I express deep gratitude and dedicate this book to those who have most inspired me, my parents, Jack and Betty Nester Weaver, who raised me to be a reader and thinker, and my siblings, Steve Weaver and Laura Garner, who teased me enough about being dumb during our childhood that I was determined to prove them wrong. I am, and always will be, deeply indebted to the incredible Dana Nelson, who was so much more than a mentor and teacher, and who by teaching me to write, think, and believe in myself, changed my life. But I reserve final thanks for Marcus Weaver-Hightower, for whose help, inspiration, love, and encouragement on this project (as in everything in life) there are not enough words.

Notes

Introduction

1. See Ashcroft, Griffiths, and Tiffin's *The Empire Writes Back* and Judie Newman's *The Ballistic Bard: Postcolonial Fictions* for further analysis of "writing back" through postcolonial counterdiscourse.

2. A partial list of revisions would include poetic versions of *Robinson Crusoe* such as Elizabeth Bishop's "Crusoe in England," St. John Perse's "Images a Crusoe," and Iain Crichton Smith's *The Notebooks of Robinson Crusoe* (1975) and novelized versions such as Michel Tournier's *Vendredi*, Muriel Spark's *Robinson*, Jean Giraudoux's *Suzanne and the Pacific*, and J. M. Coetzee's *Foe*. Rewriting *The Tempest*, in addition to Lamming's *Water With Berries*, and Cesaire's *A Tempest*, are Marina Warner's *Indigo, or Mapping the Waters* and Robertson Davies's *Tempest-Tost*. Rewriting other island narratives (some themselves revisions of *Robinson Crusoe*) are William Golding's *Lord of the Flies* (1954) and *Pincher Martin*, Marianne Wiggins's *John Dollar*, J. G. Ballard's *The Concrete Island*, and very recently Yann Martel's Man-Booker-prize-winning *The Life of Pi*. There are, of course, a few well-known examples of "writing back" to other colonial texts, specifically Jean Rhys's *Wide Sargasso Sea*, which rewrites Charlotte Bronte's *Jane Eyre*, and Maryse Condé's *Windward Heights*, which rewrites Emily Bronte's *Wuthering Heights*. (It is interesting to note that the revisions are often set on islands, even if the originals are not.) But, for sheer numbers, no other colonial texts have inspired the revisionary fervor that have *Robinson Crusoe* and *The Tempest*.

3. For analysis of the human body as cultural construct and system of representation, also see Mary Douglas's *Natural Symbols*, Andrew Blaikie's *The Body: Critical Concepts in Sociology*, Helen Thomas and Jamilah Ahmed's *Cultural Bodies: Ethnography and Theory*, Chris Shilling's *The Body and Social Theory*, Alexandra Howson's *The Body in Society: An Introduction*, Anthony Synnott's *The Body Social*, Elizabeth Grosz's *Volatile Bodies*, Peter Brooks's *Body Work: Objects of Desire in Modern Narrative*, and David Hillman and Carla Mazzio's *The Body in Parts: Fantasies of Corporeality in Early Modern Europe*.

4. Diana Loxley in *Problematic Shores: The Literature of the Islands* and Dorothy Lane in *The Island as a Site of Resistance* both examine the island as a special setting for stories of colonization and postcolonization and create a solid foundation for the work of this study. Though both focus their analysis on literature set on islands, neither takes as her purpose to delve into the psychology *behind* the use and popularity of the island form as a setting for stories of colonization, as I do. See also Chris Bongie's *Islands and Exiles* for analysis of

the island in postcolonial literature. Elizabeth Deloughry's "'The Litany of Islands, The Rosary of Archipelagoes': Caribbean and Pacific Archipelagraphy" also examines the island form, though as part of an archipelago instead of in isolation. Several critical analyses of landscape have aided my analysis of literary landscapes as highly metaphorical, including W. J. T. Mitchell's *Landscape and Power,* Denis Cosgrove and Stephen Daniels's *The Iconography of Landscape: Essays on the Symbolic Representation, Design, and Use of Past Environments,* Stephen Daniels's *Fields of Visions: Landscape Imagery and National Identity in England and the United States,* and Yi-Fu Tuan's *Topophilia: A Study of Environmental Perception, Attitudes, and Values.*

5. Few Irish texts are included in this project (only one written by an Irishman, *Gulliver's Travels,* and none set in Ireland), yet in a sense, because Ireland was the testing ground for English colonization, *all* of these imaginary islands are Ireland—as they are all also the Caribbean islands, New Zealand, Australia, and other island colonies, as well as India, Canada, most of Africa and other non-island colonies.

6. As a variety of critics have noted, some of the earliest of these fictional island narratives were based on real-world precedents. *The Tempest* is thought to be loosely based on the famous Renaissance wreck of the Sea Venture and *Robinson Crusoe* based on the shipwreck story of Alexander Selcraig (commonly called "Alexander Selkirk" in literary accounts of his story), who was marooned on an island for four years as a result of an argument he had with his ship's captain. A third equally famous maroon of the day, known as the "Moskito Indian," was island-bound for four years after accidentally being left there by Captain William Dampier. These real-world maroon tales sparked the colonial literary imagination and inspired both author and reader to fantasize about creating their own island colony. Once the story of the shipwrecked colonial entered the European imagination, it took hold and became an imperial topos, though in general the castaway myth only repeated parts of the original plot that could be construed as successful colonization.

7. For a better understanding of economic individualism, see Ian Watt's discussion of economic individualism in *The Rise of the Novel: Studies in Defoe, Richardson, and Fielding* and C. B. MacPherson's *The Political Theory of Possessive Individualism.*

8. The notion that Freud's theories recodify Western capitalism becomes more convincing when read against adaptations of psychoanalysis in colonized countries. As Christiane Hartnack (in "Vishnu on Freud's Desk") and Ashis Nandy (in "The Savage Freud") have noted, the pioneer Indian psychoanalyst, Girindrasekhar Bose, founder of the Indian Psychoanalytical Society in 1922, when describing Indian psychology, felt compelled to recast Freud's oedipal model so that the son, instead of yielding to the father, castrates him, mirroring the Indian social reality of needing to resist British imperial paternalism.

9. See Robert Young's *Colonial Desire* for discussion of *Anti-Oedipus* in relation to European colonialism. As lands were colonized, Young explains, we see the U.S./European colonizer attempt to deterritorialize the existing indigenous systems of language, education, and economy and reterritorialize them (remak-

ing these systems in the U.S./European/imperial/capitalist image). Also see John Brenkman's *Straight, Male, Modern* for more skeptical discussion of Freud's theories in terms of transference.

10. For my reading of book illustrations, I draw upon techniques pioneered by Erving Goffman in his influential book *Gender Advertisements* and by Gunther Kress and Theo van Leeuwen in *Reading Images: The Grammar of Visual Design*.

11. For more on links between masculinity and 9/11, see Marcus Weaver-Hightower's "The Gender of Terror and Heroes? What Educators Might Teach About Men and Masculinity after September 11, 2001" and Anne McClintock's "Masculinity and Other War Zones."

1. Monarchs of All They Survey

1. Verne is, of course, a Frenchman, but, as does Diana Loxley who argued in *Problematic Shores: The Literature of Islands* that Verne has become absorbed into the British literary canon, I feel comfortable analyzing him alongside British imperial writers.

2. Loxley in *Problematic Shores* argues that the characters in Verne's novel all function as different aspects of one character (with one body) and gives as evidence their strict division of labor and responsibility as well as their inability to function without Harding (the symbolic head). Wyeth's drawing of the five as one conjoined body seems to support Loxley's theory. Moreover, Wyeth's drawing positions the characters to reflect the novel's race/class/age hierarchy. Cyrus Harding stands highest in the picture, reflecting his status as group leader and highest in social class, race, and age. A bit lower stand the less-commanding characters of Pencroft and Spillet, one a journalist and one a seaman. At about the same level of elevation in the picture (though not equal in prominence—Herbert is given more space and Neb's face is not depicted) are Herbert, whose age places him lower on the hierarchy and Neb, whose race determines his position. At the bottom of the hierarchy and lowest on the picture is the dog.

3. This explanation borrows from *The Select Melanie Klein* and from the definition of "projective identification" in *The Language of Psycho-Analysis* by L. Laplanche and J. B. Pontalis.

4. By "panoptic" I allude to Jeremy Bentham's 1843 prison design that relied upon the gaze as agent of control and Foucault's analysis of it in *Discipline and Punish*. See also Timothy Mitchell's *Colonising Egypt* for discussion of the panopticon at work in the so-called margins of empire.

5. A large body of work traces historically how intellectual perceptions of the ability to view the world have been translated into visual representation, art, or culture. Among the most useful of these studies for this project are Barbara Stafford's *Voyage into Substance*, John Berger's *Ways of Seeing*, and Jonathan Crary's *Techniques of the Observer*. See also James Ryan's *Picturing Empire: Photography and the Visualization of the British Empire* for analysis of how photography captures an age's intellectual perceptions of the world.

6. For more on Mesmer's life and work see Alan Gauld's *A History of*

Hypnotism and William Kelly's *Psychology of the Unconscious: Mesmer, Janet, Freud, Jung, and Current Issues.*

7. See Kolodny, *The Lay of the Land;* McClintock, *Imperial Leather: Race, Gender, and Sexuality in the Colonial Contest;* and Rebecca Stott's "The Dark Continent: Africa as Female Body in Haggard's Adventure Fiction." Diana Loxley also argues in *Problematic Shores* that the island in *The Mysterious Island* is "progressively mapped as the female body" and that the male colonists probe the island and the cave and "implant [their] fertile reason" (54). I contend, however, that though the island might at first be mapped as a female body, it is ultimately incorporated into/as the male body, as it is disciplined and protected. The cave that Loxley sees as the female womb, I argue, becomes the metaphorical center of masculine reason and mastery, the head, and is literally the protected site of the colonist's body, as are caves in *Robinson Crusoe, The Swiss Family Robinson,* and *The Tempest.*

8. A similar map contained in a 1909 Harper and Brother's edition of *The Swiss Family Robinson* also doesn't mark the family's island. This book was illustrated by the Rhead brothers, as well, a happenstance that creates an interesting relationship between the volumes based on similarity of illustration as well as similarity of story. See David Blewett's *The Illustration of Robinson Crusoe, 1719–1920* for more in the novel's illustration history.

9. Alfred Crosby in *Ecological Imperialism: The Biological Expansion of Europe 900–1900* likewise notes that the physical transformation of the colonized landscape (domestication of animals, planting of crops) aided real-world colonization. Similarly, Jarrad Diamond's *Guns, Germs, and Steel* makes compelling arguments for agriculture and animal domestication (as well as the spread of disease) as tools of empire. See Richard Grove's *Green Imperialism: Colonial Expansion, Tropical Island Edens and the Origins of Environmentalism 1600–1860* for a further discussion of island ecosystems and of domestication as a colonial tool.

10. Consult Martin Gliserman's *Psychoanalysis, Language and the Body of the Text* for discussion of Crusoe's obsession with eating and for an extensive analysis of the novel's use of language of consumption.

11. See Eric Berne's "The Psychological Structure of Space with Some Remarks on *Robinson Crusoe*" for a fascinating discussion of Crusoe's obsessions with his body as linked to his perceptions of space. Though Berne's remarks are limited in their treatment of incorporation, they sparked my thinking in this direction. Stephen C. K. Chan's "Tactics of Space in Defoe and Foucault" also analyzes Defoe's social construction of space, though Chan focuses primarily on *A Journal of the Plague Year.*

12. See Elaine Scarry's *The Body in Pain* for further discussion of bodily discomfort as fundamental to human experience and identity.

13. These figures are reported in Murray Knowles and Kirsten Malmkjær's *Language and Control in Children's Literature.* See also Martin Green's *The Robinson Crusoe Story* and Pat Rogers's *Defoe: The Critical Heritage* for an overview of the novel's reception during and after Defoe's life.

14. This fact was reported by Patrick Keane in *Coleridge's Submerged Politics: The Ancient Mariner and Robinson Crusoe.*

2. Disciplined Islands

1. The following books (in addition to those cited throughout this chapter) were particularly helpful to my understanding of masculinity and to my use of this terminology: R. W. Connell's *Masculinities*, Anthony Rotundo's *American Manhood: Transformations in Masculinity from the Revolution to the Present Era*, and Dana D. Nelson's *National Manhood: Capitalist Citizenship and the Imagined Fraternity of White Men*. Studies of masculinity's effects on empire include Joseph Bristow's *Empire Boys: Adventures in a Man's World*, Richard Phillips's *Mapping Men and Empire: A Geography of Adventure*, and Mrinalini Sinha's *Colonial Masculinity: The "Manly Englishman" and the "Effeminate Bengali" in the Late Nineteenth Century*.

2. The publication date of *Masterman Ready* is uncertain, with many libraries listing editions as simply 1800–99. I use 1814 because it is the earliest certain publication date I have found.

3. Several postcolonial texts "writing back" to the island fantasy challenge this notion of the castaway's ability to self-discipline his body, including William Golding's 1955 novel *Pincher Martin*. Much of Golding's novel centers on Pincher's struggles to harness his body and survive on a barren piece of rock on which he lands after the sinking of the torpedoed World War II destroyer on which he served. Robert Louis Stevenson's *Kidnapped* (1886) also contains an episode that offers a story of failed island colonization, wherein David Balfour, becomes stranded on an island but instead of showing his "pluck" and natural abilities to survive, nearly starves to death before he discovers that he could have walked off the island at any time at low tide.

4. Criticism has examined some of these influences on the imperial "center" from the colonies, including Diane Sacho McLeod and Julie F. Codell's *Orientalism Transposed*, Bill Ashcroft's *On Post-Colonial Futures: Transformation of Colonial Culture*, Lydia Liu's essay "Robinson Crusoe's Earthenware Pot," which analyzes china as a colonial commodity and Michelle Maskiell's "Consuming Kashmir: Shawls and Empires, 1500–2000," analyzing the European consumption of shawls.

5. See Louis Montrose's "The Work of Gender in the Discourse of Discovery" for an excellent analysis of the historical gendered politics of Raleigh's letters from Guyana.

6. As I will discuss in chapter 5, in pantomimed theatrical performances of *Robinson Crusoe*, a different Mrs. Crusoe (Crusoe's mother) plays an important part of the story, as does Polly, Crusoe's love interest. In fact, Crusoe himself is acted by a woman, creating a range of discursive disruptions.

7. For another example of a female castaway, see also Mme. Daubenton's *Zelia in the Desert or the Female Crusoe*. Arnold Saxton's "Female Castaways" provides further analysis of the female Robinsonade. Marina Warner's 1992 novel *Indigo, or Mapping the Waters* changes and challenges the manly island myth by refocusing it on women and by creating strong female characters that resist masculine colonial domination. Muriel Spark's 1958 novel *Robinson* also challenges the ideology of natural masculine power by creating her Crusoe

as homosexual and by making her Crusoe thoroughly unlikable and untrust-worthy.

8. Giraudoux's *Suzanne and the Pacific* challenges the underlying ideology of the castaway fantasy through his Crusoe, the early twentieth-century French girl Suzanne, who does none of the things that Crusoe does to establish her authority over the island. When she swims to a nearby island and discovers the abandoned hut of a former Crusoe-esque castaway, she laughs at evidence of masculine discipline, which she calls the "lowly tasks that are allotted on desert is-lands to the strong and energetic sex" (144). As she explains, "here, where there is an abundance of fruit and shell-fish he had sown and cultivated rye; here, near two caves which are warm at night and cool during the day, he had cut joists and built a hut; here, where one learns how to climb within two hours, he had con-structed ladders" (144). Suzanne's response to island life undermines the myth of masculine discipline by helping readers see the white, male, disciplined re-action as only one socially mediated and neurotic reaction to castaway life, not as the natural or sensible way to live. Similarly, Coetzee's female castaway, Susan Barton in *Foe* views her Cruso's labor at terrace building as a self-delusional waste of time, especially in light of "the boat he would not build, and the journal he would not keep, and the tools he would not save from the wreck" (34). As well, Coetzee makes Susan and not Cruso the writer of the tale of the island castaway, making the voice of the originary myth of island colonialism and masculine self-sufficiency a woman's.

9. See Andrew Tolson's *The Limits of Masculinity* and Victor Seidler's *Redis-covering Masculinity* for further discussion of controlled or anti-emotionalism as a component of British masculinity.

10. See Klaus Theweleit's *Male Fantasies Volume 1* for discussion of how the Friecorpsmen recodified their fear of the feminized Other into a panic over dirt, slime, and feces. His *Male Fantasies Volume 2: Male Bodies: Psychoanalyzing the White Terror* continues those arguments.

11. Crusoe's description of Friday also suggests homoerotic feelings trans-ferred into acceptable homosocial feelings. Though he describes their relation-ship as that of a father/son, Crusoe also recounts Friday's handsomeness and their mutual love. Crusoe says, "I began really to love the Creature; and on his Side, I believe he lov'd me more than it was possible for him to ever love any Thing before" (154). Despite the novel's denial of a homoerotic element to their love, as Peter Hulme says, "the true romance in *Robinson Crusoe* is between Cru-soe and Friday" (*Colonial Encounters* 212).

12. See Richard Waswo's "The Formation of Natural Law to Justify Colonial-ism, 1539–1689."

13. The Australian Mabo decision in effect admitted that Aboriginal Aus-tralians did have prior access to (to remind of our Lacanian framework) the land, thus negating claims of *terra nullius*. But still individual Aboriginal groups must meet stringent criteria and sue the government in order to re-claim rights to their own land, and if the government deems the claim to be harmful to the public good, they will deny the claim. In Canada, a similar sit-uation exists in relation to treaties. The government is now recognizing that

many indigenous groups were deprived of their land without a treaty, in which case, the indigenous group still has rights to the land unless/until an official treaty is drawn up. See Christopher F. Roth's "Without Treaty, Without Conquest: Indigenous Sovereignty in Post-*Delgamuukw* British Columbia" for more on this issue.

14. See James Muldoon's "Columbus's First Voyage and the Medieval Legal Tradition" for analysis of Columbus's manipulation of legal systems.

15. See the film *Colonists for a Day* for a good introduction to the issue.

16. *The Island of Dr. Moreau* is often read as parodying the island narrative genre, but I read it as an ambivalent text that plays into some of the tropes of colonialism while critiquing others. One reading of the novel, like that presented in Cyndy Hendershot's *The Animal Within: Masculinity and the Gothic*, sees it as deconstructing European imperialism by showing imperial control and power taken too far, with disastrous results. Moreau's death, according to this logic, rightfully comes from his abuses of his white, male privilege. I read the novel, however, as also telling a lesson about the disastrous results of loss of imperial discipline. Moreau, the bad father, has lost his imperial self-discipline. Instead of protecting the bodies he governs, as would a good, white, imperial father, Moreau exploits his "children" for his own self-serving purposes. By preserving the colonial logic of the benefits of the "good" white father and the rewards of imperial discipline, Wells perpetuates imperial masculine ideology while simultaneously critiquing it. See John R. Reed's "The Vanity of Law in *The Island of Dr. Moreau*" for a reading of Wells as parodying the need both to make and break laws.

3. Voracious Cannibals, Rapacious Pirates, and Threats of Counterincorporation

1. See also E. Pearlman's "Robinson Crusoe and the Cannibals" for a reading of cannibalism in *Robinson Crusoe*.

2. I call the mutineers "pirates" because this story and others suggest that piracy will be their means of financial support after disposing of the captain, for after their mutiny, the ship would be unable to return to "civilization." Joel Baer in "The Complicated Plot of Piracy," based on a reading of Defoe's (supposed authorship) of *A General History of the Pyrates* (1724–28), similarly argues that Crusoe in *The Farther Adventures* "properly identifies the mutineers as pirates" (5). I use the term "pirate" for any criminal on the high seas, though David Cordingly reports that Henry VIII extended the denotation of piracy to any crimes committed on rivers, creeks, or sites "where the Lord High Admiral had jurisdiction" (6). A mutiny, then, under this definition, would be considered piracy, making the mutineers of *The Narrative of Arthur Gordon Pym* and *Robinson Crusoe* pirates, though they were prevented by death or intervention from progressing to robbing any passing ships.

3. A number of insightful texts analyze cannibalism and piracy as separate topics. See Carole Marsh's *In Good Taste: The History, Mystery, Legend, Lore and Future of Cannibalism*, Frank Lestringant's *Cannibals: The Discovery and Representation*

of the Cannibal from Columbus to Jules Verne, Peggy Reeves Sanday's *Divine Hunger: Cannibalism as a Cultural System,* Philip Boucher's *Cannibal Encounters: Europeans and Island Caribs, 1492–1763,* Stephen Slemon's "Bones of Contention: Post-Colonial Writing and the 'Cannibal' Question," and Maggie Kilgour's *From Communion to Cannibalism: An Anatomy of Metaphors of Incorporation,* for clear and insightful readings of cannibalism as a cultural trope. Nina Gerassi-Navarro's *Pirate Novels: Fictions of Nation Building in Spanish America,* Neville Williams's *The Seadogs: Privateers, Plunder and Piracy in the Elizabethan Age,* Hans Turley's *Rum, Sodomy, and the Lash,* and Srinivas Aravamudan's *Tropicopolitans* all present interesting and intuitive discussions of piracy.

4. If authors of island narratives didn't include pirates in the castaway story, their interest in pirates often led them to write other stories about pirates. For instance, Marryat (author of *Masterman Ready*) also wrote the novel *The Pirate* (1861); and Defoe also wrote *The King of the Pirates* (1720) and has been suspected of being the author of *A General History of the Pyrates* (1724–28). See David Cordingly's *Life Among the Pirates: The Romance and the Reality* for an outline of the debate over Defoe's authorship of the latter text (10–11).

5. See Lizabeth Paravisini-Gebert's "Cross-Dressing on the Margins of Empire: Women Pirates and the Narrative of the Caribbean" for analysis of the female pirates, Anne Bonny and Mary Read, who assumed a masculine gender to perform as pirates and a feminine gender to escape punishment.

6. Mrinalini Sinha's *Colonial Masculinity: The "Manly Englishman" and the "Effeminate Bengali" in the Late Nineteenth Century* provides a thorough investigation of the trope of the feminized indigenous Indian.

7. This reformed pirate story line resembles that of Defoe's volume 2 of *Robinson Crusoe,* in which the pirates from the end of volume 1 become reformed, model colonists. *The Mysterious Island* contains a similar story line, through the memories of the wild man of Tabor island.

8. See also Marina Warner's "Fee Fie Fo Fum: The Child in the Jaws of the Story" for more on mythological cannibalism as symbolic childbirth or as response to womb envy.

9. Gananath Obeyesekere speculates that the fictional and nonfictional practice of choosing the alien or Other as the victim of cannibalism (the Spaniard, the Portuguese, the slave, the black) stems from this same fantasy of obtaining the strength of the other. "In popular thought the black man, the Spaniard, and the Portuguese were highly sexed libidinous creatures. They represented sexuality and life power; by consumption of their flesh one could introject these powers and thus ensure strength and survival value" (640). Obeyesekere also argues that the nautical practice of eating dog meat was an expression of the fantasy to be a cannibal. Because dogs were often ship's pets, he argues, dogflesh would have been almost as taboo for food as human flesh. "The ship's officers were tantalized by Savage anthropophagy," Obeyesekere explains. "It triggered a latent wish, but, since it was impossible to consume human flesh, they chose dog meat" (642).

4. "Falling to the Lowest Degree of Brutishness"

1. Gustav Jahoda's *Images of Savages: Ancient Roots of Modern Prejudice in Western Culture* provides a gloss of the history of the literary wild man. The wild man legend, Jahoda argues, began with the Greeks, but also can be found in Nimrod, a descendant of the Biblical Ham. The wild man of the woods "gradually emerged in the literature and art of the Middle Ages and became common in European folklore by the end of the period" (5).

2. Fears of the communicability of criminality, Robert Hughes says, were also influenced by a panic over the transmission of homosexuality, for even more than criminality, convict homosexuality was feared as communicable: "The danger seemed to be that this 'contagion' would spread unchecked like an epidemic disease from [Norfolk Island] to the mainland of Australia so that, as [colonial administrator, Robert Pringle] Stuart put it, 'in future years a moral stain of the deepest dye may be impressed, perhaps immovably, on its people'" (272).

3. Annette Kobak in her introduction to *The Nomad: The Diaries of Isabelle Eberhardt* explains that Eberhardt's Muslim male "disguise" "was not so much a disguise as a reclothing of herself in her rightful mind, a becoming of the person she was underneath—the 'real me'. It also, of course, enabled her to travel freely in a way she could never have done dressed as a European or Arab woman at the end of the nineteenth century" (10). Eberhardt's dress, Kobak argues, was not motivated by European Orientalist desire to "pass" to better see hidden cultural secrets (like Richard Burton) but reflects her profound shift in identity. Of course, as Kobak notes, Eberhardt's going native didn't extend to adopting Algerian Muslim gender norms to live as a Muslim woman. Her European education and liberal upbringing gave her the intellectual and social tools to choose her situation. For further analysis of Eberhardt's interesting and controversial life, see Cecily Mackworth's study *The Destiny of Isabelle Eberhardt* and Elizabeth Kershaw's *The Nomad: The Diaries of Isabelle Eberhardt*.

4. I am grateful to Helen Tiffin for suggesting this line of thinking to me.

5. Perhaps because of this admitted pleasure and the seductions of going native, too much contact was thought inauspicious even in police work and even in the crucial enterprise of intelligence gathering, so that society deemed that "the proper venues for gathering knowledge about colonial society in the late nineteenth century" Silvestri reminds, "were censuses and social scientific fieldwork, not Strickland's [Kipling's fictional undercover policeman in India] jaunts into the bazaar" (¶ 18). Silvestri reminds that, in addition to Kipling's Strickland in *Plain Tales from the Hills,* other fictional detectives, including Conan Doyle's Sherlock Holmes and Edmund C. Cox's fictional Indian police officer John Carruthers, were given the power to don native disguise at will and pass as native in the greater service of empire.

6. See Mary Campbell's coda to *Wonder and Science* for discussion of the "wild child" phenomenon, particularly of the discovery and publicity about two feral children discovered living in the Pyrenees in the same year *Robinson Crusoe* was published. Kipling's *Kim* would provide a literary example of the wild child, which might be more acceptable to colonial culture, since he was eventually

acculturated back into "civilized" society. See also Julia Douthwaite's *The Wild Girl, Natural Man, and the Monster: Dangerous Experiments in the Age of Enlightenment.*

7. For more on links between madness and empire, see Foucault's *Madness and Civilization*, Frantz Fanon's *A Dying Colonialism* and *The Wretched of the Earth*, Octave Mannoni's *Prospero and Caliban*, and Richard Keller's "Madness and Colonization: Psychiatry in the British and French Empires, 1800–1962."

8. As Martin Crotty points out, these same conditions, centuries later, would be used by settlers to assert the superiority of settler colonies over their ancestral forebears; in the context of his argument, the sun and heat of Australia produced, supposedly, a healthier, more manly colonial subject than the sickly English reared in the damp and cold.

9. A similar scene of the simian threat or invasion of the home is found in *The Swiss Family Robinson*. When monkeys gain entrance into one of the Robinson homes, senselessly destroying all that they find there, the Robinsons are forced to defend their home by destroying the simians in one of the most horrifying and vivid scenes in the novel. The Robinson father decides to spread bird-lime over the house, its contents, and its surroundings, which mires and traps the monkeys coming after the bait the Robinsons prepared. When the monkeys become trapped in the lime, the father looses the dogs on them while he and his sons club them to death, leaving the place with "the appearance of a ghastly battlefield" (231). The novel seems to miss the irony that the only mortal violence enacted comes in the family's violence against the indigene. The monkeys' invasion of the Robinson home allegorizes similar anxious fantasies of the invasion by incorrigible natives, helping to naturalize colonial violence.

10. For background on the noble/ignoble savage dichotomy, see Hoxie Neale Fairchild's *The Noble Savage*, Gaile McGregor *The Noble Savage in the New World Garden: Notes Toward a Syntactics of Place*, and Hayden White's *Tropics of Discourse: Essays in Cultural Criticism*. Critics have discussed this noble/ignoble split since Rousseau first used the terms in the eighteenth century, though the trope existed long before Rousseau, back to Montaigne's "Of the Cannibals" (1580) and probably before. As these critics have noted, both kinds of savages justify colonization, the noble savage justifying colonial expansion through showing colonization's success, the ignoble savage justifying violence through showing the incorrigibility of the savage.

11. An interesting corollary to the noble indigene as helpmate exists in William Bingfield's 1753 tale, *The Voyages, Shipwreck, Travels, Distresses, Strange Adventures, and Miraculous Preservation of William Bingfield*, in the "amazing animal called the dog-bird" (listed later in the text's extraordinarily long and descriptive title). When stranded on an uncharted island, Bingfield and his two castaway companions encounter a large and ferocious species of bird, as he describes it "walking upon two legs, but without the least feather or down about it, its covering being of long shaggy hair" with "a short thick neck, a bony head, in make like a grey-hound's, with the sharpest and strongest teeth in its mouth, of any creature of its size that I ever saw, and a long tail, very hairy, much like a pig's" (14). This creature, which in a small pack could hunt down and kill a tiger or a

man, Bingfield domesticates by raising a few of the young found in a nest. His favorite dog bird, a female which he treats like an especially privileged spaniel, he names "Sally" for the woman he thinks he has left behind in England, but whom it turns out has also made it to the island (he rescues her from cannibals). Bingfield's treatment of and naming of the dog bird Sally suggests that she, like Beaufidell, plays the role of the noble indigene and helpmate, whom the castaway must civilize and "consume" in order to fully and legitimately command the island space.

12. See Samuel Otter's *Melville's Anatomies,* particularly his first chapter "Losing Face in *Typee*" for a particularly interesting reading of this scene.

13. For provocative studies of monsters, see Joseph D. Andriano's *Immortal Monster: The Mythological Evolution of the Fantastic Beast in Modern Fiction and Film,* Marie Hélène Huet's *Monstrous Imagination,* and Jeffrey Cohen's *Monster Theory: Reading Culture.*

14. See Marianna Torgovnick's *Gone Primitive: Savage Intellects, Modern Lives* for more on the Western desire for the savage.

15. In a curiously analogous inversion, Philip Quarll defends his choice to go naked on his island as asserting his human dominance over the island's other creatures. He discovers that the island's monkeys show him more respect when he is naked and surmises that their behavior "must be a Remnant of that Awe, intail'd by Nature upon all Animals, to that most noble and compleat Masterpiece of the Creation call'd *Man*" (Longueville, 174). Quarll explains that "appearing in the State he was first created in, and undisguis'd by Cloaths, [man] renews a Smatch of that Respect he has forfeited by his fatal Transgression" (174). Instead of clothing asserting man's civilized status, Quarll says that it "renders him ridiculous to the rest of Mankind, and generally obnoxious to all other Creatures, making a Pride of what he ought to be asham'd of" (174). But despite his elaborate reasoning, I would argue that Quarll's nakedness, like Crusoe's goatskin clothes, allows him to play native, to experience the pleasures of unbridled flesh and to allow his reader to fantasize about the same freedom. Significantly, instead of admitting this desire, Quarll must subsume it into the more traditionally acceptable assertion of colonial hegemony.

16. See Tim Barringer and Tom Flynn's *Colonialism and the Object: Empire, Material Culture and the Museum,* Michael M. Ames's *Cannibal Tours and Glass Boxes: The Anthropology of Museums* for further discussion of the nonfictional imperial museum. Also see Foucault's "Of Other Spaces" for discussion of how museums and libraries have become heterotopic spaces, that is, in museums and libraries, he says, we see "the idea of accumulating everything, of establishing a sort of general archive, the will to enclose in one place all times, all epochs, all forms, all tastes, the idea of constituting a place of all times that is itself outside of time and inaccessible to its ravages, the project of organizing in this way a sort of perpetual and indefinite accumulation of time in an immobile place" (25).

17. Frantz Fanon in *A Dying Colonialism* discusses imperial science and medicine as having a similar hegemonic purpose. As he explains, "in a non-colonial society, the attitude of a sick man in the presence of a medical practitioner is one of confidence" while in a colonized state "the sudden deaths of Algerians in

hospitals, a common occurrence in an establishment caring for the sick and the injured, are interpreted as the effects of a murderous and deliberate decision, as the result of criminal maneuvers on the part of the European doctor" (123–24). The same mistrust, Fanon explains, follows the native doctor, whom the colonized compare to "the native police, to the *caïd*, to the notable" (132).

5. Island Parodies and Crusoe Pantomimes

1. As noted in chapters 2 and 4, coevolving with these parodies were tales that adapted and challenged the castaway narrative by changing a key feature of the castaway, his race (like Albert Seguin's *The Black Crusoe*) or gender (like Charles Dibdin's *Hannah Hewitt, or The Female Crusoe*). These narratives differ from the postcolonial revisions discussed in my introduction in that they don't challenge the underlying ideology of the island fantasy but instead draw upon that ideology in the service of the disenfranchised.

2. Scholars of postcolonial literature and history have produced a number of fine examinations of specific resistance movements including Frantz Fanon's *A Dying Colonialism* and *The Wretched of the Earth*, Barbara Harlow's *Resistance Literature*, Jenny Sharpe's *"Figures of Colonial Resistance,"* and Selwyn Cudjoe's *Resistance and Caribbean Literature*.

3. See Robert Hughes's *The Fatal Shore* for more on debates over convict labor, and Adam Hochschild's *King Leopold's Ghost* for more on anticolonial debates over slavery.

4. For more information on theories of comedy, see George McFadden's *Discovering the Comic*, Paul Lewis's *Comic Effects: Interdisciplinary Approaches to Humor in Literature*, Chris Powell's "A Phenomenological Analysis of Humour in Society," and Marcel Gutwirth's *Laughing Matter: An Essay on the Comic*.

5. The one review I have found of a Robinson Crusoe pantomime, *A Short Account of the Situations and Incidents Exhibited in the Pantomime of Robinson Crusoe at the Theatre-Royal, Drury Lane* (i.e., R. B. B. Sheridan's *"Robinson Crusoe, or Harlequin Friday"*) focused on describing the production, without any clues as to audience reaction, except that they enjoyed the production and found it to be humorous.

6. For analysis of other adaptations of *The Tempest*, consult Frederick W. Kilbourne's *Alterations and Adaptations of Shakespeare*, Henry E. Jacobs and Claudia D. Johnson's *An Annotated Bibliography of Shakespearean Burlesques, Parodies, and Travesties*, and Peter Hulme and William Sherman's *'The Tempest' and Its Travels*.

7. Critics dispute the publication date of Dryden and Davenant's play. The years 1670 and 1674 are sometimes given as the publication date because significant revisions were made then, but George Robert Guffey traces the original assignment of the play to Davenant's company in the 1660s.

8. Dryden and Davenant aren't the only *Tempest* revisionists to refocus the play from politics to romance, though they were the first. *The Very Last Edition of The Tempest or The Wily Wizard, The Wensome Wench and the Wicked Willain an Original Burlesque Extravaganza in One Act*, written by an author identified only

by the initials "A.H.O." (1865) also centers the story on love interests, as does Patty Lee Clark's revision *The Admirable Miranda Written for The Hopefully Well Affected Club* (1905).

9. Ernest Renan's Tempest revision *Caliban: A Philosophical Drama Continuing 'The Tempest' by William Shakespeare* (1878) also revises Caliban's role, making him a less sympathetic character. Renan's play begins where Shakespeare's ends, with Prospero leaving the island with the other nobles, but in Renan's version, he takes Caliban and Ariel back to Milan with him. Prospero again neglects his duties, until his people revolt, making Caliban their new Duke. Prospero, finding that his magic has failed him, releases Ariel back to the elements and dies. Though Renan's play presents another defense of Caliban, the play ends with the suggestion that Caliban might become like Prospero, making the same mistakes. See Roby Cohn's *Modern Shakespeare Offshoots* for a discussion of *Caliban* and Auden's "The Sea and the Mirror" as revisions of *The Tempest*.

10. George Guffey quotes Gerard Langbaine, who reports that Duffett's aims were to compete with Shadwell and Dryden-Davenant by attempting to attract the audience from the Duke's Theatre to the Theatre-Royal (viii). Ronald Eugene DiLorenzo's notes to the play indicate that Duffett's *Mock-Tempest* parodied both the opera and the Dryden-Davenant version by recording several of Duffett's lines that are aimed at material from the Dryden-Davenant play that was not included in the opera.

11. L. W. Cowie's discussion of the history of Bridewell in *History Today* traces its fascinating evolution from royal palace to hospital, to apprentice's school, and finally to reformatory for vagrants and prostitutes. Though Bridewell was in 1675 officially a workhouse for wayward apprentices and the poor, as Cowie explains, it functioned more like "a place of detention and labour rather than of reformation and training" (354). By 1720, the establishment primarily incarcerated sex workers and petty thieves and was notorious for whipping its inmates, first publicly in the streets and then in a specially designed whipping room with a whipping post and gallery for spectators.

12. See, for example, McClintock's work in "Screwing the System: Sexwork, Race, and the Law" and "Maid to Order: Commercial S/M and Gender Power."

13. Duffett also alters Caliban and Sycorax. He introduces them only at the play's end, where (based on textual evidence) they seem to be among Prospero's subordinate prison keepers. Transforming Caliban and Sycorax from those kept in the prison/island to kindly keepers represents a significant revision and could be read as carnivalesque, as well.

14. For further information on the development of the English pantomime, see Raymond Mander and Joe Mitchenson's *Pantomime: A Story in Pictures*, R. J. Broadbent's *A History of Pantomime*, Gerald Frow's *"Oh, Yes It Is!": A History of Pantomime*, John Shand's "Pantomime," and John O'Brien's *Harlequin Britain: Pantomime and Entertainment, 1690–1760*.

15. See Peter Ackroyd's *Dressing Up* for more on the pantomime Dame.

16. Though in Defoe's version, Will Atkins is one of the pirates whom Crusoe foiled at the end of volume 1, in the pantomimes, Will Atkins is always the villain trying to steal Polly. Will Atkin's name varies from play to play, most often in

variations of the spelling of "Atkins," sometimes "Adkins," or "McAtkins." Likewise, Crusoe's love interest is most often named Polly, but she is sometimes given another name, "Alice" or "Jenny" for instance, though the characters are interchangeable.

17. Filled with advertisements and illustrations, the programs offer a brief overview of the plot and a libretto for the audience to use for following the play's dialogue and for understanding the words to songs. Some of the play's humor depended on the audience reading along with the play, as some of the jokes were based on visual word play, reliant on the audience being able to see the dialogue, such as when one cannibal says to another when discussing whether or not to eat a certain person "I shall if I *chews*" (Thorne, 33, emphasis original). The audience might miss the pun (which is typical of those in the play) if not reading along with the program during the performance. Because the programs were for use during a performance, the illustrations were likely have been in keeping with the costuming, casting, and arrangement of actors in the performance.

18. Garber's study gives an excellent background to the production and speculates on the play as a marker of a cultural crisis in masculinity. She thoroughly reads the play against Barrie's life, seeing him in multiple characters in the play. See also Andrew Birkin's *J. M. Barrie and the Lost Boys: The Love Story that Gave Birth to Peter Pan* for more on Barrie's life, and see Jacqueline Rose, *The Case for Peter Pan, or The Impossibility of Children's Fiction* for discussion of an all-woman casting of *Peter Pan.*

19. See Viola Tait's *Dames, Principal Boys—And All That: A History of Pantomime in Australia* for more on the Australian panto tradition.

20. See Laura J. Rosenthal's "'Infamous Commerce': Transracial Prostitution in the South Seas and Back" for discussion of pantomime transracial politics in John O'Keefe's panto *Omai; or, A Trip Round The World.*

21. Consult Eric Lott's *Love and Theft: Blackface Minstrelsy and the American Working Class* and Dale Cockrell's *Demons of Disorder: Early Blackface Minstrels and Their World* for more on the history of blackface theater.

22. For more on this line of argument, see James E. Gill's "Beast over Man: Theriophilic Paradox in Gulliver's Voyage to the Country of the Houyhnhnms," Claude Rowson's "Gulliver and the Flat Nosed People: Colonial Oppression and Race in Satire and Fiction," and Clement Hawes's "Three Times Around the Globe: Gulliver and Colonial Discourse."

23. Martin Green speculates that Swift and Defoe's professional rivalry spurred Swift to write his parody. According to Paul Dottin's introduction to Gildon's work, the English writer Charles Gildon was likewise inspired to write a parody of *Robinson Crusoe* for professional rivalry and the desire to ride the coattails of a hit work. Gildon published two short bits of Crusoe parody in a pamphlet entitled *Robinson Crusoe, Examin'd and Criticis'd.* The first piece in the pamphlet, "A Dialogue Betwixt D . . . . . F . . . e, Robinson Crusoe, And his Man Friday" narrates a conversation supposedly held by Defoe, Crusoe, and Friday, in which Crusoe and Friday criticize Defoe's writing, particularly his many inconsistencies and his portrayal of them as "Beings contradictory

to common Sense, and destructive of Religion and Morality" (vii). The pamphlet's second parody, "An Epistle to D . . . . . . D' F . . . e, The Reputed Author of *Robinson Crusoe*," a supposed public letter to Defoe, also criticizes the book's inaccuracies and inconsistencies.

6. The U.S. Island Fantasy, or Cast Away with Gilligan

1. The castaway story has been adapted for a variety of different genres. See Anne Hutta Colvin's *The Celluloid Crusoe: A Story of Cinematic Robinsonades* for a more complete but now slightly dated listing of these.

2. I call Hanks "all-American" because he is best known for his all-American roles (astronaut Jim Lovell in *Apollo 13*, World War II hero Captain Miller in *Saving Private Ryan*, good ol' boy Forrest Gump in *Forrest Gump*), and has become, according to Fred Pfeil, an American *icon*. See "Getting Up There with Tom" for a thorough and interesting examination of Hanks's unique place in the U.S. cultural imagination.

3. I am grateful to Peter Hulme for first pointing out to me the irony in the character's name.

4. Elleke Boehmer, agreeing with this time line, explains that "many theorists broadly agree that the decline of one sort of colonialism in the 1950s led to the rise of another, less overt, some might say more insidious, form—what has also been called a super or new imperialism. Though the betrayal of the ideals of postcolonial liberation began some time before, neo-colonial formations grew particularly pronounced in the 1970's and 1980's as recession and the burgeoning of Third World debt tightened the grip of rich Northern countries on the South" (*Colonial and Postcolonial Literature: Migrant Metaphors*, 9). Peter Hulme and Lawrence Buell have written on the idea of the United States as "postcolonial" to, as Hulme says to "include America," Hulme meaning continental America and Buell meaning the United States (Hulme "Including America"). See also Amy Kaplan's introduction to *Cultures of United States Imperialism*, in "Left Alone with America."

5. Some of these critics envision a United States empire as a potential force for good in the world, including Michael Ignatieff in, among other pieces, his *New York Times* article "The American Empire; The Burden"; Robert N. Bellah in his *Christian Century* piece "Righteous Empire: How Does a Nation that Hates Taxes and Distrusts Big Government Launch an Empire? In a State of Deep Denial"; and Max Boot in a *Weekly Standard* article "The Case for American Empire." Others express fears of negative results of a U.S. empire, including Andrew Bacevich in *American Empire: The Realities and Consequences of U.S. Diplomacy*, Chalmers Johnson in *Blowback: The Costs and Consequences of American Empire*, and István Mészáros in *Socialism or Barbarism*.

6. Among those arguing that the U.S. is not *exactly* an empire since it differs historically from empires of yesteryear, I include Leon Hadar's "U.S. Empire? Let's Get Real," John O'Sullivan's "The Reluctant Empire: The U.S. Leads the World—But Doesn't Have to Rule It," and Criton Zoakos's "Why the World Hates America: The Economic Explanation."

7. Others have noted these fantasies in relation to tourism. A number of fine analyses of tourism as it relates to empire and neo-imperialism have been published in recent years, including Jamaica Kincaid's *A Small Place* (1988), John Urry's *The Tourist Gaze: Leisure and Travel in Contemporary Societies* (1990), Tim Edensor's *Tourists at the Taj: Performance and Meaning at a Symbolic Site* (1998), and Helen Gilbert and Anna Johnston's *In Transit: Travel, Text, Empire* (2002). For a reading of *The Beach* specifically as a neo-imperial tourist fantasy, see Alex Tickell's "Footprints on The Beach: Traces of Colonial Adventure in Narratives of Independent Tourism."

8. An interesting element of the publicity surrounding the film concerned the adventures of its primary screenwriter, Bill Broyles, who participated in an island survival camp for several weeks to prepare for the writing of the film. According to several interviews, much of what Chuck faces was taken from Broyles's experiences as a willing castaway and as a conscripted Vietnam soldier. So, in essence, viewers were experiencing through the film a "real" but constructed castaway fantasy—one that was controlled both in its planning and execution. Broyles, like other U.S. castaways, was only island stranded for a brief time, returning to his U.S. home at the end of his experiment, thus dramatizing the same story of rejecting the island in favor of the more comfortable United States. See Sarah Hepola's interview with Broyles in the *Austin Chronicle*.

Works Cited

A.H.O. *The Very Last Edition of "The Tempest" or The Wily Wizard, The Wensome Wench and the Wicked Willain an Original Burlesque Extravaganza in One Act.* London: Thomas Hailes Lacy Publishers, 1865.

Abraham, Karl. *Selected Papers, with an Introductory Memoir by Ernest Jones.* Trans. Douglas Bryan and Alix Strachey. New York: Basic Books, 1927.

Achebe, Chinua. *Things Fall Apart.* New York: Anchor Books, 1994.

Ackroyd, Peter. *Dressing Up, Transvestism and Drag: The History of an Obsession.* London: Thames and Hudson, 1979.

Akhurst, W. M. *Harlequin Robinson Friday, or The Nimble Naiad, The Lonely Squatter, and the Lively Aboriginal.* Melbourne: R. Bell, 1868.

Alexander, Caroline. *Bounty: The True Story of the Mutiny on the Bounty.* New York: Viking, 2003.

Ames, Michael M. *Cannibal Tours and Glass Boxes: The Anthropology of Museums.* 2d ed. Vancouver: University of British Columbia Press, 1992.

Anderson, Benedict R. O. G. *Imagined Communities: Reflections on the Origin and Spread of Nationalism.* Rev. ed. London: Verso, 1991.

Anderson, Warwick. "'Where Every Prospect Pleases and Only Man Is Vile': Laboratory Medicine as Colonial Discourse." *Critical-Inquiry* 18 (spring 1992) 3: 506–29.

Andriano, Joseph. *Immortal Monster: The Mythological Evolution of the Fantastic Beast in Modern Fiction and Film.* Westport, Conn.: Greenwood Press, 1999.

Anzieu, Didier. *The Skin Ego.* New Haven, Conn.: Yale University Press, 1989.

Aravamudan, Srinivas. *Tropicopolitans.* Durham, N.C.: Duke University Press, 1999.

Armstrong, Diane. "The Myth of Cronus: Cannibal and Sign in Robinson Crusoe." *Eighteenth-Century Fiction* 4 (spring 1992) 3: 207–20.

Arens, William. "Rethinking Anthropophagy." In *Cannibalism and the Colonial World,* edited by Francis Barker, Peter Hulme, and Margaret Iverson. Cambridge: Cambridge University Press, 1998.

Arnold, David. *Imperial Medicine and Indigenous Societies.* Manchester: Manchester University Press, 1988.

Ashcroft, Bill, Gareth Griffiths, and Helen Tiffin. *The Empire Writes Back: Theory and Practice in Post-colonial Literatures.* London: Routledge, 1989.

Ashcroft, Bill. *On Post-Colonial Futures: Transformation of Colonial Culture.* London: Continuum, 2001.

Ashton, Philip. *Ashton's Memorial: An History of the Strange Adventures and Signal*

Deliverances of Philip Ashton, Jr. of Marblehead. 1725. Ed. Russell W. Knight. Salem, Mass.: Peabody Museum of Salem, 1976.

Auden, W. H., William Shakespeare, and C. Kirsch. *The Sea and the Mirror: A Commentary on Shakespeare's "The Tempest."* Princeton, N.J.: Princeton University Press, 2003.

Axtell, James. *The European and the Indian: Essays in the Ethnohistory of Colonial North America.* Oxford: Oxford University Press, 1982.

Azim, Firdous. *The Colonial Rise of the Novel.* London: Routledge, 1993.

Bacevich, Andrew. *American Empire: The Realities and Consequences of U.S. Diplomacy.* Cambridge, Mass.: Harvard University Press, 2002.

Baer, Joel. "The Complicated Plot of Piracy: Aspects of English Criminal Law and the Image of the Pirate in Defoe." *Studies in Eighteenth-Century Culture* 14 (1985): 3–28.

Bakhtin, Mikhail. *Rabelais and His World.* Trans. Helene Iswolsky. Cambridge, Mass.: MIT Press, 1984.

Ballantyne, R. M. *The Coral Island: A Tale of the Pacific Ocean.* 1868. London: Dean and Sons, 1958.

Ballard, J. G. *Concrete Island.* New York: Farrar, Straus, and Giroux, 1973.

Barkan, Leonard. *Nature's Work of Art: The Human Body as Image of the World.* New Haven, Conn.: Yale University Press, 1975.

Barker, Francis, Peter Hulme, and Margaret Iverson. *Cannibalism and the Colonial World.* Cambridge: Cambridge University Press, 1998.

Barrie, James Matthew. *The Admirable Crichton: A Comedy.* New York: Scribner, 1918.

———. *Peter Pan or the Boy Who Would Not Grow Up.* New York: Scribner, 1956.

Barringer, Tim, and Tom Flynn, eds. *Colonialism and the Object: Empire, Material Culture and the Museum.* London: Routledge, 1998.

Bartolovich, Crystal. "Consumerism, or The Logic of Late Cannibalism." In *Cannibalism and the Colonial World,* edited by Francis Barker, Peter Hulme, and Margaret Iverson. Cambridge: Cambridge University Press, 1998.

Bederman, Gail. *Manliness and Civilization: A Cultural History of Gender and Race in the United States, 1880–1917.* Chicago: University of Chicago Press, 1995.

Bellah, Robert N. "Righteous Empire: How Does a Nation That Hates Taxes and Distrusts Big Government Launch an Empire? In a State of Deep Denial." *Christian Century* 120 (March 8, 2003) 5: 20–25.

Benton, Gregor. "The Origins of the Political Joke." In *Humor in Society: Resistance and Control,* edited by Chris Powell and George E. C. Paton. London: Macmillan, 1988.

Berger, John. *Ways of Seeing.* London: British Broadcasting Corporation; New York: Penguin, 1972.

Berne, Eric. "The Psychological Structure of Space with Some Remarks on *Robinson Crusoe.*" *The Psychoanalytic Quarterly* 25 (1956): 349–67.

Bhabha, Homi. *Location of Culture.* London: Routledge, 1994.

———. "Of Mimicry and Man: The Ambivalence of Colonial Discourse." In *Modern Literary Theory: A Reader,* edited by Philip Rice and Patricia Waugh. London: Arnold, 1989.

————. "Signs Taken for Wonders: Questions of Ambivalence and Authority Under a Tree Outside Delhi, May 1817." In *"Race," Writing and Difference*, edited by Henry Louis Gates. Chicago: University of Chicago Press, 1986.

Bingfield, William. *The Voyages, Shipwreck, Travels, Distresses, Strange Adventures, and Miraculous Preservation of William Bingfield Esq.* London: S. Fisher, 1799.

Birkin, Andrew. *J. M. Barrie & the Lost Boys: The Love Story That Gave Birth to Peter Pan.* New York: C. N. Potter, 1979; distributed by Crown Publishers.

Bishop, Elizabeth. "Crusoe in England." *Geography III.* New York: Noonday, 1971.

Blaikie, Andrew. *The Body: Critical Concepts in Sociology.* London: Routledge, 2004.

Blewett, David. *The Illustration of Robinson Crusoe, 1719–1920.* Gerrards Cross, Buckinghamshire: Colin Smythe, 1995.

Blumstein, Alex. "Masochism and Fantasies of Preparing to Be Incorporated." *Journal of the American Psycholanalytic Association* 7 (1959): 292–98.

Boehmer, Elleke. *Colonial and Postcolonial Literature: Migrant Metaphors.* Oxford: Oxford University Press, 1995.

Bongie, Chris. *Islands and Exiles: The Creole Identities of Post/Colonial Literature.* Stanford, Calif.: Stanford University Press, 1998.

Boot, Max. "The Case for American Empire." *Weekly Standard* 7 (October 15, 2001) 5: 27–30.

Boucher, Philip. *Cannibal Encounters: Europeans and Island Caribs, 1492–1763.* Baltimore: Johns Hopkins University Press, 1992.

Bourdieu, Pierre, and Randal Johnson. *The Fields of Cultural Production: Essays on Art and Literature.* New York: Columbia University Press, 1993.

Brenkman, John. *Straight, Male, Modern: A Cultural Critique of Psychoanalysis.* New York: Routledge, 1993.

Brennan, Timothy. "The Empire's New Clothes." *Critical Inquiry* 20 (winter 2003) 2: 337–67.

Bristow, Joseph. *Empire Boys: Adventures in a Man's World.* London: Harper Collins, 1991.

Broadbent, R. J. *A History of Pantomime.* New York: Benjamin Blom, 1901.

Brooks, Peter. *Body Work: Objects of Desire in Modern Narrative.* Cambridge, Mass.: Harvard University Press, 1993.

Buell, Lawrence. "American Literary Emergence as a Postcolonial Phenomenon." *American Literary History* 4 (fall 1992) 3: 411–42.

Burg, B. R. *Sodomy and the Perception of Evil: English Sea Rovers in the Seventeenth-Century Caribbean.* New York: New York University Press, 1983.

Burroughs, Edgar Rice. *Tarzan of the Apes.* New York: A. L. Burt Company, 1914.

Burton, Richard Francis. *The Book of the Thousand Nights and a Night: A Plain and Literal Translation of The Arabian Nights Entertainments.* Printed by The Burton Club for private subscribers only, 1885.

————. *Personal Narrative of a Pilgrimage to al-Madinah & Meccah.* New York: Dover Publications, 1893.

Byron, Lord (Gordon, George). "The Island, or Christian and His Comrades." In *The Complete Poetical Works of Byron*. 1823. Boston: Houghton Mifflin, 1933.

———. "Don Juan." In *The Complete Poetical Works of Byron*. Boston: Houghton Mifflin, 1933.

Campbell, I. C. *"Gone Native" in Polynesia: Captivity Narratives and Experiences from the South Pacific*. Westport, Conn.: Greenwood Press, 1998.

Campbell, Mary. *Wonder and Science: Imagining Worlds in Early Modern Europe*. Ithaca: Cornell University Press, 1999.

Campe, Joachim Heinrich. *Robinson the Younger, or The New Crusoe*. Trans. R. Hick. London: Routlege, 1855.

Carpenter, Humphrey, and Mari Prichard. *The Oxford Companion to Children's Literature*. New York: Oxford University Press, 1984.

Carpenter, Kevin. *Desert Isles and Pirate Islands: The Island Theme in Nineteenth-century English Juvenile Fiction, a Survey and Bibliography*. Frankfort: Peter Lang, 1984.

Cassuto, Leonard. *The Inhuman Race: The Racial Grotesque in American Literature and Culture*. New York: Columbia University Press, 1997.

Cesaire, Aime. *A Tempest*. 1969. Trans. Richard Miller. New York: Ubu Repertory Theater Publications, 1985.

Chan, Stephen C. K. "Tactics of Space in Defoe and Foucault." *Studies in Language and Literature* 106 (Oct 1990): 43–57.

Clark, Patty Lee. *The Admirable Miranda: Written for the Hopefully Well Affected Club*. Westfield, Mass.: Times and News-Letter Print, 1905.

Cockrell, Dale. *Demons of Disorder: Early Blackface Minstrels and Their World*. Cambridge: Cambridge University Press, 1997.

Coetzee, J. M. *Foe*. New York: Penguin, 1986.

Cohen, Jeffrey, ed. *Monster Theory: Reading Culture*. Minneapolis: University of Minnesota Press, 1996.

Cohn, Roby. *Modern Shakespeare Offshoots*. Princeton, N.J.: Princeton University Press, 1976.

Coleridge, Samuel Taylor. *The Rime of the Ancient Mariner*. 1798. New York: Dover Publications, 1970.

Columbus, Christopher. *The Four Voyages*. Ed. and trans. J. M. Cohen. London: Penguin, 1969.

Colvin, Anne Hutta. "The Celluloid Crusoe: A Study of Cinematic Robinson-ades." Ph.D. diss., Temple University, 1989.

Condé, Maryse. *Windward Heights*. New York: Soho, 1998.

Conley, Tom. *The Self-Made Map: Cartographic Writing in Early Modern France*. Minneapolis: University of Minnesota Press, 1996.

Connell, R. W. *Masculinities*. Berkeley, Calif.: University of California Press, 1995.

———. *The Men and the Boys*. Berkeley, Calif.: University of California Press, 2000.

Connor, Stephen. "Rewriting Wrong: On the Ethics of Literary Reversion." In *Liminal Postmodernisms: The Postmodern, The (Post-) Colonial, and the (Post-)*

Feminism, edited by Theo D'Hean and Hans Bertens. Amsterdam: Rodolpi, 1994.

Conrad, Joseph, and Robert Kimbrough. *Heart of Darkness; An Authoritative Text, Backgrounds and Sources, Criticism.* Norton critical edition. 2d ed. New York: Norton, 1971.

Conquest, George, and Henry Spry. *Robinson Crusoe, the Lad Rather Loose O' and the Black Man Called Friday, Who Kept His House Tidy.* London: Phillips Brothers, 1885.

Cook, James. *A Voyage to the Pacific Ocean.* London: J. Stockdale, Scratcherd and Whitaker, J. Fielding, and J. Hardy, 1784.

Cooper, Frederick. "Colonizing Time: Work Rhythm and Labor Conflict in Colonial Mombasa." In *Colonialism and Culture*, edited by Nicolas Dirks. Ann Arbor: University of Michigan Press, 1992.

Cordingly, David. *Life Among the Pirates: The Romance and the Reality.* London: Little, Brown, 1995.

Cosgrove, Denis E., and Stephen Daniels. *The Iconography of Landscape: Essays on the Symbolic Representation, Design, and Use of Past Environments.* Cambridge: Cambridge University Press, 1988.

Cowie, L. W. "Bridewell." *History Today* 23 (1973): 350–58.

Crain, Caleb. "Lovers of Human Flesh: Homosexuality and Cannibalism in Melville's Novels." *American Literature* 66 (1994) 1: 25–53.

Crary, Jonathan. *Techniques of the Observer: On Vision and Modernity in the Nineteenth Century.* Cambridge, Mass.: MIT Press, 1990.

Crosby, Alfred W. *Ecological Imperialism: The Biological Expansion of Europe, 900–1900.* Cambridge: Cambridge University Press, 1986.

Crotty, Martin. *Making the Australian Male: Middle-Class Masculinity 1870–1920.* Melbourne: Melbourne University Press, 2001.

Cudjoe, Selwyn. *Resistance and Caribbean Literature.* Athens, Ohio: Ohio University Press, 1980.

Dampier, William. *Voyages and Descriptions.* London: Printed for James Knapton, 1700.

Daniels, Stephen. *Fields of Vision: Landscape Imagery and National Identity in England and the United States.* Cambridge: Polity Press, 1993.

Darwin, Charles. *The Origin of Species by Means of Natural Selection; or, The Preservation of Favored Races in the Struggle for Life and The Descent of Man and Selection in Relation to Sex.* New York: The Modern Library, 1936.

Daubenton, Mme. *Zelia in the Desert or the Female Crusoe.* London: Printed for G. and T. Wilkie, 1789.

Davies, Robertson. *Tempest-Tost.* Toronto: Clarke, Irwin & Co, 1951.

Davis, L. J. "Known Unknown Locations: The Ideology of Novelistic Landscape in *Robinson Crusoe.*" *Sociocriticism* 4–5 (1986–87): 87–113.

Dawson, Graham. *Soldier Heroes: British Adventure, Empire, and the Imagining of Masculinities.* London: Routledge, 1994.

De Las Casas, Bartolomé. *An Account of The First Voyages and Discoveries Made by the Spaniards in America Containing the Most Exact Relation Hitherto Publish'd, of Their Unparallel'd Cruelties on the Indians, in the Destruction of above Forty*

Millions of People; with the Propositions Offer'd to the King of Spain, to Prevent the Further Ruin of the West-Indies. London: J. Darby, 1699.

De la Mare, Walter. *Desert Islands and Robinson Crusoe.* London: Faber and Faber Limited, 1930.

Dean, Julia. *The Wonderful Narrative of Miss Julia Dean, the Only Survivor of the Steamship "City of Boston" Lost at Sea 1870.* Philadelphia: Barclay and Co., 1890.

Defoe, Daniel. *The Farther Adventures of Robinson Crusoe, Being the Second and Last Part of His Life.* London: John Stockdale, 1790.

———. *The King of the Pirates: Being an Account of the Famous Enterprises of Captain Avery, With Lives of Other Pirates and Robbers.* 1720. New York: Crosoup & Sterling, 1898.

———. *The Life and Adventures of Robinson Crusoe. With "The Life of Daniel Defoe" by George Chalmers. With Engravings after T. Stothard.* London: John Stockdale, 1804.

———. *The Life and Adventures of Robinson Crusoe.* London: Ward, Lock, and Company, 1879.

———. *The Life and Adventures of Robinson Crusoe, Illustrated by E. Nister.* New York: Dutton, 1895.

———. *The Life and Adventures of Robinson Crusoe.* New York: Harper and Brothers, 1900.

———. *The Life and Adventures of Robinson Crusoe.* London: Routledge and Sons, 1910.

———. *Robinson Crusoe: An Authoritative Text, Contexts, Criticism,* edited by Michael Shinagel. Norton critical edition. 2d ed. New York: Norton, 1994.

———. *The Robinson Crusoe Picture Book: Containing Robinson Crusoe, How Cock Sparrow Kept His Christmas. Queer Characters. Aesop's Fables.* London: Routledge, 1879.

———. *Robinson Crusoe in Words of One Syllable, With Colored Illustrations.* Philadelphia: J. B. Lippencott, 1868.

Deleuze, Gilles, and Félix Guattari. *Anti-Oedipus: Capitalism and Schizophrenia.* Minneapolis: University of Minnesota Press, 1983.

Deloughrey, Elizabeth. "'The Litany of Islands, The Rosary of Archipelagoes': Caribbean and Pacific Archipelagraphy" *ARIEL: A Review of International English Literature* 32 (January 2001) 1: 21–51.

Derrida, Jacques. "Declarations of Independence." *New Political Science* 15 (summer 1986): 7–15.

Diamond, Jared M. *Guns, Germs, and Steel: The Fates of Human Societies.* New York: W. W. Norton & Co., 1999.

Dibdin, Charles. *Hannah Hewitt, or The Female Crusoe.* In *Three Centuries of Drama, English, 1737–1800.* London: C. Dibdin, 1792.

Douglas, Mary. *Natural Symbols: Explorations in Cosmology.* New York: Pantheon Books, 1982.

———. *Purity and Danger: An Analysis of Concepts of Pollution and Taboo.* London, Routledge & K. Paul, 1966.

Douthwaite, Julia V. *The Wild Girl, Natural Man, and the Monster: Dangerous*

Experiments in the Age of Enlightenment. Chicago: University of Chicago Press, 2002.

Dryden, John, and William Davenant. *The Tempest or the Enchanted Island, A Comedy.* London: Henry Herringtoman, 1670.

Duffett, Thomas. *The Mock-Tempest, or The Enchanted Castle.* Ed. Ronald Eugene DiLorenzo. London: William Cademan, 1675.

Eberhardt, Isabelle. *The Nomad: The Diaries of Isabelle Eberhardt.* Ed. Liz Kershaw. Introduction by Annette Kobak. Chichester, West Sussex, England: Summersdale, 2001.

Edensor, Tim. *Tourists at the Taj: Performance and Meaning at a Symbolic Site.* London: Routledge, 1998.

Elias, Norbert. *The Civilizing Process.* Oxford: B. Blackwell, 1982.

Fairchild, Hoxie Neale. *The Noble Savage; A Study in Romantic Naturalism.* New York: Columbia University Press, 1928.

Fanon, Frantz. *Black Skin, White Masks.* New York: Grove Press, 1991.

———. *A Dying Colonialism.* New York: Grove Press, 1965.

———. *The Wretched of the Earth.* New York: Grove Press, 1968.

Fine, Rubin. *A History of Psychoanalysis.* New York: Columbia University Press, 1979.

Fletcher, Fineas. *The Purple Island, or The Isle of Man.* Cambridge: Cambridge University Press, 1633.

Ford, Lucy. *The Female Robinson Crusoe: A Tale of the American Wilderness.* New York: Jared Bell, 1837.

Foucault, Michel. *Discipline and Punish: The Birth of the Prison.* 2d ed. New York: Vintage Books, 1995.

———. *Power/Knowledge: Collected Interviews and Other Writings, 1972–1977.* Ed. Colin Gordon. Trans. Colin Gordon. New York: Pantheon Books, 1980.

———. "Of Other Spaces." *Diacritics* 16 (1986): 22–27.

———. *Madness and Civilization.* New York: Vintage Books, 1988.

Freud, Sigmund. *Jokes and Their Relation to the Unconscious.* 1905. Trans. James Strachey. New York: W. W. Norton, 1963.

———. *Case Histories I: "Dora" and "Little Hans."* Harmondsworth, England: Penguin, 1977.

———. *Totem and Taboo: Resemblances between the Psychic Lives of Savages and Neurotics.* Trans. A. A. Brill. New York: Vintage, 1918.

———. *The Basic Writings of Sigmund Freud.* Ed. A. A. Brill. New York: Modern Library, 1938.

Frow, Gerald. *"Oh, Yes It Is!" A History of Pantomime.* London: British Broadcasting Corporation, 1985.

Fuchs, Barbara. "Faithless Empires: Pirates, Renegadoes, and the English Nation" *English Literary History* 67 (2000) 1: 45–69.

Galligan, Edward. *The Comic Vision in Literature.* Athens: University of Georgia Press, 1984.

Garber, Marjorie. *Vested Interests: Cross-Dressing and Cultural Anxiety.* New York: Routledge, 1992.

Gauld, Alan. *A History of Hypnotism.* Cambridge: Cambridge University Press, 1992.

A General History of the Pyrates. Ed. Manuel Schonhorn. London: Dent, 1972.

Gerassi-Navarro, Nina. *Pirate Novels: Fictions of Nation Building in Spanish America.* Durham, N.C.: Duke University Press, 1999.

Gilbert, Helen, and Anna Johnston. *In Transit: Travel, Text, Empire.* New York: Peter Lang, 2002.

Gilbert, W. S., and Arthur Sullivan. *Utopia Limited, or The Flowers of Progress: An Original Comic Opera in Two Acts.* 1893. New York, London: Chappell, 1976.

Gilder, Eric, and John Crocker. *Robinson Crusoe Pantomime.* London: Evans Plays, 1972.

Gildon, Charles, and Paul Dottin, eds. *Robinson Crusoe Examined and Criticis'd or A New Edition of Charles Gildon's Famous Pamphlet Now Published with an Introduction and Explanatory Notes Together with an Essay on Gildon's Life.* London: J. M. Dent and Sons, 1923.

Gill, James E. "Beast Over Man: Theriophilic Paradox in Gulliver's Voyage to the Country of the Houyhnmhnms." *Studies in Philology* 67 (1970): 532–49.

Gilman, Sander and J. Edward Chamberlin, eds. *Degeneration: The Dark Side of Progress.* New York: Columbia University Press, 1985.

Giraudoux, Jean. *Suzanne and the Pacific.* 1923. Trans. Ben Ray Redman. New York: Howard Fertig, 1975.

Gliserman, Martin J. *Psychoanalysis, Language, and the Body of the Text.* Gainesville, Fla.: University Press of Florida, 1996.

Gluckman, Max. *Custom and Conflict in Africa.* Oxford: Blackwell, 1967.

Goffman, Erving. *Gender Advertisements.* New York: Harper, 1976.

Goldberg, Jonathan. *Sodometries: Renaissance Texts, Modern Sensibilities.* Stanford: Stanford University Press, 1992.

Goldie, Terry. *Fear and Temptation: The Image of the Indigene in Canadian, Australian, and New Zealand Literatures.* Kingston: McGill-Queen's University Press, 1989.

Golding, William. *Lord of the Flies.* New York: Putnam, 1959.

———. *Pincher Martin.* New York: Harcourt, Brace, and World, 1956.

———. Interview with James Keating. Purdue University, May 10, 1962. Casebook of William Golding's *Lord of the Flies.* New York: Putnam, 1964.

Green, Martin. *Dreams of Adventure, Deeds of Empire.* New York: Basic Books, 1979.

———. *The Robinson Crusoe Story.* University Park, Penn.: Pennsylvania State University Press, 1990.

Greenblatt, Stephen Jay. *Marvelous Possessions: The Wonder of the New World.* Chicago: University of Chicago Press, 1992.

Grosz, Elizabeth. *Volatile Bodies: Toward a Corporeal Feminism; Theories of Representation and Difference.* Bloomington: Indiana University Press, 1994.

Grove, Richard. *Green Imperialism: Colonial Expansion, Tropical Island Edens, and the Orgins of Environmentalism, 1600–1860.* Cambridge: Cambridge University Press, 1995.

Guffey, George Robert. *After The Tempest: The Tempest, or The Enchanted Island*

(1670); The Tempest, or The Enchanted Island (1674); The Mock-Tempest, or The Enchanted Castle (1675); The Tempest, an Opera (1756). Los Angeles, Calif.: William Andrews Clark Memorial Library, 1969.

Gutwirth, Marcel. *Laughing Matter: An Essay on the Comic.* Ithaca, N.Y.: Cornell University Press, 1993.

Hadar, Leon, "U.S. Empire? Let's Get Real," *Los Angeles Times.* July 2, 2003: 15.

Haggard, H. Rider. *King Solomon's Mines.* New York: Airmont, 1967.

Hall, Edward. *Narrative Discourse.* Oxford, Blackwell, 1964.

Hall, James. *Dictionary of Subjects and Symbols in Art.* New York: Harper and Row, 1979.

Hardiman, David. "From Custom to Crime: The Politics of Drinking in Colonial South Gujarat." In *Subaltern Studies IV.* Ed. Ranajit Guha. Oxford: Oxford University Press, 1985.

Hardt, Michael, and Antonio Negri. *Empire.* Cambridge, Mass.: Harvard University Press, 2000.

Harlow, Barbara. *Resistance Literature.* New York: Methuen, 1987.

Hartnack, Christiane. "Vishnu on Freud's Desk: Psychoanalysis in Colonial India." *Social Research* 57 (1990): 921–45.

Hawes, Clement. "Three Times Around the Globe: Gulliver and Colonial Discourse." *Cultural Critique* 18 (1991): 187–214.

Haynes, R. D. "The Unholy Alliance of Science in *The Island of Dr. Moreau.*" *The Wellsian: The Journal of the H. G. Wells Society* 11 (summer 1998): 13–24.

Helps, Racey. *Little Mouse Crusoe.* London: Collins, 1948.

Hendershot, Cyndy. *The Animal Within: Masculinity and the Gothic.* Ann Arbor: University of Michigan Press, 1998.

Hepola, Sarah. "Lost at Sea and Back Again: Bill Broyles' Extraordinary Adventure Story." *Austin Chronicle* (December 29, 2000): 2–8.

Herbert, T. Walter "Willie Nelson and Herman Melville on Manhood: Pierre and 'The Red-Headed Stranger.'" *Texas Studies in Language and Literature* 35 (1993) 4: 421–39.

Herodotus. *The Histories.* Trans. Aubrey De Sélincourt. Ed. John Marincola. London: Penguin Books, 1954.

Hillman, David, and Carla Mazzio. *The Body in Parts: Fantasies of Corporeality in Early Modern Europe.* New York: Routledge, 1997.

Hiltzik, Michael A. "Digital Cinema, Take 2." *Technology Review* (September 2002). Available at: http://www.technologyreview.com/articles/hiltzik0902.asp?p=1.

Hochschild, Adam. *King Leopold's Ghost: A Story of Greed, Terror, and Heroism in Colonial Africa.* Boston: Houghton Mifflin, 1998.

Homer. *The Odyssey.* New York: Farrar, Straus, and Giroux, 1998.

Horn, Andrew. "'But to Return from This Digression . . .': The Functions of Excursus in Edgar Allan Poe's *Narrative of Arthur Gordon Pym.*" *Communique* 11 (1986) 1: 7–22.

Howson, Alexandra. *The Body in Society: An Introduction.* Oxford: Polity, 2003.

Huet, Marie Hélène. *Monstrous Imagination.* Cambridge, Mass.: Harvard University Press, 1993.

Hughes, Robert. *The Fatal Shore: A History of the Transportation of Convicts to Australia, 1787–1868*. London: Guild Publishing, 1986.

Hulme, Peter. *Colonial Encounters*. London: Routledge, 1992.

———. "Including America." *ARIEL: A Review of International English Literature* 26 (January 1995) 1: 117–23.

———. "Introduction: The Cannibal Scene." In *Cannibalism and the Colonial World*, edited by Francis Barker, Peter Hulme, and Margaret Iverson. Cambridge: Cambridge University Press, 1998.

Hulme, Peter, and William Sherman. *"The Tempest" and Its Travels*. Philadelphia: University of Pennsylvania Press, 2000.

Ignatieff, Michael. "The American Empire; The Burden." *The New York Times Magazine* (January 5, 2003): 22–27, 50–54.

Indigenous Law Resources. "Kim Polak: Public Drinking." *Reconciliation and Social Justice Library*. Available at: http://beta/austlii.edu.au/au/other/IndigLRes/rciadic/individual/kimpolak/27.html.

Jacobs, Henry E., and Claudia D. Johnson. *An Annotated Bibliography of Shakespearean Burlesques, Parodies, and Travesties*. New York: Garland, 1976.

Jacobus, Mary. *Psychoanalysis and the Scene of Reading*. Oxford: Oxford University Press, 1999.

Jahoda, Gustav. *Images of Savages: Ancient Roots of Modern Prejudice in Western Culture*. London: Routledge, 1999.

James, Lawrence. *The Rise and Fall of the British Empire*. New York: St. Martin's Press, 1994.

Johnson, Chalmers. *Blowback: The Costs and Consequences of American Empire*. New York: Metropolitan Books, 2000.

Kantorowicz, Ernst Hartwig. *The King's Two Bodies; A Study in Mediaeval Political Theology*. Princeton, N.J.: Princeton University Press, 1957.

Kaplan, Amy. "'Left Alone with America': The Absence of Empire in the Study of American Culture." In *Cultures of United States Imperialism*, edited by Amy Kaplan and Donald E. Pease. Durham, N.C.: Duke University Press, 1993.

Keane, Patrick J. *Coleridge's Submerged Politics: The Ancient Mariner and Robinson Crusoe*. Columbia, Mo.: University of Missouri Press, 1994.

Keller, Arthur S., Oliver J. Lissitzyn, and Frederick J. Mann. *Creation of Rights of Sovereignty through Symbolic Acts*. New York: Columbia University Press, 1938.

Keller, Richard. "Madness and Colonization: Psychiatry in the British and French Empires, 1800–1962." *Journal of Social History* 35 (2001) 2: 295–326.

Kelly, William L. *Psychology of the Unconscious: Mesmer, Janet, Freud, Jung, and Current Issues*. Buffalo, N.Y.: Prometheus Books, 1991.

Kent, George E. "A Conversation with George Lamming." *Black World* 22 (1973) 5: 4–14, 88–97.

Khanna, Ranjana. *Dark Continents: Psychoanalysis and Colonialism*. Durham, N.C.: Duke University Press, 2003.

Kilbourne, Frederick W. *Alterations and Adaptations of Shakespeare*. Boston: The Poet Lore Company, 1906.

Kilgour, Maggie. *From Communion to Cannibalism: An Anatomy of Metaphors of Incorporation*. Princeton, N.J.: Princeton University Press, 1990.

Kimmel, Michael S. *Manhood in America: A Cultural History.* New York: Free Press, 1996.

Kincaid, Jamaica. *A Small Place.* New York: Penguin, 1988.

Kipling, Rudyard. "White Man's Burden." *McClure's Magazine* 12 (February 1899): 290.

———. *Plain Tales from the Hills.* New York: Doubleday and McClure, 1899.

———. *Kim: Authoritative Text, Backgrounds, Criticism.* New York: Norton, 2002.

Kittay, Eve Feder. "Womb Envy: An Explanatory Concept." In *Mothering: Essays in Feminist Theory,* edited by Joyce Treblcot. Totowa, N.J.: Rowman and Allanheld, 1984.

Klein, Melanie. *The Selected Melanie Klein.* Ed. Juliet Mitchell. New York: Free Press, 1987.

———. *Writings of Melanie Klein.* Vol. 1–4. New York: Free Press, 1984.

Knowles, Murray, and Kirsten Malmkjær. *Language and Control in Children's Literature.* London: Routledge, 1996.

Knowles, Ronald. *Gulliver's Travels: The Politics of Satire.* New York: Twayne Publishers, 1996.

Kolodny, Annette. *The Lay of the Land: Metaphor as Experience and History in American Life and Letters.* Chapel Hill, N.C.: University of North Carolina Press, 1975.

Kress, Gunther, and Theo Van Leeuwen. *Reading Images: The Grammar of Visual Design.* London: Routledge, 1996.

Kristeva, Julia. *Powers of Horror: An Essay on Abjection.* European Perspectives. New York: Columbia University Press, 1982.

Lacan, Jacques. *Ecrits: A Selection.* Trans. Alan Sheridan. New York: Norton, 1977.

Lamb, Charles. *Lamb's Stories from Shakespeare Put into Basic English by T. Takata.* London: Kegan Paul, 1932.

Lamming, George. *Water with Berries.* Trinidad and Jamaica: Longman Caribbean Limited, 1971.

Lane, Dorothy. *The Island as Site of Resistance: An Examination of Caribbean and New Zealand Texts.* New York: Peter Lang, 1995.

Langdon, Robert. "'Dusky Damsels': Pitcairn Island's Neglected Matriarchs of the Bounty Saga. (Statistical Data Included)." *Journal of Pacific History* 35 (2000) 1: 29–47.

Laplanche, Jean, and J. B. Pontalis. *The Language of Psycho-Analysis.* New York: Norton, 1974.

Laqueur, Thomas Walter. *Making Sex: Body and Gender from the Greeks to Freud.* Cambridge, Mass.: Harvard University Press, 1990.

Lestringant, Frank. *Cannibals: The Discovery and Representation of the Cannibal from Columbus to Jules Verne.* Berkeley, Calif.: University of California Press, 1997.

Lewcock, Dawn. "Once Upon a Time: The Story of the Pantomime Audience." In *Audience Participation: Essays on Inclusion in Performance,* edited by Susan Kattwinkel. Westport, Conn.: Praeger, 2003.

Lewin, Bertram D. *Selected Writings of Bertram D. Lewin.* Ed. Jacob A. Arlow. New York: Psychoanalytic Quarterly, 1973.

Lewis, Paul. *Comic Effects: Interdisciplinary Approaches to Humor in Literature.* Albany, N.Y.: State University of New York Press, 1989.

Lidoff, Joan. "Fluid Boundaries: The Mother-Daughter Story, the Story-Reader Matrix." *Texas Studies in Literature and Language* 35 (1993) 4: 398–420.

Lindberg, David C. *Theories of Vision from Al-Kindi to Kepler.* Chicago: University of Chicago Press, 1976.

Liu, Lydia. "Robinson Crusoe's Earthenware Pot." *Critical Inquiry* 25 (summer 1999) 4: 728–57.

Lloyd. Trevor. *Empire: The History of the British Empire.* London: Hambledon and London, 2001.

Lobanov-Rostovsky, Sergei. "Taming the Basilisk." In *The Body in Parts,* edited by David Hillman and Carla Mazzio. New York: Routledge, 1997.

Longbaine, Gerard. *An Account of the English Dramatic Poets.* 1688. New York: Garland, 1973.

Longueville, Peter. *The Hermit, or The Unparalled Sufferings and Surprising Adventures of Mr. Philip Quarll.* 1727. London: Garland, 1972.

Lott, Eric. *Love and Theft: Blackface Minstrelsy and the American Working Class.* New York: Oxford University Press, 1993.

Loxley, Diana. *Problematic Shores: The Literature of Islands.* New York: St. Martin's Press, 1990.

Mabo & Ors v. State of Queensland (no 2). (1992) 175 CLR 1, [1992] HCA 23.

Mackworth, Cecily. *The Destiny of Isabelle Eberhardt.* New York: Ecco Press, 1975.

MacLeod, Diane Sacho, and Julie F. Codell. *Orientalism Transposed: The Impact of the Colonies on British Culture.* Aldershot, England: Ashgate, 1998.

MacPherson, C. B. *The Political Theory of Possessive Individualism: Hobbes to Locke.* London: Oxford University Press, 1964.

Mandeville, John. *The Travels of Sir John Mandeville.* Trans. C.W.R.D. Moseley. London: Penguin Books, 1983.

Mander, Raymond, and Joe Mitchenson. *Pantomime: A Story in Pictures.* New York: Taplinger, 1973.

Mannoni, Octave. *Prospero and Caliban; The Psychology of Colonization.* New York: Praeger, 1964.

Marryat, Frederick. *Masterman Ready, or, The Wreck of the Pacific.* New York: Harper and Brothers, 1928.

——. *The Pirate and the Three Cutters.* London: G. Bell, 1889.

Marsh, Carole. *In Good Taste: The History, Mystery, Legend, Lore and Future of Cannibalism.* Peach Tree City, Ga.: Gallopade International, 1994.

Martel, Yann. *The Life of Pi.* New York: Harcourt, 2001.

Marx, Karl, and Friedrich Engels. *Das Kapital, A Critique of Political Economy.* Chicago: H. Regnery, 1959.

Maskiell, Michelle. "Consuming Kashmir: Shawls and Empires, 1500–2000." *Journal of World History* 13 (2002) 1: 27–65.

Maslow, Abraham. *Dominance, Self-Esteem, Self-Actualization: Germinal Papers of A.H. Maslow.* Ed. Richard J. Lowry. Monterey, Calif.: Brooks/Cole Pub. Co., 1973.

Mason, Peter. *Infelicities: Representations of the Exotic.* Baltimore: Johns Hopkins University Press, 1998.

McArdle, J. F., and Frank W. Green. *Mr. Edward Saker's Grand Comic Christmas Pantomime Entitled Robinson Crusoe, or Friday and His Funny Family.* London: Daily Post and Journal Offices, 1878.

McClintock, Anne. *Imperial Leather: Race, Gender, and Sexuality in the Colonial Contest.* New York: Routledge, 1995.

———. "Maid to Order: Commercial S/M and Gender Power" In *Dirty Looks: Women, Pornography, Power,* edited by Pamela Church Gibson. London: British Film Institute, 1993.

———. "Screwing the System: Sexwork, Race, and the Law." In *Feminism and Postmodernism,* edited by Margaret Ferguson and Jennifer Wicke. Durham, N.C.: Duke University Press, 1994.

———. "Masculinity and Other War Zones, (Or, Loving America Differently)." Visiting Distinguished Faculty Award Lecture, Lexington, University of Kentucky, January 2002.

McFadden, George. *Discovering the Comic.* Princeton: Princeton University Press, 1983.

McGregor, Gaile. *The Noble Savage in the New World Garden: Notes Toward a Syntactics of Place.* Toronto: University of Toronto Press, 1988.

Megroz, R. L. *The Real Robinson Crusoe: Being the Strange and Surprising Adventures of Alexander Selkirk of Largo, Fife, Mariner.* London: Cresset Press, 1939.

Melville, Herman. *Billy Budd and Typee.* New York: Washington Square Press, 1962.

Memmi, Albert. *The Colonizer and the Colonized.* Boston: Beacon, 1965.

Mészáros, István. *Socialism or Barbarism: From the "American Century" to the Crossroads.* New York: Monthly Review Press, 2001.

Miller, David. "The Father's Witness: Patriarchal Images of Boys," *Representations* 70 (spring 2000): 115–41.

Mitchell, Timothy. *Colonising Egypt.* Cambridge: Cambridge University Press, 1988.

Mitchell, W. J. Thomas. *Landscape and Power.* Chicago: University of Chicago Press, 1994.

Mitford, Mary Russell. *The Works of Mary Russell Mitford, Prose and Verse.* Philadelphia: James Crissy, 1841.

Montaigne, Michel. "Of the Cannibals." In *The Complete Essays of Montaigne: Essays, Travels, Journal, Letters,* translated by Donald M. Frame. Stanford: Stanford University Press, 1957.

Montrose, Louis. "The Work of Gender in the Discourse of Discovery." In *New World Encounters,* edited by Stephen Greenblatt. Berkeley, Calif.: University of California Press, 1993.

Moore, John Robert. *Daniel Defoe: Citizen of the Modern World.* Chicago: University of Chicago Press, 1958.

More, Thomas. *Utopia.* Boston: Bedford/St. Martins, 1999.

Morris, Ralph. *A Narrative of the Life and Astonishing Adventures of John Daniel.* 1751. New York: Arno Press, 1975.

Motohashi, Ted. "The Discourse of Cannibalism in Early Modern Travel Writing." In *Travel Writing and Empire: Postcolonial Theory in Transit,* edited by S. H. Clark. London: Zed, 1999.

Muldoon, James. "Columbus's First Voyage and the Medieval Legal Tradition." In *Renaissance and Discovery,* edited by Paul Maurice Clogan. Lanham, Md.: Rowman and Little Publishers, 1993.

Mulvey, Laura. "Visual Pleasure and Narrative Cinema." In *Film Theory and Criticism,* edited by Leo Braudy and Marshall Cohen. New York: Oxford University Press, 2004.

Nair, Rukmini Bhaya. *Lying on the Postcolonial Couch: The Idea of Indifference.* Minneapolis: University of Minnesota Press, 2002.

Nandy, Ashis. The Savage Freud and Other Essays on Possible and Retrievable Selves. Princeton, N.J.: Princeton University Press, 1995.

Nelson, Dana D. *National Manhood: Capitalist Citizenship and the Imagined Fraternity of White Men.* Durham, N.C.: Duke University Press, 1998.

Neville, Henry. *The Island of Pines, or a Late Discovery of a Fourth Island Near Terra Australis, Incognita.* 1668. In *Shorter Novels: Seventeenth Century.* London: Dent, 1930.

Newman, Judie. *The Ballistic Bard: Postcolonial Fictions.* London: Arnold, 1995.

Niemeyer, Carl. "The Coral Island Revisited." *College English* 22 (1961): 241–45.

Novak, Maximillian E. "The Economic Meaning of Robinson Crusoe." In *Twentieth Century Interpretations of Critical Essays,* edited by Frank H. Ellis. Englewood Cliffs, N.J.: Prentice Hall, 1969, 97–102.

O'Brien, John. *Harlequin Britain: Pantomime and Entertainment, 1690–1760.* Baltimore: Johns Hopkins University Press, 2004.

O'Sullivan, John. "The Reluctant Empire: The U.S. Leads the World—But Doesn't Have to Rule It." *National Review* 54 (November 11, 2002) 1: 42–44.

Obeyesekere, Gananath. "British Cannibals: Contemplation of an Event in the Death and Resurrection of James Cook, Explorer." *Critical Inquiry* 18: 630–54.

Orgel, Stephen. Introduction to *The Tempest,* by William Shakespeare. New York: Oxford University Press, 1987.

———. "Prospero's Wife." *Representations* 8 (fall 1984): 1–13.

Oliver, Kelly. *The Colonization of Psychic Space: A Psychoanalytic Social Theory of Oppression.* Minneapolis: University of Minnesota Press, 2004.

Orwell, George. "Funny, but Not Vulgar." In *The Collected Essays, Journalism and Letters of George Orwell. As I Please 1943–1945 III,* edited by Sonia Orwell and Ian Angus. New York: Harcourt, Brace and World, 1968.

Otter, Samuel. *Melville's Anatomies.* Berkeley, Calif.: University of California Press, 1999.

Padrón, Ricardo. *The Spacious Word: Geography, Literature, and Empire in Early Modern Spain.* Chicago: University of Chicago Press, 2004.

Paltock, Robert. *The Life and Adventures of Peter Wilkins.* London: Oxford University Press, 1973.

Paravisini-Gebert, Lizabeth. "Cross-Dressing on the Margins of Empire: Women

Pirates and the Narrative of the Caribbean." In *Women at Sea: Travel Writing and the Margins of Caribbean Discourse,* edited by Lizabeth Paravisini-Gebert and Ivette Romero-Cesareo. New York: Palgrave, 2001.

Paster, Gail Kern. *The Body Embarrassed: Drama and the Disciplines of Shame in Early Modern England.* Ithaca, N.Y.: Cornell University Press, 1993.

Paul, Adrian. *Willis the Pilot: A Sequel to the Swiss Family Robinson with Illustrations.* Boston: Mayhew and Baker, 1858.

Pearlman, E. "Robinson Crusoe and the Cannibals." *Mosaic* 10 (1976): 39–55.

Pearson, Bill. *Rifled Sanctuaries: Some Views of the Pacific Islands in Western Literature to 1900.* Oxford: Oxford University Press, 1984.

Perotin-Dumon, Anne. "The Pirate and the Emperor: Power and Law on the Seas, 1450–1850." In *The Political Economy of Merchant Empires,* edited by James D. Tracy. Cambridge: Cambridge University Press, 1991.

Perse, St. John. "Images a Crusoe." In *Eloges and Other Poems,* translated by Louise Varèse. New York: Pantheon Books, 1956.

Pfeil, Fred. "Getting Up There with Tom." In *Masculinity Studies and Feminist Theory: New Directions,* edited by Judith Kegan Gardiner. New York: Columbia University Press, 2002.

Phillips, Richard. *Mapping Men and Empire: A Geography of Adventure.* London: Routledge, 1997.

Pliny, the Elder. *Natural History.* Cambridge, Mass.: Harvard University Press, 1963.

Poe, Edgar Allan. *The Narrative of Arthur Gordon Pym.* Boston: D. R. Godine, 1973.

——— *Complete Stories and Poems of Edgar Allan Poe.* Garden City, N.Y.: Doubleday and Company, 1966.

———. "To Science." In *The Collected Tales and Poems of Edgar Allan Poe.* New York: Modern Library, 1992.

Polo, Marco. *The Travels of Marco Polo, the Venetian.* Ed. William Marsden and Jon Corbino. Garden City, N.Y.: Doubleday, 1948.

Powell, Chris. "A Phenomenological Analysis of Humor in Society." In *Humor in Society: Resistance and Control,* edited by Chris Powell and George E. C. Paton. London: Macmillan, 1988.

Prakash, Gyan. "Science 'Gone Native' in Colonial India." *Representations* 40 (fall 1992): 153–78.

Pratt, Mary Louise. *Imperial Eyes: Travel Writing and Transculturation.* London: Routledge, 1992.

Raleigh, Sir Walter. *The Discoverie of the Large, Rich and Bewtiful Empyre of Guiana.* Ed. Neil L. Whitehead. Manchester: Manchester University Press, 1997.

Reed, John R. "The Vanity of Law in *The Island of Dr. Moreau.*" In *H. G. Wells Under Revision: Proceedings of the International H. G. Wells Symposium, London, July 1986,* edited by Patrick Parrinder and Christopher Rolphe. London and Toronto: Associated University Presses, 1990.

Renan, Ernest. *Caliban: A Philosophical Drama Continuing "The Tempest" of William Shakespeare.* 1878. New York: AMS Press, 1971.

Rhys, Jean. *Wide Sargasso Sea.* New York: W. W. Norton & Co., 1966.

Richards, Thomas. *The Imperial Archive: Knowledge and the Fantasy of Empire*. London: Verso, 1993.

Rogers, Pat. *Defoe: The Critical Heritage*. London: Routledge and Kegan Paul, 1972.

Roper, Michael, and John Tosh. *Manful Assertions: Masculinities in Britain since 1800*. London: Routledge, 1991.

Rosaldo, Renato. *Culture and Truth: The Remaking of Social Analysis: With a New Introduction*. Boston: Beacon Press, 1993.

Rose, Jacqueline. *The Case of Peter Pan, or, The Impossibility of Children's Fiction*. Basingstoke, England: Macmillan, 1994.

———. *States of Fantasy*. Oxford: Clarendon Press, 1996.

Rosen, David. *The Changing Fictions of Masculinity*. Urbana: University of Illinois Press, 1993.

Rosenthal, Laura J. "'Infamous Commerce': Transracial Prostitution in the South Seas and Back." In *Monstrous Dreams of Reason: Body, Self, and Other in the Enlightenment*, edited by Laura J. Rosenthal and Mita Choudhury. Cranbury, N.J.: Associated University Presses, 2002.

Roth, Christopher F. "Without Treaty, Without Conquest: Indigenous Sovereignty in Post-*Delgamuukw* British Columbia." *Wicazo Sa Review* (fall 2002): 143–65.

Rotundo, E. Anthony. *American Manhood: Transformations in Masculinity from the Revolution to the Modern Era*. New York: Basic Books, 1993.

Rousseau, Jean Jacques. *Emile*. London: Dent; Dutton, 1974.

Rowe, John Carlos. "Melville's Typee: U.S. Imperialism at Home and Abroad." In *National Identities and Post-Americanist Narratives*, edited by Donald Pease. Durham, N.C.: Duke University Press, 1994.

Rowson, Claude. "Gulliver and the Flat Nosed People: Colonial Oppression and Race in Satire and Fiction. *Dutch Quarterly* 13 (1983) 4: 162–78.

Rutherford, Jonathan. *Forever England: Reflections on Race, Masculinity and Empire*. London: Lawrence & Wishart, 1997.

Ryan, James. *Picturing Empire: Photography and the Visualization of the British Empire*. London: Reaktion Books, 1997.

Sagan, Eli. *Human Aggression: Cannibalism and Cultural Form*. New York: Harper and Row, 1974.

Said, Edward W. *Culture and Imperialism*. New York: Vintage Books, 1993.

Sales, Roger. *English Literature in History, 1780–1830: Pastoral and Politics*. New York: St. Martin's Press, 1983.

Sanborne, Geoffrey. *The Sign of the Cannibal: Melville and the Making of a Postcolonial Reader*. Durham, N.C.: Duke University Press, 1998.

Sanday, Peggy Reeves. *Divine Hunger: Cannibalism as a Cultural System*. Cambridge: Cambridge University Press, 1988.

Saxton, Arnold. "Female Castaways." In *Robinson Crusoe: Myths and Metamorphoses*, edited by Lieve Spaas and Brian Stimpson. New York: Macmillan Press; St. Martin's Press, 1996.

Scarry, Elaine. *The Body in Pain: The Making and Unmaking of the World*. New York: Oxford University Press, 1987.

Schilder, Paul. *The Image and Appearance of the Human Body; Studies in the Constructive Energies of the Psyche.* New York: International Universities Press, 1950.

Sedgwick, Eve Kosofsky. *Between Men: English Literature and Male Homosocial Desire.* New York: Columbia University Press, 1985.

Seed, Patricia. *Ceremonies of Possession in Europe's Conquest of the New World, 1492–1640.* Cambridge: Cambridge University Press, 1995.

Seguin, Alfred. *The Black Crusoe.* New York: Books for Libraries Press, 1972.

Seidel, Michael. *Robinson Crusoe: Island Myths and the Novel.* Boston: Twayne Publishers, 1991.

Seidler, Victor J. *Rediscovering Masculinity: Reason, Language, and Sexuality.* London: Routledge, 1989.

Selvon, Samuel. *Moses Ascending.* London: Heinemann, 1975.

Shadwell, Thomas. "The Tempest." In *The Complete Works of Thomas Shadwell,* edited by Montague Summers. New York: B. Blom, 1968.

Shakespeare, William. *The Tempest.* Ed. Stephen Orgel. New York: Oxford University Press, 1987.

Shand, John. "Pantomime." In *Literary Taste, Culture and Mass Communication. Vol. 8, Theatre and Song,* edited by Peter Davison, Rolf Meyersohn and Edward Shil. Cambridge: Chadwyck-Healy, 1978.

Sharpe, Jenny. "Figures of Colonial Resistance." *Modern Fiction Studies* 35 (spring 1989) 1: 137–55.

Shilling, Chris. *The Body and Social Theory.* London: SAGE, 2003.

Shohat, Ella and Robert Stam. *Unthinking Eurocentrism: Multiculturalism and the Media.* London: Routledge, 1994.

A Short Account of the Incidents Exhibited at the Pantomime Robinson Crusoe at the Theatre-Royal, Drury Lane. London: T. Becket, 1781.

Silvestri, Michael. "The Thrill of 'Simply Dressing Up': The Indian Police, Disguise, and Intelligence Work in Colonial India." *Journal of Colonialism and Colonial History* 2 (2001). Available at: http://musejhu.edu/journals/journal_of_colonialism_and_colonial_history/002/2.2silverstri.

Simpson, A. W. Brian. *Cannibalism and the Common Law: The Story of the Tragic Last Voyage of the Mignonette and the Strange Legal Proceedings to Which It Gave Rise.* Chicago: University of Chicago Press, 1984.

Sinha, Mrinalini. *Colonial Masculinity: The "Manly Englishman" and the "Effeminate Bengali" in the Late Nineteenth Century.* New York: St. Martin's Press, 1995.

Slemon, Stephen. "Bones of Contention: Post-Colonial Writing and the 'Cannibal' Question." In *Literature and the Body,* edited by Anthony Purdy. Atlanta: Rodopi Press, 1992.

Smail, Daniel Lord. *Imaginary Cartographies: Possession and Identity in Late Medieval Marseille.* Ithaca: Cornell University Press, 1999.

Smith, Iain Crichton. *The Notebooks of Robinson Crusoe and Other Poems.* London: Victor Gollancz, 1975.

Solinus, Caius Julius. *The Excellent and Pleasant Worke, Collectanea Rerum Memorabi Lium of Solinus.* Ed. Arthur Golding. Gainesville, Fla.: Scholars' Facsimiles & Reprints, 1955.

Spark, Muriel. *Robinson: A Novel.* London: Macmillan, 1958.

Stafford, Barbara Maria. *Body Criticism: Imaging the Unseen in Enlightenment Art and Medicine.* Cambridge, Mass.: MIT Press, 1991.

———. *Voyage into Substance: Art, Science, Nature, and the Illustrated Travel Account, 1760–1840.* Cambridge, Mass.: MIT Press, 1984.

Stallybrass, Peter, and Allon White. *The Politics and Poetics of Transgression.* New York: Cornell, 1986.

Stephan, Michele. "Consuming the Dead: A Kleinian Perspective on Death Rituals Cross-Culturally." *International Journal of Psychoanalysis* 79 (1998): 1173–94.

Stevenson, Robert Louis. *Kidnapped.* 1886. New York: Scholastic, 1963.

———. *Treasure Island.* 1883. New York: Signet Classic, 1981.

———. *Treasure Island.* New York: Scribner, 1911.

Stott, Rebecca. "The Dark Continent: Africa as Female Body in Haggard's Adventure Fiction." *Feminist Review* 32 (summer 1989): 69–89.

Street, Brian. *The Savage in Literature: Representations of Primitive Society in English Fiction, 1858–1920.* London: Routledge & K. Paul, 1975.

Swift, Jonathan. *Gulliver's Travels: Complete, Authoritative Text with Biographical and Historical Contexts, Critical History, and Essays from Five Contemporary Critical Perspectives.* Ed. Christopher Fox. Boston: Bedford Books of St. Martin's Press, 1995.

Synnott, Anthony. *The Body Social: Symbolism, Self and Society.* London: Routledge, 1993.

Tait, Viola. *Dames, Principal Boys—And All That: A History of Pantomime in Australia.* Melbourne: Macmillan, 2001.

Theweleit, Klaus. "The Bomb's Womb and the Genders of War (War Goes on Preventing Women from Becoming the Mothers of Invention)." In *Gendering War Talk,* edited by Mirian Cooke and Angela Wollacoot. Princeton: Princeton University Press, 1993.

———. *Male Fantasies. Vol. 1, Women, Floods, Bodies, History.* Cambridge: Polity Press, 1987.

———. *Male Fantasies. Vol. 2, Male Bodies: Psychoanalyzing the White Terror.* Minneapolis: University of Minnesota Press, 1989.

Thomas, Helen and Jamilah Ahmed. *Cultural Bodies: Ethnography and Theory.* Malden, Mass.: Blackwell, 2004.

Thorne, Geoffrey. *The Grand Annual Christmas Pantomime Entitled Robinson Crusoe, or Harlequin Man Friday, Who Kept the House Tidy, and Polly of Liverpool Town.* Liverpool: Prince of Wales Theatre, 1895.

Tickell, Alex. "Footprints on The Beach: Traces of Colonial Adventure in Narratives of Independent Tourism." *Postcolonial Studies* 4 (2001) 1: 39–54.

Tiffin, Helen. "Metaphor and Mortality: The Life Cycle of Malaria" *Meridian* 12 (1993) 1: 46–58;

Tolson, Andrew. *The Limits of Masculinity: Male Identity and the Liberated Woman.* London: Tavistock, 1977.

Torgovnick, Marianna. *Gone Primitive: Savage Intellects, Modern Lives.* Chicago: University of Chicago Press, 1990.

Tosh, John. *A Man's Place: Masculinity and the Middle-Class Home in Victorian England*. New Haven, Conn.: Yale University Press, 1999.

Tournier, Michel. *Vendredi (Friday)*. 1967. Trans. Norman Denny. Baltimore: Johns Hopkins University Press, 1997.

Tuan, Yi-Fu. *Topophilia: A Study of Environmental Perception, Attitudes, and Values*. Englewood Cliffs, N.J.: Prentice-Hall, 1974.

Turley, Hans. *Rum, Sodomy, and the Lash: Piracy, Sexuality, and Masculine Identity*. New York: New York University Press, 1999.

Urry, John. *The Tourist Gaze: Leisure and Travel in Contemporary Societies*. London: Sage, 1990.

Verne, Jules. *The Mysterious Island. Pictures by N. C. Wyeth*. 1873. New York: Scribner, 1920.

———. *Twenty Thousand Leagues Under the Sea*. 1873. New York: Dodd, Mead, 1952.

Walcott, Derek. "The Figure of Crusoe." In *Critical Perspectives on Derek Walcott*, edited by Robert D. Hamner. Washington D.C.: Three Continents Press, 1993.

———. *Remembrance and Pantomime: Two Plays*. New York: Farrar, Straus, and Giroux, 1980.

Warner, Marina. "Fee Fie Fo Fum: The Child in the Jaws of the Story." In *Cannibalism and the Colonial World*, edited by Francis Barker, Peter Hulme, and Margaret Iverson. Cambridge: Cambridge University Press, 1998.

———. *Indigo, or Mapping the Waters*. New York: Simon and Schuster, 1992.

Waswo, Richard. "The Formation of Natural Law to Justify Colonialism, 1539–1689." *New Literary History* 27 (1996) 4: 743–59.

Watt, Ian P. *The Rise of the Novel: Studies in Defoe, Richardson, and Fielding*. London: Chatto & Windus, 1957.

Weaver-Hightower, Marcus. "The Gender of Terror and Heroes? What Educators Might Teach About Men and Masculinity after September 11, 2001." *Teacher's College Record Online* (September 9, 2002). Available at: http://www.tcrecord.org/Content.asp?ContentID=11012.

Wells, H. G. *The Island of Dr. Moreau*. 1868. London: Pan Books, 1977.

White, Hayden V. *Tropics of Discourse: Essays in Cultural Criticism*. Baltimore: Johns Hopkins University Press, 1978.

Wiggins, Marianne. *John Dollar*. New York: Harper and Row, 1989.

Williams, Carolyn. "Utopia, Limited: Nationalism, Empire and Parody in the Comic Operas of Gilbert and Sullivan." In *Cultural Politics at the Fin de Siecle*, edited by Sally Ledger and Scott McCracken. Cambridge: Cambridge University Press, 1995.

Williams, David. *Deformed Discourse: The Function of the Monster in Mediaeval Thought and Literature*. Montreal: McGill-Queens University Press, 1996.

Williams, Neville. *The Seadogs: Privateers, Plunder and Piracy in the Elizabethan Age*. London: Weidenfeld and Nicolson, 1975.

Wilson, A. E. *Pantomime Pageant: A Procession of Harlequins, Clowns, Comedians, Principal Boys, Pantomime-Writers, Producers, and Playgoers*. New York: Stanley Paul and Co., 1985.

Winkfield, Unca Eliza. *The Female American: or the Adventures of Unca Eliza Wink-field*. Ed. Michelle Burnham. Toronto: Broadview, 2001.

Woods, Gregory. "Fantasy Islands: Popular Topographies of Marooned Mascu-linity." In *Mapping Desire*, edited by David Bell and Gill Valentine. London: Routledge, 1995.

Wyss, Johan. *The Swiss Family Robinson*. 1800. Mahwah, N.J.: Watermill Press, 1980.

Young, Robert J. C. *Colonial Desire: Hybridity in Theory, Culture, and Race*. London: Routledge, 1995.

———. *Postcolonialism: An Historical Introduction*. Oxford: Blackwell, 2001.

Zoakos, Criton "Why the World Hates America: The Economic Explanation." *The International Economy* 17 (spring 2003) 2: 11.

Zwick, Jim. "An American Anti-Imperialist: Mark Twain on the Philippine-American War. *Filipinas Magazine* (September 1992): 50–54.

Films

Apollo 13. Dir. Ron Howard. Writ. William Broyles Jr. and Al Reinert. Perf. Tom Hanks, Bill Paxton, Kevin Bacon, Gary Sinise, Ed Harris. Universal Pictures, 1995.

The Beach. Dir. Danny Boyle. Fox, 1999.

The Blue Lagoon. Dir. Randal Klieser. Perf. Brooke Shields, Christopher Atkins. Columbia Tristar Pictures, 1980.

Cast Away. Dir. Robert Zemeckis. Writ. William Broyles. Jr. Perf. Tom Hanks, Helen Hunt. Twentieth Century Fox, 2000.

China Beach. Dir. Rod Holcomb. Writ. William Broyles Jr. and John Sacret Young. Warner Brothers Television, 1988.

Colonists for a Day. Writ., Dir. Alec Morgan, Prod. Chris Oliver. Narr. Paul Barry. Lindfield NSW: Film Australia, Australian Broadcast Company, 1993.

Crusoe. Dir. Caleb Deschanel. Perf. Aidan Quinn, Ade Sapara, Andrew Brauns-berg. Virgin Vision, 1988.

Forrest Gump. Dir. Robert Zemeckis. Writ. Winston Groom, Eric Roth. Perf. Tom Hanks, Robin Wright Penn, Gary Sinise. Paramount, 1994.

The Island of Dr. Moreau. Dir. Richard Stanley and John Frankenheimer. Perf. Marlon Brando, Val Kilmer. New Line Cinema, 1996.

Robinson Crusoe. Dir. Rod Hardy, George Miller. Writ. Christopher Lofton. Perf. Pierce Brosnan, William Takaku. Miramax, 1996.

Saving Private Ryan. Dir. Steven Spielberg. Writ. Robert Rodat. Perf. Tom Hanks, Edward Burns, Tom Sizemore, Matt Damon. Paramount Pictures, 1998.

Six Days, Seven Nights. Dir. Ivan Reitman. Perf. Harrison Ford, Anne Heche. Buena Vista Pictures, 1998.

Swept Away. Dir. Guy Ritchie. Writ. Lina Wertmüller, Guy Ritchie. Perf. Madonna, Adriano Giannini, Jeanne Tripplehorn. Sony Pictures, 2002.

Swept Away by an Unusual Destiny in the Blue Sea of August [*Travolti da un In-solito Destino Nell'azzurro Mare D'agosto*]. Dir., Writ. Lina Wertmüller. Perf. Giancarlo Giannini, Mariangela Melato. Cinema 5 Distributing. 1974.

Television Series

Fantasy Island. ABC. Premiered January 1977.
Gilligan's Island. CBS. Premiered September 1964.
The Real Gilligan's Island. TBS. Premiered November 2004.
Lost. ABC. Premiered September 2004.
Survivor. CBS. Premiered May 2000.
Temptation Island. Fox. Premiered January 2001.

Index

abjection, 94–98

Abraham, Karl, 116

Admirable Crichton, The (Barrie), 45, 79

alcohol: as demonstration of discipline, 59–61

Anderson, Benedict: *Imagined Communities*, 39, 194

Anderson, Warwick, "'Where Every Prospect Pleases and Only Man Is Vile': Laboratory Medicine as Colonial Discourse," 138, 141

Animal Within: Masculinity and the Gothic, The (Hendershot), 87, 235n

animals: as allowing castaway to play native, 158–61; as carriers of savagery, 144; as indigenes, 145–46; simian threat, 238n

anticolonial movements, 172–74

Anti-Oedipus: Capitalism and Schizophrenia (Deleuze and Guatarri), xxii–xxiii, 33, 230n

Anzieu, Didier, xviii–xix, 56; *The Skin Ego*, 36–37

Arens, William: "Rethinking Anthropophagy," 96

Armstrong, Diane: "The Myth of Cronus: Cannibal and Sign in *Robinson Crusoe*," 92

Ashcroft, Bill: *The Empire Writes Back*, 229n

Ashton's Memorial (Ashton), 109–10

Baer, Joel: "The Complicated Plot of Piracy: Aspects of English Criminal Law and the Image of the Pirate in Defoe," 105

Bakhtin, Mikhail, xxviii, 180, 187, 189; *Rabelais and His World*, 142–43, 178–79

Ballantyne, R. M. *See Coral Island, The*

Barrie, J. M.: *The Admirable Crichton*, 45, 79; *Peter Pan*, 78, 172, 190–93

Bartolovich, Crystal, 116

Beach, The (Garland), xxviii, 206, 210, 214–15

Between Men: English Literature and Male Homosocial Desire (Sedgwick), 47, 78–79

Bhabha, Homi, 53, 65, 77, 141; "Of Mimicry and Man," 4, 98; "Signs Taken for Wonders," 40

Bingfield, William: *The Voyages, Shipwreck, Travels, Distresses, Strange Adventures and Miraculous Preservation of William Bingfield* 238–39n

Black Skin, White Masks (Fanon), 90

Blumstein, Alex: "Masochism and Fantasies of Preparing to Be Incorporated," 110

body, human, xiv–xvi, xiii–xx. *See also* "Dark Continent, The"; *Nature's Work of Art*

Body Criticism (Stafford), xv

Body Embarrassed: Drama and the Disciplines of Shame in Early Modern England, The (Paster), xx

body image, xviii, 8, 32–33, 63

Body Social: Symbolism, Self, and Society, The (Synnott), xx

Body Work (Brooks), 10, 229n

Rebecca Weaver-Hightower is assistant professor of English and postcolonial studies at the University of North Dakota, where she teaches courses in postcolonial literatures and film. She is book review editor of the *Journal of Commonwealth and Postcolonial Studies* and has published in several journals, including the *Journal for Early Modern Cultural Studies, Journal of Popular Culture,* and *Journal of Caribbean Studies.*

"WITH ITS IMAGINATIVE USE OF CULTURAL AND PSYCHOANALYTIC THEORIES, *Empire Islands* OFFERS A TRENCHANT AND ENGAGING ANALYSIS OF CASTAWAY STORIES, ILLUMINATING THEIR HISTORICAL AND CONTEMPORARY SIGNIFICANCE FOR A WORLD NEWLY ATTUNED TO IMPERIAL ISSUES."

— f Essex

" XTS IN *Empire Islands* ARE INSIGHTFUL AND G THE STUDY OF IMPERIAL/COLONIAL IMAGINARIES ERPRETIVE IMPORTANCE."

ity of Toronto

ed unpacking of the castaway genre's appeal in , *Empire Islands* forwards our understanding of the of British Empire. Rebecca Weaver-Hightower argues by helping generations of readers to make sense of— about—imperial aggression, the castaway story in effect enabled the expansion and maintenance of European empire.

Empire Islands asks why so many colonial authors chose islands as the setting for their stories of imperial adventure and why so many postcolonial writers "write back" to those castaway narratives. Drawing on works from Thomas More's *Utopia* to Caribbean novels like George Lamming's *Water with Berries,* from canonical works such as *Robinson Crusoe* and *The Tempest* to the lesser-known *A Narrative of the Life and Astonishing Adventures of John Daniel* by Ralph Morris, Weaver-Hightower examines themes of cannibalism, piracy, monstrosity, and the concept of going native. Ending with analysis of contemporary film and the role of the United States in global neoimperialism, Weaver-Hightower exposes how island narratives continue not only to describe but also to justify colonialism.

REBECCA WEAVER-HIGHTOWER is assistant professor of English and postcolonial studies at the University of North Dakota.

University of Minnesota Press
Printed in U.S.A.
Cover design by Brian Donahue / bedesign, inc.
Cover image: *The Wild Man of Tabor Island* by N. C. Wyeth

ISBN-13: 978-0-8166-4863-4
ISBN-10: 0-8166-4863-8

9 780816 648634